Drafting Contracts

ASPEN PUBLISHERS

DRAFTING CONTRACTS
How and Why Lawyers Do What They Do

Tina L. Stark

Professor in the Practice of Law
Emory University School of Law

Wolters Kluwer
Law & Business

AUSTIN   BOSTON   CHICAGO   NEW YORK   THE NETHERLANDS

Aspen Publishers
Attn: Permissions Department
76 Ninth Avenue, 7th Floor
New York, NY 10011-5201

To contact Customer Care, e-mail customer.care@aspenpublishers.com,
call 1-800-234-1660, fax 1-800-901-9075, or mail correspondence to:

Aspen Publishers
Attn: Order Department
PO Box 990
Frederick, MD 21705

Printed in the United States of America.

1 2 3 4 5 6 7 8 9 0

ISBN 978-0-7355-6339-1

Library of Congress Cataloging-in-Publication Data

Stark, Tina L., 1953-
        Drafting contracts : how and why lawyers do what they do / Tina L. Stark.
            p. cm.
        Includes index.
        ISBN 978-0-7355-6339-1
        1. Contracts—United States. 2. Contracts—United States—Language. 3. Legal composition. I. Title.

        KF807.S73 2007
        346.7302—dc22

                                                                                        2007016511

ABOUT WOLTERS KLUWER LAW & BUSINESS

Wolters Kluwer Law & Business is a leading provider of research information and workflow solutions in key specialty areas. The strengths of the individual brands of Aspen Publishers, CCH, Kluwer Law International and Loislaw are aligned within Wolters Kluwer Law & Business to provide comprehensive, in-depth solutions and expert-authored content for the legal, professional and education markets.

CCH was founded in 1913 and has served more than four generations of business professionals and their clients. The CCH products in the Wolters Kluwer Law & Business group are highly regarded electronic and print resources for legal, securities, antitrust and trade regulation, government contracting, banking, pension, payroll, employment and labor, and healthcare reimbursement and compliance professionals.

Aspen Publishers is a leading information provider for attorneys, business professionals and law students. Written by preeminent authorities, Aspen products offer analytical and practical information in a range of specialty practice areas from securities law and intellectual property to mergers and acquisitions and pension/benefits. Aspen's trusted legal education resources provide professors and students with high-quality, up-to-date and effective resources for successful instruction and study in all areas of the law.

Kluwer Law International supplies the global business community with comprehensive English-language international legal information. Legal practitioners, corporate counsel and business executives around the world rely on the Kluwer Law International journals, looseleafs, books and electronic products for authoritative information in many areas of international legal practice.

Loislaw is a premier provider of digitized legal content to small law firm practitioners of various specializations. Loislaw provides attorneys with the ability to quickly and efficiently find the necessary legal information they need, when and where they need it, by facilitating access to primary law as well as state-specific law, records, forms and treatises.

Wolters Kluwer Law & Business, a unit of Wolters Kluwer, is headquartered in New York and Riverwoods, Illinois. Wolters Kluwer is a leading multinational publisher and information services company.

For Bobby and Mort Weisenfeld, my mother- and father-in-law, who have always treated me as if I were their daughter

For their son Dave, my best friend and beloved husband

and

For their grandson Andy, my wondrous treasure

Summary of Contents

Contents

Preface

Drafting Contracts brings a new approach to the teaching of contract drafting. It emphasizes the nexus between the business deal and the contract, both in the material taught and in the exercises students work on. In addition, it teaches students to think critically about the law and the transaction they are memorializing.

To draft a contract well, a drafter must know the rules of good writing—and more. Among other things, a drafter must

- understand the business deal;
- know how to use the contract concepts to reflect the parties' deal accurately; and
- be able to draft and recognize nuances in language that change the deal.

In addition, a good drafter knows how to add value to a deal by discerning and resolving business issues.

Drafting Contracts reflects a real world approach to contract drafting, bringing together years of real world contract drafting experience and law school teaching. Although new to the market, the materials in *Drafting Contracts* have been used in law school classrooms for more than 13 years, including use of the manuscript at more than ten schools.

Drafting Contracts teaches students through narration and drafting exercises. The exercises are numerous, permitting a professor to choose the ones most appropriate for his or her class. As designed, the exercises in later chapters incorporate material from earlier chapters, so that students practice what they have already learned while integrating new skills. Professors need not, however, teach the materials in *Drafting Contracts* in the order set out. The book is sufficiently flexible that professors can reorder the chapters to suit any curriculum.

This book's organization reflects its pedagogy. Part 1 teaches the material that is the course's foundation. Its chapters introduce students to the building blocks of contracts: representations and warranties, covenants, rights, conditions, discretionary authority, and declarations. These chapters do more, however, than define the terms. They show how and why a drafter chooses a specific contract concept by teaching the analytic skill of *translating the business deal into contract concepts*.

In Part 2, *Drafting Contracts* sets out the framework of an agreement and works through it from the preamble to the signature lines, in each instance discussing the business, legal, and drafting issues that occur in each part of a contract. After these chapters, in Part 3, *Drafting Contracts* turns to the rules for good drafting and to techniques to enhance clarity and to avoid ambiguity. Although the chapters in this Part concentrate on more traditional drafting issues, they nonetheless remain sensitive to how the business deal affects drafting in subtle ways.

In Part 4, students learn how to look at a deal from the client's business perspective and how to add value to a transaction by identifying business issues using the five-prong framework of money, risk, control, standards, and endgame.

In Part 5, students learn the drafting process, from organizing the initial contract to amending the signed agreement. Students also learn how to analyze and comment on a contract that another lawyer has drafted.

Drafting Contracts directly addresses ethical issues unique to contract drafting, both through textual material and exercises in Part 6. The book's final part, Part 7, provides supplementary exercises.

Drafting Contracts is designed for use in an upper-level drafting course but can be integrated into a variety of other courses, including a first-year writing or contracts course, a mergers and acquisitions course, a transactional simulation course, a transactional clinic, and an upper-level writing survey course. The Teachers Manual suggests appropriate chapters and exercises for each of these uses.

The Teachers Manual is detailed. For exercises that require the redrafting of a provision, the TM includes the original provision, a mark-up showing the changes, the final version, and Notes explaining the answer. For exercises that require free drafting, the TM includes an example of a good answer along with Notes explaining the answer. In addition, the TM provides answers to commonly asked questions and tips on how to present material.

The *Drafting Contracts* website will also be a resource available to professors and students. First, professors will have access to an electronic version of the TM, so anything in it can be copied and incorporated into class notes. Second, professors will be able to download PowerPoint slides and additional exercises. Third, the website will include Word and WordPerfect versions of each provision in a large, readable font. These provisions can be projected on a screen in the same way that a PowerPoint slide can be projected. Once projected, the professor and students can work through the revision together. The website will also have additional exercises to give professors even more choices for assignments. Finally, to minimize the word processing that students do, the website will include electronic versions of the longer exercises.

Drafting Contracts teaches contract drafting in a new way. It teaches students how to think like deal lawyers and how to reflect that thinking in the contracts they draft.

Tina L. Stark
May 2007

Acknowledgments

I began this book in 1993 when I first began teaching at Fordham Law School. Unfortunately, the text was only in my head. It took another ten years before I began to put the words on a page. This lengthy gestation has led to a long list of people to thank.

I begin by thanking my students. They were the first to encourage me to write this book. Through the years, their comments and insights challenged me to rethink and clarify my ideas.

While writing this book, I had the help of the following practitioners and professors: Helen Bender, Robin Boyle, Ruthie Buck, Sandra Cohen, Carl Felsenfeld, John Forry, Eric Goldman, Morton Grosz, Carol Hansell, Charles Hoppin, Vickie Kobak, Terry Lloyd, Lisa Penland, Nancy Persechino, and Sally Weaver. Their input and that of Aspen Publishers's anonymous reviewers greatly improved this book's quality.

I thank my colleague Alan Shaw for his intellectual generosity and careful review of the manuscript. In addition, I am grateful to Peter Clapp, someone whom I have never met, but who gave me line-by-line comments on almost every chapter.

Richard Green at Thelen Reid Brown Raysman & Steiner LLP was most helpful. He not only reviewed chapters, but also graciously arranged for his firm's word processing wonders to turn my typed pages into a manuscript.

While working on this book, I had the enthusiastic and dedicated support of my student research assistants: Hannah Amoah, Stephen Costa, Sarah Elkaim, and Noel Paladin-Tripp. I thank Fordham Law School for its generous support of this book.

I also thank Rick Garbarini for his good work and friendship.

Richard Neumann of Hofstra Law School played a pivotal role in this book's publication by introducing me to Richard Mixter at Aspen Publishers. I thank them and Carol McGeehan at Aspen for having had the imagination to envisage a contract drafting textbook market, even when one barely existed.

Others at Aspen also played important roles. Barbara Roth expertly shepherded me through the writing and design process, and Sarah Hains and Meri Keithley artfully designed the book's pages to showcase the contract provision examples. In addition, Kaesmene Harrison Banks skillfully guided the book through production on a tight timeframe, and Lauren Arnest meticulously copy-edited the manuscript.

Finally, I thank my husband Dave and son Andy. Their unwavering love, support, and encouragement make everything I do possible. They also make me laugh—at myself.

The author gratefully acknowledges permission from the following sources to use excerpts from their works:

American Bar Association, ABA Informal Opinion 86-1518. © 1986 by the American Bar Association. Reprinted with permission. Copies of ABA Ethics Opinions are available from Service Center, American Bar Association, 321 North Clark Street, Chicago, IL 60610, 1-800-285-2221.

American Bar Association, ABA *Model Rules of Professional Conduct*, 2006 Edition. © 2006 by the American Bar Association. Reprinted with permission. Copies of ABA *Model*

Rules of Professional Conduct, 2006 Edition are available from Service Center, American Bar Association, 321 North Clark Street, Chicago, IL 60610, 1-800-285-2221.

Gulfstream Aerospace Corporation, Gulfstream G550 photo and technical data. © Gulfstream Aerospace Corporation. Reprinted by permission.

Shaw, Alan, excerpts from Fordham Law School course materials. Reprinted by permission.

Stark, Tina L., *Thinking Like a Deal Lawyer,* 54 J. Leg. Educ. 223, 223-224 (June 2004). Excerpts appear in *Drafting Contracts* Sections 2.3 and 3.1. Reprinted by permission.

Stark, Tina L. et al. eds, *Negotiating and Drafting Contract Boilerplate,* ALM Properties, Inc. 2003. All material from *Negotiating and Drafting Contract Boilerplate* is used with permission of the publisher—ALM Publishing (www.lawcatalog.com); copyright ALM Properties, Inc. 2003. All Rights Reserved.

Drafting Contracts

PART ONE

Translating the Business Deal
into Contract Concepts

A Few Words about Contract Drafting and this Book

1.1 INTRODUCTION

A well-drafted contract is elegant. Its language is clear and unambiguous, and its organization cohesive and thoughtful. But drafting a contract requires more than good writing and organizational skills. A drafter should have keen analytical skills; a superior ability to negotiate; a sophisticated understanding of business, the business deal, and the client's business; a comprehensive knowledge of the law; and a discerning eye for details. It also helps to have formidable powers of concentration, physical stamina, mental acuity, tenacity, the ability to multitask, and a sense of humor. Finally, a drafter must enjoy working with colleagues to create a product—the contract.

1.2 WHAT DOES A CONTRACT DO?

A contract establishes the terms of the parties' relationship. It reflects their agreement as to the rules that will govern their transaction. The rules generally include

- the statements of facts that each party made that induced the other to enter the transaction;
- each party's promises as to its future performance;
- each party's rights;
- the events that must occur before each party is obligated to perform;
- each party's discretionary authority;
- how the contract will end, including the events that constitute breach and the remedies for breach; and
- the general policies that govern the parties' relationship.

These rules are the parties' private laws, which the courts will enforce, subject to public policy exceptions found in statutes and common law. Indeed, commentators speak of contracts as **private law**. They also refer to them as **planning documents**. Unlike litigation, which looks back in time, contracts look forward to the parties' future relationship and reflect their joint plans.

A contract also helps the parties to problem solve. Often parties will have the same goal but differ as to how to resolve a specific business issue. A well-written contract can bridge this difference, giving each party enough of what it needs to agree to the contract.

1.3   WHAT ARE A CONTRACT'S GOALS?

When drafting, you are trying to create a document that serves multiple purposes. Sometimes, you may not be able to accomplish all of them, but you should try. A well-written contract should do the following:

- Accurately memorialize the business deal.
- Be clear and unambiguous.
- Resolve problems pragmatically.
- Be sufficiently specific that the parties know their rights and obligations, but be flexible enough to cope with changed circumstances.
- Advance the client's goals and reduce its risks.
- Give each side enough of what it needs that each leaves the table feeling that it negotiated a good deal.
- Be drafted well enough that it never leaves the file drawer.
- Prevent litigation.

1.4   WHAT IS THE CONTEXT WITHIN WHICH CONTRACTS ARE DRAFTED?

Most contracts are drafted in a different atmosphere from that in which litigators draft memoranda and briefs. Litigators are out to win. They want to defeat their adversaries in court; cooperation is not generally a big part of their playbook. But doing deals and drafting contracts differ from litigation. Neither party wants to give away the candy store, but each looks for a way to get the deal done.

The argot of deal lawyers also differs from that of litigators. While litigators talk about their **adversaries**, those with whom they will battle through a war of words, deal lawyers and their clients talk about **the other side** or **the principals**. These phrases acknowledge that the parties are not aligned, but they are softer than *adversaries* and reflect a different relationship. The parties are competitive, but in the context of a cooperative venture.[1] Each may be willing to walk away from the deal, but each has incentive to do it.

1.5   DOES THIS BOOK COVER ALL KINDS OF CONTRACTS?

This book focuses on the drafting of **business contracts,** not standard form consumer contracts. The scope of the phrase *business contracts* is intended to be broad and encompassing. It is intended to cover all negotiated contracts, whatever the topic or dollar amount. Within its reach are contracts for the sale of a used car, the construction of an office tower, and a settlement agreement between litigating adversaries. It does not cover a standard form contract that a corporation puts to a consumer. The distinction matters because it affects a drafter's contract drafting style and a contract's substance.

Today, most consumer contracts are drafted in plain English, a style of drafting in which simplicity and clarity prevail. This book will not teach you to draft in plain English. Instead, for business contracts, this book espouses a style of drafting that this author calls **contemporary commercial drafting**. It resembles plain English, but it is not the same. It draws on the principles of plain English and promotes clarity through, among other things, simpler language, shorter sentences, and formatting. It differs from plain English, however, in important ways.

---

1. Settlement and divorce negotiations are two notorious exceptions.

First, plain English drafters make their contracts more reader friendly by, for example, adopting an informal tone. Although the business world is more informal than it used to be (think business casual dress), it is hard to imagine a multimillion dollar contract between Dell and Intel in which Dell is referred to as *we* and Intel as *you*. But more important than tone is the approach to the contract's substance. A plain English contract's provisions are pared down to their bare essentials, while a business contract's are hefty, retaining all provisions that might add value or protect against risk. Carl Felsenfeld, one of the first proponents of plain English, explained the difference between the two kinds of contracts:

> The plain English movement requires a new drafting approach. Each provision [of a consumer contract] must be analyzed one at a time against the specific transaction and the type of protection required. Many of the traditional legal provisions may well be found essentially unnecessary.
>
> It is basic to this approach that one must regard drafting for a consumer transaction as quite different from drafting for a business transaction. . . . One does not yet, for example, see it taken seriously, in the teaching of contract law. Traditionally, [promissory] notes were not divided in this way and many of the carefully drafted provisions that cluttered up consumer documents, while important, perhaps even essential, to a business transaction really added very little to the typical consumer loan. . . . The point is that consumer drafting must be regarded as a separate process from business drafting. A legal principle derived from this, while perhaps extreme, does lead the way: "In a business transaction, if a risk can be perceived draft for it. In a consumer transaction, unless a risk seems likely, forget it."[2]

1.6 WHY SHOULD YOU LEARN TO DRAFT IF YOU PLAN TO LITIGATE?

If you plan to litigate, you should learn to draft for two reasons. First, you will regularly draft contracts as a litigator. Parties who litigate settle more often than they go to trial. The settlement they reach is a business deal, just like any other, and it must be memorialized clearly and accurately. Failure to do so can lead to another dispute and further litigation. Second, knowing how to draft will make you a better litigator. Many of the cases that you litigate will grow out of contract disputes. To properly represent your client, you must be able to analyze a contract and its provisions. If you understand how and why a drafter wrote a provision in a specific way, you will be able to craft more persuasive legal arguments.

1.7 WHAT WILL THIS BOOK TEACH YOU?

This book will teach you how to write a contract and how to think about writing a contract. The first requires that you learn basic principles of contract drafting: For example, use recitals sparingly; limit the number of definitions; avoid ambiguity; do not use the false imperative; tabulate to promote clarity; and say the same thing the same way. Learning how to *think* about writing a contract will require you to learn how business people and their lawyers think about a transaction and the contract

---

2. Carl Felsenfeld, *Language Simplification and Consumer Legal Forms*, Remarks made at program on simplified legal drafting, American Bar Association, New York City, August 7, 1978, in Reed Dickerson, *Materials on Legal Drafting* 267 (2d ed., Little, Brown & Co. 1986). *See also* Carl Felsenfeld and Alan Siegel, *Writing Contracts in Plain English* 28-29 (West 1981).

that memorializes it. Some of the questions that lawyers and their clients think about include the following:

- What are the client's business goals?
- How can the contract frustrate or further those goals?
- What risks inhere in the transaction?
- What business issues does a provision raise?
- Does a provision give the other side too much control?
- Do the representations and warranties allocate too much risk to the client?
- How can the drafter change a covenant's standard of liability to reduce the client's risk?
- Should a particular event result in a breach?
- Does the contract provision resolve the client's business problem?

Asking and answering these and other questions are the fun part of contract drafting. They are what make you more than "a mere scrivener"—the ultimate insult to a contract drafter.

1.8 HOW IS THIS BOOK ORGANIZED?

Part 1, composed of Chapters 1 through 4, provides the framework for the course. It introduces you to the building blocks of contracts: representations and warranties, covenants, rights, conditions, discretionary authority, and declarations. Part 1, however, does more than define these terms. It shows how and why a drafter chooses a specific contract concept. It does this by teaching you the analytic skill of **translating the business deal into contract concepts**.

The translation skill is the analytic skill that deal lawyers use when drafting. It differs from that used in writing a persuasive document—whether a memorandum or a brief. Rather than applying the law to the facts, a deal lawyer translates the client's business concerns (a deal lawyer's facts) into contract concepts and then into contract provisions. By learning this skill in the beginning of the course, you will later be able to layer knowledge of *how* to draft on top of a framework that has taught you *what* you are drafting.

Part 2 begins with Chapter 5. It provides an overview of Part 2 by introducing you to a contract's parts:

- **Preamble**—*name of agreement, date, and the parties*
- **Recitals**—*why the parties are entering the contract*
- **Words of agreement**—*statement that the parties agree to the provisions that follow*
- **Definitions**
- **Action sections**—*promise to perform the subject matter of the contract and monetary provisions*
- **Other substantive business provisions**
- **Endgame provisions**—*provisions dealing with the contract's end*
- **General provisions**—*the "boilerplate" provisions*
- **Signature lines**

This chapter also shows you how the contract concepts you learned in Chapters 3 and 4 are integrated into a contract's parts.

In the remainder of Part 2, Chapters 6 through 17, you will learn how to draft each of the listed parts. Some of this will entail learning detailed drafting rules, but much of it will require you to learn to think like a deal lawyer.

Chapters 18 through 24, which compose Part 3, will teach you rules and techniques to enhance clarity and to avoid ambiguity. You will learn, among other things, about formatting, clarity through sentence structure, tabulation, and common causes of and cures for ambiguity. You will also learn how to draft formulas and provisions that use accounting concepts.

Chapter 25, the only chapter in Part 4, will teach you how to look at a deal from the client's business perspective and how to add value to a transaction by identifying business issues.

In Part 5, Chapters 26 through 29, you will learn the drafting process, from organizing the initial contract to amending the signed agreement. You will also learn how to analyze and comment on a contract that another lawyer has drafted. Part 6, which consists of Chapter 30, addresses ethical issues unique to contract drafting. Part 7 contains additional exercises for you to work on.

The Appendices include an Asset Purchase Agreement and a Website Development Agreement. The former is poorly drafted and the latter well drafted. As you work through the chapters, you can refer to these agreements to see the different contract concepts in action.

1.9 STYLISTIC MATTERS

As you read this book, you will see that some words and phrases are in bold and others in italics. Words or phrases in a **bold** font signal important terms, many of which are defined. *Italics* are used for three purposes: to signal contract language, to provide supplementary information, and to emphasize a word or phrase.

You will also notice that the book uses two kinds of boxes to highlight contract language. Short provisions are inside gray-shaded boxes.

> **Successors and Assigns.** This Agreement binds and benefits the parties and their respective successors and assigns.

When two or more provisions are within a gray-shaded box, each is numbered to distinguish where one ends and the other begins.

Longer provisions are inside an unshaded box—to show you how the provision would look on a contract page.

Non-competition Agreement, dated as of March 16, 20XX, between Attorney Staffing Acquisition Co., a Delaware corporation (the "Company"), and Maria Rodriguez (the "Executive").

Background

1. Attorney Staffing Inc., a Delaware corporation (the "Seller"), provides temporary lawyers to law firms in the greater Chicago area.
2. The Seller is selling substantially all of its assets to the Company in accordance with the Asset Acquisition Agreement, dated February 1, 20XX (the "Acquisition Agreement").
3. The Executive is the sole stockholder of the Seller and its President.

continued on next page >

4. The Executive has extensive knowledge of the Seller's business, including its client base and pool of temporary lawyers.

5. It is a condition to the consummation of the Acquisition Agreement that the Executive enter into this Noncompetition Agreement.

Accordingly, the parties agree as follows:

1.10 SOME FINAL WORDS

This course is a lot of work. But it is a great deal of fun (or so my students have told me). You will be learning the quintessential deal-lawyering skills: You will be learning to think and draft like a lawyer. Have fun.

The Building Blocks of Contracts: The Seven Contract Concepts

2.1 INTRODUCTION

To draft a contract, you must use contract concepts. These concepts are the foundation of every contract, the building blocks that, when properly assembled, express the parties' business deal. In this chapter, you will be introduced to those concepts. Once you understand why contract concepts are used in a specific way, you can learn how to assemble them to create a contract and how to express a contract provision clearly and unambiguously.

Here are the seven contract concepts, which when integrated into a contract's parts, result in a contract:

- Representations
- Warranties
- Covenants
- Rights
- Conditions
- Discretionary authority
- Declarations

You already know something about these concepts from your first-year contracts course. Now you will learn in more depth how deal lawyers use them.

2.2 CAPSULE DEFINITIONS

These are quick definitions of the seven contract concepts. You will learn more about each of them in Chapters 3 and 4.

- A **representation** is a statement of a past or present fact, made as of a moment in time to induce a party to act.
- A **warranty** is a promise that if a statement is false, the maker of the statement will indemnify the other party for any damages suffered because of the false statement.
- A **covenant** is a promise to do or not to do something. It creates a duty to perform.

- A **right** is the flipside of a covenant. A right entitles a party to the other party's performance.
- A **condition to an obligation** is a state of facts that must exist before a party is obligated to perform.
- **Discretionary authority** gives a party a choice or permission to act. Sometimes the exercise of discretionary authority is subject to the satisfaction of a condition.
- A **declaration** is a fact as to which both parties agree. Sometimes a declaration is subject to the satisfaction of a condition.

2.3   TRANSLATING THE BUSINESS DEAL INTO CONTRACT CONCEPTS

Each contract concept serves a different business purpose and has different legal ramifications. Accordingly, drafters choose from among these concepts when memorializing the business deal. The analytical skill of determining which contract concept best reflects the business deal is the **translation skill**; it requires the drafter to look at each specific agreement of the business deal and to translate it into contract concepts. Only then can a drafter memorialize the business deal in a contract provision.

The analytical skill of translating the business deal into contract concepts fundamentally differs from the analytical skill that litigators use. Litigators take the law and apply it to the facts to create a persuasive argument. They then memorialize that argument in a brief or a memo or otherwise use it to sway another, be it the other party or the court. In this paradigm, litigators seek a certain legal result by working backwards from the law to a static set of facts.

For example, imagine that a driver is going 80 miles an hour and hits a pedestrian; the pedestrian dies, and his heirs bring a lawsuit against the driver. The legal issue is whether the driver was negligent. To determine this, a litigator looks at the components of the cause of action for negligence and then to see whether each of the components can be matched up with the facts. The law is applied to the facts. Depending upon whom the litigator represents, the conclusion may vary.

The analytic skill of deal lawyers stands this paradigm on its head. Deal lawyers start from the business deal. The terms of the business deal are the deal lawyer's facts. The deal lawyer must then find the contract concepts that best reflect the business deal and use those concepts as the basis for drafting the contract provisions.

Chapters 3 and 4 teach the translation skill by looking at each of the contract concepts and examining its role in an agreement. Although we will be using the purchase of a house as the factual basis of much of our discussion of contract concepts, these same concepts are the building blocks of all contracts.

Translating the Business Deal into Contract Concepts: Part 1 (Representation and Warranties & Covenants and Rights)

3.1 INTRODUCTION

Before deal lawyers begin to draft, they learn the terms of the business deal. Those terms are the deal lawyer's facts. The lawyer must then find the contract concepts that best reflect the business deal and use those concepts as the basis of drafting the contract provisions. This skill is known as **translating the business deal into contract concepts**. It is the foundation of a deal lawyer's professional expertise and ability to problem solve. Without it, negotiating and drafting are abstractions. By learning this skill first, you will be able to layer knowledge of how to draft on top of a framework that has taught you what you are drafting.

This chapter and the next discuss the contract concepts in depth and demonstrate how they are used in a contract. This chapter deals with representations and warranties, then covenants and rights. Chapter 4 deals with conditions, discretionary authority, and declarations. As part of this discussion, you will learn not only the legal aspects of each contract concept, but also its business purpose. Chapter 4 ends with a chart that summarizes the material in these two chapters.

3.2 REPRESENTATIONS AND WARRANTIES

3.2.1 DEFINITIONS

Imagine that Sally Seller has listed her house for sale and that Bob Buyer is interested in purchasing it. But before Bob agrees to buy the house, he wants to learn more information about it. All that he knows now is that the house is a two-story Cape Cod painted brown. He asks Sally the following questions during a telephone call as he is out of town on business:

- When was the house built?
- How old is the roof?
- Do all the appliances work?
- Is the house wired for cable television and is the wiring functioning properly?
- Is there a swimming pool?
- Is there a swimming pool water heater? Does it use propane gas for fuel?

- How much propane gas is in the tank?
- What color are the living room walls, and when were they last painted?
- How big is the lot on which the house was built?

Sally responds to Bob by telling him the following:

- The house was built in 1953 along with other houses in the neighborhood.
- The roof is four years old.
- All the appliances are in excellent condition.
- The house is wired for cable television, and it is functioning properly.
- Yes, there is a swimming pool.
- Yes, there is a swimming pool water heater, and it uses propane gas for fuel.
- The tank is exactly one-half full with propane gas.
- The living room's walls are painted eggshell white and were painted one year ago. Sally mentions that she has been thinking of painting them a pale blue to coordinate with her furniture.
- The house was built on a one-acre lot.

After hearing Sally's responses, Bob decides that the house is perfect for him. He and Sally agree on a $200,000 purchase price. Bob then calls his lawyer and asks her to draw up the contract and to include within it the information that Sally has just told him. He tells his lawyer that the answers were an important factor in his decision to buy the house.

How does the lawyer include the information in the contract? The answer is that she will use **representations and warranties**.

A **representation**

- is a statement of fact
- as of a moment in time
- intended to induce reliance.[1]

Assume that Sally and Bob sign a contract today for the sale of the house and that in the contract Sally tells Bob the following:

- The roof is four years old.

Sally's statement is a representation. She made that statement *(a statement)* today *(a moment in time)*. (Had she made the statement a year ago, the roof would have been three years old, and if she were to make the statement in a year, it would be five years old.) In addition, she made the statement to convince Bob to purchase the house *(to induce reliance)*.

The representation that the roof is four years old is a statement about a present fact. Sally also made representations with respect to facts concerning the past: *The house was built in 1953 along with other houses in the neighborhood.* Although a party can make representations with respect to present and past facts, they generally cannot do so with respect to future facts. Those are mere statements of opinion. Chapter 9 discusses this issue in more depth.

For Bob to have a cause of action for misrepresentation, he must actually have relied on Sally's statement, and that reliance must have been justifiable.[2] That is, Bob

---

1. *See Harold Cohn & Co, Inc., v. Harco Intl., LLC*, 804 A.2d 218, 223-224 (Conn. App. Ct. 2002).
2. *See S. Broad. Group, LLC v. Gem Broad., Inc.*, 145 F. Supp. 2d 1316, 1329-1330 (M.D. Fla. 2001), *aff'd*, 49 Fed. Appx. 288 (11th Cir. 2002) (table).

must not have known that Sally's statement was false. So, for example, if Bob purchases the house after his contractor tells him that the roof is much older than four years, Bob's reliance on Sally's representation that the roof is four years old is not justifiable. Accordingly, Bob would not have a cause of action with respect to a misrepresentation as to the roof's age. He would have a cause of action, however, for breach of a **warranty** of that same statement.[3]

A warranty differs from a representation.

> A **warranty** is a promise by the maker of a statement that the statement is true.[4]

This promise will result in the maker of the statement paying damages to the statement's recipient if the statement was false and the recipient damaged. The warranty acts as an indemnity. It does not matter whether the recipient knew the statement was false.[5] The salient factor is the recipient's reliance on the promise of damages if the statement is false. Therefore, while Bob would not have a cause of action for a misrepresentation with respect to the roof's age, he would be able to sue for a breach of warranty postclosing—so long as he told Sally when they were closing that he was reserving his right to make a claim.[6]

Deal lawyers almost always negotiate for both representations and warranties. For example, in the house purchase agreement between Sally and Bob, the representations and warranties article would be introduced with the following language:

> The Seller *represents and warrants* to the Buyer as follows:

By virtue of this one line, every statement in the sections that followed would be both a representation and a warranty.[7]

In the purchase agreement between Sally and Bob, Sally's representations and warranties would resemble the following:

> **Seller's Representations and Warranties**. The Seller represents and warrants to the Buyer as follows:
> (a) The house was built in 1953, along with the other houses in the neighborhood.
> (b) The roof is four years old.
> (c) All the appliances are in excellent condition.
> (d) The house is wired for cable television, and it is functioning properly.
> (e) There is a swimming pool.
> (f) There is a swimming pool water heater, and it uses propane gas for fuel.

---

3. *Id.* at 1321-1324. *See also Shambaugh v. Lindsay*, 445 N.E.2d 124, 125-127 (Ind. Ct. App. 1983).

4. *See CBS Inc. v. Ziff-Davis Publg. Co.*, 554 N.Y.S.2d 449, 452-453 (1990).

5. *See id.* Since *CBS,* a majority of states have followed the New York rule. *See, e.g., Wikoff v. Vanderveld*, 897 F.2d 232 (7th Cir. 1990) (applying Illinois law). *But see Hendricks v. Callahan*, 972 F.2d 190 (8th Cir. 1992) (applying Minnesota law).

6. *See Galli v. Metz*, 973 F.2d 145, 150-151 (2d. Cir. 1992) (holding that where a buyer closes with full knowledge that the facts disclosed by seller are not as warranted, the buyer may not sue on the breach of warranty, unless it expressly preserves the right to do so).

7. In unusual circumstances, a practitioner might recommend to a client that it make only a warranty. See §9.4.

> (g) The tank is exactly one-half full with propane gas.
> (h) The living room's walls are painted eggshell white and were painted one year ago.
> (i) The house was built on a one-acre lot.

Finally, when determining whether a party made a misrepresentation and breached a warranty, a statement's truthfulness is always determined by comparing the statement to reality *as of the moment in time when the statement was made,* not when the determination of truthfulness is made.[8] Therefore, Sally's representation and warranty are truthful so long as the living room walls were painted eggshell white when she stated that they were that color. It would be irrelevant with respect to claims for misrepresentation and breach of warranty that she painted the walls pale blue after she made the representation in the contract for sale but before she sold the house to Bob. Of course, the painting of the walls would not be irrelevant to Bob. However, to obtain a remedy, he would need to rely on a cause of action other than misrepresentation and breach of warranty. He would need a covenant.[9]

3.2.2 REMEDIES

Representations and warranties are common law concepts. As such, they carry with them common law remedies. The differences in these remedies can directly affect which cause of action is the most favorable for a plaintiff to plead.

A party can make three types of misrepresentations: innocent,[10] negligent,[11] and fraudulent.[12] A litigation alleging any of these misrepresentations is a suit in tort.

Typically, innocent and negligent misrepresentations must be material to support a remedy.[13] The law with respect to fraudulent misrepresentations depends upon the jurisdiction. In some jurisdictions, a misrepresentation need not be material for it to constitute a fraudulent misrepresentation,[14] while in others it must.[15]

If a misrepresentation is innocent or negligent, the usual remedies are **avoidance** and **restitutionary recovery**.[16] Avoidance permits the injured party to unwind the contract.[17] Both lawyers and courts often refer to it as *rescission.* Restitutionary

---

8. *See Union Bank v. Jones,* 411 A.2d 1338, 1342 (Vt. 1980).

9. See §3.3.

10. *See Bortz v. Noon,* 729 A.2d 555, 563-564 (Pa. 1999); *Restatement (Second) of Torts* §552C (1977) (misrepresentations in sales, rental, or exchange transactions).

11. *See Liberty Mut. Ins. Co. v. Decking & Steel, Inc.,* 301 F. Supp. 2d 830, 834 (N.D. Ill. 2004); *Restatement (Second) of Torts* §552 (1977) (information negligently supplied for the guidance of others).

12. *See Skurnowicz v. Lucci,* 798 A.2d 788, 793 (Pa. Super. Ct. 2002).

13. *See Restatement (Second) of Contracts* §164 (1981).

14. *See Sarvis v. Vt. State Colleges,* 772 A.2d 494, 498 (Vt. 2001). *Compare Restatement (Second) of Contracts* §164 (1981) (providing that a fraudulent misrepresentation need not be material to make it voidable) with Restatement (Second) of Torts §538 (1977) (providing that reliance upon a fraudulent representation is not justifiable unless the matter misrepresented is material).

15. *See Skurnowicz v. Lucci,* 798 A.2d 788, 793 (Pa. Super. 2002).

16. *See Norton v. Poplos,* 443 A.2d 1, 4-5 (Del. 1981) (innocent misrepresentation); *Patch v. Arsenault,* 653 A.2d 1079, 1081-1083 (N.H. 1995) (negligent misrepresentation). Damages have been awarded in cases of innocent and negligent misrepresentation. *See Restatement (Second) of Torts* §552B and §552C (1977). *See generally* Dan B. Dobbs, *Dobbs Law of Remedies,* vol. 2, §9.2(2), 554-556 (2d ed., West 1993).

17. *See Kavarco v. T.J.E., Inc.,* 478 A.2d 257, 261 (Conn. App. Ct. 1984). *See generally* E. Allan Farnsworth, *Farnsworth on Contracts,* vol. 1, 495-496 (3d ed., Aspen 2004).

recovery requires each party to return to the other what it received, either in kind, or if necessary, in money.[18]

A misrepresentation may also be fraudulent—a misstatement made with knowledge of its falsity (**scienter**).[19] In this case, an injured party has a choice of remedies. First, it may void the contract and seek restitution,[20] just as with innocent and negligent misrepresentations. Alternatively, it may affirm the contract, retain its benefits, and sue for damages based on a claim of fraudulent misrepresentation,[21] sometimes referred to as the tort of deceit. The injured party's damages claim could also include **punitive damages**,[22] which, of course, can be significantly larger than general damages.

If an injured party decides to affirm the contract by suing for fraudulent misrepresentation, the measure of damages depends upon which state's law governs the contract. Most states use the **benefit of the bargain** measure of damages,[23] with the minority using the **out-of-pocket** measure of damages.[24]

The benefit of the bargain measure of damages results in a higher damages award and is the measure of damages that a party generally receives upon a contract breach. It is equal to the value that the property was represented to be *minus* the actual value. So, if the property was represented to be worth $10,000 but was actually only worth $3,000, the damages would be $7,000.

Value if as represented	$10,000
Actual value	-3,000
Damages	$7,000

Out-of-pocket damages are equal to the amount the plaintiff paid for the property *minus* the actual value. Thus, if the plaintiff paid $5,000 for property that was only worth $3,000, it could recover only $2,000 in damages.

Amount Paid	$5,000
Actual value	-3,000
Damages	$2,000

The difference in recovery between the benefit of the bargain damages and out-of-pocket damages can be important when a plaintiff decides whether to sue for fraudulent misrepresentation or breach of warranty. Specifically, if an injured party asserts a claim for breach of warranty, a contract claim, the remedy for that breach is full benefit of the bargain damages.[25] Therefore, in a state that follows the out-of-pocket rule of damages for fraudulent misrepresentations, a plaintiff would probably be better off pursuing a breach of warranty claim, as its benefit of the bargain damages would be

18. *See* E. Allan Farnsworth, *Farnsworth on Contracts,* vol. 1, 499 (2d ed., Aspen 2004). Some cases hold that the injured party is also entitled to reliance damages. See *In re Letterman,* 799 F.2d 967, 974 (5th Cir. 1986).

19. *See Bortz v. Noon,* 729 A.2d 555, 560 (Pa. 1999).

20. *See Smith v. Brown,* 778 N.E.2d 490, 497 (Ind. Ct. App. 2002).

21. *See Stebins v. Wells,* 766 A.2d 369, 372 (R.I. 2001).

22. *See generally* Dan B. Dobbs, *Dobbs Law of Remedies,* vol. 2, §9.2(5), 565-568 (2d ed., West 1993).

23. *See, e.g., Lightning Litho, Inc. v. Danka Indus., Inc.,* 776 N.E.2d 1238, 1241-1242 (Ind. Ct. App. 2002).

24. *See Reno v. Bull,* 124 N.E. 144, 146 (N.Y. 1919). Some states follow neither rule exclusively, but instead have a more flexible approach that varies the damage award based upon specific factors. *See, e.g., Selman v. Shirley,* 85 P.2d 384, 393-394 (Or. 1938).

25. *See Nunn v. Chem. Waste Mgt., Inc.,* 856 F.2d 1464, 1470 (10th Cir. 1988).

greater.[26] A claim for fraud might become the preferable claim, however, if a plaintiff could successfully argue for **punitive damages.**

The following chart summarizes the remedies associated with representations and warranties.

INNOCENT AND NEGLIGENT MISREPRESENTATIONS	FRAUDULENT MISREPRESENTATIONS	WARRANTIES
Avoidance and restitutionary recovery	Avoidance and restitutionary recovery *or* Damages: <ul><li>Out-of-pocket damages *or*</li><li>Benefit of the bargain damages</li><li>Punitive damages</li></ul>	Benefit of the bargain damages

In this discussion, false representations have been referred to as *misrepresentations*. Although some lawyers colloquially speak of *breaches of representations*, that terminology is incorrect. A breach is a violation of a promise. Because representations are not promises, they cannot be breached. Instead, a party makes *misrepresentations*. It is correct, however, to speak of *breaches of warranties*, as warranties are promises.

3.2.3   WHY A PARTY SHOULD RECEIVE BOTH REPRESENTATIONS AND WARRANTIES

As the preceding sections have made clear, multiple benefits accrue to a party who receives both representations and warranties. To summarize, they are the following:

- **First**, a party will have the option to void the contract and receive restitution only if that party receives representations.
- **Second**, a party may sue for punitive damages only by claiming a fraudulent misrepresentation.
- **Third**, if a party cannot prove justifiable reliance on a representation, that party can still sue for breach of warranty.
- **Fourth**, if a state follows the out-of-pocket rule for damages for fraudulent misrepresentations, a party can still recover the greater benefit of the bargain damages by suing for breach of warranty.
- **Fifth**, a breach of warranty claim may be easier to prove than a fraudulent misrepresentation claim. As noted earlier, to prove fraudulent misrepresentation, a plaintiff must demonstrate *scienter*, that the defendant knowingly made a false representation. As proving a party's state of mind can be difficult, a breach of warranty claim, which has no such requirement, may be the easier claim to win.[27]

---

26. *See Ainger v. Mich. Gen. Corp.*, 476 F. Supp. 1209, 1233-1234 (S.D.N.Y. 1979).
27. *See* W. Page Keeton, Dan B. Dobbs, Robert E. Keeton & David G. Owen, *Prosser and Keeton on Torts* §107, 741 (5th ed., West 1984).

3.2.4 RISK ALLOCATION

Each representation and warranty establishes a standard of liability. If a statement is false—if the statement does not reflect reality—then the standard has not been met and the party making the statement is subject to liability.

By establishing standards of liability, representations and warranties serve an important business purpose. They are a **risk allocation** mechanism. This means that the degree of risk that each party assumes with respect to a statement varies depending upon how broadly or narrowly the statement is drafted.

Recall that Sally told Bob that the propane gas tank was exactly one-half full. That is a precise statement. It is posited as an absolute, without any kind of wiggle room. It is a **flat representation**. It is a high-risk statement for Sally because if she is even a little wrong, Bob has a cause of action for misrepresentation and breach of warranty. Sally could have reduced her risk by making a less precise statement. She could have made a **qualified representation**. For example, she could have said that the tank was *approximately* half-filled. Then if the propane gas tank was less than one-half its capacity, Sally might still be able to contend that her statement was true. Her risk of having made a false statement is reduced. Bob, however, has now assumed a greater risk with respect to Sally's statement about the amount of fuel in the tank. Originally, Bob would have had a cause of action if the tank was even a little less than half full. Now, in order to prove a misrepresentation and breach of warranty, Bob must argue what *approximately* means. The risk allocation has shifted more of the risk to Bob.[28]

To see how risk allocation works in a more sophisticated context, imagine that you are general counsel of a $100 million company that is selling all of its shares in a wholly owned subsidiary (the Target). Your current task is to negotiate the *no litigation* representation and warranty that appears in the stock purchase agreement.[29] You know the statement needs to be qualified. But how?

Immediately following this paragraph are five versions of a *no litigation* representation and warranty. The first version is the language in the agreement. The subsequent versions represent the evolution of your thinking with respect to what kind of qualifications would be appropriate. Read all of the versions and see if you can explain how each version changes the risk allocation.

> **Version 1**
>
> **No Litigation.** No litigation is pending or threatened against the Target.
>
> **Version 2**
>
> **No Litigation.** Except as set forth in **Schedule 3.14**, no litigation is pending or threatened against the Target.

---

28. If this issue arose in the real world, the parties would most likely deal with it by a purchase price adjustment. It is used here to demonstrate risk allocation.

29. In an acquisition agreement, a *no litigation* representation and warranty details what litigation exists so that a buyer can determine if that litigation presents a significant risk to the business it is buying. Similar representations and warranties exist in other agreements. For example, in a license agreement, the licensor generally represents and warrants that there are no litigations challenging the licensor's ownership of the trademark.

Version 3

> **No Litigation**. Except as set forth in **Schedule 3.14**, no litigation is pending or, to the Seller's knowledge, threatened against the Target.

Version 4

> **No Litigation**. Except as set forth in **Schedule 3.14**, no litigation is pending or, to the knowledge of any of the Seller's officers, threatened against the Target.

Version 5

> **No Litigation**. Except as set forth in **Schedule 3.14**, no litigation is pending or, to the knowledge of any of the Seller's three executive officers, threatened against the Target. For the purpose of this representation and warranty, "knowledge" means
>
> (a) each executive officer's actual knowledge; and
>
> (b) the knowledge that each executive officer would have had after a diligent investigation.

Again, Version 1 is how the representation and warranty appears in the stock purchase agreement. It is a flat representation and warranty. You immediately recognize its most obvious flaw: it is false. Virtually every company has some litigation, and the Target is no exception. If the representation and warranty is not changed, the Seller is at great risk because it knows that the statement is false. A cause of action for misrepresentation could allege fraud. Therefore, the first qualification is that the representation and warranty must indicate pending litigations. The typical way to do this is to list them on a **disclosure schedule** and then to refer to the schedule in the representation and warranty. Version 2 does this. For a more detailed discussion of schedules, see §23.9.

The easy part is now over. Upon further review, you see that the representation and warranty actually makes two statements, one about pending litigation and the other about threatened litigation. At first, you do not see this as a concern as the disclosure schedule can qualify the representation and warranty not only with respect to pending litigation, but also with respect to known, threatened litigation. But what if the Seller does not know of an existing, threatened litigation against the Target? Perhaps someone is claiming that a product malfunctioned and intends to sue. It is an unknown, threatened litigation. After concluding that this is an unfair risk for the Seller to assume, you ask the Buyer's counsel for a knowledge qualification with respect to unknown, threatened litigation.[30] He acquiesces, and the representation and warranty is redrafted as set forth in Version 3.[31]

While the form of the Version 3 representation and warranty decreases the Seller's risk of liability, it increases the Buyer's risk. Because the Seller is no longer making a representation and warranty about unknown, threatened litigation, the Buyer will have no cause of action if unknown, threatened litigation against the Target actually exists.

---

30. Another common qualification of representations and warranties is **materiality**. That qualifier is discussed in §9.3 and is the subject of Exercise 9-1.

31. Agreeing to this qualification is so common that a buyer's first draft often includes it. The parties do, however, often negotiate the definition of *knowledge*.

Version 4 addresses the problem of what constitutes the Seller's knowledge. In the hypothetical, the Seller is a corporation, a juridical entity formed when its certificate of incorporation was filed with the appropriate governmental authority. As it is not a living, breathing human being, what constitutes its knowledge is not immediately apparent. Is it the knowledge of the company's managers, or the knowledge of everyone from the president to the employees on the shop floor?

From your perspective as general counsel (to put words in your mouth), it undoubtedly is an unfair risk for the Seller to be liable for the knowledge of every company employee. Accordingly, you request that the representation and warranty be further qualified so that the Seller is responsible only for its officers' knowledge.[32] With this change, the Seller no longer takes a risk as to the knowledge of an employee on the shop floor. However, the Seller's decrease in risk means that the Buyer's risk has commensurately increased. If an employee on the shop floor, in fact, knows of a threatened litigation, the Buyer will have no cause of action against the Seller because its representation and warranty is true: No officer knew. Thus, should the threatened litigation turn into an actual litigation and result in an award of damages, the Buyer would be obligated to pay it.

At this point, you are on a roll. You decide that even *knowledge of any of the Seller's officers* is too great a risk. Therefore, you go to the well again and ask the Buyer's counsel to change the qualification so that it reads *knowledge of any of the Seller's three executive officers.* This is the language in the first sentence of Version 5.

At this point, however, the Buyer's counsel says: "Enough. If knowledge is limited to three executive officers, they could walk around with blinders on doing their best to acquire no knowledge of threatened litigation. This is too much risk for the Buyer to assume." The Buyer's counsel instead proposes to define *knowledge* as the actual knowledge of each of the executive officers and their **imputed knowledge**; that is, the knowledge each executive would have had if the executive had performed a diligent inquiry. This is the compromise language in the remainder of Version 5. The Seller has limited its risk to the knowledge of the three executive officers, while, concurrently, the Buyer has eliminated its risk of the executive officers' intentional oblivion.

Understanding the impact of risk allocation is essential to fulfilling your role as a counselor. Clients too often misunderstand the purpose of representations and warranties and think that the time spent negotiating them is mere **wordsmithing**.[33] By explaining to a client that the wording of the representations and warranties can affect potential liability, you have explained that money is on the table, something that clients readily understand.

3.3 COVENANTS

3.3.1 DEFINITIONS AND USES OF COVENANTS

We will first look at covenants in the context of the sale of Sally's house to Bob and then in other contexts.

---

32. The qualification in Version 4 uses the phrase "to the knowledge of *any* of the Seller's officers." Thus, if any one of the Seller's officers knows of any threatened litigation, that alone creates a misrepresentation and breach of warranty. If *any* were replaced with *each,* however, then all three of the Seller's officers would have to know of the threatened litigation to cause a misrepresentation and breach of warranty. For a more detailed discussion of the proper use of *any* and *each,* see §23.16.

33. **Wordsmithing** has a pejorative connotation. It suggests that a lawyer is changing language for no substantive reason and is wasting time and money.

Imagine that after Sally and Bob have agreed to a price, Bob tells Sally that he cannot immediately purchase the house as he needs to obtain a mortgage. A delayed closing is acceptable to Sally, and they agree to close the sale on the last day of the next month. This delay creates a gap period between the signing of the purchase contract and the closing.[34] (A **closing** is when parties exchange the agreed performances. Typically, closings occur only in acquisitions and financings. In an acquisition, it would be the day the seller transfers its property to the buyer, and the buyer pays the seller; in a financing, it would be the day the bank makes the loan to the borrower, and the borrower agrees to repay it.)

As Bob and Sally finalize their agreement, Bob tells Sally that he is concerned about what will happen to the house during the gap period. Specifically, he does not want the living room walls painted, and he wants to make sure that the propane gas tank is at least one-third full with propane gas when he moves in on the closing date. Sally agrees. To incorporate Sally's agreement into the purchase contract, the lawyers use **covenants**, sometimes called **promises**.

> A **covenant** is a promise to do or not to do something. It creates a **duty** to perform.

> The duty to perform is sometimes called the **obligation** to perform.

In the purchase agreement between Sally and Bob, the covenants will resemble the following:

> **Seller's Covenants**. The Seller
>
> (a) shall not paint the walls between the signing and the Closing; and
>
> (b) shall cause the propane gas tank to be at least one-third full with propane gas on the Closing Date.

Although the need for covenants in the purchase agreement arose because of the gap period between signing and closing, covenants are not used only in this context. The need for them can arise in multiple contexts. Look at the following timelines of an acquisition agreement and a license agreement.

Example 1. Acquisition Agreement

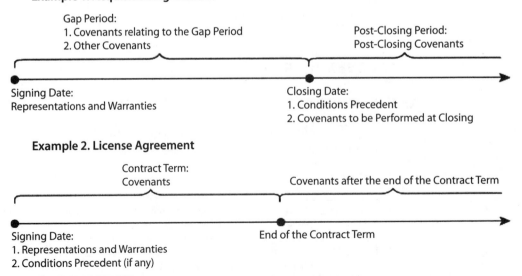

Example 2. License Agreement

34. A gap period between signing and closing is routine in acquisition transactions. It arises for multiple reasons. First, the buyer may need to obtain financing. Second, the parties may need to obtain consents to

Example 1 is the timeline of an acquisition agreement. As we have seen, in this type of transaction the parties use covenants during the gap period to control the seller's actions with respect to the subject matter of the contract (e.g., the house).[35] However, an acquisition agreement also has covenants that are unrelated to the gap period. Some covenants, such as confidentiality provisions, apply both before and after closing. Other covenants apply only at closing; for example, the promise to pay the purchase price and the promise to transfer the assets. And finally, some covenants apply only to the post-closing period. Indemnities and noncompetition provisions are classic examples.

The timeline of a license agreement, Example 2, differs from the timeline of an acquisition agreement. The license agreement has no gap period. Its term begins and ends on agreed-upon dates.[36] Each party covenants to the other as to its behavior during the term. The licensee promises to use its best efforts to manufacture and market products using the trademark, to pay license fees, and to submit for approval a prototype of each product. In turn, the licensor promises not to license the trademark to anyone else, to defend the trademark, and to promptly approve or disapprove each prototype submitted for approval. Occasionally, covenants relate to the period after the term. For example, the contract will typically set out the parties' obligations post-term with respect to any unsold inventory that the licensee owns at the end of the term.

3.3.2 DEGREES OF OBLIGATION

In the same way that representations and warranties are a risk allocation mechanism, so too are covenants. The allocation manifests itself in terms of how absolute a party's promises are. The business differences between the different ways of expressing a party's obligations are **degrees of obligation**.[37]

Consider a transaction in which the buyer hopes to acquire a lease for property that the seller uses in its business operations. To effect this acquisition, the seller must assign its rights under the lease to the buyer, but the seller's lease prohibits it from doing so. Therefore, the buyer insists that the seller must promise to obtain the landlord's consent to the assignment. Review the following covenants and see if you can determine how the risk allocation shifts depending upon the degree of the seller's obligation.[38]

Version 1

Consents. The Seller shall obtain the consent of Landlord Corp. to the Seller's assignment of the Lease to the Buyer.

the transaction or to the transfer of particular assets. Finally, the buyer may want to perform **due diligence** if it did not previously do so. (Due diligence is the corporate equivalent of test-driving a car before purchasing it. To be sure that the target company is worth purchasing, the buyer-to-be examines, among other things, the seller's contracts, equipment, and financial statements.)

35. Buyers also give covenants, such as promising to obtain any necessary consents.

36. Sometimes the parties sign on a date before the term begins. The period between the signing and the beginning of the term differs from the gap periods in acquisition agreements. During the license agreement's "gap period," generally, no covenants must be performed or conditions satisfied. Instead, the delayed beginning of the term is for administrative ease, so that the term begins either on the first day of a month or immediately after one party's relationship with a third party concludes. For example, a licensor and a licensee may negotiate and sign a license agreement in October, but the license term will not begin until January 1, the day after the licensor's current arrangement with another licensee terminates.

37. I thank my colleague, Alan Shaw, for coining this most useful phrase, *degrees of obligation.*

38. These covenants are based upon covenants that Alan Shaw drafted.

Version 2

   Consents. The Seller shall use its best efforts to obtain the consent of Landlord Corp. to the Seller's assignment of the Lease to the Buyer.

Version 3

   Consents. The Seller shall use its best efforts to obtain the consent of Landlord Corp. to the Seller's assignment of the Lease to the Buyer. For purposes of this provision, the Seller is deemed to have used its best efforts if it offers Landlord Corp. at least $10,000 as an inducement to consent to the assignment.

Version 4

   Consents. The Seller shall use commercially reasonable efforts to obtain the consent of Landlord Corp. to the Seller's assignment of the Lease to the Buyer.

Version 5

   Consents. The Seller shall request that Landlord Corp. consent to the Seller's assignment of the Lease to the Buyer.

Version 1 is the equivalent of a flat representation. It is the Seller's absolute promise to obtain consent. The promise is dangerous for the Seller to make as it has no control over the outcome: Landlord Corp. has no obligation to consent, and it could just as easily refuse consent as grant it. Because the Seller has no control, it risks breaching the covenant. The Seller, therefore, wants to reduce its risk by reducing its degree of obligation.

From the Buyer's perspective, Version 1 is a terrific covenant. If the Seller obtains Landlord Corp.'s consent, the Buyer is in position immediately to continue the Seller's business on the same premises. If the Buyer does not obtain consent, however, the Buyer should still come out whole as it has the right to sue for damages. If the current lease's rent is under market, the Buyer's damages might be equal to the rent the Buyer would have to pay for comparable leased property *minus* the rent the Seller is paying under its lease.

Versions 2 through 5 each change the Seller's risk but in a different way. Version 2 does not require the Seller to obtain consent. Instead, the standard is that the Seller must have tried to obtain consent and must have used its best efforts in that endeavor. This change substantially reduces the degree of the Seller's obligation and, therefore, its risk. Now, the focus is on the degree of effort, rather than the result. So long as the Seller uses its best efforts to obtain consent, the Buyer has no cause of action for breach if the consent is not obtained. Any difference between the cost of the existing lease and a new lease is for the Buyer's account. The decrease in the Seller's risk has shifted risk to the Buyer.

From the Seller's perspective, Version 2 is definitely better than Version 1. Nonetheless, it still sets a high standard of performance for the Seller. What does *best efforts* mean? Must the Seller spend all of its money to induce Landlord Corp. to grant consent?[39] Version 3 directly addresses this issue by capping, at $10,000, the amount that the Seller needs to spend to comply with the covenant.

---

39. *See, e.g., Bloor v. Falstaff Brewing Corp.*, 601 F.2d 609 (2d Cir. 1979).

The cap shifts risk to the Buyer. To see this more vividly, assume the Seller offers Landlord Corp. $10,000 to consent, but Landlord Corp. refuses to consent and demands $10,500. In this event, the Seller has performed its covenant and, therefore, is not in breach, even though it did not obtain consent. Accordingly, the Buyer is on the hook for any increased lease expense—even though a slightly increased payment to Landlord Corp. would have resulted in a consent.

Although Version 3 changes the Seller's risk, the Seller may not see the change as an improvement. It might not want to take on a monetary obligation. It might prefer instead to take the risk of the vague, but seemingly softer, standard set forth in Version 4. That Version arguably changes the Seller's risk by changing the standard from *best efforts* to *commercially reasonable efforts*. Thus, to comply with the covenant, the Seller must do what the reasonable businessperson would do to obtain the consent. If it does that but still cannot obtain the consent, the Buyer must pay for any increased lease expense.

Finally, Version 5 eliminates any obligation by the Seller to obtain consent. Instead, it must merely request that consent. Its degree of obligation is minimal, and the Buyer assumes almost all the risk with respect to the Seller's failure to obtain consent.

3.3.3 REMEDIES

In the same way that representations and warranties carry with them their own common law remedies, so too do covenants. In general, breach of a covenant entitles the injured party to sue for damages[40] and, if the facts are appropriate, specific performance.[41] The measure of damages is full benefit of the bargain damages. (If the breach is so material that it is a breach of the whole contract that cannot be cured, then a party may have a right to cancel as well as other remedies.[42])

If a party breaches a covenant, that party need not also have made a misrepresentation and breached a warranty. First, as is often the case, the party may not have made a representation and warranty on the same topic. Second, even if it has, the truthfulness of a representation and warranty is determined as of the time it was made. So, if a representation and warranty was true at the time that it was made, no misrepresentation or breach of warranty would occur just because the related covenant was breached.

To put this in context, assume that, at the signing of the contract, Sally represents and warrants that the walls of the living room are eggshell white and covenants to maintain their color. Then, during the gap period, Sally decides that she wants blue walls for her last few weeks in the house, and she paints them. By doing so, Sally breaches her covenant not to paint the walls, giving Bob a cause of action for breach of the covenant. Bob will not, however, have a cause of action for misrepresentation or breach of warranty because the walls were eggshell white when Sally represented and warranted their color.[43]

3.4 RIGHTS

A contract **right** flows from another party's duty to perform; that is, from a covenant. The person to whom the performance is owed has a right to that performance. There-

---

40. *See generally* Dan B. Dobbs, *Dobbs Law of Remedies,* vol. 3, §12.2, 21-50 (2d ed., West 1993).
41. *See generally id.* at §12.8, 189-245.
42. *See* U.C.C. §§2-106(4), 2-612, 2-703, U.L.A. §§2-106(4), 2-612, 2-703 (2004).
43. See §3.2.1.

fore, if there is a duty, there is a correlative right. More colloquially, the flip side of every duty is a right. Because of this relationship, a right's business purpose is the same as a duty's: to allocate risk by establishing standards of liability.

Although a duty is generally expressed as a covenant for business and legal reasons, that duty can alternatively be expressed as a right. For example:

Version 1

Payment of Purchase Price. The Buyer shall pay the Seller $200,000 at Closing. *(Drafted as the Buyer's duty.)*

Version 2

Entitlement to Purchase Price. The Seller is entitled to be paid $200,000 at Closing. *(Drafted as the Seller's right.)*

In both examples, the Buyer must pay $200,000. The difference is the focus: the Buyer's duty to pay versus the Seller's right to payment.

When determining whether a particular business point is a right, the correlative duty is not always immediately apparent. For example:

Entitlement to Deposit. If the Buyer fails to close because it did not obtain financing, the Seller is entitled to keep the deposit.

In this instance, the correlative duty would be the Buyer's obligation not to seek return of the deposit.

Translating the Business Deal into Contract Concepts: Part 2 (Conditions, Discretionary Authority, and Declarations)

4.1 INTRODUCTION

This chapter continues teaching you how to translate the business deal into contract concepts. It discusses conditions, discretionary authority, and declarations.

4.2 CONDITIONS TO OBLIGATIONS AND THE EXERCISE OF RIGHTS

4.2.1 THE BASICS

Let's continue with the hypothetical that we used in Chapter 3.

After negotiating the purchase price, Bob tells Sally that he needs to obtain a mortgage and that the application process will take about six weeks. He also tells her that while he is quite confident that he will obtain the mortgage, he does not want to be obligated to buy the house if he cannot obtain it. Sally agrees.

To establish the mortgage as a contractual prerequisite to Bob's obligation to purchase the house, the purchase contract will use a **condition.**

A **condition** is a state of facts that must exist before a party is obligated to perform.[1]

If that state of facts does not exist, the obligation to perform is not triggered. Conditions may appear in any type of agreement.

Uncertainty is a hallmark of a condition. For a state of facts to be a condition, they cannot be certain to occur. Thus, the passage of time cannot be a condition because it will occur.[2]

In the contract between Bob and Sally, the condition to the obligation and the obligation to perform might look something like the following:

---

1. The *Restatement (Second) of Contracts* § 224 (1981) defines a condition as "an event, not certain to occur, which must occur, unless its nonoccurrence is excused, before performance under a contract becomes due." However, this text will use the short-hand definition set forth above. In addition, this chapter will discuss two other types of conditions: conditions to discretionary authority and conditions to declarations.

2. *Id.,* Comment b.

> If Bob obtains a mortgage, Bob shall purchase the House.

Obtaining the mortgage triggers Bob's obligation to purchase.

The condition to an obligation and the obligation need not be in the same sentence. They can be in different sections of the contract. But for every condition to an obligation, the contract must include an obligation. They are a matched pair.

To decide whether a condition is the appropriate contract concept, determine if a relationship exists between two events and whether one must precede the other temporally. Try to fit the fact pattern into an *if/then* formulation. *If* this happens, *then* and only then is a party obligated to perform. If you can do that, draft a condition.

As a right is the flip side of a covenant,[3] the parties can provide for a condition to the exercise of a right. Here is the same business term drafted first as a condition to an obligation, along with the obligation, and then as a condition to a right, along with the right:

Version 1

> **Painting of Bedroom**. If the Seller paints the bedroom, the Buyer shall pay an additional $1,000 in purchase price.

Version 2

> **Painting of Bedroom**. If the Seller paints the bedroom, the Seller is entitled to an increase in purchase price of $1,000.

Whether the language in the first version or the second is used, the result remains the same: no additional payment unless the bedroom is painted.

4.2.2 ONGOING CONDITIONS AND WALK-AWAY CONDITIONS

Conditions can be divided into two subcategories based upon the common law consequences that flow from the failure of a condition to be satisfied:

- Conditions that if not satisfied do not affect the parties' ongoing contractual relationship **(ongoing conditions).**
- Conditions that if not satisfied permit a party to choose whether to perform or not perform **(walk-away conditions).** These conditions usually are benefits that a party wants to receive before performing the obligation memorialized in the subject matter performance provision.

This book uses the terms **ongoing conditions** and **walk-away conditions** as a pedagogical aid. They are not technical contract law terms.

Ongoing conditions are commonplace in contracts and can appear in any kind of contract. We will return once again to our hypothetical for an example.

Let's assume that the $200,000 purchase price for the house takes into account water damage to the living room ceiling resulting from a leaky roof. Not unreasonably, Bob worries that the leaks could cause extensive damage during the period between the signing and the closing. Therefore, he offers Sally the following deal: He will pay

---

3. See §3.4.

110 percent of the cost of repairs if Sally has the roof repaired no later than 10 business days after the contract's signing. Sally agrees.

In contract terms, Sally's timely repair of the roof is a condition to Bob's obligation to pay 110 percent of the cost of repairs. This condition is an ongoing condition because if it is not satisfied, the parties' relationship continues unchanged. Thus, at closing, Bob will pay the $200,000 negotiated contract price.

In contrast, Bob's securing a mortgage is a walk-away condition. If he does not secure it, so that the condition fails, he is not obligated to perform. He may, however, choose to perform. If Bob chooses to perform by buying the house,[4] he waives the failure to satisfy the condition. If he chooses not to perform, that is, not to buy the house, that nonperformance is not a breach because no obligation to perform existed. That is, the obligation to perform is never triggered because the condition to performance is never satisfied.

Deal lawyers refer to a party's choice as to whether to perform as a **walk-away right:** It is the right to walk away from the deal without performing, with that nonperformance not being a contract breach. This right arises *only* if the condition is a walk-away condition.

As a party's choice whether to perform is the common law consequence of a failed walk-away condition, most agreements do not explicitly state that the choice exists. Nonetheless, the agreement may explicitly provide additional consequences that flow from the choice not to perform.[5] For example, the agreement could automatically terminate. Or the agreement could give one or both parties the discretionary authority to terminate immediately, thereby permitting immediate termination, but not requiring it. By not requiring termination, the agreement extends the deadline by which the walk-away condition must be satisfied.[6] Often, the agreement terminates automatically if the condition is not satisfied by the new deadline.

4.2.3 RELATIONSHIP BETWEEN CONDITIONS AND COVENANTS

Walk-away conditions and walk-away rights are *sometimes* related to a party's performance of a covenant. This is particularly true in acquisitions and financings. We will use the house purchase as an example.

Suppose the kitchen is a wreck, and Bob wants Sally to refurbish it before the closing date. If Sally agrees to do the work, the parties can use both covenants and conditions to memorialize their business deal. First, Sally can promise to refurbish the kitchen before the closing date. Second, performance of the covenant can be a condition to Bob's obligation to perform.

Obligation to Refurbish the Kitchen. The Seller shall refurbish the kitchen before the Closing Date.

and

Condition to Closing. It is a condition to the Buyer's obligation to buy the House that the Seller must have complied with her covenant to refurbish the kitchen.[7]

---

4. He may have inherited money or decided to sell some stock to raise cash.

5. See §15.3.2 for an additional discussion of the consequences of a failure to satisfy a condition.

6. See §8.5 for a discussion of **rolling closing dates.**

7. Bob would probably be quite unhappy with this vague standard. In a real world situation, the parties would negotiate alternative language, providing more detailed standards.

So, on the closing date, if the walk-away condition is not satisfied, Bob may choose whether to perform or walk away. No matter which course of action he chooses, he may also sue Sally for damages because she breached her covenant to refurbish the kitchen. Two contract concepts were involved, so Bob has two sets of rights. Each contract concept exists independently of the others, so when determining a party's rights, look at each provision and its contract concept.

Section 8.2 of the Asset Purchase Agreement in Appendix A is an example of a condition based upon performance of covenants.

Although satisfaction of a condition may rest on the performance of a covenant, it need not. The condition can be unrelated to any covenant. For example, Bob might quite reasonably insist that before closing he must have received a licensed engineer's report stating that the house has no structural problems. Securing the clean report would then be a walk-away condition, giving Bob a walk-away right if not satisfied. It would not, however, be based upon Sally's performance of a covenant.

4.2.4 RISK ALLOCATION

Parties use conditions in several ways to allocate risk. First, the agreement to include a condition is itself a risk allocation. By agreeing to a condition, the parties have agreed that the "performing party" has no duty to perform if the condition is not satisfied. Thus, the contract allocates the risk of the failure to satisfy the condition to the party who would have been entitled to performance. For example, if the parties have agreed that Bob is not obligated to purchase the house if he does not obtain a mortgage, Sally takes the risk that the condition might not be satisfied.

Second, parties allocate risk by choosing to frame a business issue as a condition rather than as a covenant. A classic example occurs in the insurance context where an insured must notify its insurer of a loss.

Let's assume that Bob purchases the house and that shortly afterwards someone breaks in and steals his large-screen television. Bob reviews his homeowner's insurance policy and discovers that the insurance company must receive notice of the loss no later than 10 days after it occurs. Unfortunately, the notice Bob sends is received 10 days late. If the notice provision is a covenant, then Bob has breached the contract. In that event, the insurance company remains obligated to pay Bob for his loss, but it is entitled to damages, if any. For example, its damages might be the additional expense it incurs when it purchases the replacement television at full price, rather than at a sale that took place during the initial 10-day period.

The result differs dramatically, however, if the provision is a condition. Then, if the notice is late, Bob fails to satisfy the condition to the insurance company's obligation to perform. This failure relieves it of its obligation to pay Bob, thereby terminating Bob's right to receive the insurance proceeds. Bob forfeits his rights. Thus, the use of a condition places the risk of a late notice squarely on Bob, the homeowner.

Third, parties allocate risk by choosing the standard that establishes the state of facts that must exist before the obligation to perform arises. For example, assume that as a condition to Bob's obligation to close, Sally's lawyer must deliver an opinion dealing with, among other things, environmental matters. That condition could be formulated in several ways. Here are three. Note how even minor "drafting" revisions change the standard and shift risk.

> **Version 1**
>
> **Opinion of Seller's Counsel.** The Seller's lawyers must have delivered to the Buyer an opinion of counsel *satisfactory* to the Buyer.

> **Version 2**
>
> **Opinion of Seller's Counsel**. The Seller's lawyers must have delivered to the Buyer an opinion of counsel *reasonably satisfactory* to the Buyer.
>
> **Version 3**
>
> **Opinion of Seller's Counsel**. The Seller's lawyers must have delivered to the Buyer an opinion of counsel *substantially in the form of Exhibit B*.

Version 1 is high risk for Sally as the standard of *satisfactory to the Buyer* seems to give Bob unfettered discretion in deciding whether the opinion is acceptable. Version 2 is somewhat less risky to Sally as it constrains Bob's determination. Here, the reasonable person standard of torts has been imported into the contract. The opinion must be *reasonably satisfactory*. Version 3 substantially reduces Sally's risk as she and her lawyer will know what is required and will be able to negotiate an opinion that the lawyer can give.

Fourth, parties allocate risk by deciding whose obligations are subject to the satisfaction of which conditions. For example, Bob may insist that before he is obligated to buy the house, he wants an appropriate test to conclude that the house's water meets certain safety standards. To incorporate that requirement into the contract, the parties might use the following condition:

> **Water Safety**. It is a condition to the Buyer's obligation to close that the Buyer must have received test results that conclude that the House's water is safe to use for all residential purposes.

This condition would be a condition only to Bob's obligation to close, not Sally's. The rationale is that the test is for Bob's benefit only. It is part of his due diligence, part of his risk assessment. If the water is not satisfactory and he is willing to waive the failure of the condition, Sally should not be able to walk away without performing.

Although some conditions may be conditions for only one party, other conditions are conditions to the performance of both parties. A classic example is obtaining governmental approval.

4.3 DISCRETIONARY AUTHORITY

Discretionary authority gives its holder a choice or permission to act. The holder may exercise that authority, but is not required to do so. Once it does, the other party is bound by the holder's decision. A person who has discretionary authority is sometimes said to have a **privilege**.

As with the other contract concepts, a grant of discretionary authority allocates risk. It subjects the party without the discretion to the consequences of the actions of the party with the discretionary authority.

The following provisions from Bob and Sally's contract demonstrate how discretionary authority can be used:

> **Example 1**
>
> **Termination**. Either party may terminate this Agreement by written notice if the transactions it contemplates are not consummated on or before December 31, 20XX.
>
> **Example 2**
>
> **Notice**. A party sending notice shall use one of the following methods of delivery, but may choose which method: registered mail, personal delivery, or overnight courier.

In Example 1, both parties have the absolute discretion to terminate the contract if the house purchase is not consummated before year-end. In contrast, in Example 2, the parties have curtailed the exercise of discretion. There, the party giving notice may choose how to notify the other party, but it must be one of the previously agreed-upon methods. The notifying party has discretion, but within limited parameters.

A grant of discretionary authority often appears as an exception to a prohibition. The party exercising the discretion can be either the party prohibited from acting or the other party. Thus, the risk of how the discretionary authority is exercised depends upon how a provision is drafted.

In Versions 1 and 2 that follow, the house purchase agreement prohibits Bob from assigning his rights under the agreement, but grants Sally the discretionary authority to consent to an assignment. Thus, these versions allocate to Bob the risk of how Sally will exercise her discretionary authority. In Version 1, Bob has the greater risk because the agreement imposes no constraints on how Sally may exercise her discretion. In contrast, in Version 2, the agreement limits Bob's risk because it requires Sally to act reasonably.

Version 3 differs from the other versions because now Bob has the discretionary authority. That authority is permission to assign, which Bob may exercise without constraint. It is an exception to the prohibition against assignment, and it allocates to Sally the risk of whether Bob will exercise his discretionary authority.[8]

> **Version 1**
>
> The Buyer shall not assign any of his rights under this Agreement without the Seller's prior written consent.
>
> **Version 2**
>
> The Buyer shall not assign any of his rights under this Agreement without the Seller's prior written consent, which consent the Seller shall not unreasonably withhold.
>
> **Version 3**
>
> The Buyer shall not assign any of his rights under this Agreement, except that he may assign his rights to his wife, Lara Raskin.

---

8. In some states, a party's right to exercise its discretion is curbed by the implied obligations of good faith and fair dealing.

The exercise of discretionary authority is often subject to a state of facts having first occurred. Here, the "condition" is a **condition to discretionary authority.**

A **condition to discretionary authority** is a state of facts that must exist before a party may exercise its discretionary authority.

A classic example of the interplay between a condition and discretionary authority occurs in a loan agreement. Assume that to finance his purchase of the house, Bob takes out a loan and mortgages the house. In one of the later sections of the bank's loan agreement, that agreement lists the events that constitute an Event of Default. It then provides what happens if one of those events occurs:

> **Remedies.** If an Event of Default occurs and is continuing, then the Bank may accelerate the Loan, foreclose upon its security [Bob's house]. . . .

Here, the Bank has no authority to accelerate the Loan and to foreclose unless an Event of Default has occurred and is continuing.[9] Once this state of facts exists, the Bank must decide whether it wishes to exercise its remedies. It need not; it has discretion. Alternatively, it could sue on the note, waive the default, or grant Bob extra time to comply with the loan covenant.

A condition to discretionary authority allocates risk. Without the condition, the Bank could exercise its remedies at any time. Bob, of course, would find this unacceptable. By subjecting the exercise of remedies to the occurrence of a condition, Bob eliminates the risk of the Bank unjustifiably exercising its remedies.

In analyzing whether a party has discretionary authority, do not be lured into characterizing discretionary authority as a "right." Distinguishing the two may be difficult because parties and drafters often colloquially refer to discretionary authority as a right. For example, in the preceding example, some practitioners might characterize the Bank's choice whether to exercise its remedies as a right. But, if it were a right, the borrower would have a correlative duty, but none exists.

4.4 DECLARATIONS

A declaration is a statement of fact as to which the parties agree. But neither party has stated the fact to induce the other party to act. A party cannot sue on a declaration. No rights or remedies are associated with it.[10]

Some declarations have **legal** effect on their own, but no **substantive** effect, except when inserted into another provision; other declarations have a substantive effect on their own.

All definitions are declarations. These declarations have no substantive effect on their own. For instance, the following definition of purchase price might appear in Sally and Bob's purchase agreement:

> **"Purchase Price"** means $200,000.

---

9. The agreement's requirement that the Event of Default be continuing favors the borrower. It precludes the bank from exercising its remedies if the borrower cures the default. See §15.3.1.

10. *See Third-Party "Closing" Opinions: A Report of the TriBar Opinion Committee,* 53 Bus. Law. 592, 605-606, 620 (1998).

Although the parties have declared a legal result by including the definition in the contract, standing alone, the definition of Purchase Price has no substantive consequences within the contract. It cannot be breached because neither party has made a representation and warranty or promised to do anything. Instead, the definition must be "kicked into action" by its inclusion in another provision; for example, Bob's covenant to pay the Purchase Price at the closing.

> **Payment of Purchase Price.** The Buyer shall pay the Seller the Purchase Price at the Closing.

Only then does Bob have a duty to pay the Purchase Price and Sally a remedy upon Bob's failure to pay.

Declarations that have substantive effect on their own establish policies to which the parties must adhere during their contractual relationship. A classic example is the governing law provision.

> **Governing Law.** The laws of Michigan govern all matters with respect to this Agreement, including torts.

This provision establishes the policy that Michigan law is to be used to interpret the contract when a dispute arises.

As with a definition standing on its own, the governing law provision has no rights or remedies associated with it; it cannot be breached.[11] But, unlike definitions that must be kicked into action to have a substantive effect, the governing law provision has a substantive effect by its mere inclusion in the contract.

In the same way that obligations and discretionary authority can be subject to conditions, so too can a declaration that is a policy.

A **condition to a declaration** is a state of facts that must exist before a policy has substantive consequences.

For example:

> **Consequences of Assignment.** If any party assigns its rights under this Agreement in violation of this Section, that assignment is void.

Here, the condition and the declaration, together, establish a policy that governs the parties' relationship.

To test whether a provision is a declaration, ask yourself whether a party would want a remedy if the legal effect were not as stated. If the answer is *yes,* then the provision must be either a representation and warranty or a covenant. If the answer is *no,* then the provision is a declaration.

---

11. Although neither party could sue the other for damages based on a governing law provision, a party could sue, claiming that the governing law should be that of another state, say Georgia. The determination of that claim alone would not subject a party to liability. Liability might result, however, when the substantive claim (e.g., negligence) is adjudicated according to Georgia law, rather than Michigan law.

4.5 A CONTRACT'S BUILDING BLOCKS

Representations, warranties, covenants, rights, conditions, discretionary authority, and declarations are a contract's building blocks. Once a drafter knows which contract concept best expresses the business deal, the drafter can begin drafting the contract provision.

The following chart summarizes the salient information regarding each of the building blocks:

	DEFINITION	BUSINESS PURPOSE	REMEDY
Representation	Statement of fact as of a moment of time intended to induce reliance.	To induce reliance; to establish standards of liability; to allocate risk.	For a material, innocent or negligent misrepresentation, avoidance and restitutionary recovery. For a fraudulent misrepresentation, either • avoidance and restitutionary recovery or • damages (either out-of-pocket or benefit of the bargain) and possibly punitive damages.
Warranty	A promise that a statement is true.	To provide an indemnity if a statement is not true; to allocate risk.	Damages.
Covenant	A promise to do or not to do something. A covenant establishes a duty, also called an obligation to perform.	To require or prohibit action; to establish standards of liability; to allocate risk.	Damages and, if appropriate, specific performance. If the breach is so material that it is a breach of the whole contract that cannot be cured, then a party may have a right to cancel as well as other remedies.
Right	A party's entitlement to the other party's performance of a covenant. A right is the flip side of a covenant.	To require or prohibit action; to establish standards of liability; to allocate risk.	The same as for a covenant.

	DEFINITION	BUSINESS PURPOSE	REMEDY
Condition to an Obligation	A state of facts that must exist before a party is obligated to perform. The occurrence of the condition must be uncertain.	To establish when a party is obligated to perform a covenant; to allocate risk.	A condition to an obligation cannot be breached. Its failure to occur means that the obligation to perform is not triggered. If the failed condition does not affect the parties' ongoing relationship, the condition is an ongoing condition. If the failed condition permits one party to choose whether to perform, the condition is a walk-away condition that creates a walk-away right.
Discretionary Authority	The right to choose what action to take; permission to act.	To provide choice or permission; to allocate risk.	Not applicable.
Condition to Discretionary Authority	A state of facts that must exist before a party may exercise discretionary authority.	To establish when discretionary authority may be exercised; to allocate risk.	Not applicable.
Declaration	Statement of fact as to which the parties agree.	To create definitions and establish policies.	Not applicable.
Condition to a Declaration	A state of facts that must exist before a policy has substantive consequences.	To establish when a policy is applicable.	Not applicable.

In the next chapter, we will see how drafters integrate the building blocks into a contract's parts and assemble them to create a contract.

Drafting a Contract's Parts

A Contract's Parts

5.1 INTRODUCTION

In Chapters 3 and 4, you learned how to translate the business deal into contract concepts. This chapter introduces you to the contract parts into which the contract concepts and business deal are integrated. While subsequent chapters detail how to draft each of these parts, having an overview will give you a perspective about how the parts work together.

Look at the list of contract parts that follows. They are organized in the order in which they typically appear in an agreement. Although contracts can be on radically different topics, their organization is remarkably similar.

Parts of an Agreement

1. Preamble

2. Recitals

3. Words of agreement

4. Definitions

5. Action sections

6. Other substantive business provisions (representations and warranties, covenants, rights, conditions, discretionary authority, and declarations)

7. Endgame provisions

8. General provisions

9. Signature lines

The remainder of the sections in this chapter will introduce you to each of these parts.

5.2 INTRODUCTORY PROVISIONS

The **introductory provisions** are composed of the preamble, the recitals, and the words of agreement. They precede the agreement of the parties and provide the contract's reader with important information, such as who the parties are and why they are entering into the agreement.

5.2.1 PREAMBLE

The **preamble** is the first paragraph of the contract. Its purpose is to identify the contract. The preamble sets forth the name of the agreement, the parties, and the date the parties signed the contract. For example:

> **License Agreement**, dated April 17, 20XX, between Hong Licensing Corp., a California corporation, and Browne Manufacturing, Inc., an Alabama corporation.

5.2.2 RECITALS

The **recitals** explain the background of the contract and why the parties are entering into it. They are not enforceable provisions, so they do not provide rights or remedies. The following recitals are from a guaranty.

> **Background**
>
> 1. The Bank has agreed to lend funds to the Borrower in accordance with the Credit Agreement that they are signing today.
> 2. The Borrower is a wholly-owned subsidiary of the Parent.
> 3. The Bank will lend to the Borrower only if the Parent guarantees the Borrower's debt.
> 4. The Parent and the Borrower are engaged in related businesses, and the Parent will derive substantial direct and indirect benefit from the Bank's loans to the Borrower.
> 5. The Parent is willing to guarantee the Borrower's debt.

5.2.3 WORDS OF AGREEMENT

The **words of agreement** do what they say: they state, for the record, that the parties have agreed to the terms of the contract. Historically, these words had a secondary function, to recite the contract's consideration. But today, that recitation is archaic and superfluous in most instances. Lawyers who continue to use the more traditional language often refer to the words of agreement as the **statement of consideration**. Here are two examples:

Contemporary

Accordingly, the parties agree:

Traditional

NOW, THEREFORE, in consideration of $10 paid in hand and other good and valuable consideration, the receipt of which is hereby acknowledged, the parties hereto hereby agree as follows:

5.3 DEFINITIONS AND DEFINED TERMS

Although it is not always the case (and some contend it should never be the case), **definitions** and their **defined terms** often follow the words of agreement. Defined terms are a shorthand way of referring to complex concepts and ensure that the same concept is said the same way throughout an agreement. Definitions are used for multiple purposes, including expanding or narrowing the ordinary meaning of a word or phase. As noted in Chapter 4, definitions are drafted as declarations. An example of a definition follows:

> **"Litigation Expense"** means any expense incurred in connection with asserting, investigating, or defending any claim arising out of or relating to this Agreement, including without limitation, the fees, disbursements, and expenses of attorneys and other professionals.

5.4 ACTION SECTIONS

This textbook refers to the next part of an agreement as the **action sections**. The action sections earn their name because they are *where the action is* from the client's perspective. In the action sections, the parties

- agree to perform the main subject matter of the contract;
- agree to pay the consideration (be it purchase price, rent, or royalties);
- set forth the term of the contract (if any);
- set forth the closing date (if any); and
- list the closing deliveries (if any).

Article 2 of the Asset Purchase Agreement in Appendix A contains that agreement's action sections, Sections 2 through 5 of the Website Development Agreement in Appendix B contain that agreement's action sections.

5.4.1 SUBJECT MATTER PERFORMANCE PROVISIONS

The first section of the action sections is the **subject matter performance provision**. In this provision, each side covenants to the other that it will perform the main subject matter of the contract:

> **Example 1**
>
> **Purchase and Sale**. At the Closing, Sally Seller *shall sell* the house to Bob Buyer, and Bob Buyer *shall buy* the house from Sally Seller.
>
> **Example 2**
>
> **License**. During the term of this Agreement, the Licensor *shall license* the Trademark to the Manufacturer, and the Manufacturer *shall manufacture and market products* with the Trademark.

A subject matter performance provision does not always consist of **reciprocal covenants** of future performance. Sometimes, it is a **self-executing provision**. Then, the words are the performance:

> **Grant of Security Interest**. By signing this Security Agreement, the Borrower grants a security interest in its assets to the Bank.

Thus, the main subject matter of the contract is not to be performed in the future. Instead, the signing of the agreement effects the grant of the security interest.

5.4.2 CONSIDERATION

The next provision of the action sections usually sets out the **consideration**, be it the purchase price, salary, or royalties. Consideration is generally drafted in one of two ways. The first way states what the consideration is and then, in a separate section or sentence, a party covenants to pay the consideration. The second way combines the statement of what the consideration is with the covenant to pay it.

> **Version 1**
>
> **Royalties**. The royalties for each calendar month are the amount equal to 2 percent *times* Net Sales for that calendar month (the "**Monthly Royalties**"). The Licensee shall pay the Licensor the Monthly Royalties for each calendar month no later than the third Business Day of the following calendar month. *(Drafted as a declaration and a covenant.)*
>
> **Version 2**
>
> **Royalties**. With respect to each calendar month, the Licensor shall pay the Licensee royalties equal to 2 percent *times* Net Sales for that calendar month, payment to be made no later than the third Business Day of the following calendar month. *(Drafted as a covenant.)*

5.4.3 TERM

Another common provision of the action sections sets forth **the term of the contract**—the number of years that the contract will govern the parties' relationship. Not all contracts have terms. Some contracts contemplate a one-time transaction, such as an acquisition, and terminate upon the consummation of that transaction. Other contracts, however, are intended to govern the parties' relationship for multiple years.

Supply agreements, software licensing agreements, and leases are all agreements that commonly have terms. The following examples illustrate two of the possible ways to incorporate a term into the action sections.

Version 1

>   **Term.** The term of this Lease is three years. It begins on the date that the parties sign and deliver this Agreement and ends at 5:00 p.m. on the day immediately preceding the third anniversary of the date that the parties sign and deliver this Agreement. *(The term is stated as a declaration in a stand-alone provision.)*

Version 2

>   **Term.** The Landlord shall lease the Premises to the Tenant, and the Tenant shall rent the Premises, for a term of three years. The term begins on the date that the parties sign and deliver this Agreement and ends at 5:00 p.m. on the day immediately preceding the third anniversary of the date that the parties sign and deliver this Agreement. *(This provision integrates the contract's term into the reciprocal covenants that compose the subject matter performance provision. The next sentence, a declaration, sets forth the term's beginning and ending dates.)*

5.5 CLOSING RELATED PROVISIONS

Some transactions, not all, have a closing. Generally, they are necessary only in acquisitions and financings. When a transaction has a closing, the agreement will include a **closing date** provision and **closing deliveries** provisions. In the closing date provision, the parties state when and where the closing will take place. In the closing deliveries provisions, each party covenants to the other how it will deliver its performance at closing. In a financing agreement, the bank promises to deliver the loan amount, and the borrower promises to execute and deliver a note. Similarly, in an acquisition agreement, the seller promises to execute and deliver conveyancing documents, and the buyer promises to deliver the purchase price.

5.6 OTHER SUBSTANTIVE BUSINESS PROVISIONS

The **other substantive business provisions** follow the action sections. In our hypothetical house purchase agreement, the provisions would probably be organized by contract concept and appear in order of their chronology on the transaction's timeline: First would be representations and warranties (made at the time of the signing of the agreement), then covenants (to govern during the gap period between signing and closing), and finally conditions (to provide walk-away rights at closing). Other agreements have different organizational schemes, such as by subject matter in decreasing order of importance.[1] For example, take a look at the Website Development Agreement in Appendix B. It is organized almost wholly by subject matter. Only the parties' representations and warranties are set out by contract concept.

---

1. For a detailed discussion of how to organize a contract, see Chapter 26.

5.7   ENDGAME PROVISIONS

The **endgame provisions** are generally the next-to-last substantive provisions of a contract. They set forth the business terms that govern the end of the parties' contractual relationship. They require a drafter to determine the different ways that a contract can end and how the contract will deal with each of the scenarios.

Contracts can end either happily or unhappily. The joint venture can be successfully concluded, or the borrower can fail to pay principal when due. In either event, the contract must deal with the consequences of the end of the contract. If the contract ends happily, the endgame provisions will set out any final payments that need to be made or set forth any covenants that survive the termination of the relationship. For example, an employment agreement might include a confidentiality covenant that continues past the end of the term of the contract. If the contract ends unhappily, the endgame provisions will set forth what constitutes a default and the agreed-upon remedies. As these provisions invariably involve money, they are often hotly negotiated.

Endgame provisions are often drafted as conditions to an obligation to perform and the statement of the obligation, or conditions to discretionary authority and the statement of the discretionary authority.

Example 1

Release of Collateral. After the Borrower has paid all of the outstanding principal and accrued interest, the Bank shall sign any documents necessary to release the Collateral. *(Condition to an obligation and the statement of the obligation.)*

Example 2

Late Submission of Manuscript. If the Author does not submit his manuscript before November 1, 20XX, the publisher may refuse to publish the Book. *(Condition to discretionary authority and the statement of the discretionary authority.)*

5.8   GENERAL PROVISIONS

The final provisions of an agreement are the **general provisions**, often referred to as the **boilerplate provisions**. These provisions tell the parties how to govern their relationship and administer the contract. Classic general provisions include notice, choice of law, choice of forum, antiassignment, merger, waiver of jury trial, and severability provisions.

The phrase *boilerplate provisions* is misleading as it suggests that the provisions are standardized and in no need of tailoring. Treating these provisions in this way courts disaster. Within each of these provisions are important business and legal issues that you must address.

Some general provisions are covenants, while others are declarations:

Example 1

Assignment and Delegation. The Tenant shall not assign its rights under this Lease to any person, nor may it delegate its performance. *(A covenant.)*

> **Example 2**
>
> **Successors and Assigns**. This Agreement binds and benefits the parties and their respective permitted successors and assigns. *(A declaration.)*

5.9 SIGNATURE LINES

A contract concludes, of course, with the parties' **signatures**. While generally both parties sign a contract because both make promises, in some contracts, such as a guaranty, only one party makes promises. In that case, only that party signs.

In the following chapters, you will learn how to draft each of these parts of a contract.

CHAPTER FIVE

EXERCISES

Exercise 5-1

Draft a car purchase agreement using the following facts. Do not include any other provisions.

Facts

1. The parties are Indira Balram, the seller, and Tom Rogers, the buyer.
2. The car is a red, 20XX Acura.
3. It has been driven 26,000 miles.
4. The purchase price is $11,000. The buyer will pay the seller with a certified check.
5. The seller owns the car, and it is not subject to any liens.
6. The car has been maintained in accordance with the owner's manual and is in good operating condition, normal wear and tear excepted.
7. The closing will take place on the last day of the month that follows the month in which the car purchase agreement is signed.
8. With respect to the period beginning on the day the agreement is signed and ending on the closing date, the seller promises not to paint the car and not to drive it more than 500 miles. The seller also promises to garage the car and to continue to maintain it.
9. The buyer only has to close if the seller has performed its covenants and if the seller's representations and warranties are true on the closing date, except to the extent the agreement contemplated that specific facts might change.
10. The date of the agreement is the date that this assignment is due.

Exercise 5-2

Follow the instructions in the memorandum from the Senior Associate to the Overworked Junior Associate. For the purposes of this exercise, assume that it is March 1, 20X9.

From: Senior Associate

To: Overworked Junior Associate

Date: March 1, 20X9

     As you know, Corporate Partner went on vacation last week and left me in charge of one of his matters. As I will be conducting the negotiations, I need your assistance in churning out the documents. Please review the deal terms and determine how you would translate each of them into contract concepts. Specifically, determine which of the following contract concepts best expresses each business term. Several of the business terms require more than one contract concept. It will not help me to tell me that a business term belongs in the action sections or the endgame provisions. What I really need to know is which contract concept to use.

Put your answer on the line that follows each numbered paragraph. Don't worry about Paragraph 12. We will deal with that information later on in the transaction.

- Representation and warranty
- Covenant
- Right
- Condition
  - ➢ Condition to an obligation
  - ➢ Condition to discretionary authority
  - ➢ Condition to a declaration
- Discretionary authority
- Declaration

We will review your work as soon as you finish. (It is fine with me, in fact I prefer, if you consult with other associates in the firm.)

Our client, Healthy Hearts Inc., an immediate care medical facility, has been conducting an extensive search for a new chief executive officer. Last week, they reached a handshake deal with Adele Administrator. The salient provisions of the contract follow.

1. Healthy Hearts agrees to hire Administrator, and Administrator agrees to work for Healthy Hearts.

_____

2. Administrator will be engaged as Chief Executive Officer of Healthy Hearts.

_____

3. Administrator is currently executive vice president at Holistic Hospitals Corp. and is party to an Employment Agreement with Holistic that is dated April 1, 20X6, and purportedly ends March 31, 20X9. Healthy Hearts is very concerned about that agreement. According to Administrator, its terms do not permit her to show it to anyone other than her advisors. Healthy Hearts does not want to tortiously interfere with that agreement. Administrator insists that she is free to enter into the employment agreement with Healthy Hearts and that doing so will not breach her employment agreement with Holistic. Please see if you can put in some provision that will give Healthy Hearts comfort on this point. Specifically:

(a) Healthy Hearts wants to show that it entered into its employment agreement with Administrator in the good faith belief that it was not causing a breach.

(b) Healthy Hearts wants to be able to sue Administrator if the employment agreement with Healthy Hearts in fact causes a breach under her employment agreement with Holistic.

4. The term of employment will be for three years, beginning on April 1, 20X9.

5. Healthy Hearts negotiated for the right to terminate Administrator's employment for "cause," in which event Healthy Hearts would pay Administrator her salary through the date of termination, plus reimbursement of any expenses incurred through the date of termination. Healthy Hearts must make such payment on the date of the termination.

6. Administrator will be paid $25,000 per month, payable on the first business day of each month.

7. During her negotiations with Healthy Hearts, Administrator stated that she received her A.B. from Brown University in 20X1 and her M.D. from Harvard University in 20X5. She also advised Healthy Hearts that she is enrolled in the MBA program at Fordham University and is specializing in Hospital Administration. Healthy Hearts is very "hung up" on credentials and is also concerned about what it calls "resume fraud." It therefore wants to be able to sue Administrator if she in fact does not have the credentials she claims. In addition, Healthy Hearts does not want to be obligated under the Employment Agreement if Administrator has not been awarded her MBA by the time her employment under the Employment Agreement is to begin.

8. Administrator shall perform all duties that are customary for an officer of a corporation holding the office of Chief Executive Officer.

9. During her negotiations with Healthy Hearts, Administrator insisted upon two things to which Healthy Hearts agreed:

(a) She wants Healthy Hearts to employ Samuel Samaritan as her Administrative Assistant no later than March 31, 20X9. (Healthy Hearts agreed that Administrator would not only have the right to sue if Healthy Hearts failed to employ Samaritan by March 31, 20X9, but also the right not to go forward with Healthy Hearts.)

(b) Administrator can back out of the deal if Phil Philanthropic has not contributed $5 million to the Healthy Hearts capital fund-raising program by March 31, 20X9.

10. Administrator agreed that she would devote her attention and energies on a full-time basis to the business of Healthy Hearts.

11. If Healthy Hearts terminates Administrator's employment "without cause," it must pay Administrator any salary currently payable, plus $100,000, plus reimbursement of any expenses incurred through the date of termination. Healthy Hearts must make such payment on the date of termination.

---

12. In case you need to know for any reason, Healthy Hearts is incorporated in Michigan, and Adele Administrator lives in Detroit, Michigan.

Exercise 5-3

Exercise 5-3 once again asks you to translate the business deal into contract concepts. Please follow the instructions in the memorandum.

From: Senior Associate

To: Overworked Junior Associate

Date: April 20, 20X9

I really appreciated your help on that last project. As you know by now, the reward for excellent work is more work. . . .

Our client is Ralph Products LP. Ralph LP owns all rights in the cartoon character Ralph—a short, frumpy, bespectacled, eight-year-old for whom life never goes quite right. For reasons that no one can fathom, anything with a likeness of Ralph on it sells like hotcakes. Ralph LP has been making millions by licensing the trademark rights to use this character to different companies who manufacture and then market products bearing Ralph's likeness.

Our client and Merchandisers Extraordinaire, Inc. have agreed to enter into a license agreement with the terms set forth in this memorandum. Please tell me how you would translate these business terms into contract concepts. For each numbered paragraph, choose the correct contract concept or concepts from the list that you used in the last assignment. Then, write your answer on the lines following the paragraph. Don't worry about paragraph 11. We will deal with that information later.

---

1. Merchandiser's license will be for caps and t-shirts, and it will be able to market and merchandise them in Maine, New Hampshire, and Vermont.

---

2. As you might well understand, Ralph LP has an ongoing concern about the financial condition of its licensees. It is willing to enter into this agreement only because Merchandiser's most recent financial statements showed substantial financial strength. Ralph LP wants the contract to reflect its reliance on those financial statements. In addition, Ralph LP wants the right to terminate this agreement if Merchandiser's net worth— as at the end of any fiscal year during the term of the contract—drops below $15 million.

---

3. The agreement will have a three-year licensing term, to begin on the first day of the month after the end of this month. Please assume that we'll be able to execute this agreement tomorrow.

4. Merchandiser is to have an obligation to use its best efforts to market the Ralph merchandise. If Merchandiser has any unsold merchandise on hand at the time the term ends, Ralph LP will buy that merchandise at its cost.

5. Merchandiser wants some kind of assurance in the contract

    (a) that Ralph LP actually owns what it is licensing; and
    (b) that during the term of the license, Ralph LP will
    (i) enforce its intellectual property rights against all third parties; and
    (ii) defend its licensees against all intellectual property claims of third parties.

6. The parties have agreed that with respect to each year of the term of the contract, Merchandiser must pay royalties equal to 15 percent of all net sales.

7. Ralph LP has a reputation for being quality crazy and always requires its licensees to submit samples of any item it intends to manufacture at least 30 days before the item is to go into production. Ralph LP then must either accept or reject the item. If Ralph LP rejects the sample, the licensee may make changes and resubmit it for approval. If Ralph LP approves the item, then Merchandisers must manufacture it.

8. Merchandiser wants Ralph LP to give assurances that Merchandiser is the only one now with the right to sell caps and t-shirts in its territory and that during the term of the contract Ralph LP will not grant anyone else a competing right.

9. Merchandiser was concerned that its territory was relatively small. Our client agreed to extend the territory to include Delaware and Rhode Island if Merchandiser's sales for the first year of the term were greater than $7,000,000.

10. Please provide that Oregon law will govern.

11. In case you need to know for any reason, Ralph Products LP is a Virginia limited partnership, and Merchandisers Extraordinaire, Inc., is an Oregon corporation.

Introductory Provisions: Preamble, Recitals, and Words of Agreement

6.1 INTRODUCTION

The first three provisions of a contract are introductory and set the stage for the remainder of the contract. They identify the agreement, explain its purpose, and state that the parties agree to the provisions that follow. Although seemingly basic, they can bind the wrong party and affect a contract's meaning.

Unfortunately, many drafters continue to draft these introductory provisions in a traditional style, one that is verbose, replete with legalese, and evocative of eighteenth-century England. What follows is typical:

Version 1

THIS NONCOMPETITION AGREEMENT, made as of the 16th day of March, 20XX, by and between ATTORNEY STAFFING ACQUISITION CO., a corporation organized under the laws of Delaware (hereinafter, the "Company"), and MARIA RODRIGUEZ, residing at 21 Melmartin Road, Chicago, Illinois 60606 (hereinafter, the "Executive"),

W I T N E S S E T H:

WHEREAS, Attorney Staffing Inc., a Delaware corporation (the "Seller"), provides temporary lawyers to law firms in the greater Chicago area;

WHEREAS, the Seller is selling substantially all of its assets to the Company in accordance with the Asset Acquisition Agreement, dated the first day of February 20XX (the "Acquisition Agreement");

WHEREAS, the Executive is the sole stockholder of the Seller and its President;

WHEREAS, the Executive has extensive knowledge of the Seller's business, including its client base and pool of temporary lawyers; and

continued on next page >

> WHEREAS, it is a condition to the consummation of the Acquisition Agreement that the Executive enter into this Noncompetition Agreement;
>
> NOW, THEREFORE, in consideration of the mutual promises herein contained and other good and valuable consideration, the receipt of which is hereby acknowledged, the parties hereto hereby agree:

Note that the provisions are actually part of one long sentence:

> **This Agreement . . . witnesseth [the following things] and therefore, the parties agree to what follows:**

This format is archaic and can be revised without any change in substance or effect. For example:

Version 2

> **Noncompetition Agreement,** dated as of March 16, 20XX, between Attorney Staffing Acquisition Co., a Delaware corporation (the "Company"), and Maria Rodriguez (the "Executive").
>
> ### Background
>
> 1. Attorney Staffing Inc., a Delaware corporation (the "Seller"), provides temporary lawyers to law firms in the greater Chicago area.
> 2. The Seller is selling substantially all of its assets to the Company in accordance with the Asset Acquisition Agreement, dated February 1, 20XX (the "Acquisition Agreement").
> 3. The Executive is the sole stockholder of the Seller and its President.
> 4. The Executive has extensive knowledge of the Seller's business, including its client base and pool of temporary lawyers.
> 5. It is a condition to the consummation of the Acquisition Agreement that the Executive enter into this Noncompetition Agreement.
>
> Accordingly, the parties agree as follows:

In the remainder of this chapter, we will look at how to draft each of these introductory provisions.

6.2 PREAMBLE

The **preamble** is the first paragraph of an agreement. Some drafters refer to it as the **introductory paragraph**. It identifies the agreement by stating its name, its date, and the parties. The following is a well-drafted contemporary preamble.

> **Version 1**
>
> **SUPPLY AGREEMENT**, dated as of March 3, 20XX, between Carpetmakers, Inc., an Indiana corporation (the "Manufacturer"), and Big Retail Corp., a Florida corporation (the "Retailer").

Here are two other contemporary ways of drafting the preamble. First, the preamble can be turned into a sentence:

> **Version 2**
>
> This **SUPPLY AGREEMENT**, dated as of March 3, 20XX, is between Carpetmakers, Inc., an Indiana corporation (the "Manufacturer"), and Big Retail Corp., a Florida corporation (the "Retailer").

Second, the information can be set forth in a list format:[1]

> **Version 3**
>
> Name of Agreement: Supply Agreement
>
> Dated: As of March 3, 20XX
>
> Parties:
>
> > Manufacturer: Carpetmakers, Inc., an Indiana corporation
> >
> > Retailer: Big Retail Corp., a New York corporation

The remainder of Section 6.2 details the rules for drafting the preamble.

6.2.1 NAME OF THE AGREEMENT

Typically, the name of an agreement is indented five spaces and typed in all capital letters to make the title conspicuous. Although multiple lines of capital letters impede a document's readability, sparing use of capital letters brings attention to the capitalized words.[2] Some drafters also put the title in a bold font. An acceptable alternative is to use upper and lowercase letters and a bold font. This book uses both styles.

---

1. *See* Howard Darmstadter, *Hereof, Thereof, and Everywhereof, A Contrarian Guide to Legal Drafting* 80 (ABA 2002).

2. Carl Felsenfeld and Alan Siegel, *Writing Contracts in Plain English* 194-195 (West 1981).

> **LEASE**, dated as of November 14, 20XX, between Real Estate, Inc., a Florida corporation (the "Landlord"), and Red Shoes LLC, a Texas limited liability company (the "Tenant").

Most drafters precede the preamble with the name of the agreement on a separate line. If included, it is centered and generally in bold capital letters. The additional title further helps the reader to quickly identify the agreement. If you do this, the name of the agreement that precedes the preamble should be precisely the same as that which appears in the preamble. An additional title is particularly useful in a transaction where the parties sign multiple agreements of the same type, but where one party differs in each agreement. This might occur, for example, in a financing transaction where multiple subsidiaries guarantee the parent corporation's debt. To expedite the agreements' identification, drafters title the agreement as described and then put below the agreement's name, in brackets, the name of the subsidiary that is a party.

> **GUARANTY**
> **[Subsidiary A]**
>
> **GUARANTY**, dated as of October 15, 20XX, by Subsidiary A, an Arkansas corporation (the "Guarantor"), in favor of Big Bank, a national banking corporation (the "Bank").

An agreement's name should describe its subject matter. For example: **Supply Agreement**. Some drafters simply use *Agreement,* but that defeats the purpose of the preamble, which is to identify the agreement. A truncated agreement name is especially a problem if multiple agreements in a transaction are named *Agreement.* In that case, a reader may have to wade through the agreement to learn its subject matter. A truncated name can further frustrate a reader if one agreement refers to another. A cross-reference to the *Agreement* conveys no meaningful information.

6.2.2 DATE

Drafters can date an agreement in one of two ways:

> **Version 1**
>
> , dated January 6, 20XX,
>
> **Version 2**
>
> , dated *as of* January 1, 20XX,

Drafters use the Version 1 format when the parties reach agreement on the same day that they sign the agreement. In contrast, drafters use the Version 2 format when parties reach an agreement on the *as of* date, but do not sign their agreement until a later date.

For example, if a senior executive begins work on May 23, 20XX, without a written contract, the parties will want the agreed-upon business terms to be effective as of that date. Accordingly, the employment agreement will be dated *as of May 23, 20XX,* even if it is not signed until July 1, 20XX. That the effective date and the signing date differ causes no legal problem.[3] Nonetheless, to state what should be self-evident, an *as of* date should never be used to deceive a third party such as the government. That would be fraud.[4]

Using an *as of* date can affect the accuracy of representations and warranties and the effective date of covenants. Recall that representations and warranties speak as of the moment in time as of which they are given.[5] If a contract has an *as of* date, then the representations and warranties speak as of that date, not the date the contract is signed.

Suppose, for example, that on October 15, 20XX, Bob Buyer agreed to buy Sally Seller's car and on that day Sally represented and warranted that the fuel tank was one-half full. If the contract is signed on November 1, 20XX, without being effective as of October 15, 20XX, then the representations and warranties speak as of November 1, 20XX. In that case, the representation and warranty with respect to the fuel tank is probably wrong. Fuel may have been used or the tank refilled. Therefore, to keep the representation and warranty accurate, the parties should date the contract *as of* the date of their agreement, October 15, 20XX. Alternatively, the parties could date the contract November 1, 20XX, and update the representations and warranties.

An *as of* date can raise a similar issue with respect to covenants. Specifically, when an *as of* date is used, covenants must be effective as of that date rather than the signing date. If they are not, a party could do as it pleased from the agreement date (the *as of* date) through the signing date. So, for example, if Bob and Sally agree on October 15, 20XX, that Sally may drive the car no more than 100 miles before the closing, that covenant must limit Sally's driving beginning on that date. If instead the covenant begins on November 1, 20XX, the signing date, Sally can drive as much as she wants from October 15 to November 1 without breaching her covenant.

When drafting a contract with an *as of* date in the preamble, you should also indicate its actual signing date somewhere in the contract. This might be important for tax or other reasons. Some drafters put a date line under each signature.

> Cartoon Characters LLC
>
> By: _____
>   Ann Chin, Manager
>   February 27, 20XX

Although this approach is common, at least one court has decided that it creates an ambiguity as to the contract's effective date.[6] As an alternative include the *as of* date and the signing date in the concluding paragraph:

> To evidence the parties' agreement to this Agreement's provisions, the parties have executed and delivered this Agreement *on February 27, 20XX, but as of the date set forth in the preamble.*

---

3. *See Brewer v. National Sur. Corp.*, 169 F.2d 926, 928 (10th Cir. 1948).

4. *See U.S. v. Bourgeois*, 950 F.2d 980, 982-983 (5th Cir. 1992).

5. See §3.2.1.

6. *Sweetman v. Strescon Indus., Inc.*, 389 A.2d 1319, 1322 (Del. Super. Ct. 1978).

As a second alternative, state the signing date in the preamble and include an effective date provision in the action sections.

> **SETTLEMENT AGREEMENT**, dated February 27, 20XX, between Cartoon Characters LLC, a Pennsylvania limited liability company ("Cartoon"), and Specialty Manufacturing, Inc., a Texas corporation ("Specialty").
>
> *and*
>
> **Effective Date**. This Agreement is effective as of January 10, 20XX.

Do not put a future date in the preamble. If parties want an agreement to be effective on a future date, use the signing date in the preamble and include an effective date provision in the action sections.

Whether an agreement is dated the agreement date or the signing date, drafting the date is straightforward. Either offset the date with two commas, or use no commas. Either style is acceptable.

> **Version 1**
>
> . . ., dated January 6, 20XX, . . ., dated as of January 1, 20XX, . . .
>
> **Version 2**
>
> . . . dated January 6, 20XX . . . dated as of January 1, 20XX . . .

6.2.3 PARTIES

After the date, the preamble states who the parties are.

> **SETTLEMENT AGREEMENT**, dated as of January 10, 20XX, *between Cartoon Characters LLC, a Pennsylvania limited liability company ("Cartoon"), and Specialty Manufacturing, Inc., a Texas corporation ("Specialty").*

Although some drafters precede the first party's name with *by and between,* the words *by and* are superfluous, and you should omit them.

Some lawyers use *between* if a contract has two parties and *among* if it has three or more. This is wrong. *Between* is correct whenever two or more parties are in a direct reciprocal relation with each other. In contrast, *among* should be used to express a less direct relationship with a group.[7]

Consider the example of a stockholders' agreement whose parties are the seven stockholders and the corporation. In this instance, an agreement exists between each stockholder and each of the other stockholders and between each stockholder and the corporation. Accordingly, *between* is the correct preposition to use in the pre-

---

7. *The Oxford English Dictionary* 154-155 (2d ed., Clarendon Press · Oxford 1989). *See also* H. W. Fowler, *A Dictionary of Modern English Usage* 57 (Sir Ernest Gowers ed., 2d ed., Oxford U. Press 1965). In New York City, lawyers used to circulate a Cleary Gottlieb newsletter from 1981. In it, one of the firm's lawyers argues fervently in favor of the use of *between* in all instances in a preamble, regardless of whether the number of parties is two or more. *See* Andrew Kull, *Between You, Me and the Gatepost* in *Cleargolaw News,* Vol. XXIII, No. 4, March 19, 1981 (copy on file with the author).

amble. Distinguish this example from the following: *The Clean Air Act is among the environmental laws that have been enacted.* Here, the laws do not have a direct, reciprocal relationship with each other. Instead, they are members of a group. Thus, *among* is correct.

If you intend to use *between* in all instances in a preamble, beware. You may have an uphill battle convincing your colleagues that you are right. The improper use of *among* in this context is deeply ingrained. But, keep in mind that using *between* or *among* in the preamble does not affect a contract's substance.[8] Therefore, do not waste negotiating capital on this point.

6.2.3.1 Identifying the Parties

When drafting the preamble, take the time to be sure that you properly identify the parties. Using the wrong name may mean binding the wrong party. To accurately ascertain an entity's name, check its organizational document; for example, its certificate of incorporation. That will give you the entity's legal name, including such details as whether a comma precedes *Inc.* If the party is an individual, confirm that you have that person's full legal name, rather than a nickname or professional name.[9] Some drafters put the parties' names in all capital letters, but this is unnecessary.

After an entity's name, state what type of entity it is, along with its jurisdiction of organization (together, its **organizational identity**). Some drafters omit this information, believing it to be inappropriate in a preamble. That may be correct in the context of consumer agreements being drafted in plain English. However, in the context of sophisticated parties entering into a complex commercial agreement, other concerns take priority.

Specifically, the jurisdiction of organization may be necessary to identify an entity and to prevent confusion as to which entity is a party to the contract. Although no two entities organized in the same state may have the same name, entities organized in different states may have the same name. Indeed, some holding companies intentionally give their subsidiaries the same name so that they have the same public persona.

For example, ABC Inc., a holding company incorporated in Delaware, may have 49 subsidiaries, each of which is named ABC Inc., and each of which is incorporated in a different state. If the preamble lists ABC Inc. as a party, but omits its state of incorporation, a nonparty might not know which ABC Inc. was the party to the agreement. Including an entity's organizational identity clears up any ambiguity. Here are two examples of an entity's name followed by its organizational identity.

Example 1

Internet Inc., a Delaware corporation,

Example 2

Colossal Construction LP, a New York limited partnership,

---

8. The choice between these terms can matter in a contract's substantive provisions, so make sure you understand when each should be used.

9. Some women use their given surname for professional purposes, but their married name for all other purposes.

Note that a comma precedes and follows the organizational identity. Grammar dictates this punctuation because the organizational identity is an appositive—a word or phrase following a noun that further describes the noun. Note also that neither *corporation* nor *limited partnership* is capitalized. Capitalize these terms only if they are part of an entity's name:

> **Correct**
>
> Hong Corporation, a California corporation,

In addition, avoid the old-fashioned, elongated version of an entity's organizational identity:

> **Wrong**
>
> Internet Inc., a corporation organized under the laws of the State of Delaware,

Instead, truncate the appositive as in the previous examples.

Including an entity's organizational identity in the preamble does not substitute for including that information in an agreement's representations and warranties. There, it becomes a substantive provision, giving a party a remedy if the information is incorrect. Banks, for example, often want this information so that they know where to file to perfect their security interests in a borrower's assets.

When one of the parties is an individual, some drafters state that the party is an individual and give the state where the individual lives:

> Maria Rodriguez, an individual residing in Illinois,

Although this is appropriate from a technical perspective so that a company and an individual are treated in a parallel manner, generally the information is not necessary for identification in the same way that a state of incorporation is. Accordingly, many drafters choose to omit this information.

Drafters also have different views on including the parties' addresses in the preamble. The better practice is to put that information in the notice section or another appropriate substantive provision. This is good practice even if one of the parties is a natural person. It keeps the preamble short and easy to read. It also reduces the likelihood of inadvertently including multiple inconsistent addresses.

6.2.3.2 Defining the Entity

To define the parties in the preamble (which is the usual practice), first, insert parentheses after the organizational identity. By inserting the parentheses, the second comma of the appositive would precede the open parenthesis. (Version 1.) But this placement violates the stylistic rule that a comma never precedes an open parenthesis. Therefore, move that comma so that it immediately follows the close parenthesis. (Version 2.)

> **Version 1—Wrong**
>
> Colossal Construction LP, a New York limited partnership**,** (defined term to
> be inserted)
>
> **Version 2—Correct**
>
> Colossal Construction LP, a New York limited partnership (defined term to
> be inserted)**,**

Next, with respect to the first party, choose a defined term that either relates to the party's role in the transaction or is a shorthand name for the individual or entity. Good shorthand names include an individual's last name and a significant word from an entity's name. Be careful when choosing a defined term that is role related as the term can affect the agreement's interpretation.[10] Capitalize the defined term and then use it capitalized throughout the agreement to signal that it is a defined term.

> **Example 1**
>
>   Contractor
>
> **Example 2**
>
>   Dell
>
> **Example 3**
>
>   Josephson

Avoid acronyms—a word formed from initials. Readers generally find it difficult to remember what the letters stand for. However, if an entity is commonly referred to by an acronym (e.g., IBM), then you may use it.

As a guiding principle in choosing defined terms, choose a term that makes it easy for the reader to follow who is doing what to whom. First, consider who the audience is. Ask yourself, "Which will be easier for the audience— names or role-related terms?" Whatever the answer is, you can easily change an agreement's existing defined terms by using a word-processing program's "Find and Replace" function.

Next, consider whether the terms relating to the parties' roles are confusing. Classic baffling terms are *mortgagor* and *mortgagee, lessor* and *lessee,* and *licensor* and *licensee.* Instead of these terms, use the parties' names or other terms that indicate a party's role, such as *bank* and *borrower* or *landlord* and *tenant.* These alternative terms can also reduce typographical errors.

Also take into account the number of parties. If more than two, using role-related defined terms is often the better choice. For example, in a credit agreement, the parties often include the borrower, multiple lending banks, and an agent bank (a bank

---

10. *See In re Taxes, Aiea Dairy, Ltd.*, 380 P.2d 156, 160-161 (Haw. 1963) (finding that the parties' choice of role-related defined terms (producer and distributor) was evidence that the parties had an agency relationship, rather than that of buyer and seller).

that acts on behalf of the other banks). In this instance, a reader will probably find it easier to keep track of the parties if the contract uses role-related defined terms.

Finally, consider whether others will use this agreement as a precedent. If so, role-related terms are preferable, as they will facilitate the drafting of future agreements.

Once you choose the first party's defined term, choosing the other parties' defined terms is easy. Choose a term that parallels the term chosen for the first party.

Example 1

Landlord and Tenant

Example 2

IBM and General Foods

If you choose a role-related defined term, you must decide whether the word *the* will precede each use of it within the agreement.

Version 1

    Rent. *The* Tenant shall pay *the* Landlord the Rent no later than the first business day of each month.

Version 2

    Rent. *Tenant* shall pay *Landlord* the Rent no later than the first business day of each month.

Both formats are acceptable, although drafters disagree over which to use. Some drafters omit *the* on the theory that it shortens the agreement. Other drafters include it, reasoning that the agreement will not be that much shorter and that its absence is jarring to lay readers who are accustomed to it preceding a noun. This author prefers the use of *the*.

If *the* will precede the defined term, insert it before the defined term inside the parentheses. Otherwise, only the defined term should be inside the parentheses.

Version 1

    (the Executive)

Version 2

    (Executive)

As the final step in creating defined terms, insert quotation marks before and after the defined term, *excluding* the word *the* if you are using it.

Example 1

    (the "Executive")

Example 2

("Executive")

Example 3

("GM")

Do not precede the defined term with *hereinafter referred to as* or some variant. The language is legalese and surplussage. Also, do not create two defined terms for a party, such as *IBM* and the *Company*. That will confuse the reader. Create only one defined term, and then use it capitalized, without quotation marks in the rest of the contract.

The punctuation at the end of the preamble is a period.

The following are examples of complete preambles, each of which uses a different style for the defined terms.

Version 1

Employment Agreement, dated October 10, 20XX, between Internet Inc., a Delaware corporation (the "Company"), and Joe Hacker (the "Executive").

Version 2

Employment Agreement, dated October 10, 20XX, between Internet Inc., a Delaware corporation ("Company"), and Joe Hacker ("Executive").

Version 3

Employment Agreement, dated October 10, 20XX, between Internet Inc., a Delaware corporation ("Internet"), and Joe Hacker ("Hacker").

Occasionally, an agreement will have multiple parties in the same role. In this event, define each party by name and include a defined term for all the parties in the same role.

Version 1

Shareholders' Agreement, dated July 18, 20XX, between Paper Products Inc., a Georgia corporation (the "Corporation"), and Investment Corp., an Ohio corporation ("Investment"), Barbara Steckler ("Steckler"), Shanice Washington ("Washington"), and Andrew Yates ("Yates") (Investment, Steckler, Washington, and Yates, individually, a "Shareholder" and collectively, the "Shareholders").

As an alternative to listing in the preamble all the parties in the same role, put the information concerning those parties in an exhibit and refer to the exhibit in the preamble. It unclutters the preamble, making it easier to read.

> **Version 2**
>
> **Shareholders' Agreement**, dated July 18, 20XX, between Paper Products Inc., a Georgia corporation (the "Corporation"), and each shareholder listed in **Exhibit A**[11] **(individually, a "Shareholder" and collectively, the "Shareholders").**

6.2.4 DEFINING THE *AGREEMENT*

You may define the agreement being drafted either in the preamble or in the definition section.

> *In the preamble*
>
> **Version 1**
>
> **Shareholders' Agreement** (the "Agreement"), dated as of July 18, 20XX, between Paper Products Inc., a Georgia corporation (the "Corporation"), and each shareholder listed in **Exhibit A** (individually, a "Shareholder" and collectively, the "Shareholders").
>
> **Version 2**
>
> **Shareholders' Agreement** (including all schedules, exhibits, and amendments, the "Agreement"), dated as of July 18, 20XX, between Paper Products Inc., a Georgia corporation (the "Corporation"), and each shareholder listed in **Exhibit A** (individually, a "Shareholder" and collectively, the "Shareholders").
>
> *In the definition section*
>
> **"Agreement"** means this Shareholders' Agreement and all Schedules, Exhibits, and amendments, as each is amended from time to time.

Some drafters prefer to define the agreement in the definition section because it shortens the preamble, especially if the definition includes schedules, exhibits, and amendments. They will do this even if they use the defined term *Agreement* in the recitals or the words of agreement. Although this violates the traditional rules relating to the drafting of definitions, it is customary in the legal community. If an agreement does not have a definition section, define the agreement in the preamble.

6.3 RECITALS

Recitals follow the preamble. They describe the background and purpose of a contract. For example:

---

11. Many drafters bold references to Schedules and Exhibits. This makes it easier for the reader to determine what other documents need to be read and easier for the drafter when collating the full agreement. See §§23.9.2 and 23.9.3.

ESCROW AGREEMENT, dated July 1, 20XX, between Pretty Pearls, Inc., a Delaware corporation ("Pearls"), Bijoux Extraordinaires Co., a New York corporation ("Bijoux"), and Big Bank Corp., a New York banking corporation, as escrow agent (the "Escrow Agent").

Background

1. Each of Bijoux and Pearls is a general partner in Gems & Jewels, a New York general partnership (the "Partnership").
2. Bijoux and Pearls have decided to dissolve the Partnership and have memorialized their decision in the Dissolution Agreement, dated the date of this Agreement (the "Dissolution Agreement").
3. In accordance with the Dissolution Agreement,

   (a) Bijoux has executed and delivered to Pearls a certificate, dated the date of this Agreement and attached as **Exhibit A** (the "Warranty Certificate"), in which Bijoux makes representations and warranties with respect to specific matters; and

   (b) Bijoux and Pearls have agreed that the Partnership will deposit with the Escrow Agent into the Escrow Account (as defined in Section 2(f)) $250,000 that the Partnership would otherwise pay to Bijoux as a distribution in respect of Bijoux's general partnership interest in the Partnership.

Accordingly, the parties agree as follows:

If this escrow agreement had no recitals, its title would give information as to the agreement's general purpose, but not its specific purpose. By using recitals, the drafter explains to the reader the parties' relationship and *why* they have entered into the escrow agreement. Recitals are particularly useful if the parties want to inform interested third parties about an agreement's purpose.[12]

Drafters also use recitals to buttress a contract term that might otherwise be unenforceable. Look again at the first example of introductory provisions in this chapter. Here, the recitals tell the reader that the noncompetition agreement is part of a larger transaction, the sale of a business. As courts are more likely to enforce restraints on a person's ability to work if they arise in the context of an acquisition,[13] this information could tip the balance in favor of enforceability. Therefore, by setting the stage for a provision in the recitals, a drafter can explain its factual predicate, giving the court a basis on which to ground its decision.

Recitals are also used to clarify the parties' intent. This can occur either because the parties explicitly state their intent in the recitals or because the courts use the recitals to interpret ambiguous operative provisions.

---

12. *See Ohio Valley Gas, Inc. v. Blackburn*, 445 N.E.2d 1378, 1383 (Ind. Ct. App. 4th Dist. 1983).
13. *See Purchasing Associates, Inc. v. Weitz*, 196 N.E.2d 245, 247 (N.Y. 1963).

A classic example of the use of recitals to interpret a contract's provisions is *Wood v. Lucy, Lady Duff-Gordon*,[14] a case you may recall from your contracts course. In that case, Lady Duff-Gordon granted Wood an exclusive license to market her designs and to place her endorsement on the designs of others. The contract, however, did not include a return promise that Wood would use his best efforts in this endeavor. Nonetheless, the court held that the contract included an implied promise to this effect, and relied, in part, upon the contract's recitals to reach its decision.[15]

Drafters may also use recitals to identify a contract's consideration. For example, when a party guarantees another person's debt, the return consideration to the guarantor may not be immediately apparent. In this case, the drafter should specify the consideration in the recitals to dispel any notion that the consideration flows in only one direction.[16] For example:

Guaranty, dated March 18, 20XX, by Handicrafts Corp., a Missouri corporation (the "Guarantor"), in favor of Big Bank Corp., a Missouri banking corporation (the "Lender").

Background

1. Baskets Inc., a Missouri corporation (the "Borrower"), and the Lender have entered into a loan agreement, dated March 18, 20XX (the "Loan Agreement"), under which the Lender will make loans to the Borrower.
2. The Guarantor owns all of the issued and outstanding shares of the Borrower.
3. The Guarantor and the Borrower are engaged in related businesses, and the Guarantor will derive substantial direct and indirect benefit from the Lender's loans to the Borrower.
4. The Loan Agreement requires as a condition to the making of any loans by the Lender that the Guarantor guarantee the Borrower's obligations under the Loan Agreement.

Courts differ as to whether recitals are part of a contract. The issue is a red herring. The real issue is how recitals may or may not be used. On this, the courts are consistent. Recitals are not enforceable, operative provisions of a contract, unless the parties explicitly incorporate them into the contract.[17] Therefore, do not put representations and warranties, covenants, or conditions in the recitals. For example, return to the recitals in the Escrow Agreement at the beginning of this section. If the following "recital" were added to the recitals already in that agreement, a court would probably not enforce what is actually a covenant:[18]

---

14. *Wood v. Lucy, Lady Duff–Gordon*, 118 N.E. 214 (N.Y. 1917).

15. *Id.* at 214.

16. *See State v. Larsen*, 515 N.W.2d 178, 180-181 (N.D. 1994).

17. *See In re Taxes, Aiea Dairy Ltd.*, 380 P.2d 156, 163 (Haw. 1963).

18. Of course, if the operative provisions of the contract restate or incorporate what is in the recitals, those provisions are enforceable.

> 5. The Escrow Agent shall release funds to Bijoux only if
>
>   (a) Pearls delivers a certificate to the Escrow Agent stating that the Warranty Certificate has no misrepresentations or breaches of warranties; or
>   (b) Pearls and Bijoux deliver a certificate to the Escrow Agent stating the amount that the Escrow Agent should release to Bijoux.

Finally, the recitals and the operative provisions of a contract are sometimes inconsistent. In that case, the following rules of interpretation govern:

> If the recitals are clear and the operative part is ambiguous, the recitals govern the construction. If the recitals are ambiguous and the operative part is clear, the operative part must prevail. If both the recitals and the operative part are clear, but they are inconsistent with each other, the operative part is to be preferred.[19]

Use the following guidelines when drafting recitals.

Guidelines for Recitals

1. *Do not overuse recitals.* Use them only if they add something to the agreement. Lawyers have a long and sordid history of overusing recitals. The practice began in England hundreds of years ago when clients paid their lawyers by the length of the document.[20]

2. *Determine the content of the recitals by their purpose.* Thus, as with the drafting of anything else, you must determine what you want to accomplish before you write. Consider who the audience is. It may be only the parties and their lawyers. However, it may also include, among others, the parties' shareholders, financial analysts, a judge, and the judge's clerk. If the audience is only the parties and their lawyers, the recitals may be quite short or even omitted. For example, some bank loan agreements no longer include recitals. After reading the agreement's title, no one needs to know much more about the background of the agreement. However, if the anticipated audience is wider, the recitals should be expansive enough to explain the contract's background and the parties' intent.

3. *If the agreement includes expansive recitals, they should tell a story.*

4. *When stating facts in the recitals that relate to the party's past relationship, make sure that they are accurate.* If they are wrong, they might damage your client's case in a litigation. Courts have held recitals to be conclusive evidence of the material facts stated.[21] Specific recitals, rather than general recitals, are more likely to be deemed conclusive evidence of the facts stated.[22]

5. *If the background surrounding the agreement is complicated, consider stating the facts in chronological order.* Chronology can often be a helpful organizing principle.

---

19. *Jamison v. Franklin Life Ins. Co.*, 136 P.2d 265, 269 (Ariz. 1943), quoting *Williams v. Barkley*, 58 N.E. 765, 767 (N.Y. 1900), quoting English case law (citations omitted).

20. David Mellinkoff, *The Language of the Law* 190-191 (Little, Brown & Co. 1963).

21. *See Union Pacific Resources Co. v. Texaco, Inc.*, 882 P.2d 212, 222 (Wyo. 1994).

22. *See Detroit Grand Park Corp. v. Turner*, 25 N.W.2d 184, 188 (Mich. 1946).

6. *Do not put operative provisions in the recitals.* Representations and warranties, covenants, and conditions all belong in the body of the agreement—after the words of agreement. A court will not enforce operative provisions that are in recitals.

7. *Do not put information concerning the consideration in the recitals,* unless the consideration's adequacy is unclear. Then, use the recitals to explain what the consideration is and why it is adequate. For example, look at the recitals for the Guaranty set out earlier in this section.

8. *Draft recitals in a contemporary format.*

    (a) Do not introduce recitals with the archaic *Witnesseth.* Instead, either proceed directly from the preamble to the recitals or indicate that the recitals follow by using either the word *Recitals* or *Background.*

    (b) Do not precede each recital with *Whereas.* As with *Witnesseth,* it is archaic. Instead, write a well-drafted paragraph or a series of numbered sentences.

9. *Avoid drafting the recitals as reciprocal statements of the parties:*

> **Wrong**
>
> The Company desires to employ the Executive, and the Executive desires to work for the Company.

It is archaic. Try a simpler sentence:

> **Correct**
>
> This Agreement provides for the Company's employment of the Executive.

In either event, if this recital were the only one in the employment agreement, it would be superfluous as the title of the agreement would convey the necessary information.

10. *If you define a term in the recitals, put the defined term inside quotation marks inside parentheses and precede the defined term with the word* the, *unless the defined term is a person's name.*

> **Example 1**
>
> (the "Defined Term")
>
> **Example 2**
>
> ("Danowski")

The recitals in the introductory provisions of the Escrow Agreement at the beginning of this section have several examples of how to define terms in recitals.

11. *Avoid using defined terms in the recitals if they are not defined in the preamble or recitals.* Occasionally, it is appropriate to use a defined term in the recitals, even though the definition for that term appears in the definition section. Do this *only* if the defined term clearly conveys the definition's substance, and if including the definition in the recitals is awkward. Any defined term used without a definition should cross-reference the definition immediately following the defined term's first use. The cross-reference should be inside a set of parentheses. Look at the recitals in the introductory provisions of the Escrow Agreement at the beginning of this section. There, *Escrow Account* is used as a defined term, but without definition.

6.4 WORDS OF AGREEMENT

The **words of agreement** follow the recitals. Some drafters refer to them as the **statement of consideration**, a term that reflects their historical role. These provisions are often verbose and replete with legalese. For example:

Example 1

NOW, THEREFORE, in consideration of the premises[23] and of the mutual agreements and covenants hereinafter set forth, the Owner and the Contractor hereby agree as follows:

Example 2

NOW, THEREFORE, in consideration of $10 paid in hand, and other good and valuable consideration the receipt of which is hereby acknowledged, the parties agree as follows:

Example 3

NOW, THEREFORE, in consideration of the mutual representations, warranties, covenants, and agreements, and upon the terms and conditions hereinafter set forth, the parties hereto do hereby agree as follows:

Example 4

NOW, THEREFORE, in consideration of the mutual promises set forth in this Agreement, the parties agree as follows:

Do not use these provisions—unless you are working for a superior who has one foot rooted in the eighteenth century. Of the four examples, Example 4 is the least offensive because it is the simplest and most likely reflects the actual consideration. Usually, a better choice is the following:

Example 5

Accordingly, the parties agree as follows:

Look again at Examples 1 through 4. Each provision has two parts:

- A recitation of the consideration.
- A statement that the parties agree to the provisions that follow.

---

23. *Premises* is not a typographical error. It means that which came before—i.e., the information provided in the recitals.

The first part is archaic and in most states no longer serves a legal purpose. A drafter cannot turn into consideration something that cannot be consideration. As stated by Professor Farnsworth, "[An] employer cannot transform an unenforceable promise to give an employee a gold watch into an enforceable one simply by reciting, 'In consideration of your past service, I promise. . . .'"[24] Similarly, although a recitation of consideration may create a presumption of consideration, that presumption is rebuttable.[25] Accordingly, unless the consideration's adequacy is uncertain, omit the recitation of consideration from the words of agreement. But, if the consideration's adequacy is in doubt, draft recitals explaining what the consideration is and tailor the words of agreement to reflect the recitals. Drafters do this regularly with guaranties and options where the return consideration for the guaranty and option is unclear.[26] Look, for example, at the recitals of the Guaranty in Section 6.3.

The second part of the words of agreement is useful. It evidences the parties' agreement to the contract provisions that follow. This statement can be quite simple as in Example 5.

---

24. E. Allan Farnsworth, *Farnsworth on Contracts,* vol. 1, 157 (3d ed., Aspen 2004).

25. *See, e.g., Earl v. St. Louis U.,* 875 S.W.2d 234, 237 (Mo. Ct. App. 1994); *Finegan v. Prudential Ins. Co.,* 14 N.E.2d 172, 175-176 (Mass. 1938). In some states, statutes provide that a written instrument is presumptive evidence of consideration. *See Okla. Stat. tit.* 15, §114 (1996); *Idaho Code* §29-104. *See also* Farnsworth, *supra* n. 24, at vol. 1, 158 and the cases cited therein.

26. *See* Arthur L. Corbin, *Corbin on Contracts,* vol. 2, 84-88 (Joseph M. Perillo and Helen Hadjiyannakis Bender eds., rev. ed., West 1995). In some states, it may also be necessary to recite the consideration in land contracts. *See generally* W. W. Allen, *Necessity and Sufficiency of Statement of Consideration in Contract or Memorandum of Sale of Land, Under Statute of Frauds,* 23 A.L.R.2d 164 (1952).

EXERCISES

Exercise 6-1

Return to Exercise 5-3, and using the facts in that exercise, draft the preamble to the agreement described in that Exercise.

Exercise 6-2

Memorandum[27]

To: Leslie Lawyer

From: Brad S. Dennison

Subject: Indemnity Agreement

As you know, I am Vice President in charge of sales for Locomotive Transportation, Inc., a New York corporation (Locomotive). Three months ago, after negotiations with Rapid Trains Corp., a Massachusetts corporation (Rapid), Locomotive sold Rapid 2,100 30-ton coal cars—everything that we had in stock. About a week later, Anne Winsom (a new sales representative) met with Coal Transportation, Inc., a New Jersey corporation (Coal Transportation), and signed a contract with Coal Transportation. That contract committed Locomotive to deliver 300 30-ton coal cars within one week. Obviously, we didn't meet that schedule, as we had no more cars in stock. Coal Transportation sued, alleging breach of contract.

Yesterday, I got a call from Sally Milton, President of Rapid. According to Sally, Rapid would love to purchase an additional 300 cars. As we now have at least that number of cars in stock, I want to do this deal. The proverbial fly in the ointment is that Rapid has heard about Coal Transportation's suit against us and is afraid Coal Transportation will sue Rapid for tortious interference. After I told Rapid that Locomotive would indemnify them, Sally agreed that Rapid would do the deal. (I'm not worried about the lawsuit. According to David Fein in your Litigation Department, the damages we may have to pay are minimal. Our profit on the deal will more than cover anything we have to pay to Coal Transportation. Apparently, they purchased the cars from another manufacturer at approximately the same price as our contract price.)

Please draft the preamble, recitals, and the words of agreement for the indemnity agreement. I would like to review the draft as soon as possible. Please be sure that the agreement is effective as of today, no matter when we sign it.

B.S.D.

---

27. This exercise is based on *Hocking Valley Ry. Co. v. Barbour*, 192 N.Y.S. 163 (App. Div. 3d Dept. 1920), *aff'd without op.*, 130 N.E. 909 (N.Y. 1921).

Exercise 6-3

Memorandum

To: A. Barrister

From: H. Flighty

Date: August 31, 20XX

Re: Purchase of Sam Samson's G550

Last evening, while sharing a bottle of Chablis with Sam Samson, I finally agreed to buy his jet for $21 million! The Chablis must have been a better vintage than I thought, because I had no intention of agreeing to a price in excess of $15 million. Nonetheless, I signed a Purchase Offer in my capacity as President of Fly-by-Night Aviation, Inc. (Aviation). (A copy of the Purchase Offer is attached.) In my current financial situation, I am simply unable to consummate this transaction. It would, of course, be most embarrassing if I had to admit my current financial straits to Sam.

There is a solution.

I know that Sam's archrival, Rob Robertson, has coveted Sam's Gulfstream G550 for years and that Robertson would be willing to purchase the G550 for a price in excess of $21 million. I'm sure that I can strike a deal with him pursuant to which Aviation will

(a)   assign all of its rights in the Purchase Offer to Robertson's holding company, The Robertson Jet Corp., a Delaware corporation (Robertson Jet); and

(b)   delegate its performance to Robertson Jet, which would assume Aviation's performance under the Purchase Offer and contemporaneously pay Aviation $1,000,000.

I plan to speak to Robertson about this transaction in the next week or so. When I meet with him, I would like to show him at least part of the Assignment and Assumption.

Accordingly, please draft the preamble, recitals, and words of agreement for the Assignment and Assumption and have it ready for my review as soon as possible. Also, be sure to check whether my company can delegate its duty to pay a portion of the purchase price with a promissory note. If there's an issue, write me a one-paragraph explanation of the law and how we can deal with the problem.

H.F.

Purchase Offer Attached

Fly-by-Night Aviation, Inc.
987 West 48th Street
New York, New York 10036

Purchase Offer August 30, 20XX

Fly-by-Night Aviation, Inc. ("Buyer") hereby offers to purchase the Gulfstream Aerospace Corporation G550 Aircraft, bearing United States Registration No. N765BW and Manufacturer's Serial

No. 8181, equipped with two Rolls-Royce Tay engines, model number MK611-8, Serial Numbers 72725 and 72726 (the "Aircraft"), from Supersonic Wings Corp. ("Seller") for $21,000,000, subject to the following terms and conditions:

1. Negotiation and execution of a definitive Aircraft Purchase Agreement satisfactory to both parties.
2. $5,000,000 of the purchase price shall be paid by delivery of Buyer's promissory note to Seller. The note will bear interest at 9% per annum and will be due in a single bullet payment on December 31, 2012.
3. Aircraft to be delivered with title free and clear of all liens and encumbrances of any nature whatsoever.
4. At Closing, Aircraft to have no more than 2,500 hours total flying time, exclusive of any flying time necessary to deliver the Aircraft to the location specified in paragraph 5.
5. On the Closing Date, the Aircraft must be at National Airport in Washington, D.C., or such other reasonable and mutually convenient location as Buyer shall designate.
6. Seller to execute any and all bills of sale, certificates of title, etc., necessary to convey good title to the Buyer.
7. Maintenance Agreement, dated as of April 3, 20XX, with Greasemonkeys, Inc., to be assigned by Seller to Buyer. Buyer is to assume all liabilities as of the date of execution of the definitive aircraft purchase agreement.
8. Pilot Agreement, between Ace Pilots, Inc. and Seller, dated as of May 12, 20XX, to be assigned to Buyer. Buyer is to assume only those liabilities that arise after the closing date.
9. Closing to occur on November 25, 20XX, at the offices of Workhard & Playlittle LLP, 1133 Avenue of the Americas, New York, New York, or on another date to which the parties agree. If the Closing does not occur on or before November 29, 20XX, because of the fault of Buyer, Buyer shall pay Seller a $3,000,000 termination fee.

Upon acceptance of this offer, Buyer will cause a deposit of $300,000 to be placed in escrow with Harold C. Astor & Associates, Oklahoma City, Oklahoma (HCA). (The escrow deposit will be governed by the terms of the escrow agreement being entered into by the parties and HCA no later than two days after the execution of this Purchase Offer. The form of Escrow Agreement is attached.) The deposit will be used in partial payment of the purchase price. If the Closing does not occur and Buyer is not at fault, then Buyer is entitled to the return of its deposit.

Very truly yours,

Fly-By-Night Aviation, Inc.

By: _Horatio Flighty_____
Horatio Flighty, President

Accepted by:

Supersonic Wings Corp.

By: _Sam Samson_____
Sam Samson, President

ESCROW AGREEMENT[28]

Escrow Agreement (the "Escrow Agreement"), dated [date to be inserted], between Supersonic Wings Corp., a Delaware corporation (the "Seller"), Fly-by-Night Aviation, Inc., a New York corporation (the "Buyer"), and Harold C. Astor & Associates, an Oklahoma partnership (the "Escrow Agent").

Background

The Seller and the Buyer have executed a Purchase Offer dated August 30, 20XX (the "Purchase Offer"), that provides for the Seller's sale to the Buyer of a Gulfstream Aerospace Corporation G550 aircraft. Among other things, the Purchase Offer requires the Buyer to deposit $300,000 in escrow with the Escrow Agent. This Escrow Agreement sets forth the terms relating to the escrow.

The Seller, the Buyer, and the Escrow Agent agree as follows:

1. **Escrow Deposit.** Simultaneously with the execution and delivery of this Escrow Agreement, the Buyer shall deliver $300,000 in immediately available funds to the Escrow Agent. The $300,000 delivered to the Escrow Agent, together with all interest that it earns, is referred to as the "Escrow Amount." Immediately upon receipt of the Escrow Amount, the Escrow Agent shall invest it in an interest-bearing money market account at the Bank of Oklahoma City. Afterwards, the Escrow Agent shall hold and dispose of the Escrow Amount as provided in this Escrow Agreement.

2. **Payment of the Escrow Amount.** The Escrow Agent shall dispose of the Escrow Amount in one of the following two ways:

   2.1 **Pursuant to Notice of the Seller and Buyer.** The Escrow Agent shall dispose of the Escrow Amount in the manner instructed pursuant to a notice, substantially in the form of **Exhibit A,** that both the Seller and the Buyer sign.

   2.2 **Pursuant to a Court Order.** The Escrow Agent shall dispose of the Escrow Amount when and in the manner that a court of competent jurisdiction instructs in an order that is final and no longer subject to appeal in the opinion of the Escrow Agent's counsel.

3. **Compensation.** The Escrow Agent's fees for its services under this Escrow Agreement are to be determined in accordance with its publicly announced fee schedule as in effect from time to time. The Seller and the Buyer shall each

   3.1 pay 50% of the Escrow Agent's fees for its services under this Escrow Agreement; and

   3.2 reimburse the Escrow Agent for 50% of the Escrow Agent's reasonable out-of-pocket expenses incurred in providing its services under this Escrow Agreement.

4. **Indemnification.**

   4.1 **Indemnity Obligation.** The Seller and the Buyer, jointly and severally, shall indemnify and defend the Escrow Agent against any loss, liability, obligation, claim, damage, or expense (including, without limitation, reasonable attorneys' fees and expenses) arising from or relating to acting under this Escrow Agreement, unless caused by the Escrow Agent's gross negligence or willful misconduct.

   4.2 **Right of Setoff.** Without limiting the Escrow Agent's other rights and remedies against the Seller and the Buyer, the Escrow Agent may satisfy all or part of the Seller and the Buyer's indemnity obligations under subsection 4.1 by setoff against the Escrow Amount. The Escrow Agent shall promptly notify the Seller and the Buyer of any setoff.

---

28. This Escrow Agreement is based, in part, on an Escrow Agreement that my colleague Alan Shaw drafted.

5. **Escrow Agent's Role.** The Seller and the Buyer acknowledge that the Escrow Agent is acting solely as a stakeholder and that, in this capacity, it is not the Seller's or the Buyer's agent. The Escrow Agent has no obligations under this Escrow Agreement, except as expressly stated in this Escrow Agreement.

6. **Escrow Agent's Liability.**

   6.1 **Gross Negligence and Willful Misconduct.** The Escrow Agent is not liable for any loss arising because it acted or refrained from acting in connection with the transactions this Escrow Agreement contemplates, except for any loss arising because of its gross negligence or willful misconduct.

   6.2 **Advice of Counsel.** The Escrow Agent is not liable for any loss arising because it acted or refrained from acting in connection with the transactions this Escrow Agreement contemplates if it relied in good faith upon its counsel's advice.

7. **Resignation and Discharge of the Escrow Agent.**

   7.1 **Resignation.** The Escrow Agent may resign from its duties under this Escrow Agreement by notifying the Seller and the Buyer in writing that it is resigning and stating in that notice the effective date of the resignation.

   7.2 **Discharge.** The parties may discharge the Escrow Agent from its duties under this Escrow Agreement by a written agreement that

       7.2.1 the Seller and the Buyer sign;

       7.2.2 is delivered to the Escrow Agent; and

       7.2.3 states the effective date of the discharge.

   7.3 **Successor Escrow Agent.** If the Escrow Agent resigns or is discharged, the Seller and the Buyer shall jointly and promptly appoint a successor escrow agent. If they are unable to agree, then a court of competent jurisdiction is to appoint the successor escrow agent.

8. **General Provisions.**

   8.1 **Assignment and Delegation.** The Escrow Agent shall not assign its rights or delegate its performance under this Escrow Agreement without the other parties' written consent. The Seller and the Buyer may each assign its rights and delegate its performance under this Escrow Agreement. Any assignment or delegation in violation of this Section is void.

   8.2 **Amendments.** The parties may not amend this Escrow Agreement, except by an agreement that all the parties sign.

   8.3 **Merger.** This Escrow Agreement is the final and exclusive expression of the parties in connection with the transactions this Escrow Agreement contemplates.

Fly-By-Night Aviation, Inc.

By: _____
    Horatio Flighty, President

Supersonic Wings Corp.

By: _____
    Sam Samson, President

Harold C. Astor & Associates,
a general partnership

By: _____
    Harold C. Astor, general partner

Exhibit A

Harold C. Astor & Associates
1911 Main Street
Oklahoma City, Oklahoma 73110

_____, 20XX

Ladies and Gentlemen:

We refer to the Escrow Agreement (the "Escrow Agreement"), dated as of [date to be inserted], between Supersonic Wings Corp., a Delaware corporation (the "Seller"), Fly-by-Night Aviation, Inc., a New York corporation (the "Buyer"), and Harold C. Astor & Associates, an Oklahoma partnership (the "Escrow Agent").

Each capitalized term used in this letter without definition has the meaning assigned to it in the Escrow Agreement.

By this letter, the Seller and the Buyer instruct the Escrow Agent to wire transfer the Escrow Amount in immediately available funds in [insert city and state] to the [Seller's] [Buyer's] bank account as follows:

[Bank account information to be inserted.]

Very truly yours,

Supersonic Wings Corp.

By: _____
Title:

Fly-By-Night Aviation, Inc.

By: _____
Title:

Definitions and Defined Terms

7.1 INTRODUCTION

7.1.1 DEFINITIONS

A definition states the meaning of a word or phrase. Drafters use them primarily to create clarity and prevent ambiguity. They do so in the following ways:

First, a definition may expand or limit the dictionary meaning of a word. So, for example, the dictionary meaning of *lake* is "a considerable inland body of standing water."[1] In a contract dealing with the bottling of water from a specific lake, the definition of *lake* might limit its meaning to the specific lake from which water is to be taken for bottling.

Second, a definition may clarify the meaning of a word or phrase, such as *business day*. Although Monday, Tuesday, Wednesday, Thursday, and Friday are typically thought of as business days, the parties might want to clarify that if a holiday falls on any of those days, that day is not a business day.

Third, a definition may resolve the meaning of a word that is ambiguous. The word *dollar* is a classic example. In a contract between two U.S. companies, *dollar* would clearly refer to U.S. money. But in a contract between a Canadian and a U.S. company, *dollar* would be ambiguous. It could refer to either Canadian or U.S. dollars. A definition would eliminate this ambiguity by stipulating the correct meaning.

Fourth, a definition may explain the meaning of a technical word or phrase. For example, *capitalized lease* has a specific meaning under the accounting rules. To avoid any doubt as to the meaning of this phrase, the parties might want to spell out the specifics of those rules or refer to them.

Fifth, a definition can be used to express a concept that is specific to the transaction. For instance, in a loan agreement, the bank might want to limit the borrower's investments to those that are liquid, that is, easily convertible into cash.[2] This is a contract-specific concept. To draft the definition for this concept, the parties might list all of the permitted investments.

---

1. *Merriam-Webster's Collegiate Dictionary* 652 (10th ed. 1999).

2. A bank would want a borrower's investments to be liquid so that the borrower would always have ready access to cash to pay the bank.

Sixth, as indicated in the immediately preceding paragraph, a definition can list all the things to which a word or phrase refers. This list might specify only one thing, such as the pledge agreement between a bank and its borrower, or it could specify multiple things, such as all of the permitted investments.

Seventh, a definition can explain the meaning of a word or phrase by listing its significant characteristics. For example, the dictionary defines *computer* to be "a programmable electronic device that can store, retrieve, and process data."[3]

7.1.2 DEFINED TERMS

Defined terms are shorthand expressions of definitions. Drafters use them as an easy way of saying the same thing the same way. Failure to say the same thing the same way is an open invitation to the other side and the court to construe two provisions differently. Moreover, without defined terms, drafters would have to repeat the full-blown definition each time a concept was needed in a contract. This would make the agreement onerous to read. For instance, compare the following two versions of the same provision.[4] The first version does not use a definition for *storage space,* while the second does.

> **Version 1**
>
> **Condition of Storage Space**. When the Tenant takes possession of the 2,500 square feet of storage space shown on the drawing attached to this Lease as Exhibit A, that possession is conclusive evidence that the 2,500 square feet of storage space shown on the drawing attached to this Lease as Exhibit A was in the condition that the Tenant and Landlord agreed upon.
>
> **Version 2**
>
> *The definition*
>
> **"Storage Space"** means the 2,500 square feet of storage space shown on the drawing attached to this Lease as Exhibit A.
>
> *The provision*
>
> **Condition of Storage Space**. When the Tenant takes possession of the Storage Space, that possession is conclusive evidence that the Storage Space was in the condition that the Tenant and Landlord agreed upon.

Now imagine what Version 1 would be like if Tenant and Landlord had not been defined!

7.2 STRATEGIC CONCERNS IN DEFINING TERMS[5]

Strategic concerns affect how a term is defined. For example, consider the strategic concerns that might come into play when parties decide whether to define *force*

---

3. *Merriam-Webster's Collegiate Dictionary* 237 (10th ed., 1999).
4. These provisions are based upon a provision in Mark A. Senn, *Commercial Real Estate Leases: Preparation, Negotiation, and Forms* 4-29 (3d ed., Aspen 2004).
5. This section was suggested by class materials created by Alan Shaw.

majeure event by listing the events that constitute a *force majeure* event or by listing the criteria that an event must meet. Look at the following two definitions:[6]

Definition 1

"*Force Majeure* Event" means war, flood, lightning, drought, earthquake, fire, volcanic eruption, landslide, hurricane, cyclone, typhoon, tornado, explosion, civil disturbance, act of God or the public enemy, terrorism, military action, epidemic, famine or plague, shipwreck, action of a court or public authority, or strike.

Definition 2

"*Force Majeure* Event" means any act or event, whether foreseen or unforeseen, that meets all three of the following tests:

(a) The act or event prevents a party (the "Nonperforming Party"), in whole or in part, from

    (i) performing its obligations under this Agreement; or

    (ii) satisfying any conditions to the obligations of the other party (the "Performing Party") under this Agreement.

(b) The act or event is beyond the reasonable control of and not the fault of the Nonperforming Party.

(c) The Nonperforming Party has been unable to avoid or overcome the act or event by the exercise of due diligence.

Which of these definitions is better depends upon whether your client is more likely to be the nonperforming party or the performing party. If your client is more likely to be the nonperforming party, Definition 2 may be more appealing. Because it lists criteria, Definition 2 is elastic without clear limits. This might enable your client to argue that a *force majeure* event includes an event not listed in Definition 1. If Definition 1 with its exclusive list of *force majeure* events had instead been included as the definition, your client would have no basis for its argument—which is exactly why the party most likely to be the performing party would prefer it.

7.3 DEFINITIONS AS STANDARD-SETTING TOOLS

Definitions establish standards that affect the parties' rights and obligations. For example, assume that a stockholders' agreement has a defined term *Affiliate* and that a contract provision prohibits assignments *except to Affiliates*. In this context, *Affiliates* is a standard that is integral to the contract's business purpose. Depending upon whether the term is defined broadly or narrowly, the brother of the president of a subsidiary might or might not be included within the scope of the definition. Therefore, you must exercise great care when crafting definitions and think through the ramifications of each definition the same way you would if you were crafting a full provision.

---

6. These definitions are from Nancy F. Persechino, *Force Majeure*, in *Negotiating and Drafting Contract Boilerplate* 201-202 (Tina L. Stark et al. eds., ALM Publg. 2003).

7.4 PLACEMENT OF DEFINITIONS

If an agreement is short or informal, or has only a few definitions, drafters often omit a separate definition section and define terms in context—that is, where they are used. But, most sophisticated commercial transactions do not fall within this category, thus inexorably leading to the question: where do the definitions go?

Commentators and drafters disagree as to the answer to this question. Some lawyers champion putting the definition section immediately after the words of agreement, so that the definitions appear in the beginning pages of an agreement. Others urge that the definition section appear as the next to last section of an agreement, preceding the contract's general provisions. Finally, some lawyers advocate that definitions should appear in context, even if the contract is lengthy and sophisticated. Let's look briefly at the pros and cons of each approach.

The most common approach is to put the defined terms and their definitions in a separate section after the words of agreement. This way, terms used throughout the body of an agreement are easily accessible at the beginning of the contract, facilitating a reader's ability to find them. This placement also reminds a reader who might otherwise ignore the definitions that they often contain deal-critical concepts. A reader cannot help but to stumble upon them. Finally, having all of the definitions in one place near the front permits the sophisticated practitioner to skim them to see how the contract treats specific issues. For example, loan agreements often include financial covenants, such as requiring the borrower to maintain a certain ratio of cash flow to its debt obligations. As these financial covenants generally are drafted using defined terms, a practitioner can often quickly learn about the covenants by reading the definitions.

Some drafters disagree with this approach. They propose that each term be defined the first time it is used in the body of the agreement. They believe this format yields at least three benefits. First, readers will garner a better understanding of a defined term by seeing its definition in context. Second, readers will no longer need to shuffle through a contract's pages looking for a term's definition in the definition section. Third, the definition section will no longer interrupt the flow of the contract. Instead, the business provisions of the action sections would immediately follow the words of agreement.

Although this approach has a superficial appeal, a realistic concern is that defining terms in context can lead to ambiguity. Specifically, the parameters of the definition may be unclear because of the defined term's placement. Generally, the problem relates to how much of the preceding or succeeding language is intended to be included in the definition. Look at the following recital, where an ambiguity concerning two definitions led to litigation:

> WHEREAS, Seller possesses technical information and know-how (the "Technical Information") relating to the production and manufacture of food products which look similar to the thin, crispy crust of 'french bread' from which the dough has been removed (the "Products"). . . .[7]

---

7. *G. Golden Assocs. of Oceanside, Inc. v. Arnold Foods Co., Inc.*, 870 F. Supp. 472, 474 (E.D.N.Y. 1994).

In the lawsuit over the meaning of *Products,* the plaintiff argued that the definition of *Products* began with the words *food products* and that *Products* was not limited to *Products* produced in accordance with the *Technical Information* being transferred. The defendant, however, asserted that *Products* was limited to those produced in accordance with the *Technical Information.* Realistically, it is likely that neither party noted this issue when drafting the recital. It was a subtlety that both sides missed. But if the parties had been forced to construct a definition for a definition section, they would have been much more likely to confront the issue.

If you define terms in context, one possible way to reduce the risk of ambiguity is to put the defined term at the end of the sentence and indicate within the parentheses the noun or phrase as to which the defined term refers. Yet even when this approach works, it is not a panacea. Sometimes too much information needs to be included inside the parentheses. For example, assume that the recital from the litigated case was rewritten as follows:

> WHEREAS, Seller possesses technical information and know-how relating to the production and manufacture of food products which look similar to the thin, crispy crust of 'french bread' from which the dough has been removed *(the technical information and know-how, the "Technical Information;" the food products manufactured in accordance with the Technical Information, the "Products").* . . .

Here, the parenthetical is almost as long as the recital. It is cumbersome and interrupts the flow of the contract. An alternative would be to write the recital without any definitions, but then to include the definitions in the definition section. These definitions would trump any ambiguity in the recitals.

Drafters who prefer not to define terms in context also point out that doing so does not end the shuffling of pages to find the appropriate definition. Specifically, a reader who wants to check the meaning of a term previously defined must still find where in the 100-page document it was first used. Those who prefer to define terms in context address this concern by creating an alphabetical index of all the defined terms and listing the page on which each term is defined. Arguably, this index increases a reader's work. Rather than simply turning to the definition section and then returning to the contract provision, a reader must go to the index, then back to the body of the agreement where the term is defined, and finally back to the provision that includes the defined term. This may even need to be done the first time a reader encounters a defined term because, in some instances, a term is not defined the first time it is used.

Drafters promote two other alternative locations for definitions. Some drafters put them in a separate section at the end of the contract. They agree that it is easier for the reader if all of the definitions are in one place but believe that they should be at the end of the contract. This way, they will not hinder the reader who wishes to read the action sections immediately. These drafters also often believe that placing the definitions at the end of the contract expedites negotiations by making the parties focus first on substantive provisions rather than the definitions.

The second alternative is to put the definitions in an appendix or other stand-alone document. Drafters often do this in transactions in which multiple agreements rely on the same definitions. For example, a credit agreement, security agreement, and a pledge agreement all need terms to refer to the debt outstanding, the agent bank, and the maturity of the loan. If the defined terms are not the same in all three agreements, litigation is almost inevitable. To ensure that the agreements all use the same defined terms with the same definitions, the parties use an appendix whose defined terms are incorporated into each agreement.

So, what do you do if you are a junior lawyer and the designated drafter? The real world answer is that you follow the precedent you are given or the style of the person for whom you are working. You should be a chameleon until you are in charge. Then, you can decide.

On balance, this author believes that, in most instances, definitions should be placed in a separate section at the beginning of the contract—where they are easy to find and hard not to trip over. Readers who wish to begin with the action sections, or any other section, may easily do so by obtaining the appropriate page number from the contract's table of contents.

There are some exceptions to this general rule. In the appropriate transaction, defining the terms in an appendix or other stand-alone document is a viable option. In addition, it may make sense to define all the terms in context if an agreement is short, informal, or includes only a few definitions.

Even if a contract includes a definition section, it is appropriate to define a particular term in context in two instances.

- First, when the words of a provision cannot be easily reordered to turn them into an independent definition and defined term.
- Second, when a defined term is used multiple times, but in only one section.[8]

7.5 GUIDELINES FOR DRAFTING DEFINITIONS AND DEFINED TERMS

7.5.1 GENERAL GUIDELINES

There is no hard-and-fast rule about when definitions should be drafted. If you use a precedent to draft the agreement, you will begin your draft with some definitions that probably work perfectly well—that is one of the benefits of using a precedent. (Of course, you can only be sure that no change is required by reviewing each instance in which the defined term is used.) Other definitions in the precedent will need to be tailored to the specific transaction. For example, in a contract for the sale of real property, the definition of *Premises* will need to be changed (obviously) so that it refers to the property being sold in that transaction. Finally, you will be able to craft some definitions only in the middle of the drafting process when you discover that you have a new concept (the definition) for which you need a new defined term.

Before finalizing a defined term and its definition, check every use of it. Sometimes a definition that works perfectly in three provisions does not work in the fourth. The computer is a terrific tool for this task. Most word processing applications can search a document for specific words. This automates the task, making it much easier to complete. If you subsequently decide to change a definition, repeat the search to make sure that each provision still makes sense with the new definition.

7.5.2 SPECIFIC GUIDELINES: DEFINING TERMS IN THE DEFINITIONS SECTION

Here are guidelines for drafting definitions and defined terms in a definition section. Of course, depending upon a contract's organization, the definitions and their defined terms may appear in their own article.

---

8. See §7.5.3. Guideline 1.

1. *Introduce the definitions and their defined terms with words to the following effect:*

> **Definitions**. Terms defined in the preamble and the recitals of this Agreement have their assigned meanings, and the following terms have the meanings assigned to them:

If no terms are defined in the recitals, do not refer to the recitals in this introductory language. Many drafters continue to use the term *recitals* although the information is contained in the *Background*.

2. *Do not create a defined term unless you will use it more than once, and once you create it, use it each time the definition is appropriate.* Despite the preceding sentence, you may use a defined term only once if its use will enhance a provision's readability. Specifically, sometimes a concept is so complicated that putting it in the middle of a provision makes the provision difficult to understand. If the defined term sufficiently encapsulates the concept, using it in the provision may permit a reader to understand better an otherwise thorny provision. If you do this, break the provision down into two subsections. Put the defined term and its definition in the first subsection and the substantive provision in the second.[9] Drafters sometimes take this approach in credit agreements when stating complex accounting concepts.[10]

3. *Create only one defined term for each definition, and use it exclusively.*

4. *List the defined terms alphabetically.* Including subsection referents, such as (a), (b), or (c), is unnecessary.

5. *Include all terms defined in the agreement in the list of defined terms, other than terms defined in the preamble or the recitals.* If you define a term in context,[11] the alphabetical listing should cross-reference the definition's location.

> **"Rent"** has the meaning assigned to it in Section 2.2.

6. *When defining a term, capitalize the first letter of each word. Put the entire defined term in bold or italics and surround it with quotation marks:*

> **"Mechanical Failure"**

If you are working for a firm that drafts in a plain English style, that style might include omitting the quotation marks. Some drafters underline the defined term rather than putting it in boldface or italics. But boldface is the preferred way to make words prominent. Underlining is a holdover from the days when contracts were typed on typewriters, and boldface was not an option.[12]

---

9. See §7.5.3, Guideline 1, for an example.

10. For an example, see §22.3.3, the text accompanying n. 6.

11. See §7.5.3.

12. Bryan A. Garner, *Legal Writing in Plain English: A Text with Exercises* §44, 126-127 (U. Chicago Press 2001).

7. *When in the body of a contract, signal that a term is defined by capitalizing the first letter of each word*—just as was done when the term was defined in the definition section.

Be careful. Occasionally, a defined term should not be capitalized because it is not intended to signal a definition. For example, *Agreement* is generally the word chosen as the defined term that refers to the parties' contract. Capitalizing *agreement* would be incorrect, however, in the following representation and warranty:

> **Agreements. Schedule 4.12** lists each agreement to which the Borrower is a party.

In this instance, *agreement* refers to contracts other than the parties' contract.

8. *Follow the defined term with the verb* means. *Shall mean* is incorrect. *Shall* is the language of obligation, and only parties can be obliged to do something.[13] As the defined term is not promising to do anything, *shall* is wrong. If it is used, it is known as the *false imperative*.

> **Correct**
>
> **"Mechanical Failure"** means

9. *If a definition is not intended as an exclusive listing or description, follow the defined term with the verb* includes.

> **"Breach"** includes a cross-default.[14]

10. *Never use* means and includes. If *means* is the verb, it signals that the defined term and the definition are equivalents. Logically, no additional matters can be part of the definition. *Includes* indicates that the defined term refers not only to matters stated in the definition, but also to matters outside the definition. Therefore, *means* and *includes* are inconsistent and cannot be used together.

11. *To exclude something that would ordinarily be within the contemplation of a defined term, follow the defined term with* excludes.

> **Version 1**
>
> **"Telephone"** excludes a cellular telephone that takes photographs.

Note that this definition does not state what a *telephone* is. It relies on the parties' understanding of this everyday term. An alternative is to state what a telephone is and to follow it with the exclusion.

---

13. See §10.2, Guideline 1.

14. A **cross-default** is a default that occurs in the subject agreement because of a default in another agreement. For example, a credit agreement may specify that a default under that agreement occurs if a borrower fails to pay when due any material liability under any other agreement.

> **Version 2**
>
> **"Telephone"** means an instrument for reproducing sound at a distance,[15] but excludes a cellular telephone that takes photographs.

12. *Choose as the defined term words that convey information to the reader about the substance of the definition.* Thus, *Residence* would be a good defined term if the definition were *house, townhouse, apartment, cooperative, houseboat, and condominium.*

Similarly, the substance of a definition should not include concepts unrelated to the other concepts in a definition. Thus, the definition of *Residence* should not include *office towers.*

13. *If a definition varies the usual meaning of a word or phrase, choose a defined term that signals the variation.* For example, a good defined term for an electronic book would be *E-book,* not *Book.*

14. *Include a defined term in the definition of another defined term if one definition builds on another definition.* For example, the following definition is from a website-linking agreement pursuant to which one company agrees to include in its website a hyperlink to another company's website:[16]

> **"Company A Users"** means users accessing Company B's Website through the Link.

If the definition of *Company A Users* could not include the defined terms *Company B's Website* and *Link,* then, upon eliminating the defined term *Company A Users,* the replacement language would be as follows:

> . . . users accessing [definition of *Company B's Website*] through [definition of the *Link*]

Great care would be required to ensure that the definitions were completely and accurately transferred each time the concept of *Company A Users* was needed. Any deviation would open the door to a claim that the parties intended the deviation to be a substantive change. In addition, integrating the definitions would make the provision lengthier and more difficult to understand. As drafted, the defined terms nicely signal their meaning, permitting a short definition.

Although including a defined term in another defined term's definition is a useful drafting technique, it can be overdone, forcing a reader to go on a scavenger hunt to understand a defined term's definition. If the defined term in the definition is used only in that definition, follow the exception to Guideline 15.

Do not cross-reference a defined term in a definition even if it is defined later in the definition section. Cross-references are unnecessary because the language introducing the definitions tells a reader that this is where the agreement's definitions

---

15. "an instrument for reproducing sound at a distance" is a quotation from Merriam-Webster's Collegiate Dictionary 1211 (10th ed., 1999).

16. This definition is based on a definition in *License Agreements: Forms and Checklist* 4-27 (Gregory J. Battersby and Charles W. Grimes eds., Aspen 2003).

are. (This practice differs from what you should do if you use a defined term without definition in the recitals.[17] Then, you must tell the reader where to find the definition of any undefined terms, as the recitals precede the language introducing the definitions.)

> **Wrong**
>
> **"Consent"** means any consent, approval, authorization of, notice to, designation, or filing with any Person (as subsequently defined in this Article 1).
>
> **Correct**
>
> **"Consent"** means any consent, approval, authorization of, notice to, designation, or filing with any Person.

15. *Do not define a defined term in another term's definition.* If you do, you will frustrate the poor reader who searches for the definition after reading its defined term later in the contract. The reader will look for the defined term and its definition in the alphabetical list of defined terms, but they will not be where they should. They will be hidden in another definition.

> **Wrong**
>
> **"Closing Date"** means the day that the transactions contemplated by this Agreement are consummated (the "Closing").
>
> **Correct**
>
> **"Closing"** means the consummation of the transactions that this Agreement contemplates.
>
> *and*
>
> **"Closing Date"** means the day of the Closing.

Despite the general rule, you may define a defined term within a definition if that term is used only in that definition. Alternatively, put the definition in a paragraph immediately following the definition:

> For the purposes of the preceding definition of [the defined term], **"X"** means . . .

If you take advantage of the exception, do not include the defined term in the alphabetical list of defined terms as the reader will have no reason to look for it there.

16. *Avoid definitions that apply to more than one person at one time.* For example, the definition of Contracts in a share purchase agreement is often intended to apply to the Seller, the Buyer, and the Target. This definition can be cumbersome:

---

17. See §6.3, Guideline 11.

Version 1

"Contract" means any contract, lease, arrangement, commitment, or understanding to which the Seller, the Buyer, or the Target is a party or by which the Seller, the Buyer, or the Target or any of their respective properties or assets may be bound or affected.

A simpler version applies the definition to *a Person,* thereby applying it to only one person at a time, but making the definition generally applicable.

Version 2

"Contract" means, with respect to a Person, any contract, lease, agreement, license, arrangement, commitment, or understanding to which that Person is a party or by which that Person or any of its properties or assets is bound or affected.

17. *Do not define a term when the ordinary meaning of the word or phrase expresses the concept.* For example, the following definition of *Resume Performance* is superfluous.

"Resume Performance" means to recommence performance after it was suspended because of a *Force Majeure* Event.

Similarly, a definition of *Parties* is generally unnecessary.[18]

18. *Write a definition as narrowly as possible so that additional information may be included as part of a substantive provision, such as a representation and warranty or a covenant.* A party may sue on a representation and warranty or a covenant, but not on a definition.

Wrong

Definition

"Shares" means the 1,000 issued and outstanding common shares of the Company, par value $1 per share.

and

Representation and Warranty

The Company has 1,000 issued and outstanding Shares [1,000 issued and outstanding common shares of the Company, par value $1 per share], each of which has a par value of $1 per share.

Because the information as to the number of shares and their par value is included in the definition of *Shares,* a representation and warranty as to the number and par

---

18. One instance when it might be useful to define *parties* is if Nebraska law governs the contract and the contract includes a third-party beneficiary provision. *See Props. Inv. Group of Mid-America v. Applied Commun., Inc.*, 495 N.W.2d 483, 489-490 (Neb. 1993) (holding that *party* refers to nonsignatories).

value of the *Shares* has the information twice, explicitly and through the use of the definition of *Shares*. If the number of issued and outstanding shares and the par value are omitted from the definition of Shares, then the representation and warranty works as it should.

> **Correct**
>
> *Revised definition*
>
> **"Shares"** means the Company's common shares.
>
> *and*
>
> *Representation and Warranty*
>
> The Company has issued and outstanding 1,000 Shares [the Company's common shares], each of which has a par value of $1 per share.

19. *Do not create a circular definition; that is, do not define a term by using the same term.* For example, do not do the following:

> **Wrong**
>
> **"Subsidiary"** means a subsidiary.

A better definition is:

> **Correct**
>
> **"Subsidiary"** means any corporation with respect to which the Seller owns more than 50 percent of the issued and outstanding shares.

Despite the general rule, you may include the defined term in the definition *if* the definition is intended to narrow the general meaning of the term so that it applies to a specific instance. For example:

> **"Song"** means any song that the Beatles recorded and included in any of their albums.

20. *Do not include substantive provisions, such as representations and warranties, covenants, and conditions, in a definition.* Their inclusion may create an ambiguity as to the substantive provision's purpose. For example, consider the following definition of *Intellectual Property* from an agreement of sale:

> **"Intellectual Property"** means patents, copyrights, trade secrets, registered trademarks and service marks, trade names, and Internet domain names, *all of which are to be unencumbered as of the Closing Date.*

Are the italicized words a condition to closing or a preclosing covenant, or both? The proper way to draft the definition would be to omit the italicized words. Then, insert them into the appropriate article or articles of the agreement.

Including substantive provisions in a definition increases the likelihood that a reader will miss the provision when reviewing the contract. For example, a reader trying to find all of the conditions to closing in an acquisition agreement will look at the conditions article, not the definitions article. If the reader has a wonderful memory, she may remember that a definition had a substantive provision. But that's if she remembers. Far better to put the substantive provision where it belongs.

21. *Be leery of defining a term by referring to a source outside the contract if the information in that source can be easily restated in the contract.* A reference to an outside source means that the contract does not stand on its own, making it more difficult for a reader to understand the contract's full implications.

Sometimes, however, it is appropriate to define a term by referring to an outside source. For example, a real estate lease may need to refer to various environmental laws. As restating those laws in the contract would be unwieldy, a cross-reference is appropriate. If the outside source changes over time, the definition must indicate whether it is referring to the source as it exists on the day of the agreement's signing or as it exists from time to time (e.g., including any amendments).

> **"CERCLA"** means the federal Comprehensive Environmental Response, Compensation and Liability Act of 1980, as amended [as of the date of this Agreement] [from time to time].

22. *Define an agreement, other than the agreement being drafted by using the information in the preamble of the agreement being defined: the name of that agreement, its date, and the parties.* Some drafters precede the name of the agreement in the definition with the words *that certain.* Those are **pointing words**, and they make the definition no more specific. Omit them.

> **Wrong**
>
> **"Credit Agreement"** means *that certain* Credit Agreement, dated April 11, 20XX, between the Borrower and the Lender, as amended from time to time.
>
> **Correct**
>
> **"Credit Agreement"** means the Credit Agreement, dated April 11, 20XX, between the Borrower and the Lender, as amended from time to time.

The definition should indicate whether references to the agreement are to the agreement's provisions as they exist on the day of that agreement's signing (Version 1) or as they may exist from time to time (Version 2).

> **Version 1**
>
> **"Credit Agreement"** means the Credit Agreement, dated April 11, 20XX, between the Borrower and the Lender as of the date of its signing.
>
> **Version 2**
>
> **"Credit Agreement"** means the Credit Agreement, dated April 11, 20XX, between the Borrower and the Lender, as amended from time to time.

Which version is used has substantive ramifications. For example, pledge agreements and other security agreements often incorporate by reference the credit agreement's definitions. This saves time and paper and ensures that the definitions in the two agreements are exactly the same.

> **Definitions**. Capitalized terms used in this Pledge Agreement without definition have the meanings assigned to them in the Credit Agreement.

The definitions of the two agreements will fall out of synch if the pledge agreement includes a definition of *Credit Agreement* that freezes it as of the date of signing (Version 1) and if the parties subsequently amend the credit agreement's definitions. This disconnect could cause conflicting obligations. To ensure that the two agreements always work in tandem, the pledge agreement's definition of the *Credit Agreement* must refer to that agreement *as it exists from time to time* (Version 2).

A different approach may be appropriate, however, when drafting an acquisition agreement. Then, the buyer may want to freeze the provisions of the seller's contracts so that it knows what is being assigned to it. Accomplishing this business goal requires a two-step process. First, the parties must narrowly define the contracts, so that their definitions exclude future amendments; and second, the seller must promise that it will not amend the contracts.

> **Wrong**
>
> **"Maintenance Agreement"** means the Maintenance Agreement, dated March 13, 20XX, between the Seller and ABC Inc., as amended from time to time.
>
> **Correct**
>
> **"Maintenance Agreement"** means the Maintenance Agreement, dated March 13, 20XX, between the Seller and ABC Inc., as amended to the date of this Agreement.

23. *Once a term is defined, do not repeat any part of the definition when using the defined term.* For example, assume that a contract includes the following definition of *Shares:*

> **"Shares"** means the issued and outstanding common shares of the Company.

In the substantive provisions that follow, the phrase *of the Company* should not be included when the defined term *Shares* is used.

> **Wrong**
>
> *A* shall deliver 500 Shares *of the Company* to *B.*
>
> **Correct**
>
> *A* shall deliver 500 Shares to *B.*

7.5.3 SPECIFIC GUIDELINES: DEFINING TERMS IN CONTEXT

1. *To define a term in context, define it in the sentence in which the definition appears.* The format is fairly straightforward. Follow the rules for defining parties in the preamble. Capitalize the defined term, surround it with quotation marks, put it in bold, and precede it with *the* if it is a noun other than a person's name.

> **Version 1**
>
> **Post-decree Sale of the House.** Lisa and Edward Boswick shall put their house at 496 Maple Avenue, Glen Street, Maryland (the "**House**") on the market no later than 30 days after their divorce decree is final.

Alternatively, carve the section into subsections and put the definition in the first subsection and the substantive provision in the second subsection. Also use this format if a defined term is used multiple times but only used in one section.

> **Version 2**
>
> **3.2 Sale of the House.**
>
> **(a) Definition.** "**House**" means 496 Maple Avenue, Glen Street, Maryland.
>
> **(b) Post-decree Sale of the House.** Lisa and Edward Boswick shall put the House on the market no later than 30 days after their divorce decree is final.

As discussed earlier in this chapter, the key to defining terms in context is their proper placement. Be sure to look carefully at any sentence that includes a definition for any possible ambiguities.

2. *List alphabetically in the definition section any term defined in context and include a cross-reference to the section in which the term is defined.*

> "**Competition**" has the meaning assigned to it in Section 5.3.

By including the cross-reference, the reader will be able to find the defined term's definition easily.

7.6 OTHER PROVISIONS IN THE DEFINITIONS SECTION

In many sophisticated commercial agreements, the definitions section has a second part. Often entitled *Interpretive Provisions* or *Other Definitional Provisions*, these provisions are of general applicability. The following is typical:

> **2.2 Other Definitional Provisions.**
>
> (a) Each term defined in this Agreement has its defined meaning when used in any other Deal Document, unless the term is otherwise

defined in that Deal Document. In that event, the term has the meaning that the Deal Document assigns it.

(b) References to "Sections," "Exhibits," and "Schedules" are to Sections, Exhibits, and Schedules of this Agreement, unless otherwise specifically provided.

(c) The words "including," "includes," and "include" are deemed to be followed by the words "without limitation."

(d) References to a Person include that Person's permitted successors and assigns and, in the case of any governmental Person, the Person succeeding to the relevant functions of that governmental Person.

(e) All references to statutes and related regulations include

(i) any past and future amendments of those statutes and related regulations; and

(ii) any successor statutes and related regulations.

(f) All references in this Agreement to "Dollars" or "$" refer to lawful currency of the United States of America.[19]

---

19. This subsection is generally needed only in agreements with non–U.S. parties.

CHAPTER SEVEN

EXERCISES

Exercise 7-1

Return to Exercise 5-3. Define the territory that Merchandisers will have under the license agreement.

Exercise 7-2

Draft a defined term and definition for a definition section for the financial statements described in the following representation and warranty. In addition, mark up the provision so that the financial statements are defined in context.

> **Financial Statements.** The balance sheet of the Company as of December 31, 20X4 and December 31, 20X3 and the related statements of income, cash flows, and shareholders' equity for each of the two years in the period ended December 31, 20X4, reported on by Debit & Credit LLP, independent accountants, present fairly, in all material respects, the financial position of the Company as of December 31, 20X4 and December 31, 20X3, and the results of its operations and its cash flows for each of the two years in the period ended December 31, 20X4, in conformity with accounting principles generally accepted in the United States of America.

Exercise 7-3

Create a defined term for *Purchase Price* based upon the sentence that follows. In addition, state where you would place the defined term if you were to define it in context.

The purchase price for the House is $250,000.

Exercise 7-4

Assume that your client wants to exclude industry-wide strikes from the definition of *Force Majeure* Event. How would you redraft this provision?

> **"*Force Majeure* Event"** means any act or event that
>
> (a) prevents the affected party, in whole or in part, from
>
> (i) performing its obligations under this Agreement or

(ii) satisfying any conditions required by the other party under this Agreement;

(b) is beyond the reasonable control of and not the fault of the affected party; and

(c) the affected party has been unable to avoid or overcome by the exercise of due diligence,

including, without limitation: war, flood, lightning, drought, earthquake, fire, volcanic eruption, land-

slide, cyclone, typhoon, tornado, explosion, civil disturbance, act of God or the public enemy,

epidemic, famine or plague, shipwreck, action of a court or public authority, or strike, work-to-rule

action, go-slow or similar labor difficulty, each on an industry-wide, region-wide or nation-wide

basis.[20]

Exercise 7-5

Review the definition of *Excluded Assets* in the Asset Purchase Agreement in Appendix A and determine the drafting error based upon the Guidelines.

Exercise 7-6

In choosing between the following definitions, what would you consider?

Version 1

"Breach" means a misrepresentation, breach of warranty, and breach of covenant.

Version 2

"Breach" includes any breach of warranty or covenant.

---

20. This definition is from Nancy F. Persechino, *Force Majeure,* in *Negotiating and Drafting Contract Boilerplate* 201-202 (Tina L. Stark et al. eds., ALM Publg. 2003).

Exercise 7-7

Memorandum

To: A. Barrister

From: H. Flighty

Date: September 14, 20XX

Re: Purchase of Aircraft

As it is our responsibility to draft the purchase agreement, we need to get moving on it. To save some money and give you a head start, I wrote some of the contract last night. Please take a look at it. I think I did a pretty good job, but if you find any errors, correct them.

Remember that you have the Purchase Offer if you need it (Exercise 6-3). One other thing: I used an October 30 date in the preamble because that's the date Samson and I want to sign the agreement.

AIRCRAFT PURCHASE AGREEMENT

AGREEMENT, dated October 30, 20XX, by and among Supersonic Wings Corp., a Delaware

corporation, (the "Seller") and Fly-by-Night Aviation, Inc., a New York corporation having its principal

place of business at 987 East 48th Street, New York, New York 10036 ("Buyer").

WHEREAS, the Seller desires to sell to Buyer, and Buyer desires to purchase from the Seller,

the Aircraft; and

WHEREAS, the Buyer hereby agrees to pay the Seller $23,000,000 in immediately available

funds.

NOW, THEREFORE, in consideration of the mutual promises herein set forth and subject to the

terms and conditions hereof, the parties agree as follows:

Article 1

Definitions

1.1. Defined Terms. As used in this Agreement, terms defined in the preamble and recitals of this Agreement have the meanings set forth therein, and the following terms have the meanings set forth below:

"Agreement" means this Agreement of Sale and all Schedules and Exhibits hereto, as the same may be amended from time to time.

"Aircraft" means the Airframe, equipped with two Rolls-Royce Tay engines model number MK611-8 bearing Serial Numbers 72725 and 72726, together with all appliances, avionics, furnishings, and other components, equipment, and property incorporated in or otherwise related to the Airframe or engines.

"Airframe" means the Gulfstream Aerospace Corporation G550 aircraft, bearing United States Registration No. N765BW and Manufacturer's Serial No. 8181.

"Assigned Contracts" means the Maintenance Agreement (as hereafter defined) and the Pilot Agreement (as hereafter defined).

"Assumed Liabilities" means, collectively, all liabilities and obligations of the Seller that arise under either (i) the Maintenance Agreement on or after the date hereof or (ii) the Pilot Agreement on or after the date of the Closing.

"Aviation Fuel" means any gas or liquid that is used to create power to propel an aircraft. At the time of the Seller's delivery of the Aircraft to Buyer, the fuel gauge of the Aircraft shall register as full.

"Closing" means the closing of the sale of the Aircraft contemplated by this Agreement in New York, New York on the Closing Date.

"Closing Date" has the meaning specified in Section 2.04(a).

"Consent" shall mean any consent, approval, authorization of, notice to, or designation, registration, declaration or filing with, any Person.

"Contract" shall mean any contract, lease, agreement, license, arrangement, commitment or understanding to which the Buyer or any Seller is a party or by which it or any of its properties or assets may be bound or affected.

"Engines" means the two Rolls-Royce Tay engines model number MK611-8, bearing Serial Numbers 72725 and 72726.

"Laws" means all Federal, state, local or foreign laws, rules and regulations.

"Lien" means any lien, charge, encumbrance, security interest, mortgage, or pledge.

"Maintenance Agreement" means that certain Maintenance Agreement, dated as of April 3, 20XX between Greasemonkeys, Inc., and Seller, as the same may be amended from time to time.

"Note" means the Buyer's 9 percent promissory note, payable to the order of the Seller, in the principal amount of $5,000,000, due on December 31, 2012, substantially in the form of Exhibit A to this Agreement.

"Order": any judgment, award, order, writ, injunction or decree issued by any Federal, state, local or foreign authority, court, tribunal, agency, or other governmental authority, or by any arbitrator, to which any Seller or its assets are subject, or to which the Buyer or its assets are subject, as the case may be.

"Person" shall mean any individual, partnership, joint venture, corporation, trust, unincorporated organization, government (and any department or agency thereof) or other entity.

"Pilot Agreement" means that certain Pilot Agreement between Seller and Ace Pilots, Inc. dated as of May 12, 20XX, as the same may be amended from time to time.

Action Sections

8.1 INTRODUCTION

The **action sections** tell the parties how to perform the principal objective of the contract. The two primary components are

- the provisions in which the parties agree to perform the main subject matter of the contract; and
- the consideration provisions, generally the payment of money.

If appropriate, the action sections also include the closing date, the closing deliveries, and a contract's term.

Reminder: "Action sections" is not a technical contract term. This book uses that phrase to refer to the provisions that this chapter discusses.

8.2 SUBJECT MATTER PERFORMANCE PROVISION

The first section of the action sections is always the **subject matter performance provision**. In this provision, the parties promise to accomplish a contract's primary objective.

Imagine that a client receives her dream job offer and that her prospective employer asks her to sign an employment agreement. The primary subject matter of that agreement is her employment. The contract will deal with other significant topics, such as salary, duties, and benefits, but the agreement's primary purpose is to obligate the employer to hire your client and to obligate her to work for the employer. These obligations are the promises that comprise the subject matter performance provision. Similarly, if a client decides to write a book, the primary subject matter of the agreement with the client's publisher is the book's publication. So, in this instance, the subject matter performance provision contains the client's agreement to write the book and the publisher's agreement to publish it. Here are these provisions as they would appear in a contract:

> **Example 1**
>
> **Employment**. Subject to the provisions of this Agreement, the Company shall hire the Executive, and the Executive shall work for the Company for the Term.
>
> **Example 2**
>
> **Agreement to Write and Publish**. Subject to the provisions of this Agreement, the Author shall write a book on seals in the Galapagos Islands, and the Publisher shall publish that book.

Note that both provisions include **reciprocal promises** and are introduced with qualifying language, *Subject to the provisions of this Agreement*. The reciprocal promises reflect the mutuality of the transaction. The qualifying language clarifies that the reciprocal promises must be read in conjunction with the contract's other provisions. Thus, the Publisher's promise to publish the book may be subject to a condition—for example, the Author must have written a précis that the Publisher finds acceptable.

Although the subject matter performance provision often takes the form of mirror image reciprocal promises that reflect the flip sides of a transaction—*hire* and *work for, write* and *publish*—this is not always the case. In some agreements, a party's principal promise cannot be reduced to a few words that can easily be juxtaposed with the other party's promise. The return promise may be much more elaborate and require multiple provisions. In addition, the structure of the transaction may not allow for the mirror image promises. Thus, in a loan agreement, while the bank promises to lend money, the borrower does not promise to borrow it. Instead, it generally has the discretion to borrow on an as-needed basis. The borrower's reciprocal promise would be its promise to repay the principal with interest.

Finally, not all contracts have subject matter performance provisions that are promises. In these provisions, rather than promising to perform in the future, a party performs when it signs the contract. The words in the subject matter performance provision constitute the performance. These provisions are **self-executing**. Classic examples are guaranties, waivers, releases, options, and grants of security interests.

> **Example 1**
>
> **Guaranty**. By signing this Guaranty, Conglomerate Corp. guarantees to Big Bank the debt of its subsidiary, Oliveira Manufacturing, Inc.
>
> **Example 2**
>
> **Grant of Security Interest**. By signing this Security Agreement, the Borrower grants the Lender a security interest in the Borrower's assets.
>
> **Example 3**
>
> **Appointment of Escrow Agent**. By signing this Agreement, the parties appoint Vivienne Kim as Escrow Agent.

8.3 CONSIDERATION PROVISIONS

The consideration provision of a contract sets forth its financial terms. In this section, one party promises to pay the other in exchange for whatever that party has promised to do. In a publishing agreement, the publisher promises to pay the author royalties for the book the author will write; while in a lease, the tenant promises to pay the landlord rent in exchange for the use of the leased premises.

Money is not the only form of payment that parties use. They can also pay with monetary equivalents such as shares, a promissory note, an assignment of rights, an assumption of liabilities,[1] or any other agreed-upon medium of exchange.[2] This section will refer to the different forms of payment, when referred to together, as *consideration*.

Every consideration provision must state the amount of the consideration and include a promise to pay it. You can draft the provision as two sentences or sections, one a declaration stating the amount of the consideration, and the other a promise to pay it. Alternatively, you can combine the statement of the amount and the promise to pay into a single sentence.

> **Example 1**
>
> **Rent**. The rent is $2,500 per month (the "Rent"). With respect to each month of the Lease, the Tenant shall pay the Landlord the Rent no later than the first day of that month.
>
> **Example 2**
>
> **Fee**. The Owner shall pay the Contractor a $35,000 fee for renovating the House, $10,000 contemporaneously with the signing of this Agreement and $25,000 upon completion of the renovation.

When drafting the monetary provision, keep the following guidelines in mind.

Guidelines for Considering Provisions

1. *Follow the cash.*[3] Make certain that you keep track of all the money in the transaction: Make a flowchart so that you can visualize the flow of money. Who has it? Why? What triggers its payment? Is there a deposit? Who is entitled to it when the contract ends? Are multiple payments being made to one or more parties?

2. *The consideration provision should answer the questions of **who** is paying **what** to **whom, when, why,** and **how**.* Create a chart that lists each payment and how it is to be made. If money is to be deposited to a bank account, include the name of the bank and the account number.

---

1. See §8.3, Guideline 3 for an explanation of *assumed liabilities*.

2. Although this section discusses payments, a transaction need not involve money or a monetary equivalent. For example, parties could agree to a barter exchange in which one party promises to deliver ten bushels of apples in exchange for five bushels of corn. Similarly, Henry can promise to paint Moesha's living room in return for Moesha's promise to tutor Henry's son.

3. The phrase, *follow the cash,* is the mantra of my former partner, Donald Schapiro.

3. *State the* **amount** *of consideration payable.* (This answers the question of *what?*)

Example 1

Purchase Price. The purchase price is $40 million.

Example 2

Rent. The monthly rent is $2,500.

Example 3

Purchase Price. The purchase price is 20,000 shares of the Company's Class A Common Stock.

Some drafters put defined terms relating to the payment of consideration in the consideration provision as this is often the only place they are used. To prevent ambiguity, avoid defining terms in context. Instead, define any needed terms in a separate section or subsection.

If the transaction involves international parties, state the currency in which payment is to be made.

As noted earlier, consideration is typically money, shares, or promissory notes, but it can also be an assignment of rights or an assumption of liabilities. If a party assigns its rights, it transfers its right to the other party's performance to a third person. Imagine that Colossal Construction Corp. owes Tong's Machinery LLC $100,000, but the payment is not due until year-end. If Tong's Machinery needs cash immediately, it can assign to its bank its right to payment from Colossal Construction. In exchange, the bank will pay Tong's Machinery a discounted amount, say, $90,000. The consideration is the assignment of the right to payment and the return payment of $90,000. Big Bank earns a $10,000 profit when Colossal Construction Corp. pays it the $100,000 originally owed to Tong's Machinery LLC.

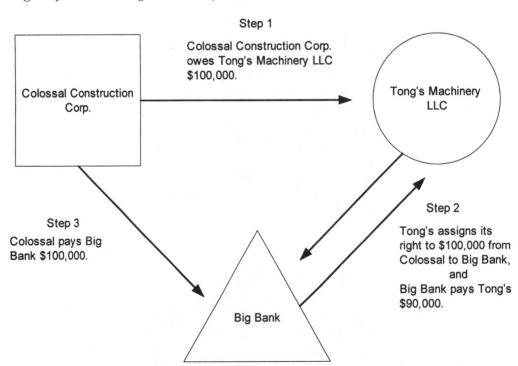

An assumption of liabilities is the converse of an assignment of rights. In this situation, a third party takes on a party's duty to perform. To see how this works, we will first look at a transaction without an assumption, and then, we will compare it to the same transaction but with an assumption.

Imagine that Darnell Winston purchased Blackacre last year for $75,000 and paid $50,000 with his own money and the remaining $25,000 with money that he borrowed from a bank. Upon completing the purchase, Darnell has a $25,000 liability, the amount he owes to the bank. Because the real estate market is hot, Darnell decides a year later to sell Blackacre for $100,000 to Phyllis Wright. If Phyllis pays Darnell $100,000, Darnell must use $25,000 of that amount to repay the bank. After that payment, he nets $75,000.

Darnell receives	$100,000
Darnell pays the bank	(25,000)
Darnell nets	$ 75,000

Alternatively, if the bank agrees, Phyllis could assume Darnell's liability to the bank. Phyllis will stay pay $100,000, but she will pay part of that amount to Darnell and the rest to the bank. More specifically, Phyllis will pay Darnell $75,000, the same amount he would have netted if Phyllis had paid him $100,000 in cash. In addition, she will pay the bank the $25,000, plus interest, that Darnell owed. So, whether the consideration is $100,000 in cash, or $75,000 in cash, plus the assumption, both parties end up in essentially the same financial position.[4]

When stating what the consideration is, think through whether a contract term's midyear start date requires a stub period payment. A **stub period** is a period less than a calendar year that occurs when a contract term begins or ends in the middle of a calendar year. For example, if an executive begins work on September 15, the midyear start date creates two stub periods. The first occurs in the first year of the contract term. It begins on September 15 and ends on December 31. The second stub period occurs in the contract's final year. It begins on January 1 and ends on September 14, the last day of the contract term. In both instances, if the executive is entitled to a bonus based on the company's performance for each calendar year, the parties might need to provide special rules to calculate the bonus for the stub periods.

4. State **who** is paying **what** to **whom**. Draft a party's obligation to pay in the active voice.

> **Payment of Rent.** With respect to each month of the Term, the Tenant shall pay the Rent to the Landlord.

Some drafters violate this rule by providing that a payee has a right to payment. Although this is technically correct as every obligation to perform includes a right to that performance, stating the obligation more clearly expresses who must pay what to whom.

---

4. In the real world, a buyer is in a slightly different financial position if it assumes a seller's liabilities to third parties. First, a buyer may not have to pay the seller's liabilities immediately. Instead, the buyer may be able to pay them over time, either in accordance with the seller's agreements with the third parties or in accordance with an arrangement it can negotiate. This delayed payment could be a substantial advantage to a buyer. Second, a buyer could also negotiate with the third parties to reduce the amount to be paid, thus obtaining a discount. Third, a buyer may have to pay interest that it would not have had to pay if it had paid the full amount owed.

Do not use euphemisms for an obligation to pay. State explicitly that *X shall pay Y.*

> **Wrong**
>
> **Fee**. The Producer is responsible for paying the Screenwriter $6,000 for the script.
>
> **Correct**
>
> **Fee**. The Producer shall pay the Screenwriter $6,000 for the script.

5. *Calculate any amounts that can be calculated before signing rather than including a mathematical formula.* For example, if possible, state the amount each party is to be paid, rather than stating each party is to be paid its allocable share. This should reduce the likelihood of a dispute as the parties will check the calculations before signing the agreement. Do not state the formula and the results of the formula; it may create an ambiguity.

If a party must pay more than one form of consideration to more than one party, create a chart that specifies the type and amount of consideration payable to each party. For example:

> **Wrong**
>
> **Consideration**. The Purchase Price is $100 million in immediately available funds,[5] $25 million in subordinated debt, and 5 million Class A Shares, each Shareholder to be paid that Shareholder's allocable share.
>
> **Correct**
>
> **Consideration**. The Purchase Price is $100 million in immediately available funds, $25 million in subordinated debt, and 5 million Class A Shares, payable to each Shareholder as follows:

	IMMEDIATELY AVAILABLE FUNDS	SUBORDINATED DEBT	EQUITY
Shareholder A	$20 million	$5 million	1 million Class A Shares
Shareholder B	$70 million	$17.5 million	3.5 million Class A Shares
Shareholder C	$10 million	$2.5 million	.5 million Class A Shares

6. *State **when** the consideration is payable:*

> **Rent**. With respect to each month of the term, the Tenant shall pay the Rent to the Landlord *no later the first day of that month.*

---

5. See Guideline 8.

7. *If a contract term creates any stub periods, provide for appropriate payment dates.* Also, consider what timing issues are created if the contract term does not coincide with the fiscal year.[6] If a license agreement term begins on March 15, are payments to be made

- at the end of every three months based on a term beginning on March 15 (i.e., June 14, September 14, December 14, and March 14), or
- at the end of each calendar quarter (i.e., March 31, June 30, September 30 and December 31)?

Consider also whether any payment should be accelerated or delayed. Loan agreements often require mandatory prepayments of principal if the borrower sells equity securities, borrows more money, or sells substantially all of its assets.

8. *State **how** a party is to pay money: personal check, company check, bank check, certified check, or immediately available funds.*

> **Rent**. With respect to each month of the Term, the Tenant shall pay the Rent to the Landlord *by certified check* no later than the first day of that month.

The form of payment determines when a recipient has access to the money and reflects an allocation of risk between the parties. Some forms of payment are more risky for a recipient than others. The most risky are personal checks and company checks. When a party pays by check, the recipient does not have immediate access to the funds. It must first deposit the check at its bank, and that bank must (technically) receive payment from the paying party's bank. The delay that this process entails creates a credit risk: The paying party may not have money in its account at the time payment is required. Thus, even if the recipient has performed, it might not get paid. Despite this risk, many recipients are willing to accept a personal or company check. For example, Internet providers, telephone companies, and electric utilities all accept their customer's personal checks.

Less risky for a payee are cashier's checks (also known as bank checks) and certified checks. A **cashier's check** is a check that a bank issues from its own account. It is the bank's promise to pay the recipient.[7] (The paying party applies to its bank for a cashier's check, at which time the bank takes the money from that party's account and issues its own check to the order of the recipient.) Thus, when a recipient accepts a cashier's check as payment, it no longer takes a risk as to the paying party's creditworthiness. Instead, its credit risk is the bank's creditworthiness. Although the recipient's credit risk is significantly reduced, it still does not have access to the funds until the business day after the banking day on which they were deposited.[8] In addition, the check is subject to final clearing and reversal if it is dishonored because of fraud or some other issue.

A **certified check** is a check as to which a bank has set aside sufficient funds from the paying party's account to ensure full payment of the check. The bank "certifies" the check by having an authorized employee sign the check.[9] Again, while the

---

6. A company's fiscal year is the one-year period that the company uses to determine its annual revenues, etc. Generally, the fiscal year is a calendar year, but that does not hold true in all industries.

7. 12 C.F.R. §229.2(i) (2006).

8. 12 C.F.R. §229.10(c)(v) (2003).

9. 12 C.F.R. §229.2(j) (2006).

recipient has reduced its credit risk, the funds are not available until the business day after the banking day on which the funds were deposited.[10] In addition, the bank can take back its payment if it discovers the check was fraudulently issued.

Parties often use cashier's checks or certified checks when the parties know the payment amount several days before the transaction, the amount is relatively large, and the recipient wants to reduce its credit risk. Car dealers often insist on one of these forms of payment.

In complex, sophisticated transactions with significant sums at risk, many recipients refuse to take any risk of nonpayment and, in addition, want immediate access to the money for investment or other purposes. In these transactions, the paying party can **wire transfer** immediately available funds from its bank account to the recipient's. The recipient need not make a deposit because the wire transfer accomplishes that. Technically, a wire transfer is an irrevocable, electronic transfer of immediately available funds using a system that the Federal Reserve System maintains.[11] Parties speak colloquially of a **Fed funds transfer.**

If a wire transfer involves multinational parties or parties located in different cities, determine where the funds are to be sent. Are they being transferred to an account in New York City, Detroit, or Tokyo? Funds immediately available in New York City are not immediately available in Tokyo because of the difference in time zones. An obligation to pay by a Fed funds wire transfer is generally along the following lines:

> **Payment of Purchase Price**. The Buyer shall pay the Seller the Purchase Price by wire transfer of immediately available funds in Chicago. The Seller shall notify the Buyer of the bank account into which the funds are to be transferred no later than two business days before the Closing.

Some drafters provide that a paying party must pay the consideration in *cash*. Do not do this. **Cash** is currency (bills and coins), and it is most unlikely that the parties intend the paying party to arrive with bushels of dollar bills. Although courts have interpreted *cash* to mean immediately available funds,[12] other courts have held that *cash* means currency.[13] While using the word *cash* is unlikely to cause a problem, when drafting, say what you mean.

9. *If money is payable for more than one reason, make sure that the terms for each payment conform to this section's guidelines.* For example, if a company is obligated to pay an executive both a salary and a bonus, create separate payment sections for each payment, and then in each section, state the appropriate amount, when the payment is due, etc. Treating the two types of payments separately will help you analyze the possibly different business issues associated with each of the payments (e.g.: When is the bonus paid?).

10. *If payment is based on a formula, state the formula accurately.* While a formula may appear simple at first, it often requires sophisticated drafting.[14]

---

10. 12 C.F.R. §229.10(c)(v) (2003).

11. *See generally* Federal Reserve Board, *Fedwire and National Settlement Services,* http://www.federalreserve.gov/paymentsystems/fedwire/default.htm (accessed Nov. 16, 2006).

12. *Upchurch v. Chaney*, 635 S.E.2d 124, 125 (Ga. 2006) (holding that in context of a judicial sale "cash" meant immediately available funds).

13. *Nance v. Schoonover*, 521 P.2d 896, 897 (Utah 1974) (holding that parties intended *cash* to mean *currency*).

14. See Chapter 22, Numbers and Financial Provisions, and Chapter 25, Adding Value to the Deal, §25.2.4.

8.4 TERM

Some contracts relate to a specific transaction, for example, the sale of Blackacre. Although it may take time for the parties to consummate this transaction, their contract has a limited time horizon. In other contracts, however, the parties anticipate a relationship that will span an extended time period. Their contract will govern their relationship for a **term of years.** Leases and license agreements are examples.

When drafting a contract for a term of years, the beginning and ending dates of the term must be unambiguous. The easiest way to accomplish this is to state the term's beginning and ending dates.[15] You may do this either by drafting a stand-alone section or by incorporating the dates into the subject matter performance provision. In either case, drafters often define *Term* in the action sections.[16]

> **Example 1**
>
> **Term**. This Agreement's term begins on January 1, 20X5 and ends on December 31, 20X7 (the "Term"). *(Stand-alone section.)*
>
> **Example 2**
>
> **Term**. Subject to the provisions of this Agreement, the Supplier shall supply the Manufacturer with the Materials listed in **Exhibit A**, and the Purchaser shall purchase those Materials, for a three-year term beginning on January 1, 20X5 and ending on December 31, 20X7 (the "Term"). *(Incorporated into the subject matter performance provision.)*

If you are drafting a precedent for use in multiple transactions, you may want a contract that requires minimal changes each time it is used. In this case, key the beginning of the term to the date the parties sign the contract. The ending date then keys off the anniversary date of the contract's signing.

> **Term**. This Agreement's term begins on the date that the parties execute and deliver this Agreement and ends at 5:00 p.m. on the day preceding the third anniversary of the date the parties execute and deliver this Agreement (the "Term").

A contract need not state the specific date as of which a term is to begin. Instead, the contract can provide that the first day of the term coincides with a future event. Here, the parties distinguish the creation of a binding contract from the first day of the term. That is, although a binding contract comes into existence on the date the parties sign the contract, the term does not begin until a later date when a specified event occurs. For example, a lease term may begin on the day the tenant pays its deposit.

When drafting the ending date of the contract, some drafters provide for the contract's early termination.

---

15. Provisions dealing with dates are, unfortunately, often rife with ambiguity. Chapter 21 discusses how to avoid ambiguity when drafting contract provisions that include time periods.

16. If you define *Term* in the action sections, remember to include it in the contract's alphabetical listing of defined terms, along with a cross-reference to the section where you define it.

> **Term**. The Agreement's term begins on the date that the parties execute and deliver this Agreement and ends at 5:00 p.m. on the day preceding the third anniversary of the day the parties execute and deliver this Agreement, *unless sooner terminated in accordance with the provisions of this Agreement.*

Other drafters believe the additional language is superfluous. The better practice is to explicitly state that the term is subject to early termination, but this can be done in either in the term provision or in the endgame provisions.

When drafting contracts with a term, discuss with the client whether the contract should include an **evergreen provision**. These provisions automatically renew a contract's term. When drafting an evergreen consider the following issues:

- Does the term automatically renew, unless one party notifies the other that it is terminating the contract?
- Does the term automatically end, unless a party exercises its option to renew?
- Does each party have the authority to renew?
- How long should the renewal period be: the same length of time as the original period or shorter?

The following is an example of an evergreen provision:[17]

> **Term**. This Agreement's term begins on January 1, 20X5 and ends on December 31, 20X7. It automatically renews for successive one-year terms, unless either party exercises its option to terminate this Agreement. (The initial three-year period and each successive one-year renewal, a "**Term**.") To exercise its option to terminate at the end of a Term, a party must deliver a written notice of termination to the other party that is received no later than thirty days before the last day of the then existing Term.

When drafting an evergreen provision, do not provide that the parties will agree upon a price increase at the time of a renewal. Agreements to agree are unenforceable.[18] Instead, provide a contractual mechanism for determining the amount of the increase (e.g., a stated percentage increase or a percentage increase tied into cost-of-living increases). If the parties want to be able to negotiate the increase at the end of a term, the contract can require the parties to negotiate in good faith. Counsel should advise the parties, however, that if they do not reach an agreement, the renewal may be unenforceable.[19]

8.5 CLOSINGS AND THE CLOSING DATE

Recall from Chapter 3 that you learned that a closing was the consummation of a transaction at which time the parties exchanged consideration. It is the final step in actuating a transaction. In the context of the Sally and Bob house sale described in Chapter 3, the closing will occur when Sally delivers the deed, and Bob pays the purchase price.

---

17. For an excellent discussion of term provisions, *see* David C. Burgess, *Duration of the Agreement,* in *Drafting Business Contracts: Principles, Techniques, and Forms* ch. 6 (Continuing Ed. Bar Cal. 2006).

18. *Joseph Martin, Jr., Delicatessen, Inc. v. Schumacher,* 417 N.E.2d 541, 543-544 (N.Y. 1981).

19. *Id.* at 544.

In a financing, the closing occurs when the bank funds the loan and the borrower signs the note.

Not every transaction requires a formal closing. Usually, closings are necessary only in complex commercial transactions where the parties sign multiple documents. Transactions that typically require closings are acquisitions, underwritings, and financings. Most other transactions do not. For example, the Website Development Agreement in Appendix B does not require a closing. Similarly, no closing is necessary in many leasing transactions. All that is required is that the parties sign the lease and the tenant pay the deposit. The parties need not even get together to sign the lease; they can exchange signature pages by fax.

If the transaction will have a closing, the contract should give its place, date, and time. The statement of the time should indicate which time zone governs the time of the closing. If both parties are in the same time zone, a reference to *local time* is sufficient. In addition, when drafting that provision, consider whether the closing date should be fixed or whether it should be determined by the happening of an event. For example, the closing date in the following provision is tied into the date that the parties receive all the consents to their transaction.

> **Closing**. The consummation of the transactions that this Agreement contemplates is to take place at the offices of Workhard & Playlittle LLP, 8000 Sears Tower, Chicago, Illinois, at 10:00 a.m. Chicago time on the third business day after the parties receive the last of the consents listed in **Schedule 3.7**.

If the contract provides for a specific closing date, determine whether the parties must close on that date. If so, consider a time-of-the-essence clause, but be sure that you understand the consequences of that provision in your jurisdiction. If time is not of the essence, provide that the parties may jointly postpone the closing date. It is awkward to need an amendment or a waiver if documenting the transaction takes longer than expected. Many deals have what are colloquially referred to as **rolling closing dates**. The parties agree to close, say, on March 15, but the documentation is not ready then, so the parties postpone day by day until they are ready to close.

If the agreement permits postponements, consider whether the contract should include a **drop-dead date**, a date after which the parties may no longer postpone the closing. A drop-dead date might be appropriate, for instance, in an acquisition that needs to close before year-end so that the seller can include the income in its year-end financial statements. A drop-dead date might also be appropriate in the purchase and sale of a house where a seller has another buyer waiting in the wings. The following provision provides for a rolling closing date with a drop-dead date.

> **Closing**. The consummation of the transactions that this Agreement contemplates (the "Closing") is to take place at the offices of Workhard & Playlittle LLP, 200 Peachtree Street, Atlanta, Georgia 30303, on June 15, 20XX, at 10:00 a.m. local time or on another date and time as to which the parties agree, but in no event later than June 30, 20XX (the date and time of the Closing, the "Closing Date").

If a contract includes a drop-dead date, include endgame provisions that provide for the contract's termination and that spell out the consequences of a failure to close. Do not put this information in the action sections.

8.6 CLOSING DELIVERIES

The phrase **closing deliveries** has both a narrow and a broad meaning. Its narrow meaning arises in the context of an acquisition or a financing agreement and refers to the exchange of documents and consideration necessary to consummate the transaction. Thus, in a sale of assets, the seller's closing deliveries include the bill of sale, an assignment of contracts, and any deeds. The buyer's closing deliveries are the delivery of the purchase price and, if appropriate, an assumption of liabilities. Deal lawyers also use *closing deliveries* in a broader sense in acquisitions and financings to refer to any documents that a party delivers at closing. These documents include bring-down certificates,[20] incumbency certificates, certified resolutions, and opinion letters.

Where the closing deliveries are listed depends upon the closing deliveries being referred to. In an acquisition agreement, the action sections will include a closing delivery section in which the buyer and seller obligate themselves to exchange the documents and consideration necessary to consummate the transaction. These are the *closing deliveries* as that term is used in its narrow sense. For example, the following closing delivery section excerpt comes from an acquisition agreement. As you read the provision, note the italicized language that establishes the standard as to the form of the conveyancing document. Which form gives the Seller the most latitude? Which form best protects the Buyer?

Closing Deliveries

(a) **Seller's Deliveries.** At the Closing, the Seller shall deliver to the Buyer the following:

   (i) *A bill of sale* for the Purchased Assets.

   (ii) An assignment of each real property lease under which the Seller is lessee, *in form satisfactory to the Buyer.*

   (iii) Assignments for all funds on deposit with banks or other Persons which are Purchased Assets, *in form reasonably satisfactory to the Buyer.*

   (iv) A general warranty deed for each real property interest owned by any Seller, *in the form customarily used in commercial transactions in the place where the real property is located.*

   (v) Assignments for each Assigned Contract, each to be *substantially in the form of* **Exhibit C.**

As to the other closing deliveries (*closing deliveries* as used in its broader sense), some are included in the action sections and others in the conditions article. The decision as to where a closing delivery should be listed reflects the contractual

---

20. In a bring-down certificate, a party certifies that the representations and warranties that were made on the signing date are also true on the closing date. Section 8.3 in the Asset Purchase Agreement in Appendix A provides for a bring-down certificate.

ramifications of listing the delivery in one place or the other. If the delivery is listed in the action sections, a party covenants to deliver the document. Any failure to deliver it breaches the agreement, entitling the other party to damages. In addition, the other party would have a walk-away right as, in an acquisition agreement, a breach of any of these covenants results in a failure to satisfy a condition. (See, for example, Section 8.2 in the Asset Purchase Agreement in Appendix A.) The contractual consequences differ, however, if the closing delivery is listed only in the conditions article. Then, the buyer's sole remedy is a walk-away right.

In deciding where to list a closing delivery, determine whether the party responsible for the delivery has control over its delivery. If the party can control its delivery, list the closing delivery in the action sections. In this event, the delivering party accepts the risk of breaching its covenant to deliver the document. If the party cannot control the delivery, list it as a condition to closing, so that a walk-away right is the other party's only remedy.

For example, drafters always carefully provide that the delivery of a legal opinion is a condition to closing, not a covenant. This protects the parties, as they cannot control whether their lawyers will deliver the opinion. A peculiarity in the transaction's structure or a new court opinion can make an opinion difficult, if not impossible, to deliver. By listing the delivery of the opinion in the conditions article, an opinion's nondelivery creates only a walk-away right, not a right to damages.

In contrast, deliveries that properly appear in the action sections include certified resolutions of a party and agreements that the delivering party must sign, for example, a noncompetition agreement. These are documents the delivery of which a party can control.

EXERCISES

Exercise 8-1

If you represented a supplier of sheet metal and the contract's pricing terms provide for annual generous increases that continue in any extended term, which type of evergreen would you recommend to your client and why?

Version 1

An evergreen provision that automatically renews the contract's term, unless one party notifies the other that it is terminating the contract.

Version 2

An evergreen provision that automatically ends the contract's term, but which permits a party to extend the contract by exercising an option to renew.

Exercise 8-2

Memorandum

To: Portia Porter

From: Sam Samson

Date: September 22, 20XX

Re: Sale of Aircraft

While we can't take over the drafting of the whole agreement, I convinced Flighty to let us draft the action sections. I told him that it would save him money. That guy is so cheap, he said yes immediately. Of course, the real reason I want you to do the drafting is that I don't trust Flighty. He is just a little too "sharp."

You may recall that several years ago his company bought a helicopter from Rich Lefkowitz's company. The purchase price was to be paid partially in cash and the rest in notes. In addition, as part of the business deal, Flighty was supposed to personally guarantee his company's notes. As I heard the story, he signed the guaranty and then took it off the table while the money was being wired. It wasn't until Lefkowitz threatened to sue for fraud that Flighty delivered the guaranty. What a bum.

I would appreciate your getting me the draft of the action sections as soon as possible. You probably know this, but to draft those provisions, you will need information from the Purchase Offer and the Escrow Agreement (Exercise 6-3) and a few defined terms from the first draft of the Aircraft Purchase Agreement (Exercise 7-7). Thanks.

Exercise 8-3

Below are five versions of the same provision based on the facts that follow. Read each version and compare it to the others. Be prepared to discuss how the versions differ and why one version is better than the others. Some of the versions have substantive and nonsubstantive drafting errors. Determine the errors and how you would correct them.

Facts

1. Assume that it is October 18, 2006. Your client, the employer, is entering into an agreement on this day for the employment of an executive.
3. The executive is to begin work on January 1, 2007. The last day of the employment term is December 31, 2009.
4. The salary is at a rate of $85,000 per year for the first year. The company will pay the employee every two weeks. The salary will increase each year over the previous year's salary by at least 7 ½ percent. The increase takes effect on January 1 of each year.
5. The executive is entitled to a bonus of $15,000 each year. The bonus will be paid on December 31, 2007, December 31, 2008, and December 31, 2009.
6. The company will pay the executive with its company check.

Version 1

From the Definition Section

"Employment Term" means the three-year period beginning on January 1, 2007 and ending on December 31, 2009.

The contract provision

    3.1 Salary. For the first year of the Employment Term, the Company shall pay the Executive a salary of $85,000 (the "Base Salary") in biweekly installments of $3,269.23. Beginning on the first anniversary of this Agreement and on each subsequent anniversary during the Employment Term, the Base Salary of the Executive increases by an amount not less than 7 ½ percent of the preceding year's Base Salary.

    3.2 Bonus. In addition to the Base Salary, with respect to each year that the Executive is employed under this Agreement, the Company shall pay the Executive a $15,000 bonus (the "Bonus") on the last day of that year.

Version 2

From the Definition Section

"Employment Term" means the three-year period beginning on January 1, 2007 and ending on December 31, 2009.

---

continued on next page >

The contract provision

3.1 Salary.

(a) **Obligation to Pay.** During the Employment Term, the Company shall pay the Executive an annual base salary (to be computed as set forth in Section 3.1(b)) in biweekly installments.

(b) **Calculation of Annual Base Salary.** For the first year of the Employment Term, the annual base salary is $85,000. Commencing on the first anniversary of the Employment Term and on each subsequent anniversary during the Employment Term, the Company shall increase the base salary by an amount not less than 7 ½ percent of the preceding year's base salary.

3.2 Bonus. In addition to the annual base salary, the Company shall pay the Executive a $15,000 bonus (the "Bonus") on December 31 of each year of the Employment Term.

Version 3

From the Definition Section

"Employment Term" means the three-year period beginning on January 1, 2007 and ending on December 31, 2009.

The contract provision

3.1 Compensation. During the Employment Term, the Company shall pay the Executive

(a) an annual base salary (to be computed as set forth in this Section 3.1) in biweekly installments; and

(b) a $15,000 bonus on December 31 of each year.

For the first year of the Employment Term, the annual base salary is $85,000. Beginning on the first anniversary of the Employment Term and on each subsequent anniversary during the Employment Term, the base salary increases by an amount not less than 7 ½ percent of the preceding year's base salary.

Version 4

From the Definition Section

"Base Salary" means $85,000.

"Employment Term" means the three-year period beginning on January 1, 2007 and ending on December 31, 2009.

"Minimum Salary Increment" means, with respect to each year of the Employment Term, an amount not less than 7 ½ percent of the preceding year's Salary.

"Salary" means, with respect to each year of the Employment Term, the Executive's aggregate annual salary.

The contract provision

3.1 Compensation.

(a) **Salary for the First Year.** With respect to the first year of the Employment Term, the Company shall pay the Executive a Salary equal in amount to the Base Salary in biweekly installments.

(b) **Salary for the Second and Third Years.** Beginning on the first anniversary of the Employment Term and on each subsequent anniversary during the Employment Term, the Company shall increase the Salary by an amount not less than the Minimum Salary Increment and pay that Salary to the Executive in biweekly installments.

(c) **Bonus.** During the Employment Term, the Company shall pay the Executive a bonus in an amount not less than $15,000 no later than the last day of each year of the Employment Term.

Version 5

From the Definition Section

"Employment Term" means the three-year period beginning on January 1, 2007 and ending on December 31, 2009.

The contract provision

3.1 Compensation.

(a) **Salary.** During the Employment Term, the Company shall pay the Executive a salary (the "Salary") in an amount computed as follows:

   (i) With respect to the first year of the Employment Term, the Salary is $85,000.

   (ii) With respect to each year of the Employment Term, other than the first year of the Employment Term, the Salary is the amount equal to the *sum* of

      (A) the Salary for the immediately preceding year *plus*

      (B) an amount equal to 7 ½ percent of the Salary for the immediately preceding year or such greater amount as the Company determines in its sole discretion. The Company shall pay the Executive the Salary in equal, biweekly installments.

(b) **Bonus.** During the Employment Term, the Company shall pay the Executive a $15,000 bonus (the "Bonus") no later than the last day of each year of the Employment Term.

Representations and Warranties

9.1 INTRODUCTION TO CHAPTERS 9 THROUGH 14

As you learned in Chapters 3 and 4, the building blocks of contracts are the following contract concepts: representations and warranties, covenants, rights, conditions, discretionary authority, and declarations. By using these building blocks as the starting point for the drafting of contract provisions, a drafter can accurately memorialize the parties' business deal.

Chapters 9 through 12 discuss the drafting of the building blocks from two perspectives. First, when appropriate, a chapter explains the considerations to take into account from a business perspective. Second, it details the rules relating to the drafting of each building block—for example, what tense and voice are appropriate. Chapter 13 explains when you can use *will* and provides a nongrammatical framework for determining whether the use of *shall* is correct. Chapter 14 provides a chart that summarizes the key information in Chapters 9 through 13.

Each chapter, other than Chapter 13, has exercises that apply to the material in that chapter. Chapter 14's exercises require you to draft and mark-up provisions using all the contract concepts.

9.2 GENERAL COMMENTS ON DRAFTING REPRESENTATIONS AND WARRANTIES

The language introducing representations and warranties is simple and results in each statement of fact being both a representation and a warranty.

> Party A represents and warrants to Party B as follows:

Nothing else is needed, and individual statements of fact do not need to reiterate that a party is making both representations and warranties.

Using *represents and warrants* together, rather than either term alone, precludes any ambiguity as to the contract's meaning. It plainly states the parties' intent: that a party both represents and warrants the statements that follow.

The phrase *represents and warrants* differs from other couplets and triplets where the words are synonymous.[1] With respect to those phrases, a drafter can safely omit all but one of the words without changing the phrase's meaning. But using just *represents* or just *warrants* could create different legal consequences because those terms do have different substantive meanings. Using only one of them raises the possibility that the parties intended the consequences of only that term. It invites litigation. However, preventing litigation is one of a drafter's crucial jobs.[2] A careful drafter anticipates the business and legal problems that a provision might pose and then drafts to foreclose the possibility of that problem occurring. By using both *represents* and *warrants,* a drafter reduces a client's litigation risk by explicitly saying what the parties mean—a cardinal principle of good drafting.

The standard language introducing the representations and warranties makes them speak as of the date in the preamble. The parties, however, might want a different or additional date. For example, if a bank and its borrower are restating their credit agreement,[3] absent any change in the introductory language, the representations and warranties would speak as of the date in the restated agreement's preamble. The bank, however, might insist that the borrower's representations and warranties be true as of two dates: the date of the restated agreement and the date of the original credit agreement. This way the restated agreement does not eliminate any of the bank's rights or remedies arising from any misrepresentation or breach of warranty in the original credit agreement. Revised introductory language might look like the following:

> The parties represent and warrant the following as of the date of this Restated Agreement and as of the date of the Original Agreement:

The following sections discuss considerations specific to representations and warranties.

9.3 DRAFTING THE SUBSTANCE OF REPRESENTATIONS

This section discusses what you should consider when drafting the statements of fact that constitute representations. By virtue of the introductory language referred to earlier, these statements do double duty and will also serve as warranties. This section focuses, however, on how to craft the representations, the statements of fact, from a client's business perspective.

When drafting a representation, remember that it allocates risk by establishing a standard of liability. That standard is the statement of fact. If it is false, the maker of the representation is liable. Recall from Chapter 3 how the standard of liability—and, therefore, the risk—shifted each time the knowledge qualifier in the no litigation representation changed. The same process of risk allocation occurs each time a drafter changes a representation. If the statement changes, the standard changes, and the risk shifts. Therefore, when drafting the substance of representations, look closely at each word and ask whether it establishes the appropriate standard.

---

1. See §18.3

2. *See* Louis M. Brown, *The Law Office—A Preventive Law Laboratory,* 104 U. Pa. L. Rev. 940, 945-946 (May 1956).

3. For a discussion of restated agreements, see §29.3.

When drafting representations, your strategic approach will differ, depending upon whether you represent the party making the representations or receiving them. If you represent the party making the representations, minimize the number of representations, and qualify them as much as possible. This reduces your client's potential liability. But, if you represent the party receiving the representations, your client's business interests are best served by receiving representations that are as broad and as unqualified as possible. These representations increase the risk that the maker will misstate a fact, thereby making it easier for the recipient to claim a misrepresentation.

As noted, drafters often use knowledge qualifiers to reduce a maker's risks. They also frequently use **materiality qualifiers**. A materiality qualifier reduces a maker's risks by limiting a representation's focus to the most important facts. Something is material if it would affect a person's decision.[4] Compare the following:

> **Version 1**
>
> **Defaults**. The Borrower is not in default under any agreement.
>
> **Version 2**
>
> **Defaults**. The Borrower is not in default under any *material* agreement.

Under Version 1, a borrower with $200 million in sales misrepresents the facts if it has failed to pay the rent for even one month on one of its 450 photocopiers. But it will not have misrepresented the facts if the representation is that in Version 2. Exercise 9-1 looks at the various ways in which materiality qualifiers can be drafted.

9.3.1 REPRESENTATIONS WITH RESPECT TO THE PAST, PRESENT, AND FUTURE

Generally, the facts in a representation must relate to a state of affairs that exists in the present or existed in the past.[5] With respect to those facts that presently exist, draft the representation and warranty in the present tense.

> **Organization; Good Standing**. The Seller *is* a corporation duly organized, validly existing and in good standing under the laws of the state of its incorporation as set forth in **Schedule 4.1**, with all requisite corporate power and authority to own, operate, and lease its properties, and to carry on its business as now being conducted.

Be careful not to use *currently* or *presently* in a representation. Their use affects the meaning of a condition that provides that representations must also be true on the closing date. If a representation includes one of these words, the maker probably intends that the representation speak *only* as of the date of signing. But a condition that requires a repetition of the representation as of the date of the closing would frustrate the maker's intent because the condition would require the representation to be true *currently*, that is, as of the date of the closing. With respect to those facts

---

4. *See Barrington Press, Inc. v. Morey*, 752 F.2d 307, 310 (7th Cir. 1985).
5. *Restatement (Second) Contracts* § 159 cmt. c (1981).

that relate to the past, draft the representation in a tense that expresses that time horizon.[6]

> **Tax Returns and Payments.** The Parent and each Subsidiary *have duly filed* all federal, state, and local tax returns and reports required to be filed and each of them *has duly paid or established* adequate reserves for the proper payment of all taxes and other governmental charges upon it or its properties, assets, income, franchises, licenses, or sales.

The question arises: Can representations be drafted with respect to the future? Typically, the cases say *no,* holding that statements about future events are opinions or speculation.[7] Thus, a recipient of a representation with respect to the future usually cannot justifiably rely on it.[8]

There are, of course, exceptions. A recipient of a representation may rely on a future "fact"—an opinion—if the speaker purports to have special knowledge of the "fact," stands in a fiduciary relationship to the recipient, and has secured the recipient's confidence.[9] In addition, a statement has been held to be one of existing fact if

> a quality is asserted which inheres in the article so that, at the time the representation is made, the quality may be said to exist independently of future acts or performance of the one making the representation, independently of other particular occurrences in the future, and independently of particular future uses or requirements of the buyer.[10]

Moreover, a party has a cause of action when another party promises to perform, but knows it will not.[11] This is known as **promissory fraud**. In this context, the promise as to the future fraudulently misrepresents a present fact—the misrepresenting party's state of mind.[12] While this cause of action exists, courts disfavor it because it risks converting ordinary breach of contract claims into tort actions, which bring with them the potential award of punitive damages.[13]

The following representation from an acquisition agreement shows an error with respect to "future facts" that drafters commonly make.

> **Wrong**
>
> **3.8 Consents**. The Seller has obtained all consents required in connection with the execution and delivery of this Agreement. The Seller *will have obtained* before Closing all consents required in connection with the consummation of the transactions that this Agreement contemplates.

---

6. Representations with respect to the past are generally drafted in the past tense (The Borrower's board of directors *authorized* the Borrowings on September 26, 20XX.) or the present perfect tense (The Executive *has completed* her doctoral dissertation in biochemical engineering.) It is not necessary to remember the names of the tenses. Instead, remember that a party may make a representation with respect to the past.

7. *See, e.g., Next Cent. Commun. Corp. v. Ellis*, 171 F. Supp. 2d 1374, 1379-1380 (N.D. Ga. 2001).

8. *Glen Holly Entertainment, Inc. v. Tektronix, Inc.*, 100 F. Supp. 2d 1086, 1093 (C.D. Cal. 1999).

9. *Outlook Windows Partn. v. York Intl. Corp.*, 112 F. Supp. 2d 877, 894 (D. Neb. 2000) (citing *Burke v. Harman*, 574 N.W.2d 156, 179 (Neb. App. 1998)).

10. *Nyquist v. Foster*, 268 P.2d 442, 445 (Wash. 1954).

11. *Levin v. Singer*, 175 A.2d 423, 432 (Md. 1961); *but see Bower v. Jones*, 978 F.2d 1004, 1011-1012 (7th Cir. 1992) (stating that Illinois does not recognize promissory fraud as a cause of action, except if the promise is part of a scheme to accomplish fraud; but noting, however, that the exception has been viewed as swallowing the rule).

12. *Palmacci v. Umpierrez*, 121 F.3d 781 786-787 (1st Cir. 1997).

13. *See Rosenblum v. Travelbyus.com, Ltd.*, 2002 WL 31487823, *3 (N.D. Ill.).

As the second sentence is with respect to the future, a recipient cannot justifiably rely on it. That sentence was included, however, with the best of intentions. The seller intended to comfort the buyer by stating that it would obtain all the consents before closing, even though it had not yet done so. In essence, the seller was *promising* the buyer that it would obtain them. Indeed, representations with respect to the future are generally disguised covenants. Therefore, to carry out the seller's intent, the provision should be redrafted as two provisions—one a representation and the other, a covenant.

> **Correct**
>
> **3.8 Consents**. The Seller has obtained all consents required in connection with the execution and delivery of this Agreement. Except as listed in **Schedule 3.8**, the Seller has obtained all consents required in connection with the consummation of the transactions that this Agreement contemplates. *(The representation.)*
>
> **4.6 Consents**. The Seller shall obtain all the consents listed in **Schedule 3.8** before the Closing. *(The covenant.)*

By breaking out the covenant from the representation, a risk hidden in the representation becomes evident. The seller courts danger with the covenant as drafted because it cannot control whether it will receive all the consents. To protect itself, the seller must change the covenant's degree of obligation so that it promises to exert a stated degree of effort to obtain the consents.[14]

9.3.2 ACTIVE V. PASSIVE VOICE

Treatises and commentators usually advise drafters to prefer the active voice over the passive. When using the active voice, the subject of the sentence acts upon an object. In the passive voice, the subject of the sentence is acted upon by an actor. Sometimes the actor is even dropped from the sentence, creating the possibility of an ambiguity. Sentences in the active voice tend to be shorter, easier to read, and have a stronger impact.

> **Active**
>
> **Taxes**. The Seller paid its taxes when due.
>
> **Passive**
>
> **Version 1**
>
> **Taxes**. The taxes were paid when due by the Seller.
>
> **Version 2**
>
> **Taxes**. The taxes were paid when due.

While you should generally draft representations in the active voice, that is not always the case. Sometimes the voice used makes a substantive difference: A change

---

14. With the change in the covenant, a buyer would probably insist on a condition that all consents be obtained by closing. This would be its ultimate protection with respect to the consents.

in the subject of the sentence can change its meaning. For example, when purchasing a used parachute, a buyer wants to know the total number of times the parachute has been used, not how many times the seller has used it.

> **Active**
>
> **Prior Use**. The Seller has used the parachute three times.
>
> **Passive**
>
> **Prior Use**. The parachute has been used five times.

When the issue is the action rather than the actor, the passive voice is appropriate.

You can use settings in a word-processing application to help you spot the use of the passive voice so that you can use it appropriately.

9.4 WARRANTIES

9.4.1 WARRANTIES WITH RESPECT TO THE FUTURE

When a warranty is coupled with a representation, one party promises to indemnify the other with respect to a state of facts currently existing or that existed in the past. A party may also warrant that a state of facts will exist in the future.[15] It may do so because the issue of the recipient's justifiable reliance disappears with respect to a warranty.

For example:

> **Warranty**. The Manufacturer warrants to the Retailer [and the eventual consumer] that the Product as packaged and shipped from the Manufacturer's plant *will be free* from defects in material and workmanship and *will function and perform* in accordance with Manufacturer's specifications for a period of one year from the date of retail purchase.

Here, the Retailer is not relying on the truthfulness of the underlying statements (the future facts) but instead on the Manufacturer's promise that it will pay damages if the state of facts does not exist in the future.[16] Thus, a statement that cannot be a representation because it deals with the future can be a warranty.

---

15. *See S. Cal. Enterprises, Inc. v. D.N. & E. Walter & Co.*, 178 P.2d 785, 757-758 (Cal. Dist. App. 1947).

16. *See Wright v. Couch*, 54 S.W.2d 207, 209-210 (Tex. Civ. App. 1932).

9.4.2 RISK ALLOCATION

Occasionally, but not often, as a matter of risk allocation, a party might make only a warranty. Typically, this occurs when a party refuses to represent a "fact" because it is false, but the parties agree that the would-be maker should be liable if the fact is not as stated.

For example, suppose the buyer of a manufacturing business asks the seller to represent and warrant that existing claims under the seller's warranties for its products do not exceed $1.5 million. If the seller does not know, it might quite reasonably refuse to make the representation. Nonetheless, the parties might agree that, as a matter of risk allocation, the seller should be financially responsible for any claims on the product warranties that exceed $1.5 million. In this circumstance, some lawyers would permit their clients to make the requested representation and warranty without qualification. As an alternative, the seller could warrant, but not represent, the dollar amount of the claims. This would accomplish the risk allocation, without the seller making a misrepresentation.

This author believes that the better practice is not to make the representation, but to accomplish the desired risk allocation through alternative means.[17] First, as a matter of policy, parties should understand that truthfulness in a contract matters. Second, a seller could be blindsided if its buyer "forgets" that the representation was merely risk allocation and sues for fraudulent misrepresentation, including punitive damages. Third, a buyer might not even have a cause of action for misrepresentation if its seller successfully argues that the buyer could not justifiably rely on the representation. Ironically, in that event, the buyer ends up where it could have started—with a cause of action for breach of warranty.

---

17. The parties could address this matter in two additional ways. First, the seller could make the representation and warranty to its knowledge—assuming it had the knowledge. Then, it could indemnify the buyer with respect to the representation and warranty, but without regard to the knowledge qualifier. That is, for the purposes of the indemnity, the representation and warranty would be flat. Second, the parties could address this issue only in the indemnity, where the seller would agree to indemnify the buyer for claims in excess of $1.5 million. Both these methods accomplish the parties' business goals without the seller misrepresenting the facts.

CHAPTER NINE

EXERCISES

Exercise 9-1

In the same way that parties use a knowledge qualification as a risk allocation mechanism, they also use a **materiality** qualification. Materiality is a vague term, requiring a facts and circumstances test. There is no easy or pat definition. What may be material in one context may not be material in another. Generally, something is material if it would affect a person's decision. In essence, a materiality qualification means that the parties will not nitpick. The focus is on the important issues.[18]

The provisions that follow in the examples are representations and warranties and a definition from a loan agreement. In a loan agreement, a bank requires representations and warranties from a borrower in the same way that a buyer requires representations and warranties from a seller. Both the buyer and the bank are making investments. The buyer is investing in the seller by buying it, and the bank is investing in the borrower by making a loan to it. Both the buyer and the bank need as much information as possible before they make their respective decisions to invest. In addition, the bank will use the representations and warranties as a risk allocation mechanism, to establish standards of liability, which, if breached, will provide the bank with remedies.

Each of the examples has a materiality qualification, but each differs from the others. This Exercise is intended to familiarize you with these differences and how they affect the business deal. Although most of the examples are of different representations and warranties, several examples are different versions of the same representation and warranty. In reality, of course, only one version would actually appear in an agreement.

Part 1

Review Examples 1 through 3. Is Example 1 a flat or qualified representation and warranty? Would the bank or the borrower have asked for the change in language from Example 1 to Example 2? What would have been its argument to support its request for the change? If the first draft of the contract used the representation and warranty in Example 2, which party would have asked to change it to the language in Example 3? If the bank were to agree to the language in Example 3, what risk would it be taking?

Example 1

> **Purchase and Sale Orders.** Listed in **Schedule 3.10** is each purchase and sale order to which the Borrower is a party.

Example 2

> **Purchase and Sale Orders.** Listed in **Schedule 3.10** is each material purchase and sale order to which the Borrower is a party.

---

18. *See Barrington Press, Inc. v. Morey*, 752 F.2d 307, 310 (7th Cir. 1985).

Example 3

Purchase and Sale Orders. Listed in **Schedule 3.10** is each purchase and sale order to which the Borrower is a party and that involves future payments in excess of $100,000.

Part 2

The representations and warranties in Examples 4 and 5 both deal with the possibility of defaults. Example 4 answers the question of whether entering into the agreement creates a conflict or a default under any other agreement to which the Borrower is a party. Example 5 answers the question of whether the Borrower is currently in default under any other agreement to which it is a party. Both Examples include materiality qualifications. Which qualifications are more favorable to the borrower and why?

Example 4

Non-contravention. The Borrower's execution and delivery of this Agreement do not conflict with or create a default under any agreement to which the Borrower is a party, except for any conflict or default that would not materially adversely affect the business or financial condition of the Borrower.

Example 5

From the Definitions

"Material Agreement" means any agreement that involves future payments in excess of $50,000.

The provision

Other Material Agreements. The Borrower is not in default under any Material Agreement, except for any default that does not materially adversely affect the Borrower.

Part 3

Would the borrower prefer the language in Example 6 or Example 7? Why?

Example 6

Regulatory Compliance. The Borrower is in compliance in all material respects with all federal, state, local, and foreign laws and regulations applicable to it.

Example 7

Regulatory Compliance. The Borrower is in compliance with all federal, state, local, and foreign laws and regulations applicable to it, except for those instances of noncompliance that would not materially adversely affect the Borrower's financial condition, business, or results of operations.

Part 4

In Example 8, would the borrower prefer the *material adverse change* qualification in subsection (a) or subsection (b)? Why? What is the effect of the words *severally or in the aggregate* in Example 9?

Example 8

> **No Material Adverse Change.** Since the date of the Financial Statements,
> (a) no material adverse change has occurred in the financial condition, opera-
>   tions, or business of the Borrower and the Subsidiaries taken as a whole; and
> (b) no property or asset of the Borrower or any Subsidiary has suffered material
>   damage, destruction, or loss.

Example 9

> **Leases.** With respect to each lease listed in **Schedule 3.11**,
> (a) no default has occurred and is continuing; and
> (b) no event has occurred and is continuing which, with notice or lapse of time
>   or both, would constitute a default on the Borrower's part, except for those
>   defaults, if any, that
>   (i) are not material in character, amount, or extent; and
>   (ii) do not, severally or in the aggregate, materially detract from the value, or
>   interfere with the present use of, the property subject to the lease.

Part 5

List all of the qualifications in Example 10. What are the most important words or
phrases in the definition of "Material" in Example 11?

Example 10

> **Litigation.** Except as set forth in **Schedule 3.14**, no litigation is pending
> or, to the knowledge of any of the Borrower's officers, threatened that might,
> severally or in the aggregate, materially adversely affect the financial condition
> of the business, assets, or prospects of the Borrower and the Subsidiaries taken
> as a whole.

Example 11

> **"Material"** means an event, condition, matter, change, or effect (either
> alone or in combination with any one or more other events, conditions, mat-
> ters, changes, or effects) that impacts or that is reasonably likely to impact the
> Borrower's condition (financial or otherwise), in an amount in excess of $10,000.

Exercise 9.2

Determine the drafting errors and mark-up the provisions to correct the errors.

> **Compliance with Applicable Law.** The Seller has complied with, is currently in compliance
>
> with, and will be in compliance with on the Closing Date, all laws, rules, and regulations, except for
>
> any noncompliance that would not have a material adverse effect on the Seller.

_____

_____

Unacceptable Content. The Book will contain no matter that invades any person's privacy or that is scandalous, libelous, obscene, or otherwise unlawful.

Exercise 9-3

If you were selling the Horse, which of the following two representations and warranties would you prefer and why?

Version 1

Additional Races. Sam Jockey has not raced the Horse since the Kentucky Derby.

Version 2

Additional Races. The Horse has not raced since the Kentucky Derby.

Covenants and Rights

10.1 DRAFTING THE SUBSTANCE OF COVENANTS

As with representations and warranties, covenants allocate risk and establish standards of liability. Recall from Chapter 3 how a drafter can change a covenant's import by using different degrees of obligation.[1] Should the equipment be maintained *in good condition, ordinary wear and tear excepted,* or should it be maintained *in accordance with industry standards*? As the obligation changes, so too does the standard of liability. The covenant becomes harder or easier for the promissor to perform, and, therefore more or less likely that the promissor could be found in breach of the standard. Good drafting requires that you carefully examine each covenant in the context of the client's business deal to determine the appropriate standard of liability. As a general rule, if your client is making the covenant, the degree of obligation should be as weak as possible, while the reverse would be true if your client has the right to the performance.

To help you determine the substance of a covenant, use the *who, what, when, where, why, how, and how much* tests. Each time you answer one of the questions, ask yourself whether a variation might be more helpful to your client.

- **Who**: Who is obligated to whom?
- **What**: What is the obligation?
- **When**: By when must the obligation be performed?
- **Where**: Where will the performance take place?
- **Why**: Why must a party perform?
- **How**: How is the obligation performed?
- **How much**: If performance involves money or goods, how much?

Example 1

Samples. No later than 60 days before an Item is to be shipped to the Retail Stores *[when—Should it be shorter or longer?]*, the Manufacturer *[who]* shall submit a sample of that Item *[what]* to the Licensor *[to whom]*

---

1. See §3.3.2.

for its approval. The Licensor *[who]* shall approve or reject the sample and notify *[what]* the Manufacturer *[who]* of its decision by telephone *[how]* no later than three business days after the date of its receipt of the Item *[when]* for approval.

Example 2

Delivery of Disputed Amount. No later than five days after its receipt of the Release Notice *[when—Should it be later or sooner?]*, the Escrow Agent *[who]* shall deliver *[to whom?]* a certified check *[how—Would a wire transfer be better?]* in an amount equal to the Disputed Amount *[how much?]*, payable to the order of the party set forth in the Release Notice.

Example 3

Condition of Premises at End of Term. The Tenant *[who]* shall leave the Premises broom clean *[what—Is this the proper standard if representing the Landlord?]* when it vacates the Premises at the end of the Term *[when and why—What if the Tenant leaves earlier?]*.

When analyzing the substance of a covenant, be wary if it asks your client to promise something that it cannot control. This is a high-risk covenant because an outside event or third party controls whether your client breaches it. For example, imagine that Giants Stadium Productions asks your client, Preston Presentations Inc., to sign a contract that includes the following provision:

McCartney Concert. Preston Presentations Inc. shall present a concert on July 4, 20XX at Giants Stadium at which Paul McCartney is the lead act.

This covenant presents no problem if your client has already arranged that Sir Paul will perform. If it has not . . .

10.2 DRAFTING GUIDELINES

Adhere to the following guidelines when drafting covenants.
1. *To obligate a party to perform, use* **shall.**

Regular Exercise. The Athlete *shall* exercise regularly in order to maintain himself in top physical condition.

Some drafters no longer use *shall* to signal a covenant. Instead, they use *will*. They worry that *shall* has become ambiguous because of the plethora of cases that construe *shall* to refer to the future or to signal discretionary authority. But the suggested solution replaces one set of problems with another.

Assume that drafters banish *shall* from their contracts. In that event, a drafter would need to use either *will* or *must* to signal a covenant. But as *will* is already reserved for the future,[2] it would then need to do double duty, creating again the

---

2. See Chapter 13.

possibility of ambiguity. The issue of whether *shall* signals the future or discretionary authority will not go away if *will* is used instead of *shall*. It will merely be transformed. Instead, courts will need to construe *will*. Imagine the irony of a court using as precedent the cases analyzing whether *shall* was intended to signal a covenant, the future, or discretionary authority. To cure the problematic use of *shall*, drafters must reform and reserve the use of *shall* for duties.

Here is one example of the proper use of *will*. It appears in a covenant, but does not signal the obligation. Instead, it is part of the promise of what the General Partner will do in the future.

> **Obligation to Find Investors**. The General Partner *shall* use its best efforts to find at least 10 limited partners each of whom *will* invest $1 million in the Partnership.

2. *As a general rule, do not state what a party has a right to; state what the other party's obligation is.* Recall from Chapter 3 that a right is the flip side of a covenant. Therefore, you could draft these provisions as either a covenant or a right. You should, however, draft them as covenants for two reasons:

- **First**, a covenant is easier to litigate because it explicitly states that a party has an obligation to perform. The statement of a right does not always do so. When a provision is cast as a right, a litigator must first establish who has the obligation to perform. While hardly an insurmountable task, it adds an unnecessary issue to the litigation.
- **Second**, a covenant facilitates the drafting of the full contours of a party's obligations.

> **Wrong**
>
> **Air-conditioning**. The Tenant *is entitled* to air conditioning for the Premises in the summer.
>
> **Correct**
>
> **Air-conditioning**. The Landlord *shall air condition* the Premises during the summer.

If a party insists on a statement of its rights, state the right but pair it with a covenant—except as discussed next:

> **Author's Access to Publisher's Records**. The Author *is entitled* to review the Publisher's records as to the Book's sales, and the Publisher *shall provide* the Author access to those records during its regular business hours upon the Author's request.

Generally, you may state just a party's rights if you are stating its remedies.

> **Equitable Relief**. If the Employee breaches its duty of confidentiality, the Company *is entitled* to equitable relief.

The flip side of the right is the Employee's promise not to contest that equitable relief is appropriate.[3]

3. *Do not use any form of* **agree.** It is superfluous because the words of agreement state that *the parties agree.*

Wrong

   Capital Contribution. Each Limited Partner *agrees* to contribute $100,000 to the limited partnership before January 1, 20XX.

Correct

   Capital Contribution. Each Limited Partner *shall* contribute $100,000 to the limited partnership before January 1, 20XX.

---

4. *Do not say that a party* **is responsible** *for doing something.*

Wrong

   Costumes. The Performer *is responsible* for designing and making her own costume.

Correct

   Costumes. The Performer *shall* design and make her own costume.

---

5. *To obligate a party not to do something, use* **shall not,** *except as stated in Guideline 6.*

   Participation in Other Sports. The Athlete *shall not* participate in any sport other than baseball.

---

6. *If the sentence uses a negative subject, use* **may,** *instead of* **shall not.** Negative subjects include *neither party* and *no party.*

   Antiassignment. Neither party may assign any of its rights under this Agreement.

If *shall* were used instead of *may,* the substantive meaning of the sentence would change: *Neither party shall assign any of its rights under this Agreement* means that neither party is obligated to assign its rights. It does not prohibit assignments.

7. *To negate a duty to perform, use either* **is not required to** *or* **is not obligated to.**

   Landlord's Consent. The Seller shall use commercially reasonable efforts to obtain the Landlord's consent, but in using those efforts, the Seller *is not obligated to* spend more than $10,000.

---

3. *See* Thomas R. Haggard, *Legal Drafting: Process, Technique, and Exercises* 409 (West 2003).

8. *Draft covenants using the active voice.*

> **Wrong**
>
> **End of Term Repairs.** The premises *shall be painted* by the Tenant in the last month of the lease term.
>
> **Correct**
>
> **End of Term Repairs.** The Tenant *shall paint* the premises in the last month of the lease term.

9. *Beware of covenants posing as declarations.* Sometimes drafters write a provision so that it appears to be a declaration. Test whether a declaration is appropriate by asking whether remedies should flow from the provision. If so, recast the provision as a covenant.

> **Version 1—Wrong**
>
> **Security Deposit.** The security deposit will be $3,000 due immediately in full upon signing of the Agreement.

A quick read of Version 1 gives the impression that the provision is a declaration, that it defines the amount of the security deposit. However, a closer read reveals that the provision should be drafted to include both a declaration and a covenant, as in Version 2, or as a covenant that includes the information in the declaration, as in Version 3.

> **Version 2—Correct**
>
> **Security Deposit.** The security deposit is $3,000, and the Tenant shall pay the security deposit to the Landlord by certified check upon the parties' execution and delivery of this Agreement.
>
> **Version 3—Correct**
>
> **Security Deposit.** The Tenant shall pay the Landlord a $3,000 security deposit by certified check upon the parties' execution and delivery of this Agreement.

10. *Do not draft a provision so that it appears to bind a nonparty.* For example, contracts often include arbitration provisions in which the parties state the arbitrators' obligations. A typical provision might be as follows:

> **Version 1—Wrong**
>
> **Choice of Law.** The arbitrators shall interpret all controversies relating to this Agreement, including torts, in accordance with the laws of Missouri.

The use of *shall* is inappropriate because the arbitrators are not parties to the agreement and cannot be obligated to do anything. Here is an appropriate redraft:

> **Version 2—Correct**
>
> **Choice of Law.** The arbitrators are to interpret all controversies relating to this Agreement, including torts, in accordance with the laws of Missouri.

This wording creates a declaration, a policy statement. As an alternative, the agreement can obligate the parties to instruct the arbitrators how to act:

> **Version 3—Correct**
>
> **Choice of Law.** The parties shall instruct the arbitrators to interpret all controversies relating to this Agreement, including torts, in accordance with the laws of Missouri.

A similar problem occurs when a parent corporation sells the shares of a subsidiary. A buyer often wants the subsidiary to take various actions during the gap period. But the subsidiary is not a party to the agreement. To deal with this issue, have the parent cause the subsidiary to perform in a certain way:[4]

> **Equipment.** The Seller shall cause the Target to maintain its equipment in accordance with industry standards.

The covenant is the seller's. Its obligation is to cause the target to take the actions that the buyer desires.

---

4. As an alternative, some buyers require the target to become a party to the stock purchase agreement and to agree to perform certain obligations during the gap period.

CHAPTER TEN

EXERCISES

Exercise 10-1

Which of the following covenants would a seller prefer and why? Which would a buyer prefer and why?

Version 1

Maintenance. Seller shall maintain its plants, structures, and equipment in good operating condition and repair.

Version 2

Maintenance. Seller shall maintain its plants, structures, and equipment in good operating condition and repair, subject only to ordinary wear and tear.

Version 3

Maintenance. Seller shall maintain its plants, structures, and equipment in customary operating condition and repair.

Version 4

Maintenance. Seller shall maintain its plants, structures, and equipment in accordance with industry standards.

Version 5

Maintenance. Seller shall steam clean, oil, and otherwise maintain each piece of equipment as prescribed in Exhibit B.

Version 6

Maintenance. Seller shall not permit its plant, structures, and equipment to be in a state of operating condition and repair that would materially and adversely affect the operations of Seller.

Exercise 10-2

Mark up the following sentences to correct the drafting errors:

Capitalization. All of the capital stock of the Company is owned beneficially and of record by

Barbara Ballard.

Fees and Expenses. The fees of the Escrow Agent and all expenses reasonably incurred by the Escrow Agent in performing its obligations hereunder shall be borne one-half by Rapid Transportation and one-half by Eagle.

Discharge. No employee may be discharged without two weeks notice.

Conditions to an Obligation

11.1 INTRODUCTION

For the purposes of this chapter, a condition is a state of facts that must exist before a party is obligated to perform. Chapter 12 discusses conditions to discretionary authority and to declarations.

11.2 DRAFTING THE SUBSTANCE OF A CONDITION

Once the parties have decided that a condition is appropriate, they must decide on the state of facts—the standard—that must exist before a party is obligated to perform. Each party's risk then depends upon how difficult or easy it is to meet the standard.

For example, assume that a landlord and a tenant (a store owner) have agreed that the landlord will maintain the premises in the ordinary course of business, but that it will make immediate repairs under certain circumstances. The parties and the drafter must then determine those circumstances—the standard. Here is the provision before the parties have negotiated the standard.

> **Maintenance of the Premises**. The Landlord shall maintain the Premises in the ordinary course of business. Despite the preceding sentence, if [the state of facts], the Landlord shall make immediate repairs.

The tenant, wary of liability, might propose that the landlord's obligation be activated whenever an *unsafe condition* exists. The landlord might object to this standard, noting its vagueness and failure to consider a danger's extent or immediacy. Consistent with these concerns, the landlord might propose instead that its obligation be activated only when a *significant, imminent danger* exists. This alternative standard would reduce the landlord's risk that it would be obligated to perform. Here are the two versions of the provision:

Version 1

    Maintenance of the Premises. The Landlord shall maintain the Premises in the ordinary course of business. Despite the preceding sentence, if an unsafe condition exists, the Landlord shall make immediate repairs.

Version 2

    Maintenance of the Premises. The Landlord shall maintain the Premises in the ordinary course of business. Despite the preceding sentence, if a significant, imminent danger exists, the Landlord shall make immediate repairs.

Although many conditions depend upon facts occurring, a condition can also be based upon the failure of facts to occur. For example, a condition to a bank's obligation to lend could be the absence of product liability litigation.

When deciding the substance of a condition, keep in mind the following:

- A party's own actions cannot be a condition to its obligations. If they could, the party could decide never to act, making it impossible to trigger its obligation to perform.
- The passage of time cannot be a condition because it is certain to occur.

11.3   HOW TO SIGNAL A CONDITION

The manner in which a drafter signals a condition depends upon whether it is within or outside a conditions article. The following sections describe how to draft each type of condition.

11.3.1   LANGUAGE THAT SIGNALS A CONDITION OUTSIDE A CONDITIONS ARTICLE

When a drafter wants to craft a condition outside a conditions article, she usually uses one of the following words or phrases: *if/then, must, when, subject to, provided that, if, conditioned upon, and upon.*[1] Unfortunately, using these words does not guarantee that a court will construe the provision as a condition.[2] Courts dislike conditions because they often result in a party forfeiting a right.[3] So, when given a choice between construing a provision as a condition or a covenant, courts regularly interpret the provision to be a covenant. Then, the nonbreaching party must still perform, but the breaching party must pay it damages.

To ensure—as much as possible—that a court will construe a provision as a condition, do one or more of the following:

- State that a provision is a condition.
- Use *must.*

---

1. *Ross v. Harding*, 391 P.2d 526, 531 (Wash. 1964).

2. *Cedar Point Apartments, Ltd. v. Cedar Point Investment Corp.*, 693 F.2d 748 n. 9 (8th Cir. 1982), *cert. denied*, 461 U.S. 914 (1983).

3. See §4.2.4 for an example of how a condition can result in a forfeiture.

- Include an interpretive provision that *must* signals a condition.
- Construct the sentence using an *if/then* formulation.
- State the consequences of the failure to satisfy a condition.

Example 1

Conversion of Preferred Stock. To convert its preferred stock to common stock, a preferred stockholder must submit the Required Documents to the Corporation no later than May 15, 20XX.

and

As part of the general provisions or the interpretive section of a definition article

The use of *must* in this Agreement signals a condition.

Example 2

Excerpt from an insurance agreement

Claims. If the Owner suffers a loss because of theft or unintentional damage, then the Owner must give the Insurer written notice of the claim no later than 10 days after the loss. The Owner's failure to deliver a timely notice relieves the Insurer of its obligation to pay the Owner for any loss.

Example 3

Excerpt from an insurance agreement

Claims. It is a condition to the Insurer's obligations under this Agreement that the Owner give the Insurer written notice of any Loss no later than 10 days after the Loss.

Example 4

Termination. If the Contractor completes construction before the Deadline, then the Owner shall pay the Contractor a $5,000 bonus no later than five Business Days after the construction is complete.

Example 2 uses an *if/then* formulation and establishes the condition and its consequences in its two sentences. It does not, however, obligate the Insurer to pay if the condition is satisfied. That appears elsewhere in the contract. Example 4 also uses an *if/then* formulation, but in this instance, the Owner's obligation to pay appears in the *then* clause. It signals that obligation by using *shall.*

Note that the *if* clauses in Examples 2 and 4 are properly drafted in the present tense. The *if* clause in the following provision incorrectly uses *shall* because it is not signaling a covenant.

Wrong

Notice. If the Owner *shall have suffered* a loss because of theft or unintentional damage, the Owner must give the Insurer written notice of the claim no later than 10 days after the loss.

When drafting a provision that uses an *if/then* formulation, the sentence typically begins with the *if* clause that establishes the condition to reflect the temporal sequence of events.[4] But if the *if* clause contains multiple conditions, the sentence may become difficult to read because too much information precedes the *then* clause. In this instance, the order of the clauses should be reversed.[5]

11.3.2 LANGUAGE THAT SIGNALS A CONDITION IN A CONDITIONS ARTICLE

The agreements that most commonly have conditions articles are acquisition and financing agreements. The proper way to signal a condition in a conditions article is to join the word *must* with another verb in one of three ways:

- *must + be,* to indicate a fact that must exist on the closing date.
- *must + have + the past tense of a verb,* to indicate something that someone must have caused to happen after the signing date but no later than the closing date.
- *must have been + the past tense of a verb,* to indicate something that must have occurred after the signing date but no later than the closing date; this is the passive version of the preceding use of *must* and should be used when the issue is the action, not the actor.

The following is a series of conditions from an acquisition agreement. The sentence following the heading for Section 13 establishes two legal matters: first, that each section that follows contains a condition to the buyer's obligation to perform; and second, that the buyer may waive the failure to satisfy any condition. The contractual statement that the buyer may waive is not technically necessary as the buyer may waive as a matter of common law.

---

13. Conditions to the Buyer's Obligations.

The Buyer is obligated to consummate the transactions that this Agreement contemplates only if each of the following conditions has been satisfied or waived on or before the Closing Date.

13.1. Seller's Representations and Warranties. The representations and warranties of the Seller set forth in this Agreement *must be* true on and as of the Closing Date with the same force and effect as though made on and as of the Closing Date, except as affected by transactions that this Agreement contemplates.

13.2. Seller's Covenants. The Seller *must have performed* all of its covenants contained in this Agreement to be performed by it on or before the Closing Date.

13.3. Seller's Closing Certificate. The Buyer *must have received* a certificate of the Seller, executed on behalf of the Seller by the President or any Vice President of the Seller, dated the Closing Date, in form and substance satisfactory to the Buyer's counsel, certifying the satisfaction of the conditions in Section 13.1 and Section 13.2.

13.4. Seller's Trademark and Patent Counsel's Opinion. The Seller's trademark and patent counsel *must have delivered* to the Buyer an opinion, dated the Closing Date, in form and substance reasonably satisfactory to the Buyer's counsel.

13.5. The Manufacturing Facility. The Manufacturing Facility *must have been* demolished and all debris cleared away.

---

4. Section 21.5 discusses how an *if/then* formulation can create an ambiguity.
5. See §20.3.2 for an example.

Although *must* is the correct word choice, most drafters use *shall*. Analytically *shall* is incorrect because conditions do not establish obligations. They establish facts that must exist before performance is required.

The following provisions are substantively the same as the preceding provisions, except they demonstrate the drafting that you are most likely to see in practice.

---

13. Conditions to the Buyer's Obligations.

The Buyer is obligated to consummate the transactions that this Agreement contemplates only if each of the following conditions has been satisfied or waived on or before the Closing Date.

13.1. Seller's Representations and Warranties. The representations and warranties of the Seller set forth in this Agreement *shall* be true on and as of the Closing Date with the same force and effect as though made on and as of the Closing Date, except as affected by transactions contemplated by this Agreement.

13.2. Seller's Covenants. The Seller *shall have performed* all of its covenants contained in this Agreement to be performed by it on or before the Closing Date.

13.3. Seller's Closing Certificate. The Buyer *shall have received* a certificate of the Seller, executed on behalf of the Seller by the President or any Vice President of the Seller, dated the Closing Date, in form and substance satisfactory to the Buyer's counsel, certifying the satisfaction of the conditions in Section 13.1 and Section 13.2.

13.4. Seller's Trademark and Patent Counsel's Opinion. The Seller's trademark and patent counsel *shall have* delivered to the Buyer an opinion, dated the Closing Date, in form and substance reasonably satisfactory to the Buyer's counsel.

13.5. The Manufacturing Facility. The Manufacturing Facility *shall have* been demolished and all debris cleared away.

In the preceding examples, the introductory language specifies the Closing Date as the date by which all of the conditions must have been satisfied. This specificity eliminates the need to include a deadline in each condition. It does presuppose, however, that all of the conditions must be satisfied by the same date. If one or more of the conditions has its own deadline, then the introductory language must be general and the individual conditions specific:

13. Conditions to the Buyer's Obligations.

All of the following conditions must have been satisfied or waived before the Buyer is obligated to close the transactions that this Agreement contemplates. . . .

13.5. The Manufacturing Facility. The Manufacturing Facility must have been demolished and all debris cleared away *on or before the Closing Date.*

13.6 Shareholder Approval. The Seller's shareholders must have authorized the sale that this Agreement contemplates *no later than December 23, 20XX.*

11.4 CONTRACTUAL CONSEQUENCE OF A FAILED CONDITION

When drafting conditions in a conditions article, do not state in that article any contractual consequences of failing to satisfy a specific condition. The language introducing the conditions already provides that a party is not obligated to perform if all of the conditions are not satisfied. Put all other consequences relating to the failure to satisfy a condition in the endgame provisions.

11.5 RELATIONSHIP BETWEEN COVENANTS AND CONDITIONS

In some contracts, performing a specific covenant is a condition to performing some other covenant. For example, in an acquisition agreement, a common condition to the buyer's obligation to close is that the seller must have performed all of its covenants to be performed before the closing.[6]

Not every condition in an acquisition agreement is based upon a preclosing covenant. Sellers often try to limit their risk by insisting that certain matters be handled with just a condition, not a condition and a covenant. For example, delivery of an opinion letter from the seller's lawyers is generally a condition to a buyer's obligations to close. A seller is generally willing to risk the buyer's refusal to close if the seller's lawyers refuse to deliver their opinion. If that happens, the seller's risk may be limited to its transaction costs. But if the seller also *promises* that its lawyers will deliver their opinion letter, the seller's risk substantially increases. Then, the lawyers' failure to deliver their opinion puts the seller in breach, making it liable for damages to the buyer.

---

6. Section 4.2.3 also discusses this relationship. Acquisition agreements generally also provide that as a condition to the buyer's obligation to perform, all of the representations and warranties must be true on the closing date. This condition usually provides an exception for any change in facts that the parties anticipate. See the Asset Purchase Agreement in Appendix A, §§7.1, 7.2, 8.1, and 8.2.

EXERCISES

Exercise 11-1

Tom Payne and Georgia Washington are negotiating their prenuptial agreement. Tom has agreed to pay Georgia $100,000 if they divorce before they have been married five years. They have agreed, however, that Tom is not obligated to pay Georgia if the couple divorces because Georgia wants to marry someone else.

Draft the provision.

Exercise 11-2

Ralph LP owns all rights in the cartoon character Ralph—a short, frumpy, bespectacled, eight-year-old for whom life never goes quite right. Ralph LP has agreed to indemnify its licensee, Merchandisers, Inc., if a third party claims that Merchandisers, Inc., is violating that party's trademark in Ralph. Ralph LP insists that it will be liable, however, only if it receives notice from Merchandisers, Inc. no later than 10 business days after it receives notice of the claim.

Draft this provision.

Exercise 11-3

Big Bank NA is willing to lend New Venture, Inc. $250 million only if the Equity Investors have contributed at least $20 million on or before Closing.

Draft the condition assuming that it will appear in the conditions article of the loan agreement.

Discretionary Authority and Declarations

12.1 DISCRETIONARY AUTHORITY

12.1.1 DRAFTING THE SUBSTANCE OF A DISCRETIONARY AUTHORITY PROVISION

A provision grants discretionary authority if it gives a party a choice or the permission or authorization to do something. Occasionally, the exercise of discretionary authority is subject to the satisfaction of a condition.

When drafting a provision that grants discretionary authority, consider how broad or narrow the grant should be. If your client will be exercising the discretionary authority, then draft the grant as broadly as possible; that is, to give the client as much discretionary authority as possible. Also, draft broadly any condition to the exercise of discretionary authority, so that it can be easily satisfied. If the other party will be exercising the discretionary authority, narrow the grant as much as possible. In addition, draft any condition to the exercise of the discretionary authority so that it applies only in the most limited circumstances.

When drafting a grant of discretionary authority, you must determine whether to provide for

- an unfettered grant of discretionary authority (Version 1); or
- a grant that constrains discretion by requiring that a party be reasonable in the exercise of its discretion (Version 2).

> **Version 1**
>
> **Antiassignment**. The Tenant shall not assign its rights under this Lease, without the prior written consent of the Landlord, and the Landlord may give or withhold that consent in its sole discretion. *(Unfettered grant of discretion.)*
>
> **Version 2**
>
> **Antiassignment**. The Tenant shall not assign its rights under this Lease, without the prior written consent of the Landlord, and the Landlord shall not unreasonably withhold that consent. *(Exercise of discretion subject to reasonableness standard.)*

In some jurisdictions, courts hold that public policy considerations override an unlimited grant of discretionary authority. These courts have concluded that such grants must be exercised in good faith in order to effect the parties' intent.[1]

12.1.2   USE OF *MAY* TO SIGNAL DISCRETIONARY AUTHORITY

Use *may* to signal the grant of discretionary authority.

> **Example 1**
>
> **Events of Default**. If an Event of Default occurs and is continuing, the Bank *may* waive the Event of Default or exercise its remedies. *(Choice.)*

> **Example 2**
>
> **Capital Expenditures**. The Borrower shall not make any capital expenditures, except that it *may* make capital expenditures in connection with the Bridge Project. *(Permission/authorization.)*

Occasionally, using *may* alone does not properly express the parties' intent. Assume that a retailer and a manufacturer agree that the latter will manufacture a product in one of two colors, with the manufacturer to decide which color. Look at the proposed provision:

> **Wrong**
>
> **Color of the Product**. The Manufacturer may manufacture the Product in green or blue.

This provision does not say what it means: that the Manufacturer is obligated to make the Product in one of the two colors, but it may choose between the two. As drafted, the provision does not prohibit the Manufacture from making the Product in colors other than green or blue. In similar situations, courts have refused to interpret a provision as if the word *only* had been included in the sentence.[2] Inserting *only* does not fix the problem:

> **Wrong**
>
> **Color of the Product**. The Manufacturer may manufacture the Product *only* in green or blue.

Now the provision limits the colors, but it still does not obligate the manufacture to make the Product in green or blue. Using *shall* does not work either. Now, the pro-

---

1. *See e.g., White Stone Partners, LP v. Piper Jaffray Cos., Inc.*, 978 F. Supp. 878, 882 (D. Minn. 1997).

2. *See Pravin Banker Assoc., Ltd. v. Banco Popular Del Peru*, 109 F.3d 850, 856 (2d Cir. 1997).

vision does not state who has the discretionary authority to determine the Product's color:

> **Wrong**
>
> **Color of the Product.** The Manufacturer shall manufacture the Product in green or blue.

Curing this drafting problem is actually simple . . . the provision should say what it means:

> **Correct**
>
> **Color of the Product.** The Manufacturer shall manufacture the Product in green or blue and may choose which color.

Although most provisions use *may* to signal a grant of discretionary authority, sometimes a provision only implies that grant. Look at the following antiassignment provision:

> **Antiassignment.** The Tenant shall not assign its rights under this Lease, without the prior written consent of the Landlord.

Here the Landlord's right to consent implies a grant of discretionary authority to decide whether it will permit the assignment.

12.1.3 CONDITIONS TO DISCRETIONARY AUTHORITY

A party's exercise of discretionary authority may be subject to the satisfaction of one or more conditions. Drafters often establish the relationship between a condition and the exercise of discretionary authority by using an *if/then* formulation. Draft the *if* clause in the present tense.

> **Example 1**
>
> **Sales to Other Persons.** If the Manufacturer *builds* more than 500 units of the Product in any month, the Manufacturer *may* sell the units in excess of 500 to a Person other than the Retailer. *(Permission.)*
>
> **Example 2**
>
> **Publication of Paperback Edition.** If the Book *earns* gross sales in excess of $30 million, the Publisher *may* publish the paperback edition of the Book at any time afterwards. *(Permission.)*

12.1.4 DISCRETIONARY AUTHORITY POSING AS A DECLARATION

In the same way that covenants can pose as declarations, a grant of discretionary authority can pose as a declaration.

> **Wrong**
>
> **Counterparts**. Execution of this Agreement in counterparts is permissible.
>
> **Correct**
>
> **Counterparts**. The parties may execute this Agreement in counterparts. (*Permission* to execute in counterparts and the *choice* whether to execute in counterparts.)

12.2 DECLARATIONS

Declarations should be drafted in the present tense as these provisions have continuing effect throughout a contract's life. As stated by Reed Dickerson:

> [A provision should speak] as of the time it is being read, not merely as of the time it took effect.[3]

If drafted this way, a declaration always applies to the current situation, no matter when it occurs during the life of the contract and the transaction.

> **Example 1**
>
> **Governing Law**. The laws of Idaho govern all matters arising under this Agreement, including torts.
>
> **Example 2**
>
> **Salary.** The Executive's salary is at the rate of $3,000 per week.[4]
>
> **Example 3**
>
> **Successors and Assigns.** This Agreement binds and benefits the parties to this Agreement and their respective permitted successors and assigns.

Some declarations have substantive consequences only if a condition is satisfied. Here, the full second sentence is the policy, but the policy only applies if the condition is satisfied. In these instances, the condition and the declaration are drafted in the present tense, as in the second sentence of the provision that follows.

> **Antiassignment.** Neither party may assign its rights under this Agreement. If any party purports to assign its rights under this Agreement, that purported assignment is void.

---

3. Reed Dickerson, *The Fundamentals of Legal Drafting* 185 (2d ed., Little Brown & Co. 1986).

4. As discussed in § 8.3, this declaration must be paired with a covenant obligating the Company to pay the Executive.

CHAPTER TWELVE

EXERCISES

Exercise 12-1

Mark up the following provisions to correct the drafting errors:

Alterations. The Tenant shall be permitted to alter the Premises if the Tenant shall have submitted its architectural plans to the Landlord at least 60 days before it wants to begin construction.

Termination. If the Retailer shall fail to pay the Manufacturer when Payment is due, the Manufacturer shall be entitled to terminate this Agreement.

Will and Shall

13.1 INTRODUCTION

This chapter discusses when to use *shall* and when to use *will*. It also gives you a non-grammatical framework for testing whether you are using *shall* properly.

The basic rules are simple. Use *shall* to indicate a covenant and *will* to indicate the future. If you do that, you will create a bright line distinction in meaning between the two words. If you do not follow this rule, you will eventually draft an ambiguous provision. The only exception is a covenant with a negative subject. Then, you should use *may.*[1]

13.2 WHEN TO USE *WILL*

Although you should not use *will* in representations or to signal a covenant, you may use it in limited circumstances:

1. If a provision states a party's opinion, determination, or belief about the future.

> **Amendments.** As a condition to the effectiveness of each amendment, each party must obtain the authorization of
>
> (a) its Board of Directors and
>
> (b) its stockholders
>
> if, in the judgment of that party's Board of Directors, the amendment *will* have a material adverse effect on the benefits intended under this Agreement to that party and its stockholders.

---

1. See §10.2.

2. If a provision is a covenant that includes a statement about the future.

> **Subcontractor for Painting**. The Contractor shall use its best efforts to find a subcontractor who *will* paint the House for less than $5,000.

3. If a provision is a right that includes a statement about the future.

> **Right to Deposit upon Termination**. When the Lease terminates, the Landlord is entitled to retain the Deposit to the extent required to reimburse itself for expenses that it has incurred or *will* incur to repair the Tenant's damage to the Premises.

4. If a provision grants a party discretionary authority with respect to some future event.

> **Choice of Color**. The Owner may choose the color that the Contractor *will* paint the House.

5. If a declaration includes a statement about intent.

> **Construction of House**. Shoshanna and Chaim intend to build a house that *will* be their home after they marry. Each of them shall contribute 50 percent of the cost to build the house. *(From a prenuptial agreement.)*

6. If a provision warrants performance or a future state of facts.

> **Warranty**. The Manufacturer warrants to the Retailer [and the eventual consumer] that the Product as packaged and shipped from the Manufacturer's plant *will be free* from defects in material and workmanship and *will function and perform* in accordance with Manufacturer's specifications for a period of one year from the date of retail purchase.

In this provision, the manufacturer promises that if a state of facts does not exist in the future, then it is responsible as described in the warranty's other provisions. *Shall* would be incorrect in this provision because the Product is not promising anything about its future performance.

13.3 WHEN TO USE *SHALL* AND TESTING WHETHER *SHALL* IS CORRECT

As discussed in Section 10.2, you should use *shall* only to signal an obligation. But drafters incorrectly use *shall* so frequently that they think they are using it correctly, even when they are not. Although you could rely on grammatical tests to confirm whether you are using *shall* correctly, this Section provides easy, nongrammatical rules to help you. To ensure that you correctly apply these rules, use your word-processing application to find each instance of *shall*.

Here are the rules:

Rule 1

If a party does not precede the word shall, *then* shall *is wrong.* Different corrections are appropriate depending upon the parties' intent and the sentence's construction. Specifically, you must determine whether the parties intended the sentence to be

- a covenant (as in Example 1);
- a statement of discretionary authority or permission (as in Example 2);
- a present tense declaration (as in Example 3);
- a provision purporting to bind a nonparty (as in Example 4); or
- a condition (as in Example 5).

Example 1

Wrong

> **Maintenance of the Premises**. The outside of the Premises shall be maintained by the Landlord, and the inside of the Premises shall be maintained by the Tenant.

Correct

> **Maintenance of the Premises**. The Landlord shall maintain the outside of the Premises, and the Tenant shall maintain the inside of the Premises.

With the change, the provision is now in the active voice, rather than the passive voice.

Example 2

Wrong

> **Forum**. An action shall be permitted to be filed to enforce this Agreement in the Supreme Court of the State of New York.

Correct

> **Forum**. A party may file and maintain an action to enforce this Agreement in the Supreme Court of the State of New York.

With the change, the provision is now in the active voice and uses the correct verb (may) to signal permission.

Example 3

Wrong

> **Governing Law**. This Agreement shall be governed by the laws of Nebraska, without regard to its conflict of laws principles.

> **Correct**
>
> **Governing Law**. Without regard to its conflict of laws principles, the laws of Nebraska govern all matters with respect to this Agreement, including torts.

With the change, the provision becomes a declaration stated in the present tense. It also makes a substantive change by adding "including torts."[2]

> **Example 4**
>
> **Wrong**
>
> **Arbitration.** The arbitrators shall render a decision promptly.
>
> **Correct**
>
> Version 1
>
> **Arbitration.** The parties shall instruct the arbitrators to render a decision promptly.
>
> Version 2
>
> **Arbitration.** The arbitrators are to render a decision promptly.

With the change, the first revision properly requires the parties to perform, rather than the arbitrators, who, as nonparties, cannot be bound. The second revision restates the provision as a declaration.

> **Example 5**
>
> **Wrong**
>
> **Notice.** The Event Notice shall be given to the Insurance Company no later than ten days after the Insured Event.
>
> **Correct**
>
> **Notice.** The Insured must give the Event Notice to the Insurance Company no later than ten days after the Insured Event.

With the change, the provision unambiguously states that the giving of the Event Notice is a condition to the Insurance Company's performance.

Rule 2

If a party precedes the word shall, shall *is usually correct, but there are at least three exceptions.*

First, the use of *shall* is wrong if a party precedes *shall* and *shall* is coupled with a form of the verb *to have*.[3] Different corrections are appropriate depending upon the

---

2. See §16.4.

3. Technically, *to have* as used in this way is an **auxiliary verb**, also known as a **helping verb**.

intent and construction of the sentence. For example, if the parties intended to create a condition, replace *shall* with *must.*

> **Wrong**
>
>   **Consent.** The Seller shall have obtained the Landlord's consent.
>
> **Correct**
>
>   **Consent.** The Seller must have obtained the Landlord's consent.

Alternatively, if the parties intended the sentence to be a statement of discretionary authority, replace *shall* with *may.*

> **Wrong**
>
>   **Termination**. The Publisher *shall have the right* to terminate this Agreement if the Author does not complete the Work by the Deadline.
>
> **Correct**
>
>   **Termination**. The Publisher *may* terminate this Agreement if the Author does not complete the Work by the Deadline.

Second, the use of *shall* is wrong if a party precedes *shall* and *shall* is coupled with a form of the verb *to be.*[4] Delete *shall* and change the verb *to be* to its present tense form.

> **Wrong**
>
>   **Suspension of Performance**. If a *Force Majeure* Event occurs and is continuing, the Affected Party shall be excused from the performance to the extent prevented from performing.
>
> **Correct**
>
>   **Suspension of Performance**. If a *Force Majeure* Event occurs and is continuing, the Affected Party is excused from the performance to the extent prevented from performing.

Once redrafted, you can see that the provision is a condition to a declaration and the declaration. (The full sentence is the policy, but that policy applies only if the condition is satisfied.)

Third, the use of *shall* is wrong if a party precedes *shall* in a clause that establishes the circumstances under which an event may occur. Clue words and phrases that begin these clauses include *when, if, in the event of,* and *that.* These clauses are properly drafted in the present tense so that the clause reads as presently applying whenever the circumstances occur.

---

4. *To be* when used in this way is also an auxiliary verb. See n. 3.

> **Wrong**
>
> **Late Payment**. If the Borrower shall fail to pay interest when due, the Bank may declare the Borrower to be in default.
>
> **Correct**
>
> **Late Payment**. If the Borrower fails to pay interest when due, the Bank may declare the Borrower to be in default.
>
> **Wrong**
>
> **Deposit of Funds**. The Bank shall deposit the funds to any account that the Borrower shall designate in a written notice.
>
> **Correct**
>
> **Deposit of Funds**. The Bank shall deposit the funds to any account that the Borrower designates in a written notice.

Finally, do not consider these three exceptions the only exceptions. Drafters can be inventive. Always test each use of *shall* by asking whether a party is promising to do or not to do something. If no party is making a promise, the use of *shall* is incorrect.

The chart that follows summarizes the tests in this Section 13.3.

A Party Does Not Precede *Shall*	A Party Precedes *Shall*
Shall is always wrong.	*Shall* is generally correct, but there are at least three exceptions: 1. If *shall* is coupled with the verb *to be*, *shall* is wrong. 2. If *shall* is coupled with the verb *to have*, *shall* is wrong. 3. If *shall* is in a clause that establishes a circumstance, *shall* is wrong (clue words include *when, if, in the event of,* and *that*).

Drafting the Contract Concepts— A Summary Chart

The following chart summarizes the material in Chapters 9 through 13. Reading it does not replace reading the chapters. Use it as a handy, quick reference tool.

Contract Concept	Drafting Considerations
Representations and warranties	■ If representing the maker, draft the representations and warranties narrowly, and qualify them as much as possible. ■ If representing the recipient, draft the representations and warranties broadly and with as few qualifications as possible. ■ Representations and warranties may deal with past or the present facts, but not with future "facts." ■ Draft in the active voice, unless the focus is on the action rather than the actor. Then, use the passive voice.
Covenants	■ Determine the appropriate degree of obligation, using qualifiers as appropriate. ■ Use the *who, what, when, where, why, how,* and *how much* tests to help determine a provision's substance. ■ Use *shall* to signal a covenant, except if the sentence has a negative subject. Then use *may.*

Conditions to an Obligation	■ If your client must satisfy the condition, draft it so that the client can satisfy it easily. If the other party must satisfy the condition, consider how difficult it should be in the context of the transaction.
	■ Outside a conditions article,
	  ➢ use *must;*
	  ➢ state that a provision is a condition;
	  ➢ state the consequences of the condition;
	  ➢ include an interpretive provision; or
	  ➢ use some combination of these methods.
	■ Inside a conditions article, use *must* with another verb in one of three ways:
	  ➢ *must + be,* to indicate a fact that must exist on the closing date.

continued on next page >

Contract Concept	Drafting Considerations
	➤ *must + have* + the *past tense of a verb,* to indicate something that someone must have cause to happen after the signing date but no later than the closing date. ➤ *must have been* + the *past tense of a verb,* to indicate that the issue is the action, not the actor; this is the passive version of the preceding use of *must.* ■ Real-world note: Most firms continue to use *shall* instead of *must* within condition articles.
Discretionary Authority	■ Consider how broad or narrow the grant of discretionary authority should be. Will your client have the discretionary authority (a broad grant) or will the other party have the discretionary authority (a narrow grant)? ■ Use *may* to signal discretionary authority. ■ If a party may exercise discretionary authority only upon the satisfaction of a condition, consider how difficult it should be to satisfy it. Again, consider whether it is your client or the other party that must satisfy the condition.
Declarations	■ Draft declarations in the present tense. Any condition to a declaration should also be drafted in the present tense. ■ Determine whether the declaration needs to be kicked into action and if so, draft the associated provision.
Proper Use of *Shall*	■ If a party does not precede *shall, shall* is always wrong. ■ If a party precedes *shall, shall* is generally correct with three exceptions: ➤ If *shall* is coupled with the verb *to be, shall* is wrong. ➤ If *shall* is coupled with the verb *to have, shall* is wrong. ➤ If *shall* is in a clause that establishes a circumstance, *shall* is wrong (clue words include *when, if, in the event of,* and *that*).
Proper Use of *Will*	Use *will* in the following circumstances: ■ If a provision states a party's opinion, determination, or belief about the future. ■ If a provision is a covenant that includes a statement about the future. ■ If a provision is a right that includes a statement about the future. ■ If a provision grants a party discretionary authority with respect to some future event. ■ If a declaration includes a statement about intent.

CHAPTER FOURTEEN

EXERCISES

Exercise 14-1

Draft the employment agreement in Exercise 5-2. Use the facts in the exercise. Do not change the facts to reflect any discussions that you have had in class.

Before beginning to draft, review the numbered paragraphs that contain the information to be incorporated into the representations and warranties and underline each statement of fact in those paragraphs. Think through whether HHI would be better served with broad or narrow representations and warranties. If you need definitions, create a definition section. (Leave the definition for "Cause" blank.)

Exercise 14-2

Mark up the following provisions so that they use the proper verb forms. Make any other appropriate changes.

Effects of Termination. If the transactions that this Agreement contemplates shall not have been consummated on or before July 18, 20XX, this Agreement shall terminate on July 18, 20XX, and thereafter, neither party shall have any rights or obligations under it, and Buyer will continue to perform all of its obligations under the Confidentiality Agreement.

Publicity. The parties agree that no publicity release or announcement concerning the transactions contemplated hereby shall be issued by any party without the advance consent of the other, except as such release or announcement may be required by law, in which case the party making the release or announcement shall show the release or announcement in advance to the other party.

Delays. The Contractor agrees that it shall be accountable for promptly notifying the Owner in writing of any event that may delay completion of the Building. The notice shall explain why the delay has occurred and its estimated duration.

Compliance. The Tenant must comply in all material respects with any law the violation of which could have a material adverse effect on the Landlord.

Article and Section Headings. Article and Section headings and the Table of Contents contained in this Agreement shall be for reference purposes only and shall not affect in any way the meaning or interpretation of this Agreement.

Change of Control. A change in control of the Licensee will constitute a default under this License.

Restrictions on Transfer. During the term of this Agreement, none of the Shares now owned or hereafter acquired by any of the Stockholders may be transferred unless such transfer of Shares shall be made in accordance with the provisions of this Agreement. *(This provision is from a Stockholders' Agreement.)*

Endgame Provisions

15.1 INTRODUCTION

A contract may end for a myriad of reasons, some friendly, some unfriendly: the successful conclusion of a joint venture, the end of a lease term, the consummation of a transaction, the sale of a partnership interest, the breach of an agreement, the death of a party. The **endgame provisions** establish the terms on which the parties' contractual relationship ends. They define default, provide remedies, detail continuing obligations, establish the financial terms of exit strategies, and otherwise tie up loose ends. Many lawyers use the phrase *termination provisions* to refer to these provisions. Often, this refers only to default and remedy provisions, and provisions dealing specifically with the contract's end.[1] This book uses the phrase *endgame provisions* to reflect the broader scope of topics covered. It also echoes the argot clients often use.

The remainder of this chapter discusses the business and legal issues associated with drafting the endgame provisions, as well as where to locate and how to organize them. As you should separately analyze the issues associated with friendly and unfriendly terminations, the chapter deals with each of these terminations in turn.

15.2 FRIENDLY TERMINATIONS

Before drafting a friendly termination provision, you and your client must decide what constitutes a friendly termination. Typically, it results from the successful consummation of a transaction or the conclusion of a multiyear relationship: Parties close an acquisition or a lease term ends. Additionally, parties can agree that a specific event triggers the contract's termination. Employment agreements for senior executives sometimes provide that the company's sale terminates the executive's employment. This can be a very friendly termination if the executive's contract includes a **golden parachute**—a great deal of money to ensure a happy landing.

---

1. Some contracts distinguish between **termination** and **expiration.** Specifically, a contract terminates if it ends prematurely because a specified event occurs. In contrast, a contract expires on the last day of its term. See U.C.C. §2-106, U.L.A. §2-106 (2004), which distinguishes *termination* from *cancellation.* Here, termination occurs when a party ends a contract other than for breach, while cancellation occurs when a party ends a contract because of a breach. *Termination* is not used in either of its technical senses in this chapter. Instead, it refers to the end of a contract for any reason.

Friendly terminations can also result from a unilateral action. For example, a supplier may choose not to renew the contract term despite an evergreen provision.[2] Although an acrimonious relationship with the buyer may have precipitated the supplier's decision not to renew, the reason could have been innocuous—the supplier decided to discontinue the product.

Contracts sometimes provide that the parties may agree to terminate. Often such a provision appears as part of a section that lists the ways that the agreement can terminate. Under the common law, the provision is superfluous; parties may agree to terminate without it. Nonetheless, parties include these provisions to memorialize their intent and to put third parties on notice of that intent.

Once you determine what constitutes a friendly termination, you and your client must decide the consequences. They usually fall into one of four categories:

- Termination of the parties' rights and obligations
- Obligations that return the parties to their *status quo* before the contract
- Substantive obligations that continue
- Exit strategies

Examples of obligations that return the parties to their pretransaction *status quo* include the following:

- Upon payment in full of its loan, a bank's obligation to release the collateral it holds and to execute any documents necessary to reflect its release of the collateral
- An obligation to return a security deposit (for example, in connection with the termination of a lease)

Substantive obligations that continue are manifold:

- Noncompetition obligations (for example, in connection with an acquisition)
- Confidentiality obligations (for example, in connection with a termination of employment)
- Monetary obligations (for example, final, post-term payments by a licensee to its licensor)
- Further assurances obligations (for example, in connection with an acquisition)

Common exit strategies include the following:

- Going public (a favorite of venture capitalists)
- Take-out financing (for example, long-term lenders take over the debt of a lender that provided construction financing)
- Buyouts (for example, shareholders purchasing another shareholder's equity interest)
- A drop-dead date (for example, parties agreeing that their rights and duties end if they cannot consummate the sale of a house before an agreed-upon date)

15.3 UNFRIENDLY TERMINATIONS

Clients do not always want to discuss or negotiate the endgame provisions that deal with unfriendly terminations. When negotiating the contract, they are anticipating

---

2. See §8.4.

a successful working relationship. Either consciously or unconsciously, they prefer to avoid or postpone thinking about what could go wrong. As a counselor, you must ensure that your client understands the consequences of the business transaction succeeding or failing.

The content of unfriendly termination provisions can be divided into three topics: defaults, remedies, and dispute resolution provisions. This section addresses each of these topics in order.

15.3.1 EVENTS PRECIPITATING UNFRIENDLY TERMINATIONS

When drafting the endgame provisions dealing with unfriendly terminations, first think through what could go wrong. Unfriendly terminations can result from a panoply of causes:

- Misrepresentation
- Breach of warranty
- Breach of covenant
- Failure to satisfy a condition
- Cross-default
- *Force majeure* event
- Violation of law
- Failure to obtain governmental approval
- Death
- Bankruptcy
- Merger or change of control
- Business dispute
- Occurrence of specified event
- Failure to maintain corporate existence

This list is general. To make it work for your contract, go through the contract section by section and ask, *what if? What if* this representation and warranty is not true? *What if* this covenant is breached? *What if* a party fails to perform because a *force majeure* event occurs? *What if* this condition is not satisfied? *What if* a particular event occurs?

As part of this *what if* exercise, think through what your client's assumptions and expectations are and what could frustrate them.[3] For example, if a pharmaceutical company hires a sales representative, it expects that he will generate a certain sales volume. If he does not, the client's expectations are frustrated, and it will want the right to terminate the contract, so it can cut its losses. This analysis requires more than looking at a specific provision and determining how it works. You must imagine a successful relationship and think about what would undermine it.

Deal lawyers often speak of misrepresentations and breaches of covenants and warranties as **breaches**—something that a party has done wrong. Breaches are a subcategory of **defaults**—any act or event that permits a party to exercise its remedies. A default need not be contract related. For example, death, bankruptcy, merger, change of control, and **cross-defaults** are often included as events giving rise to remedies. (A cross-default is a default that arises under an agreement because a party is in default under another agreement.) Therefore, when thinking through what events might entitle your client to remedies, think beyond the four corners of the contract.

---

3. My colleague Alan Shaw suggested this analysis.

Next consider whether the contract should provide the defaulting party with notice and an opportunity to **cure** the default—that is, the right to fix the problem and preclude the exercise of remedies. Credit agreements often permit the borrower a **grace period** during which the borrower can fix the problem causing the default. For example, a credit agreement may provide the borrower with a three-day grace period to cure any breach arising from a failure to pay interest. If the borrower makes the payment within the three-day grace period, the bank will not exercise its remedies. Similarly, if a borrower fails to deliver its quarterly financials, the loan agreement may require the bank to give the borrower notice of the failure and a grace period. The length of the grace period may vary, depending upon the type of default.

If the endgame provisions provide for notice of a default, a grace period, or both, the contract may distinguish a **default** from an **event of default**. An offending event is a default before the notice and grace period. After the nonbreaching party gives notice and the grace period expires without any cure, the default ripens into an event of default, entitling the nondefaulting party the right to exercise its remedies. As another way of achieving the same result, some agreements limit the exercise of remedies by requiring that the default have *occurred* and be *continuing*.

Not all defaults are susceptible of a cure. Death, for example, is final. Similarly, if a borrower did not meet a financial covenant, it cannot turn back the clock and manage the business differently. In these instances, a default cannot ripen into an event of default. The default, when it occurs, is an event of default.

Depending upon the contract, the events that permit a termination may not be termed *defaults*. Instead, the contract may list the events that permit termination without categorizing them.

As part of your analysis of what events should result in termination, analyze whether those events should be the same for both parties. They need not be. A credit agreement is an extreme example of where the termination events differ. Those agreements will have an entire article devoted to the borrower's defaults, but be silent with respect to the lender's defaults.

15.3.2 REMEDIES

Once you create the list of defaults, you must decide the appropriate remedy for each item on the list. Will common law remedies suffice or should the contract provide remedies? Contractual remedies include damages, contract termination, and indemnification. In financing agreements, a default typically gives the lender the right to accelerate the payment date of any outstanding principal amount, to receive **default interest** (a higher rate of interest than the borrower was paying the lender before the default), and to foreclose on any security. An agreement may also provide for injunctive relief in appropriate circumstances. Confidentiality agreements often do so as a way of limiting unauthorized disclosures. In addition, as with friendly terminations, a party may be obligated to return money that it previously received.

When deciding the appropriate remedy, analyze whether the contract should provide different remedies for different unfriendly termination events. For example, if a condition is not satisfied, the remedy could vary, depending on the reason the condition is not satisfied. If the condition fails because a party breached a covenant, that party could be obligated to pay liquidated damages, and, in addition, the contract could terminate. In contrast, if the condition fails because of a reason other than a covenant breach, the contract could automatically terminate on a stated date, or one or both parties could have the discretionary authority to terminate the contract. If time is not of the essence, the contract could also extend the date by which the condition must be satisfied.

Parties can also fashion remedies that are transaction specific. For example, if a partner breaches a provision of a partnership agreement, the nonbreaching partners could have the right to buy the equity interest of the breaching partner. Similarly, an employment agreement might provide a golden parachute on a change in control.

Some remedies, though conceptually perfect, may be unenforceable. Classic examples are liquidated damages provisions that are really penalties and endgame provisions that kick in on bankruptcy.[4]

Drafters and their clients must also think through whether the contract remedies are exclusive or cumulative. Parties to an acquisition agreement usually agree that indemnity provisions are the exclusive remedy and supersede any common law remedies. Nonetheless, buyers might want to provide specifically for the right to avoid the contract if the seller fraudulently induced it to enter into the agreement.[5]

15.3.3 DISPUTE RESOLUTION PROVISIONS

Unfortunately, parties end up litigating many contractual disputes. In anticipation of that litigation, many parties want their contracts to include dispute resolution provisions, provisions that will govern some of the procedural and substantive aspects of the litigation.

Preliminarily, the parties must decide whether they want to adjudicate or arbitrate any disputes or rely on some other dispute resolution mechanism. If the parties agree to adjudicate their disputes, the dispute resolution provisions should include governing law, forum selection, and service of process provisions. Other provisions to consider are a waiver of venue objections, a waiver of the right to a jury trial,[6] and a provision requiring the losing party to pay the prevailing party's attorneys' fees and other expenses. The last is often difficult to obtain.

If the parties agree to arbitrate their disputes, the provisions with respect to the arbitration can be short (a simple statement of the agreement to arbitrate) or detailed. A detailed provision will specify, among other things:

- The disputes to be arbitrated
- The rules that will govern the arbitration
- The location of the arbitration
- The governing law
- The qualifications of the arbitrators
- The method of choosing the arbitrators
- The payments of expenses relating to the arbitration
- The finality of the arbitration

---

4. *See generally* 11 U.S.C. § 362(a) (prohibiting any act to obtain or control possession of property after a party enters bankruptcy) and § 365(e) (prohibiting the termination or modification of any executory contract or any provision in an executory contract solely because of a provision in the contract that is conditioned upon a party's bankruptcy or financial condition).

5. *See Abry Partners V, L.P. v. F & W Acq. LLC*, 891 A.2d 1032, 1064 (Del. Ch. 2006).

6. Although a waiver of the right to a jury trial is enforceable in most states, some states prohibit a waiver. *See e.g.,* Mont. Code Ann. 28-2-708 (Westlaw current through 2005 Regular Session of the 59th Legis. and the Dec. 2005 Spec. Session).

15.4   LOCATION OF THE ENDGAME PROVISIONS

Endgame provisions are almost always found at the end of the contract. The beginning of the contract has the parties' plan for a successful transaction or relationship. The conclusion of the relationship, whether good or bad, is relegated to the end of the contract. It reflects the chronology of a transaction.

Endgame provisions usually appear together in one section or article. This makes it easy for a reader who wants to know what happens upon the contract's termination. Occasionally, drafters integrate an endgame term with substantive business provisions. For example:

> **Certificate of Occupancy**. The Owner shall try to obtain a certificate of occupancy for the new family room before October 1, 20XX. If the Owner does not do so, the Buyer may terminate this Purchase Agreement.

If endgame provisions are to be scattered throughout the contract, consider nonetheless including a stand-alone endgame section or article with cross-references to the endgame provisions, wherever they are. This will help the reader who has turned to the back of the contract looking for the endgame provisions in their usual place.

One remedy commonly found outside the endgame section or article is the walk-away right that arises from a failure to satisfy a condition to closing (generally, in an acquisition or a financing agreement). This remedy is generally embedded in the introductory language that precedes the listing of the conditions.

> **Conditions**. All of the following conditions must have been satisfied before the Buyer is obligated to close the transactions that this Agreement contemplates *(This is the walk-away right.)*. The Buyer may waive any failure to satisfy any one or more of the conditions.

Although the preceding provision specifically states that the buyer may waive the failure to satisfy a condition, the provision need not do so. It is a common law consequence of the failure to satisfy a condition. If any other consequence flows from the failure of a condition, do not include it in the conditions article. Instead, insert it into the endgame article.

15.5   DRAFTING THE ENDGAME PROVISIONS

Conceptually, endgame provisions are a series of *if/then* propositions:[7]

- If this good event happens, then this is the consequence.
- If this bad event happens, then this is the consequence.

While the consequences differ from contract to contract based upon the parties' business concerns, they generally fall into one of three categories:

---

7. Section 21.5 discusses how an *if/then* formulation can create an ambiguity.

- An obligation to perform. (The Borrower shall pay default interest.)
- The grant of discretionary authority. (The Bank may foreclose.)
- A declaration. (The contract terminates upon a party's delegation of its performance without the other party's consent.)

An obligation to pay money is a common endgame provision. When drafting these provisions, make sure to *follow the cash* and answer the *who, what, when, where, why, how,* and *how much* questions, just as in drafting the monetary provisions of the action sections.[8]

The organization of endgame provisions depends upon the contract. If they deal with defaults (something has gone wrong), two schemes are common. The first puts a list of the offending events into one section and the consequences into another. Credit agreements and employment agreements often follow this scheme, as the agreements have default provisions relating to only one party. The second scheme creates an endgame article that has separate sections for each party's defaults. If the consequences of both parties' defaults are the same, a third section can detail the remedies. Otherwise, each party's section should be broken down into subsections, with the first subsection listing the defaults and the second listing the consequences. Remember, these organizational schemes may not be appropriate for all contracts and are merely guidelines.

If the endgame provisions are not related to defaults (a happy endgame), create separate sections or articles as needed to address specific business issues. For example, Article 11 of the Asset Purchase Agreement in Appendix A includes two subsections that assume the transaction has been successfully consummated. The first section requires the seller to change its name postclosing so that the buyer can use it, while the second requires the seller not to compete.

---

8. See § 8.3.

EXERCISES

Exercise 15-1

In addition to the endgame provisions mentioned in the last section of the chapter, what are the other endgame provisions in the Asset Purchase Agreement in Appendix A? What are the endgame provisions in the Website Development Agreement in Appendix B?

Exercise 15-2

Draft the endgame provisions of the Aircraft Purchase Agreement. Use the information from the Purchase Offer and the Escrow Agreement, found in Exercise 6-3, and the defined terms that were included in the Aircraft Purchase Agreement excerpt in Exercise 7-7.

Exercise 15-3

Read the excerpt from an employment agreement and then answer the questions that follow.

Excerpt from an Employment Agreement

10.   Termination. This Agreement terminates before the termination date set forth in Article 2 as follows:

    10.1   Death or Disability. If the Executive dies or becomes permanently disabled, this Agreement terminates effective at the end of the calendar month during which his death occurs or when his disability becomes permanent.

    10.2   Cause. If a majority of the disinterested directors of the Company's board of directors vote to remove the Executive from his duties for Cause, this Agreement terminates and the Executive ceases to be an officer of the Company effective on the date specified by the directors. For purposes of this Agreement, "Cause" means the occurrence of any one or more of the following events:

        10.2.1   The Executive has been convicted of or pleaded guilty or no contest to

            10.2.1.1   any misdemeanor reflecting unfavorably upon the Company; or

            10.2.1.2   any felony offense.

        10.2.2   The Executive has committed fraud or embezzlement, that determination to be made by a majority of the disinterested directors of the Company's board of directors in their reasonable judgment.

        10.2.3   A majority of the disinterested directors of the Company's board of directors has determined in their reasonable judgment that

            10.2.3.1   the Executive has breached one or more of his fiduciary duties to the Company or has made an intentional misrepresentation to the Company; and

10.2.3.2 the breach or misrepresentation has had or is likely to have a material adverse effect upon the Company's business operations or financial condition.

10.2.4 The Executive has failed to obey a specific written direction from the board of directors consistent with this Agreement and the Executive's duties under this Agreement.

10.2.5 After written notice and a 30-day cure period, the Executive has materially neglected or failed to satisfactorily discharge any of his duties or responsibilities, that determination to be made by a majority of the disinterested directors of the Company's board of directors in their reasonable judgment.

Questions

1. Section 10.1 provides for termination upon death or permanent disability. While death is relatively certain, the Company and Executive might dispute whether the Executive's disability has become permanent. If you represented the Executive, what substantive changes could you recommend that would provide greater certainty as to when a disability would become permanent?

2. Why are fraud and embezzlement treated differently from misdemeanors and felonies that require conviction?

3. Does subsection 10.2.3 adequately protect the Company if the Executive makes misrepresentations or breaches his fiduciary duties? What if he lied on his resume? Will this lead to a material adverse effect on the Company's financial condition?

4. If you represented the Executive, what change could you ask for in subsection 10.2.4 that would provide your client with greater protection? Use the other subsections as a guide.

5. Assume that the Company pays the Executive an annual salary and a guaranteed bonus of $10,000, and reimburses his expenses. The guaranteed bonus increases each year by 5 percent on a compounded basis. If you represented the Company, what would you suggest that the Company pay the Executive upon termination for each of the scenarios in the excerpt? Not precise dollar amounts, but conceptually. What would you recommend if you represented the Executive?

General Provisions

16.1 INTRODUCTION[1]

Drafters often refer to the **general provisions** at the back of the contract as the *boilerplate* provisions. Typical provisions include amendment, governing law, severability, and waiver of jury trial.

These provisions supply a road map, telling the parties how to govern their relationship and administer the contract. The provisions are said to serve housekeeping functions, arguably matters of secondary importance. The placement of these provisions towards the end of the contract, under a caption of *Miscellaneous* or *Administrative Provisions,* furthers the impression that these provisions are but an afterthought. Consequently, lawyers often ignore them, and legal commentators and critics lampoon them.

The term *boilerplate* suggests standardized provisions that can be used in all circumstances. But they cannot. You will regularly find key business issues hidden in these provisions, and they will get you into trouble if you do not redraft them. By learning the business and legal implications of the general provisions, you will know when and how to modify them.

Each section that follows discusses one of the general provisions and begins with an example of the relevant provision. These provisions are not paradigms of perfect drafting. Instead, they are intended to give you a sense of the provisions that you will typically see. As a drafting exercise, you can mark up each of the provisions to take into account the information you learn.

One general point: If parties are executing multiple agreements as part of a single transaction, make sure that the general provisions are the same in each agreement. For example, when a party borrows money, it may sign not only a credit agreement,

---

1. Each Section in this chapter is based on a chapter in *Negotiating and Drafting Contract Boilerplate* (Tina L. Stark et al. eds., ALM Publg. 2003). The text in this chapter either quotes or paraphrases the relevant chapter. At the beginning of each section, the author of the relevant chapter is named. I thank each of the authors for their contributions to *Negotiating and Drafting Contract Boilerplate* and to this textbook.

Section 16.1 is based on Chapter 1 in *Negotiating and Drafting Contract Boilerplate,* author, Tina L. Stark.

All material from *Negotiating and Drafting Contract Boilerplate* is used with permission of the publisher—ALM Publishing (www.lawcatalog.com); copyright ALM Properties, Inc., 2003. All Rights Reserved.

but also a security agreement and a pledge agreement. All of these agreements should use exactly the same general provisions. Any divergence creates the potential for litigation.

16.2 ASSIGNMENT AND DELEGATION[2]

> **Assignment and Delegation**. This Agreement cannot be assigned or delegated by the parties.

The assignment and delegation provision is one of the general provisions that you will tailor most often. When you do, remember that you must deal with both assignments and delegations, not just assignments. Many provisions in precedents do not even mention delegation.

16.2.1 THE BASICS OF ASSIGNMENTS AND DELEGATIONS

Recall from Chapter 3 that the flip side of every covenant is a right.[3] An assignment is a transfer of those rights to a third party. For example, if Leslie has an obligation to pay Ibrahim $100, Ibrahim has a right to be paid $100, and he may transfer that right, for example, to Mark. Ibrahim is the **assignor**; Mark is the **assignee**, and Leslie is the **nonassigning party**.

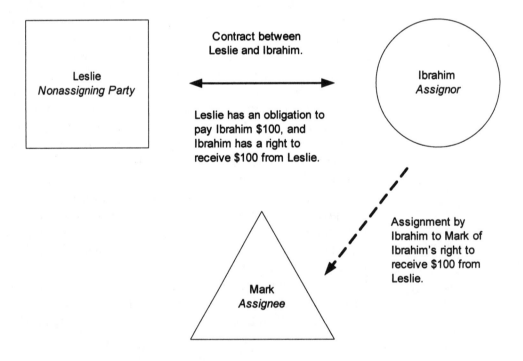

Once Ibrahim assigns his rights, he no longer has a right to Leslie's performance. Instead, Mark has that right, and Leslie has a duty to perform in his favor.

---

2. Section 16.2 is based on Chapter 3 in *Negotiating and Drafting Contract Boilerplate,* author, Tina L. Stark.

3. See §3.4.

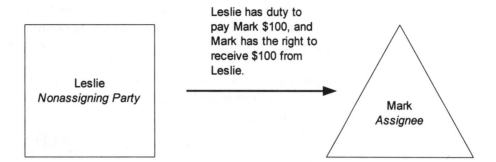

Note that the arrow goes in only one direction. Mark has no duty to perform in favor of Leslie as Ibrahim did not delegate his performance contemporaneously with the assignment—which leads us neatly to delegations.

A party delegates its performance when it appoints someone else to perform in its stead. The party who delegates its performance is the **delegating party**. The person to whom it delegates its performance is the **delegate**, and the other party to the original contract is the **nondelegating party**. Performance refers not only to duties, but also to conditions.[4]

Not all duties are delegable. If a duty is personal in nature or requires the delegating party's unique skills, the would-be delegating party cannot delegate. For example, Billy Joel could not delegate his duty to perform at Madison Square Garden to your professor. Among the nondelegable duties is a party's obligation to pay under a promissory note. If it were delegable, the delegating party could delegate its duty to someone who has no ability to pay. That duty would become delegable, however, if the delegate were willing and able to tender cash to the nondelegating party at the time of the delegation.

Returning to our earlier hypothetical, assume that Ibrahim has a right to the $100 only if he delivers two boxes of multipurpose paper to Leslie. That is, Ibrahim has not only a right, but also a duty to perform. A delegation would consist of Ibrahim delegating to Mark the former's duty to deliver the paper to Leslie.

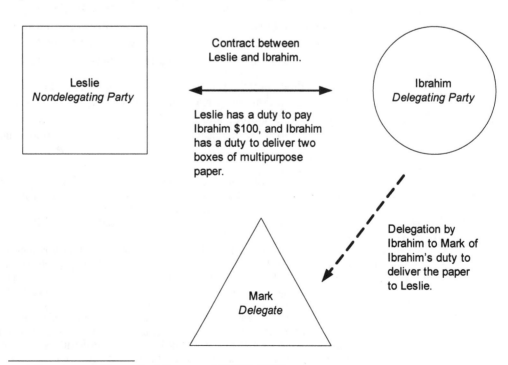

---

4. *Restatement (Second) of Contracts* § 319(1) (1981).

Delegation alone does not bind a delegate to perform in favor of the nondelegating party. If it did, anyone could become obligated to perform anything even though that person had not agreed to do so. Thus, the delegate must agree with the delegating party that it will perform in favor of the nondelegating party. It must **assume** the delegating party's duties to the nondelegating party. When it does so, the nondelegating party becomes a third-party beneficiary of that assumption.

Delegation of a duty does not discharge the delegating party's performance obligation. Rather, the delegating party remains secondarily liable. Were it otherwise, the delegating party could effectively eliminate its performance obligation by delegating it to someone unable to perform.

16.2.2   ANTIASSIGNMENT PROVISIONS

An antiassignment provision is what it sounds like: a provision that prohibits a party from assigning its rights under a contract. Parties insert these provisions to prevent assignments that would materially change the nonassigning party's duties or materially increase its risks.[5] In addition, parties pair them with antidelegation provisions to ensure that they need to deal with only one party—the one with whom they originally contracted.

Making an antiassignment provision enforceable requires a detailed, carefully drawn provision, and it often does not work. The reasons are twofold. First, the provisions of the Uniform Commercial Code (the "U.C.C.") render ineffective any antiassignment provisions subject to the U.C.C.[6] So, no matter how careful you are, the provision will be ineffective. Second, even if the U.C.C. is inapplicable, courts are hostile to these provisions, and judges are willing to write tortured opinions to find the provisions unenforceable. The hostility stems from their belief that antiassignment provisions inappropriately restrain commerce.[7]

To prohibit a transfer of rights, draft the antiassignment provision to prohibit *an assignment of rights under the agreement.* If the provision prohibits only *the assignment of the agreement,* courts generally interpret the provision as an antidelegation provision. Indeed, both the U.C.C. and the *Restatement (Second) of Contracts* specifically provide canons of interpretation to that effect.[8]

In making their decisions, courts determine whether the parties intended an antiassignment provision or an antidelegation provision. As stated by Professor Corbin:

> [If] a building contract provides that the builder shall not assign the contract, it is almost certain that the parties intend that he shall not delegate supervision of the work wholly to another, and leave the job himself. In the absence of very apt words to the contrary, they do not intend that the builder shall not assign his right to instal-

---

5. For example, in one line of cases, the antiassignment provisions were held enforceable because assignment would increase the risk that the nonassigning party would lose certain tax benefits. *See e.g. Grieve v. Gen. Amer. Life Ins. Co.*, 58 F. Supp. 2d 319, 323 (D. Vt. 1999).

6. *See* U.C.C. § 2-210(2), U.C.C. U.L.A. § 2-210(2) (2004), U.C.C. §§ 9-406–9-409, U.C.C. U.L.A §§ 9-406–9-409 (2002).

7. The following is an example of how an antiassignment provision can impede commerce. Assume that Rancher Rob sells Stockyard Sue 10 head of cattle for $500 and that the contract provides that Stockyard Sue can pay Rancher Rob at a later date. Assume further that before the payment date, Rancher Rob needs cash to make an investment. One way that Rancher Rob can fund that investment is to assign his $500 account receivable to Credit Bank. In exchange, Credit Bank would pay Rancher Rob a discounted amount, say $450. The benefit of this assignment is that it gives Rancher Rob access to funds that he would not otherwise have. Thus, the assignment permits a new commercial venture. That venture is not possible, however, if Rancher Rob's contract with Stockyard Sue has an enforceable antiassignment provision.

8. U.C.C. § 2-210(4), U.L.A. U.C.C. § 2-210(4) (2004); *Restatement (Second) of Contracts* § 322(1) (1981).

ments [sic] of the price as they fall due. It may be of great importance to have the personal supervision of the builder; but it is of much less importance to whose hands the money is to be paid. If the owner desired to deprive the builder of the power to assign his right to the money, he would have said that the builder's right to the money shall not be assigned, not that the builder shall not assign the "contract."[9]

This reasoning may seem as if the courts are turning themselves inside out to conclude what they want. They are. They dislike antiassignment provisions and, therefore, as a policy matter, construe them narrowly.

Generally, a simple prohibition against the assignment of rights does not suffice when drafting an antiassignment provision. You must also reckon with the distinction between the **right** and the **power** to prohibit an assignment. An antiassignment provision that only prohibits an assignment takes away only the right to assign. In that instance, any assignment would be enforceable, although the nonassigning party would have a cause of action for breach against the assignor. That might not be worth much, however. Nonassigning parties generally suffer little damage as their performance usually does not change.

To create an antiassignment provision that renders an assignment void, you must take away not only the right to assign, but also the power to assign.[10] To do this, a contract must prohibit the assignment of rights under the contract and declare that any purported assignment is void. You do not need to add *null* or *of no further force and effect*. They are synonyms, and *void* suffices.

Finally, in drafting an antiassignment provision, you must take into account that courts narrowly construe the meaning of the verb *assign*. If you want to prohibit assignments by merger or by operation of law, explicitly prohibit these types of assignment. A general prohibition on assignments does not include them. Indeed, do not rely on the general antiassignment language if the parties agree that a specific assignment is prohibited. Be specific.

Consistent with this advice, explicitly prohibit a **change of control.** A change of control occurs, for example, if a shareholder sells more than 50 percent of a company's shares to another person. Parties worry about such a change because a new person controlling the other party can dramatically change the parties' relationship.

To prohibit a change of control, provide either that a change of control is deemed an assignment for purposes of the antiassignment provision or that a change of control is a default. In addition, consider whether the agreement should define change of control.

16.2.3 ANTIDELEGATION PROVISIONS

Unlike antiassignment provisions, antidelegation provisions are generally enforceable and may be drafted in a straightforward manner by stating that neither party may delegate performance.[11] Just as with an antiassignment provision, include a declaration that any purported delegation in violation of the parties' agreement is void.

If the parties desire an antidelegation provision but wish to permit a specific delegation, consider whether the right to delegate should be subject to any conditions. A common one requires the delegate to be creditworthy. In addition, drafters often

---

9. Arthur L. Corbin, *Corbin on Contracts,* vol. 9, § 872, 427-428 (Interim ed., LexisNexis 1951, renewed 1979).

10. *See Bel-Ray Co., Inc. v. Chemrite (Pty) Ltd.*, 181 F.3d 435, 442 (3d Cir. 1999).

11. *Performance* is a better word choice than duty because technically it is broader, referring not only to duties, but also to conditions.

require the delegate to assume, in writing, the delegating party's performance obligations. If you represent a client that is likely to be the delegating party, secure an agreement that the delegating party is deemed released from its performance obligations upon the signing of the delegation documents. Otherwise, it remains secondarily liable.

16.3 SUCCESSORS AND ASSIGNS[12]

> **Successors and Assigns.** This Agreement binds and benefits the parties and their respective successors and assigns.

The successors and assigns provision is a staple of commercial contracts. Although inserted almost ritualistically, its function and effect are rarely understood. It is sometimes confused with the assignment and delegation provision. But that provision deals with whether the contract permits assignments and delegations, while the successors and assigns provision, properly understood, deals with the consequences of an assignment or delegation.

The case law regarding the successors and assigns provision is muddy, with courts differing as to the provision's purpose and effect. To understand the issues, some additional detail on the law of assignments and delegation is helpful.

As noted in Section 16.2.1, when a party assigns its right under a contract to a third party, the nonassigning party becomes bound to perform for the benefit of the assignee. But an assignment confers only the benefits of the rights being assigned, not any performance obligations. The assignee is only an assignee, not an assignee and a delegate. Acceptance of the assignment does not create performance obligations.

An assignee may concurrently be a delegate. If a party simultaneously assigns it rights and delegates it performance, the assignee becomes a delegate upon assuming the delegating party's duties to the nondelegating party. Unfortunately, assignments are often ambiguous and do not clearly state whether the assignor is simultaneously delegating its performance. In these cases, the courts look to whether the assignee assumed its assignor's performance. If it did, then the court will find a contemporaneous delegation. Unfortunately, no consensus exists as to whether an assumption must be express or whether an implied assumption is also permissible.

The modern approach is set forth in the *Restatement (Second) of Contracts* and the U.C.C. Both provide that broad, general words of assignment constitute not only an assignment, but also a delegation.[13] The rationale is that both are generally intended, despite the drafting. So, for example, an assignment *of all my rights under the contract* would be both an assignment and a delegation, even though the delegation was unstated and the assumption implied. Courts have created an exception if evidence demonstrates that the parties intended something different, such as when an assignment is a grant of a security interest. The less modern cases hold that assumptions must be express.

---

12. Section 16.3 is based on Chapter 4 in *Negotiating and Drafting Contract Boilerplate,* author, Tina L. Stark.

13. *Restatement (Second) of Contracts* § 328(1) (1981); U.C.C. § 2-210(4), U.L.A. U.C.C. § 2-210(4) (2004).

Enter the successors and assigns provision. The better view is that this provision

- eliminates the necessity of an express assumption, binding the assignee to perform as it is also a delegate; and
- restates the common law that the nonassigning party must give the benefit of its performance to the assignee.

Some courts have held, however, that an assignment does not bind an assignee simply because of the presence of a successors and assigns provision. Other cases have held that the provision demonstrates that the parties intended that contract rights be assignable and performance obligations be delegable. In the face of these different holdings, you rely on this provision at your risk. The better approach is to draft a provision that says exactly what the parties intend.

If you do use the traditional version, include the word *permitted* before *successors and assigns.* That should prevent a party from successfully arguing that the successors and assigns provision allows assignments and delegations.

16.4 GOVERNING LAW[14]

> **Governing Law**. This Agreement is to be governed by and construed in accordance with the laws of Arkansas, without regard to its conflict of law principles.

A **governing law** provision, also known as a **choice of law** provision, establishes the law that governs a dispute arising from an agreement. In its absence, common law conflicts of law principles govern. In that event, the governing law is the state with the most substantial relationship to the transaction. In a litigation, the parties may disagree which state that is, particularly when the law in one state favors one party. By choosing the governing law when drafting the contract, the parties may forestall a dispute on this issue. To complement the governing law provision, also include a choice of forum provision that chooses a forum in the state whose law will govern. This enhances the likelihood that a court will enforce the governing law provision.

When choosing which state's law should govern, consider several factors. First, evaluate whether the law of the jurisdiction under consideration is well developed and predictable. Delaware and New York, for example, both have well-developed bodies of corporate law, making an agreement's interpretation more predictable than might be true in other jurisdictions. In addition, evaluate whether the particular body of state law is hostile or friendly to the type of client (and the subject matter) being represented. For example, while California courts have upheld significant punitive damages awards for bad faith denials of insurance coverage, New York courts, as a general matter, prohibit such awards.

When drafting a governing law provision, pay attention to the language defining the scope of the provision. Despite the plain meaning of the words, the following provision is not as broad in scope as it seems to be:

---

14. Section 16.4 is based on Chapter 6 in *Negotiating and Drafting Contract Boilerplate,* authors, Brad S. Karp and Shelly L. Friedland.

> **The laws of Kentucky govern all matters with respect to this Agreement.**

All matters excludes torts, including the tort of fraudulent inducement. To bring that cause of action within the provision's embrace, choose one of two options: either add *including torts* at the end of the sentence, or, alternatively, replace *with respect to* with the phrase *arising under or relating to*. The second option may be startling since it uses a couplet. Generally, couplets should be banished from contracts as legalese.[15] Here, however, the couplet has meaning.

In many commercial transactions, the parties wish New York or Delaware law to govern, even though the transaction has no relationship with the chosen state. This can be done if the amount of the transaction meets statutory thresholds set forth in New York and Delaware law.[16]

If you go this route, pair the New York or Delaware governing law provision with a New York or Delaware choice of forum provision so that the litigation is in a forum that will enforce the governing law provision.[17] For New York, be careful to check the dollar threshold because the amount required for the choice of forum provision exceeds that for a governing law provision.[18]

Some choice of law provisions deal with *renvoi. Renvoi* is French for *return* or *send back*. It occurs when one state's conflict of law principles require that a second state's principles be used, but that second state's principles require that the first state's principles be used. This referral from one state's principles to another and back to the first creates an endless cycle of return.

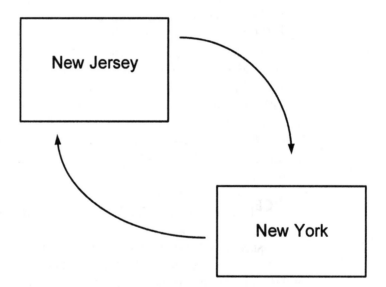

To break this cycle, some lawyers qualify the governing law provisions with the clause, *without regard to its conflict of law principles*. (See the provision introducing this section.) In reality, this clause is unnecessary as most courts routinely apply their state's conflict of law principles. However, it has become so commonplace that you will be hard-pressed to convince someone that the provision is superfluous.

---

15. See §18.3.
16. N.Y. Gen. Oblig. L. § 5-1401(1) (McKinney 2001) and Del. Code Ann. tit. 6 § 2708(c) (Lexis 2005).
17. *But see Nutracea v. Langley Park Invs. PLC*, 2007 WL 135669 (E.D. Cal.) (slip copy).
18. *See* N.Y. Gen. Oblig. L. § 5-1402 (McKinney 2001).

16.5 **WAIVER OF JURY TRIAL**[19]

> **Waiver of Jury Trial.** The Borrower waives its right to trial by jury in all matters regarding this Agreement.

The United States Constitution and many state constitutions guarantee the right to a jury trial. In most states, a party may waive this right.[20] But before inserting a waiver of jury trial provision into a contract, first consider whether a waiver benefits your client. If your client is a large, commercial corporation, a waiver of jury trial provision might be provident. Jury members often harbor a visceral dislike of large, commercial corporations or see them as deep pockets.

Because the right to a jury trial is a constitutional right, courts disfavor a waiver of this right and require that a waiver be *knowing, intentional, and voluntary*. The key, of course, is to draft the waiver in such a way that a court will reach the "appropriate" conclusion. The following are several drafting guidelines based on the case law:

1. *Put the waiver of jury trial provision as the last of the general provisions, so that it immediately precedes the signature lines.*

2. *Make the provision prominent by putting it in a bold font and a font size that is larger than that used in the rest of the contract.*[21]

3. *Use a caption that indicates that the right to a jury trial is being waived.*

4. *List the provision in the table of contents, using the caption that indicates the right to a jury trial is being waived.*

5. *Make the provision bilateral.*

6. *If the other party is a natural person,*
  (a) *require that person to initial the provision;*
  (b) *include a statement that the waiver is knowing, voluntary, and intentional;*
  (c) *require that person to acknowledge that her lawyer explained the provision; and*
  (d) *require that person's lawyer to sign a form stating that he has explained the provision and its ramifications to his client.*

16.6 **NOTICE**[22]

> **Notice.** All notices under this Agreement shall be given in writing.

Notice provisions are ubiquitous. Nearly every contract has one. They do more, however, than list the addresses to which parties should send their notices. They allocate the risk of a notice's nonreceipt.

---

19. Section 16.5 is based on Chapter 7 in *Negotiating and Drafting Contract Boilerplate,* authors, Lauren Reiter Brody and Frances Kulka Browne.

20. *But see* Mont. Code Ann. 28-2-708 (Westlaw current through 2005 Regul. Session of the 59th Legis. and the Dec. 2005 Spec. Session).

21. You may also consider putting the provision in all capital letters. Although some commentators believe that all capital letters are difficult to read, courts have nonetheless suggested that they are an acceptable way to make the waiver of jury trial provision prominent.

22. Section 16.6 is based on Chapter 15 in *Negotiating and Drafting Contract Boilerplate,* author, Steven R. Berger.

Traditional notice provisions usually state that a notice is effective three days after its deposit in a U.S. Postal Service mailbox. This means that, even if the notice is lost, the sender of the notice has rights against the recipient three days after mailing. The risk of nonreceipt is on the recipient. As this can lead to inequitable results, many parties now insist that the risk of nonreceipt should be on the sender. To do so, notice must be effective only upon its receipt.

A well-drafted notice provision should state the modes by which a party may give notice. Typically, a provision permits notices to be given by fax, personally, or overnight courier. The sender can easily monitor these modes to determine whether the other party has received the notice. Many notice provisions no longer permit delivery by first class mail because of its unreliability. If the parties insist on delivery through the U.S. Postal Service, a common compromise is delivery by certified or registered mail. The benefit of these two forms of delivery is that a sender can request a return receipt. Although some drafters provide for the delivery of notice by e-mail, it is not yet common. This may change, however, as parties become more comfortable with Internet technology.

A notice provision should also indicate whether delivery of a notice is a covenant or a condition to the notice's effectiveness, or both. In addition, it should state how a party may change its address for purposes of the contract.

16.7 SEVERABILITY[23]

> **Severability.** If any provision of this Agreement is illegal or unenforceable, that provision is severed from this Agreement and the other provisions remain in force.

Courts will not enforce obligations arising out of illegal agreements. A contract that contains one illegal provision may, however, also contain legal, enforceable provisions. In these situations, a refusal to enforce the entire contract might prove unduly harsh. Instead, courts often strike the offending provisions, allowing the rest of the agreement to stay in force.

The purpose of a severability provision is to express the parties' intent that a court enforce the valid provisions of a contract, even if it finds a provision to be illegal or unenforceable. Usually, the provision is similar to one that begins this section.

Unfortunately, this typical provision rarely reflects the parties' actual intent. For example, imagine a noncompete agreement that requires an employer to pay an employee $3 million, in return for which the employee agrees not to compete anywhere in the world for 10 years. Imagine further that the court holds that the noncompete is overly broad and unenforceable. With the standard severability provision, the noncompete would be severed, but the payment obligation would remain. The likelihood that this would effect the parties' intent is low. More likely, they intended that the nonsevered provisions would remain in effect only if the essential provisions of the agreement for each party remained binding and enforceable.

While this rewriting of the more standard formulation may not preclude all intent-related issues, at least it explicitly expresses that the parties cannot do without some

---

23. Section 16.7 is based on Chapter 17 in *Negotiating and Drafting Contract Boilerplate,* authors, C. James Levin and Avery R. Brown.

provisions. In addition, it gives them the opportunity to argue which provisions are essential in the context of any later dispute.

Keep one other thing in mind when drafting severability provisions: The way you draft the provision should reflect whether the governing law is that of a state that follows the **blue-pencil rule** or that of a state that follows the **rule of reasonableness**.

Under the traditional blue-pencil rule, a court will delete portions of an otherwise unenforceable provision if the deleted portions can be clearly—and grammatically—separated from the remainder of the provision (i.e., if the provision will still be grammatically correct after the offending terms have been deleted). For example, an overbroad covenant forbidding future employment in Connecticut could not be reduced to cover one county in a blue-pencil jurisdiction. By contrast, that result could be reached if the covenant had separately listed each county in Connecticut. Then, a court could salvage the noncompete by deleting specific counties until the list was no longer overbroad. States that have adopted this approach include Colorado, Connecticut, Indiana, and North Carolina.

The *Restatement (Second) of Contracts* has rejected the blue-pencil approach in favor of the more flexible rule of reasonableness. Under this rule, a court may reform an unenforceable provision to the extent reasonable under the circumstances and then enforce it as so reformed.[24] States that have adopted this approach include Delaware, Florida, New Jersey, New York, Pennsylvania, and Tennessee. Courts have sought to limit the risk of overreaching that this approach might entail by requiring proof that the offending provisions were drafted in good faith and in accordance with standards of fair dealing.

16.8 AMENDMENTS[25]

> **Amendments**. This Agreement may be amended only by an agreement in writing.

The no oral amendments provision is classic boilerplate–always present, rarely negotiated. It is also generally unenforceable under the common law. In a Texas case, the court stated that a written contract "is of no higher legal degree than an oral one, and either may vary or discharge the other."[26] Similarly, in a New York case, Judge Cardozo said:

> Those who make a contract may unmake it. The clause which forbids a change, may be changed like any other. . . . What is executed by one act is restored by another. . . . Whenever two [persons] contract, no limitation self-imposed can destroy their power to contract again.[27]

To bring greater predictability to contractual relations, some states have enacted laws providing that no oral amendment provisions are enforceable.[28] The courts, however, have undermined these statutory provisions by finding that parties can modify

---

24. *Restatement (Second) of Contracts* § 184 (1979).
25. Section 16.8 is based on Chapter 16 in *Negotiating and Drafting Contract Boilerplate*, author, Brian A. Haskel.
26. *Mar-Lan Industries, Inc. v. Nelson*, 635 S.W.2d 853, 855 (Tex. App. 1982).
27. *Beatty v. Guggenheim Exploration Co.*, 122 N.E. 378, 381 (N.Y. 1919).
28. *See e.g.* Cal. Civ. Code Ann. § 1698 (West 1985); N.Y. Gen. Oblig. L. § 15-301 (McKinney 2001).

the underlying agreement by an executed oral amendment, a course of conduct, or estoppel.

A nationwide solution has also been attempted through U.C.C. § 2-209(2), which provides that no oral amendment provisions are enforceable in contracts. Unfortunately, this solution is limited in scope to contracts subject to U.C.C. Article 2 and is not bulletproof. Specifically, under U.C.C. § 2-209(4) a purported amendment that does not satisfy the requirements of the statute of frauds can operate as a waiver of the no oral amendments provision. The rationale is that course of performance during the term of the contract either represents a waiver or is relevant in determining whether a particular act affects the agreement's meaning. In essence, U.C.C. § 2-209(4) codifies the estoppel theory under which courts have enforced oral amendments despite contractual prohibitions against them.

With all these obstacles to an enforceable no oral amendments provision, the obvious question is whether it makes sense to try to include one. The answer is *yes*. These provisions evidence the parties' agreement and their intent at the time the contract was executed. Many parties use them as guideposts for their actions during the life of the contract. If a dispute arises as to whether a purported amendment is enforceable, these provisions set the starting point for a court's analysis because they reflect the parties' understanding when they made their agreement.

The no oral amendments provision can be very simple. It needs to state that the parties may amend the provision only by written agreement. You may tailor the provision by specifying who must sign on behalf of each party. You may also include as a condition to the enforceability of the amendment that each party must deliver to the other a board resolution authorizing the amendment.

16.9 MERGER[29]

> **Merger.** This Agreement states the full agreement between the parties and supersedes all prior negotiations and agreements.

A **merger provision** is sometimes called an **integration provision** or a **zipper clause**. Generally speaking, it is the best way to make sure that a contract will not be altered or supplemented through parol evidence. In the absence of a merger provision, courts will examine a contract to determine whether it is a final and exclusive expression of the parties' agreement. A writing that is a final expression of the parties' agreement is said to be partially integrated, while a writing that is both a final and exclusive expression of the parties' agreement is said to be fully integrated.

Under the parol evidence rule, if a writing is integrated, whether fully or partially, a term that contradicts the existing writing cannot be admitted into evidence. If the writing is partially integrated, evidence of prior negotiations and agreements are admissible to supplement the writing, but not to contradict it. (Remember: If the agreement is partially integrated, it is not the exclusive statement of the parties' agreement. Therefore, consistent provisions can supplement it.) But if the writing is fully integrated (final and exclusive), generally, not even evidence of an additional, consistent term is admissible.

---

29. Section 16.9 is based on Chapter 18 in *Negotiating and Drafting Contract Boilerplate,* authors, Ronald B. Risdon and William A. Escobar.

Despite these rules, parol evidence is always admissible to explain an ambiguous contract term. In addition, courts generally permit a party to introduce parol evidence that the other party fraudulently induced it to enter into the contract. A number of courts have prohibited the introduction of this evidence if the allegedly defrauded party disclaimed reliance in the contract on the representation that it now claims was the basis of the fraud.

When drafting a merger provision, describe the agreement being signed as *final and exclusive* to signal that the parties intend the agreement to be fully integrated. Also state the ramifications of the agreement being final and exclusive: that all prior negotiations and agreements are merged into the agreement being signed. If the agreement being signed does not supersede an existing agreement, such as a confidentiality agreement, state the exception.

If the parties are signing multiple agreements contemporaneously, use a defined term to refer to all the agreements. For example, use *Transaction Documents*. The merger provision should then state that those documents together constitute the final and exclusive agreement of the parties. Be sure that each of the other agreements being executed includes a merger provision that is exactly the same as the one in the primary agreement.

16.10 COUNTERPARTS[30]

> **Counterparts**. This Agreement may be executed in one or more counterparts, each of which is an original, and all of which constitute only one agreement between the parties.

A **counterpart** is a duplicate original that parties sign. Drafters use them to expedite transactions when not all the parties attend the agreement's signing and to create multiple originals so that each party can have a fully executed original.

Historically, the rationale for using multiple counterparts was to create an antifraud measure for contracts. The use of counterparts originated in real property conveyancing in England. Under English common law, an indenture was used to memorialize an agreement for the purchase or lease of real property. The indenture, or deed indented, takes its name from the practice of writing as many copies of the deed as there were parties on one large sheet of parchment, and then cutting them apart in a notched or wavy line. Thus, each document was a counterpart to the other. This practice was particularly useful in transactions where one or more parties had continuing covenants, because in these situations each party desired its own copy of the agreement.

The counterparts were signed in one of two ways. The first was for the landlord to sign the portion of the document that contained his promises, and the tenant to sign the portion with his promises.[31] Then they would swap their respective signed

---

30. Section 16.10 is based upon Chapter 19 in *Negotiating and Drafting Contract Boilerplate*, author, Frances Kulka Browne.

31. The following is a counterparts provision from the Indenture, dated January 25, 1694, between Joseph Reynolds and John Balderston and the Fellows and Scholars of Emanuel College:

> In Witness Whereof to one part of these Indentures remaining with . . . Joseph Reynolds[,] the . . . Fellows and Schollars [*sic*] have put their common seale [*sic*] [; and] to the other parte [*sic*] thereof remaining with the . . . Fellows and Schollars [*sic*][,] . . . Joseph Reynolds hath put to his hand and seale [*sic*] the day and year first above written.

documents. (Traditionally, the portion of the indenture that the landlord executed was called the *original*, and the remaining sections were termed the *counterparts*.) The second way that indentures could be signed was for all the parties to execute the identically drafted segments of parchment, thereby rendering them all "originals."[32] In either case, in the event of a dispute, the counterparts could be physically pieced together to verify that they came from the same parchment.

The typical counterparts provision in a modern contract provides that the parties may execute the contract in one or more counterparts. This is usually interpreted in two ways: first, to permit each party to sign separate counterparts, which, when collated, together constitute a fully executed original; second to permit multiple originals, each of which is signed by all the parties. In this event, each party leaves the signing with a single document that is a fully executed original. Some drafters prefer to spell out each of the two possibilities.

A well-drafted counterparts provision also states that the counterparts *constitute only one agreement.* This means that each party makes only one set of promises even though the parties may have executed multiple counterparts, creating multiple fully executed originals. That is, neither party promises to do something as many times as it has executed counterparts.

For details concerning the signing of counterparts, see Section 17.5.2.

Contemporary English redraft:

> In Witness Whereof, the Fellows and Scholars have executed the part of this Indenture remaining with Joseph Reynolds; and Joseph Reynolds has executed the part of this Indenture remaining with the Fellows and Scholars.

[Contract from the collection of Tina L. Stark.]

32. For example, in a 1773 indenture, both parties signed the same counterpart after the contract recited the following: "In witness whereof the partys [*sic*] first above named to these presents interchangeably have set their hands and Seals the day and year first above written." Articles of Agreement, May 27, 1773, between Ann Gibbons and William Wells. [Contract from the collection of Tina L. Stark.]

CHAPTER SIXTEEN

EXERCISES

Exercise 16

The following provision comes from an agreement between an interactive game developer and a publisher. As drafted, what does the provision prohibit the Developer from doing? Mark up the provision so that it states what you think the parties intended, and make any other appropriate changes.

Because the Developer has unique qualifications and capabilities that were important to the

Publisher when deciding to hire the Developer, it is expressly understood that the Developer is not

allowed to assign this Agreement to a third party, nor delegate any of its obligations hereunder, and

if the Developer tries to do so, the attempt shall be null and void. However, Publisher will be fully

entitled to do so without Developer's consent.[33]

Exercise 16-2

Section 12.7 of the Asset Purchase Agreement in Appendix A contains that agreement's merger provision. Redraft it so that it applies to that agreement and to the related agreements that the parties are executing contemporaneously. Make any other changes necessary to preclude parol evidence from being introduced.

Exercise 16-3

Mark up the following provision so that it applies if one of the parties is an individual. *Clue:* When the words *successors* and *assigns* are used in tandem, *assigns* denotes a party to whom a voluntary transfer of rights has been made. *Successor* does not usually mean *assignee.* Instead, the classic definition of a *successor* is a corporation that by merger, consolidation, or other legal succession has been transferred rights and has assumed the performance obligations of another corporation. What should replace *successor* with respect to a person? Is *assigns* still appropriate?

This Agreement binds and benefits the parties and their respective permitted successors and

assigns.

---

33. This provision is based upon a provision in Thomas F. Villeneuve, Robert V. Gunderson, Jr., Daniel M. Kaufman, *Corporate Partnering: Structuring & Negotiating Domestic & International Strategic Alliances* 2003 Supplement, 22-34 (3d ed., Aspen 2004).

Exercise 16-4

Mark up the following provisions to correct any drafting errors. Assume that they appear in the same agreement.

12.4 Jury Trial. The Borrower waives its right to a trial by jury in connection with any litigation

concerning the subject matter of this Agreement.

12.5 Governing Law. This Agreement shall be governed by the laws of the State of Michigan,

without giving effect to its conflicts of law principles.

Exercise 16-5

Redraft the following provision so that

- each party promises to deliver notice by the means listed in the provision;
- compliance with the promise is a condition to the notice's effectiveness; and
- a notice is effective only upon receipt.

Any notice required under this Agreement is to be delivered only in person, by recognized over-

night courier, or by facsimile.

Exercise 16-6

Redraft the notice provision in Section 12.6 of the Asset Purchase Agreement in Appendix A to correct the drafting errors. Assume that your client is the party most likely to receive notice. Also, provide that each party's lawyer is to receive a copy of each notice. Do not make any other substantive changes.

Exercise 16-7

Mark up the following provision to require the parties to negotiate in good faith to modify any illegal or unenforceable provision so that the revised provision approximates as much as possible the parties' original intent.

If any provision of this Agreement is determined to be illegal or unenforceable, the remaining

provisions continue to be legal and enforceable.

Exercise 16-8

Draft a no oral amendments provision that includes a condition that a vice president of each party needs to sign each amendment.

Exercise 16-9

How would you draft the notice provision if

- multiple agreements were being executed as party of a single transaction, and
- the general provisions were to be stated only in the principal agreement?

Exercise 16-10

Read the following memorandum and follow its instructions.

Memorandum

To: Neurotic Associate

From: Petulant Partner

Re: Rail Transportation Agreement

Attached are excerpts of a draft of the Rail Transportation Agreement (RTA) that we have received from opposing counsel. Our client, ABC Movers, Inc. (ABC), has used a series of expletives to express its view about the drafting. ABC has requested that we revise the #&^*!!# excerpts in order to fix what it perceives to be the problems. Specifically:

1. The preamble is old-fashioned and grammatically incorrect.
2. Something "seems wrong" with one of the recitals. (No, I don't know which recital. Did you really expect me to read the RTA?)
3. The definitions don't seem to follow any format.
4. There is legalese galore.
5. The antiassignment provision borders on unintelligible. (Among other things, we're supposed to make sure that the legal and business terms are used appropriately and that only a party who should be entitled to request something has the right to make that request. (Yes, I know that that is somewhat unclear, but I am only repeating what the client said. Read the RTA. Maybe you can figure it out.))

No doubt, it would be helpful if you knew what the business deal was supposed to be. I was told the following:

6. Either party may assign its rights or delegate its duties under the Agreement if the other party consents.
7. ABC will consent in the RTA to an enumerated list of acceptable assignees. (Does the use of the word *assignees* make business sense in the context of the draft? If not, please fix it.)

Please do this mark-up as soon as possible.

P.P.

RAIL TRANSPORTATION AGREEMENT

THIS RAIL TRANSPORTATION AGREEMENT (the "Agreement") is made and entered into as of

this 21st day of October, 20XX, by and among the CLIFF COAL COMPANY, a Delaware corporation,

with a principal business office at _____ (hereinafter referred to as "Industry"), and ABC

MOVERS, INC., a Delaware corporation, with a principal business office at _____

(hereinafter referred to as "Carrier").

WITNESSETH:

WHEREAS, Industry and Carrier desire to enter into a contract pursuant to which Carrier will transport Coal for Industry; and

WHEREAS, Carrier agrees to provide transportation of Coal and to furnish and maintain necessary railroad rolling stock as stated herein.

NOW THEREFORE, in consideration of the premises and the mutual covenants and obligations contained herein, it is agreed as follows:

1.   Definitions

The following capitalized terms shall be defined as follows:

1.1.   Agreement—Shall mean this Rail Transportation Agreement, including all Appendices attached hereto, as it may be amended from time to time.

1.2   Facility—That certain cogeneration plant located in Energytown, Georgia.

1.3   Facility Owners—Shall mean any person or entity that owns the Facility.

1.4   Parties—Industry and Carrier.

[Sections Intentionally Omitted]

12.   Binding Effect; Assignment

12.1   Binding Effect—This Agreement shall be binding upon, and inure to the benefit of, the Parties hereto and their respective successors and assigns.

12.2   Assignment—

(a)   Permitted Assignments. Either Carrier or Industry may assign or otherwise convey any of its rights, titles, interests, or obligations under this Agreement with the prior written consent of the other party hereto, which consent shall not be unreasonably withheld. Carrier hereby consents to the assignment by Industry or its successor or permitted assignee of any or all of Industry's rights, titles, interests, and obligations hereunder to

(i)   an affiliate whose net worth is at least $20,000,000;

(ii)   to any person, corporation, bank, trust company, association, or other business or governmental entity as security in connection with obtaining financing for the Facility; or

(iii)   any person, corporation, bank, trust company, association or other business or governmental entity in order to enforce any security assignment described in Subsection 12.2(b); or

(iv)   any entity which owns the Facility or any interest therein; or

(v)   any successor entity (whether by merger, by consolidation, or by sale of substantially all the assets).

(b)   **Assumption of Obligations.** Upon each permitted assignment described herein (other than in Section 12.2(b) above), the assignee of such party shall expressly assume in writing all of the obligations of such party hereunder. Industry and Carrier hereby agree that upon assignment of the Agreement to Facility Owners, Industry shall be released from all obligations under this Agreement. In such case, Industry's assignee shall be solely responsible for performance of Industry's obligations hereunder.

(c)   **Written Acknowledgment.** Upon request of either party, the other party shall acknowledge and consent in writing to any permitted assignment and the right of any permitted assignee to enforce this Agreement against such other party.

Signatures

17.1 INTRODUCTION

With a few exceptions,[1] creation of a contract requires neither a writing nor a signature.[2] Instead, contract formation requires offer, acceptance, consideration, and mutual assent to the agreement's essential terms.[3] But the drafter must make sure that the signature lines are correct if the parties want a written contract to memorialize their contract and intend that signatures evidence their agreement. If done improperly, the signatures could bind the wrong entity, make a corporate officer personally liable, or make the agreement effective only in part. Attention to detail is essential.

The formal name for the language introducing the signature blocks is the **testimonium clause**. This book refers to it as the **concluding paragraph**. The following is typical:

> In Witness Whereof, the parties have executed and delivered this Agreement as of the date hereof.

This chapter will first address the meaning of *executed* and *delivered* and then the benefits of a more contemporary concluding paragraph. It concludes with a discussion of e-signatures, the drafting of signature blocks, and a variety of issues related to signature pages.

17.2 EXECUTION AND DELIVERY

17.2.1 DEFINITIONS

Parties have repeatedly litigated the meanings of *executed* and *delivered* and whether both of these actions are necessary to create an enforceable contract. The case law is messy.

---

1. Among the exceptions are contracts subject to the statute of frauds. *See e.g.* N.M. Stat. § 55 2-201 (2003).

2. *See e.g. Schaller Tel. Co. v. Golden Sky Sys., Inc.*, 298 F.3d 736, 743 (8th Cir. 2002).

3. *See e.g. Fant v. Champion Aviation, Inc.*, 689 So. 2d 32, 37 (Ala. 1997).

Older, but not overruled, cases distinguish the verb *to execute* from the verb *to sign*. *To sign* means to affix one's name in one's own handwriting, while *to execute* is broader and connotes affixing a signature either in one's one handwriting or through a representative.[4] Other cases use the verbs synonymously.[5] Statutes can also be determinative. The Uniform Commercial Code provides that a signature includes the signing by a person and that person's authorized representative.[6]

In some instances, cases distinguish execution from delivery,[7] while others interpret execution broadly to include signing and delivery.[8] When the terms are differentiated, *delivery* means the exchange of signed copies of the agreement. That and the exchange of consideration are the final steps that consummate a transaction.

17.2.2 DELIVERY AND CONTRACT FORMATION

Delivery is not required for an agreement to be effective,[9] except for a few documents, such as deeds,[10] contracts under seal,[11] negotiable instruments,[12] and documents of title.[13] Nonetheless, if parties intend that delivery should be an element of formation, courts will effectuate that intent.[14] Similarly, if they intend that signing is sufficient, courts will effectuate that intent.[15]

Parties generally intend that the agreements to be signed at the closing of a sophisticated commercial transaction be both signed and delivered. These closings can be tumultuous, with negotiations and drafting continuing up until the last minute. Adding to the tumult, the parties must sign multiple copies of the dozens of documents needed to memorialize the business deal.[16] As a logistical matter, the parties cannot postpone signing the agreements until everything else is done. So, they begin to sign the agreements while they are nailing down the final business points. After each agreement is signed, it is placed in its own spot around the perimeter of a closing table or in a file.

As a closing is not certain until the parties successfully complete their negotiations, the signed agreements on the closing table must remain ineffective until the actual closing. To do this, delivery becomes an additional element of the agreements' formation, and delivery is postponed until the parties agree they are ready to close. Then, they exchange consideration and deliver the agreements. Although many transactions rely on this type of arrangement, it is almost never memorialized in writing. It is an unstated understanding.

---

4. *Wamesit Natl. Bank v. Merriam*, 96 A. 740, 741 (Me. 1916).

5. *Elliott v. Merchants' Bank & Trust Co.*, 132 P. 280, 281 (Cal. App. 2d Dist. 1913).

6. U.C.C. § 3-401, U.L.A. U.C.C. § 3-401 (2004).

7. *See Brown Bros. Lumber Co. v. Preston Mill Co.*, 145 P. 964, 966-967 (Wash. 1915).

8. *Hayes v. Ammon*, 85 N.Y.S. 607, 608 (N.Y. App. Div. 1st Dept. 1904).

9. *See Hunts Point Tomato Co., Inc. v. Roman Crest Fruit, Inc.*, 35 B.R. 939, 944-945 (Bankr. S.D.N.Y. 1983).

10. *See Herr v. Bard*, 50 A.2d 280, 281 (Pa. 1947).

11. *See Restatement (Second) of Contracts* § 95 (1981). Some states still recognize the vitality of a seal and its consequences, although most states have abolished seals or the distinction between sealed and unsealed agreements. See Eric Mills Holmes, *Corbin on Contracts*, vol. 3, § 10.18 (Joseph M. Perillo ed., rev. ed., West 1996).

12. U.C.C. § 3-201, U.L.A. U.C.C. § 3-201 (2004).

13. U.C.C. § 7-501, U.L.A. U.C.C. § 7-501 (2005).

14. *See Schwartz v. Greenberg*, 107 N.E.2d 65, 67 (N.Y. 1952).

15. *See Bohlen Indus. v. Flint Oil & Gas, Inc.*, 483 N.Y.S.2d 529, 530 (App. Div. 4th Dept. 1984).

16. In addition to the agreements, other documents need to be signed: for example, U.C.C. financing statements and closing certificates.

You can directly address the issue of intent in the contract by stating when the contract becomes effective: upon signing, or upon signing and delivery. Requiring both elements presents the parties with an additional hurdle to contract formation. Whether that will help or hurt your client is generally unfathomable because of the inability to see what future factual circumstances will create the issue. On balance, this author prefers to require delivery as an element of contract formation. People change their minds. Signing an agreement and putting it in a briefcase is different from handing a signed agreement to someone else.

If you decide to address the effective date through a contract provision, insert a declaration into the action sections stating when the agreement is effective. Do not rely on the dates listed below the signature lines or in a concluding paragraph[17] that states that the agreement is being executed and delivered as of a specific date.

As an alternative, some drafters include the effective date in the counterparts provision. They generally do this when they know that parties will be signing the agreement in counterparts. The usual options for effectiveness are *the date that the last party signs* or *on delivery of one signed counterpart from each party to the other parties*. If the contract is to be effective on the date that the last party signs the contract, insert a line for the signing date under each signature line. In addition, conform the concluding paragraph, so that it states that each party is signing on the date set forth under that party's signature.

> **FURNITURE BY FRANK, INC.**
>
> By: ___*Frank Rabb*___
> Frank Rabb, President
>
> Dated: ___4-13-20XX___

No matter which option is stated in the counterparts provision, include a declaration in the action sections that the Agreement is effective as provided in Section __ [the counterparts section]. It will help the reader find what may be an important provision. See Section 16.5.2 for a further discussion of counterparts.

17.3 THE CONCLUDING PARAGRAPH

As noted in Section 17.1, the concluding paragraph generally resembles the following:

> **Wrong**
>
> In Witness Whereof, the parties hereto have executed and delivered this Agreement as of the date hereof.

This language is, of course, replete with legalese and technically unnecessary. It is not, however, without purpose. It evidences that the parties have intentionally signed the agreement, and it reminds them that they have agreed to bind themselves.[18] A more contemporary version follows:

---

17. For a discussion of concluding paragraphs, see §17.3.

18. *See* Lon Fuller, *Consideration and Form,* 41 Colum. L. Rev. 799, 800 (1941).

> **Correct**
>
> To evidence the parties' agreement to this Agreement, they have executed and delivered it on the date set forth in the preamble.

This version retains both *executed* and *delivered* to reflect the historical distinction between the terms. It also echoes the traditional language that more senior lawyers are used to, perhaps making it easier to convince them of a change.

If you have more flexibility in the drafting of a contract, as an alternative to the preceding language, you could replace *executed* with the simpler and more contemporary *signed*. This continues to recognize the historical distinction between *executed* and *delivered* but further modernizes the concluding paragraph. Make this change, however, *only* if you change all of the contract's provisions that use *executed* or a form of it. For example, many contracts include a representation and warranty that a party has the power and authority to execute, deliver, and perform the agreement. Legal opinions may also need to be changed. Be careful. Not saying the same thing the same way invites litigation.[19]

The proposed concluding paragraph assumes that the parties wish to retain the historical distinction between *execution* and *delivery*. If they do not, use just *executed* or just *signed*. If you use *signed*, again, be sure to conform the contract's other provisions. Remember, however, that some case law does give *execute* a broad meaning that encompasses delivery.

The concluding paragraph also deals with the date of signing and delivery. The proposed language refers to execution and delivery *on* the date set forth in the preamble. If that date is an *as of* date,[20] draft the concluding paragraph as follows:

> To evidence the parties' agreement to this Agreement, they have executed and delivered it *on [insert date of actual execution], but as of the date set forth in the preamble.*

This language establishes for the record the actual date that the signing took place. This might be important for tax or other reasons.

17.4   DRAFTING THE SIGNATURE BLOCKS

Before drafting the signature blocks, make sure that you have the correct name of each party. Related parties often have similar names. For example, one party's name may be Web Design, Inc., and its corporate parent's name may be Web Designers Corp.—similar, but not the same. As the potential for mistakes is high, check the organizational documents of each party to confirm the details of each name, including any commas and where they go. Then confirm that the name in the preamble is the same as the name in the signature block.

Next, check an entity's organizational documents and bylaws to find out whether more than one signature is necessary. Sometimes two or more signatures may be

---

19. See §21.8.

20. See §6.2.2 for a discussion of *as of* dates; §8.4 for a discussion of effective dates in contracts for a term of years; and §16.10 and §17.5.2 for a discussion of effective dates with respect to contracts executed in counterparts.

required for a particular kind of contract, such as a loan, or if the contract involves more than a certain amount of money.

Finally, if an entity is signing the agreement, obtain an incumbency certificate—a document that states who has signing authority. It should include an original signature of each person with signing authority, so that you can compare the signature of the person signing the documents with the signature on the incumbency certificate. If the entity is a corporation, the corporate secretary should sign the certificate. In addition, an officer other than the corporate secretary needs to certify the portion of the incumbency certificate relating to the corporate secretary.

Signature blocks are typically placed on the right half of a page, one above the other if more than one person is signing. Some drafters precede each signature block with the role-related defined term for the party, although this is unnecessary. For example:

TENANT

Tanya Williams
Tanya Williams

LANDLORD

ROCHESTER REALTY CORP.

By: _James Tao_
James Tao, President

17.4.1 DRAFTING THE SIGNATURE BLOCK OF AN INDIVIDUAL

The signature line for an individual is easy to draft. It is a line with the individual's name typed directly under it. The individual then "signs on the dotted line."

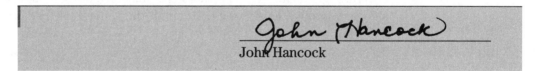
John Hancock
John Hancock

17.4.2 DRAFTING THE SIGNATURE BLOCK OF A CORPORATION

The signature block for a corporation must reflect that it acts through its officers. To do this, first put the name of the corporation on a separate line. Most drafters put the name in all capital letters; some also use a bold font. Both are stylistic. Four lines down, insert the line on which the officer will sign and precede it with _By_. Then, immediately beneath that line, put the officer's name and title.[21] Failure to draft the signature line this way could result in personal liability for the officer.

Example 1 shows what the signature block would look like if the drafter had all the information relating to the signatory at the time of drafting. Although that it is optimal, it is not always possible. Examples 2 and 3 show alternatives that you can

---

21. _See 780 L.L.C. v. DiPrima_, 611 N.W.2d 637, 644-645 (Neb. Ct. App. 2000).

use, depending upon what you know. If you draft the signature blocks as in Example 2 or 3, be certain that you fill in any blanks when the parties sign the agreement.

Example 1

SWEAT & TOIL, INC.

By: *Elizabeth N Workhorse*
Elizabeth N. Workhorse, Vice President

Example 2

SWEAT & TOIL, INC.

By: *Elizabeth N Workhorse*
Name: Elizabeth N. Workhorse
Title: Vice President

Example 3

SWEAT & TOIL, INC.

By: _____
Name:
Title:

17.4.3   DRAFTING THE SIGNATURE BLOCKS OF A GENERAL PARTNERSHIP, A LIMITED PARTNERSHIP, AND A LIMITED LIABILITY PARTNERSHIP

In the same way that a corporation's signature line must reflect that the corporation acts through its officers, a partnership's signature block must reflect that the partnership acts through its general partners. If the general partner is an individual, use the following format:

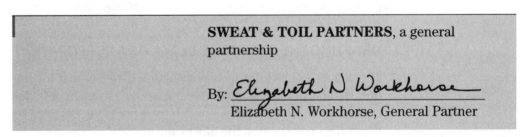

SWEAT & TOIL PARTNERS, a general partnership

By: *Elizabeth N Workhorse*
Elizabeth N. Workhorse, General Partner

If the general partner is a corporation, then you must add an additional layer to the signature block. The signature block must reflect that the partnership is acting through its general partner, a corporation, which is acting through its officer. Some drafters reflect the relative relationship between the partnership and the corporate partner by indenting the information with respect to the corporate officer as follows:

> **SWEAT & TOIL LP**, a limited partnership
> By: SWEAT INC., General Partner
>
> By: *Elizabeth N Workhorse*
> Elizabeth N. Workhorse, Vice President

Many personal service businesses, such as law firms and accounting firms, are organized as limited liability partnerships. A proper signature block for an LLP uses the following format:

> **SWEAT & TOIL LLP**, a limited liability partnership
>
> By: *Elizabeth N Workhorse*
> Elizabeth N. Workhorse, [General] Partner

Although LLPs are a kind of general partnership, a law firm's signature line may follow the signer's name with the title *partner* rather than *general partner.* In part, this is because many law firms are two-tier partnerships that do not want the outside world focusing on how they classify their partners.[22]

If the signature line uses *partner* rather than *general partner,* the other party to the contract relies upon the apparent authority of the person holding himself out as a partner. The cure for any concern regarding apparent authority is to ask for a copy of the partnership agreement and then to make sure that the partner signing is duly authorized to act on behalf of the partnership in that transaction. This capacity issue is usually more important in the context of commercial dealings with the LLP (e.g., bank loans, leases, and major commercial contracts) than in professional dealings with the LLP (e.g., opinions, pleadings, confidentiality agreements, and formal advice to clients).

17.4.4 DRAFTING THE SIGNATURE BLOCK OF A LLC

Limited liability companies may be managed by their members or by managers.[23] In each case, the signature block must reflect who manages the LLC.

> **SWEAT & TOIL, LLC**
>
> By: *Elizabeth N Workhorse*
> Elizabeth N. Workhorse, Member

---

22. In these partnerships, some partners' pecuniary interest in the firm is based wholly on a share of the profits. (These partners are what one ordinarily considers partners in a general partnership.) Other partners' pecuniary interest in the firm is only partially dependent upon profits. The rest is usually some form of guaranteed amount. These latter partners are authorized by the firm to hold themselves out as partners and are generally permitted to sign opinions and some agreements.

23. 6 Del. Code Ann. tit. 6, § 18-402 (Westlaw current through 75 Laws 2006, ch. 441).

SWEAT & TOIL, LLC

By: _Elizabeth N Workhorse_

Elizabeth N. Workhorse, Managing Director

17.5 MODE OF EXECUTION

Generally, most parties use a pen to sign an agreement, but anything that makes a mark and is identifiable to a party usually suffices. The following sections discuss e-signatures and execution in counterparts.

17.5.1 E-SIGNATURES

In the Internet age, lawyers are called upon to draft contracts that become legally binding electronically. These documents present a modern spin on the classic evidentiary problem of authentication. In today's world, what constitutes a valid **e-signature**, and what safeguards ensure its authenticity?

In the United States, enforceability of e-signatures is principally governed by two pieces of legislation: the federal Electronic Signatures in Global and National Commerce Act (the E-Sign Act),[24] and the Uniform Electronic Transactions Act (UETA),[25] a uniform state law adopted by almost all of the states as of this writing. In accordance with a provision of the E-Sign Act, UETA supersedes the E-Sign Act, but only if a state enacts the uniform law in the form recommended by the National Conference of Commissioners on Uniform State Laws.[26] Therefore, make sure you know which statutory framework governs.

UETA's stated purpose is "to remove barriers to electronic commerce by validating and effectuating electronic records and signatures."[27] It then defines an e-signature as "an electronic sound, symbol, or process attached to or logically associated with a record and executed or adopted by a person with the intent to sign the record."[28] Practically, e-signatures usually take the form of now-familiar electronic modes of confirmation, such as clicking on an *I Accept* button.

Internationally, different legislative bodies have developed their own laws, such as the European Union's Electronic Commerce Directive. In addition, the United Nations Commission on International Trade Law Working Group on Electronic Commerce has issued model legislation addressing electronic commerce and electronic signatures.

A detailed discussion of how to create e-signatures is beyond the scope of this book. If you need to create an electronic signature, be sure to research the law as it is evolving.

17.5.2 COUNTERPARTS

As discussed in Chapter 16, parties cannot always convene to sign an agreement. In these circumstances, lawyers often arrange for each party to sign a separate, dupli-

---

24. The Electronic Signatures in Global and National Commerce Act, 15 U.S.C.A. §§ 7001-7031 (Westlaw current through P.L. 109-363 (excluding P.L. 109-295, P.L. 109-304, P.L. 109-347, P.L. 109-351).

25. Unif. Electronics Transactions Act, §§ 1-21, U.L.A. Elec. Trans. § 1-21 (2002).

26. 15 U.S.C.A. § 7002(a).

27. Unif. Electronics Transactions Act, Prefatory Note, U.L.A. Elec. Trans., Prefatory Note.

28. *Id.* at § 2(8).

cate original—a counterpart. Once each party has signed its counterpart, the lawyer assembles them to produce a fully executed original counterpart agreement.

Parties also use counterparts to create multiple originals, so that each party to a transaction has its own fully executed original. To do this, each party signs as many counterparts as the number of parties. So, if there are eight parties, each party signs eight counterparts.

For a more detailed discussion of counterparts, see Chapter 16, Section 16.10.

17.5.3 STAND-ALONE SIGNATURE PAGES

Occasionally, drafters create signature pages without text from the agreement. Generally, they do this to resolve a logistical problem. It permits a party who cannot attend a closing to sign while the lawyers continue to draft the agreement. The party's lawyer then holds the signature pages until the closing and, at that time, appends them to the final version of the agreement.

While convenient, this practice involves risk. First, the parties may dispute whether the signed pages constituted execution and delivery of the contract or whether they were a mere logistical convenience.[29] Second, a drafter risks a malpractice claim. A client could allege that the lawyer had no authority to append the signature pages because it never would have assented to the final version of the agreement had it known and understood its terms. To prevent such a claim, send your client the final text by fax or e-mail, and get its approval of any last minute changes.

17.6 ANTIFRAUD MECHANISMS

As signatures can create an enforceable contract, their misuse can create a contract that at least one party did not intend. You can address this potential fraud in several ways.

Although stand-alone signature pages can be helpful logistically, they also create the possibility of fraud: A nefarious person could attach them to a different document.[30] If all the parties can attend a signing, format the agreement so that the signature lines are on the same page as the final provisions or at least begin on that page. If the signature lines naturally fall on a separate page, stop the text of the agreement about half way down the previous page, space down several lines and insert in bold letters "**INTENTIONALLY LEFT BLANK**" or draw an X through the blank space. Then, on the following page of the agreement, conclude the text of the agreement and add the signature lines.

As another antifraud mechanism, the parties should initial each interlineation. It should act as an estoppel, precluding a party from successfully claiming that it did not agree to the interlineation. In addition, have the parties initial each page of the agreement if a client worries that the other side might replace a page with one that included "nonagreed to" provisions. As initialing every page of a long agreement is onerous, reserve this procedure for the appropriate situations (e.g., separation agreements and settlement agreements with respect to contentious litigation).

Although initialing each page is not typical practice in significant commercial transactions in the United States, parties in some foreign jurisdictions almost always do it. Accordingly, be sure to check local custom and practice.

---

29. *See Midwest Mfg. Holding, L.L.C. v. Donnelly Corp.*, 1998 WL 59500 (N.D. Ill. Feb. 6, 1998).
30. *See Winston v. Mediafare Ent. Corp.*, 777 F.2d 78, 79-80, 83 (2d Cir. 1985).

17.7 INITIALING OTHER THAN AS AN ANTIFRAUD MECHANISM

Parties occasionally initial a contract not as an antifraud mechanism but to indicate that they have read and understood a provision. For example, a drafter sometimes requires a party to initial a jury waiver provision.[31] The lawyer can then use the initials as evidence that the waiver was knowing, voluntary, and intentional—the standard that courts insist upon before enforcing a waiver.

17.8 ACKNOWLEDGMENTS

An acknowledgment is a party's formal declaration before an authorized public official that it voluntarily executed an agreement.[32] In some states, it authenticates an agreement,[33] while in others it makes the agreement effective.[34] You need to use an acknowledgment only when a statute requires one, as in connection with real estate conveyances and mortgages. Because the laws with respect to acknowledgments differ from state to state, check the law in your jurisdiction. If an acknowledgment is required, it follows the signature lines. It may also be on a separate page attached to the agreement.

---

31. *See Coop. Fin. Assn. v. Garst*, 871 F. Supp. 1168, 1172, n. 2 (N.D. Iowa 1995).
32. *Estate of Burleson*, 210 S.E.2d 114, 114 (N.C. Ct. App. 1974).
33. *Webster Bank v. Flanagan*, 725 A.2d 975, 980 (Conn. App. Ct. 1999).
34. *Lewis v. Herrera*, 85 P. 245, 246 (Ariz. 1906).

EXERCISES

Exercise 17-1

Nathan Nocturne is Managing Director of Nocturne LLC, a manager-managed LLC. Nocturne LLC is the general partner of Nocturne Luminescence LP, which is in turn the general partner of Nitelite LP. Draft the signature line for Nitelite LP.

PART THREE

Drafting Clearly and Unambiguously

Legalese

18.1 INTRODUCTION

Legalese annoys almost anyone who reads contracts—whether client, lawyer, or judge. Obscure words and phrases, hailing from times past, clutter provisions and make them difficult to understand. Not surprisingly, commentators have disparaged legalese for centuries:

> Swift's acid phrase was "a peculiar Cant and Jargon of their own, that no other Mortal can understand." Bentham had a bag of phrases, applied with uncomplimentary impartiality: *law jargon, lawyers' cant, lawyers' language, flash language. . . .* With more or less politeness, [others have complained that lawyers are wordy]. "Words multiplied for the Purpose," "a vicious sea of verbiage," repetitious, verbose, prolix.[1]

Despite this harsh criticism, legalese remained the norm until 1975 when Citibank lawyers rewrote their consumer promissory note.[2] These lawyers did more than revise the bank's contracts. They reconceived how consumer contracts should be written. They began by eliminating legalese and provisions appropriate only for commercial contracts. In addition, they improved the contracts' appearances by using white space and easily readable fonts. They also turned full-page sentences into short, clear sentences and adopted a more informal tone, making the contracts less intimidating. Together, these changes resulted in a new style of contract drafting, dubbed **plain English**.

The benefits of plain English drafting are so apparent and so appealing that some states have statutorily mandated that plain English be used in consumer contracts.[3] No such laws have been passed with respect to sophisticated commercial contracts, but, over time, drafters have incorporated plain English concepts into their contracts.[4]

In this chapter and Chapters 19 and 20, you will learn how to replace legalese with ordinary words, format provisions to make complicated material easier to assimilate, and redraft long, dense sentences into shorter, simpler ones.

---

1. David Mellinkoff, *The Language of the Law* § 2, 3-4 and § 19, 24 (Little, Brown & Co. 1963) (emphasis in the original) (footnotes omitted).

2. *See* Carl Felsenfeld and Alan Siegel, *Writing Contracts in Plain English* 27-30 (West 1981).

3. *See, e.g.,* N.Y. G.O.L. § 5-702 (Westlaw current through L. 2006, ch. 646).

4. Federal regulations do, however, mandate the use of plain English principles in a prospectus. 17 C.F.R. § 230.421 (Westlaw current through October 19, 2006).

18.2 FORMAL AND ARCHAIC WORDS

Legalese creeps into contracts in several ways. One of the most common is the use of formal, archaic words, such as the following:[5]

> above (as an adjective)
> above-mentioned
> aforementioned
> aforesaid
> before-mentioned
> henceforth
> hereby
> herein
> hereof
> hereto
> hereinafter
> hereinbefore
> herewith
> said (as a substitute for "the," "that," or "those")
> same (as a substitute for "it," "he," "him," etc.)
> such (as a substitute for "the," "that," or "those")
> thereof
> therewith
> whatsoever
> whensoever
> wheresoever
> whereof
> whosoever
> within-named
> witnesseth

Some drafters complain that some of these terms are actually helpful and should be used. In fact, in almost all instances, acceptable alternatives are available.

Drafters often use *hereof, hereto,* and similar words to indicate the section, schedule or exhibit to which a provision is referring. To eliminate these words easily, include an interpretive provision either in the definition section or with the general provisions:

> **Internal References**. Unless otherwise stated, references to Sections, subsections, Schedules, and Exhibits are to Sections, subsections, Schedules, and Exhibits of this Agreement.

Hereby is also easily replaced. Replace it with the thing to which *hereby* is referring.

---

5. This list is based on a list from Reed Dickerson, *The Fundamentals of Legal Drafting* 207 (2d ed., Little, Brown & Co. 1986).

> **Wrong**
>
> **Waiver of Jury Trial**. Each party waives its right to a jury trial with respect to the transactions contemplated *hereby*.
>
> **Correct**
>
> **Waiver of Jury Trial**. Each party waives its right to a jury trial with respect to the transactions [contemplated by this Agreement] [that this Agreement contemplates].

The second bracketed phrase is preferable as it changes the phrase from the passive to the active voice.

Thereof can often be replaced with *its*. Alternatively, determine to what *thereof* refers and create a prepositional phrase beginning with *of* and ending with the thing to which *thereof* is referring:

> **Wrong**
>
> **Escrow Fund**. The Escrow Fund shall be held by the Escrow Agent under the Escrow Agreement pursuant to the terms *thereof*.
>
> **Correct**
>
> **Escrow Fund**. The Escrow Agent shall hold the Escrow Funds under the Escrow Agreement pursuant to its terms.
>
> **Better**
>
> **Escrow Fund**. The Escrow Agent shall hold the Escrow Funds pursuant to [the terms of the Escrow Agreement] [the Escrow Agreement's terms].

This redraft also changes the sentence from the passive to the active voice. Look also at this example of how to eliminate *thereof*:

> **Wrong**
>
> Without limiting the generality *thereof*. . .
>
> **Correct**
>
> Without limiting the generality of the preceding sentence. . .[6]

Said and *such* are pointing words. They refer to something previously stated. Replace them with *the, a, that,* or *those.*

---

6. Drafters use this phrase when they establish a rule in one sentence and then, in a subsequent sentence, want to list specific matters that come within the rule.

Wrong

> **Bonus**. With respect to each year of the Term, the Company shall pay the Executive a bonus equal to 10 percent of [*such*] [*said*] year's Net Profits, except that the Company is not obligated to pay [*such*] [*said*] bonus with respect to any year of the Term in which Net Profits are less than $1 million.

Correct

> **Bonus**. With respect to each year of the Term, the Company shall pay the Executive a bonus equal to 10 percent of *that* year's Net Profits, except that the Company is not obligated to pay *the* bonus with respect to any year of the Term in which Net Profits are less than $1 million.

18.3 COUPLETS AND TRIPLETS

Contracts are often replete with redundancies. A classic example is *null and void*. Drafters frequently fear paring down these couplets and triplets, terrified that any deletion will result in an unknown, disastrous substantive change. This fear is usually unreal.

The profusion of couplets and triplets reflects the evolution of the English language.[7] After the Normans invaded England in 1066, French slowly became the language used in English courts and contracts. It predominated from the mid-thirteenth century to the mid-fifteenth century. Not unexpectedly, the English came to resent the use of French and began once again to use English for legal matters. As the use of law French began to wane, English lawyers were faced with a recurring problem. When they went to translate a French legal term into an English legal term, they were often unsure whether the English word had the same connotation. The solution was obvious: Use both the French and the English word. For example, *free and clear* is actually a combination of the Old English word *free* and the French word *clair*. Here are a few other examples:[8]

• acknowledge and confess	Old English and Old French
• breaking and entering	Old English and French
• goods and chattel	Old English and Old French
• right, title, and interest	Old English, Old English, and French

Compounding this penchant for joining French and English synonyms was the English custom of joining synonyms, especially those that were alliterative and rhythmic:[9]

- to have and to hold
- aid and abet
- part and parcel
- rest, residue, and remainder

---

7. This discussion of the history of the English language is based on the materials in David Mellinkoff, *The Language of the Law* ch. 9 (Little, Brown & Co. 1963).

8. *Id.* at 121-122.

9. *Id.* at 42-46 and 120-122.

The bottom line is that most couplets and triplets reflect our linguistic heritage and not legal distinctions. Therefore, they should be pared down to one word—unless the drafter intends a substantive difference, as in the phrase *represent and warrant.*

The following is a list of word combinations that should not be used:[10]

all and every (use the term appropriate for the context)
any and all
alter or change
amend, modify, or change
bind and obligate
by and between
by and with
convey, transfer, and set over
covenant and agree
due and owing
each and all (use the term appropriate for the context)
each and every (use the term appropriate for the context)
final and conclusive
for and in behalf of
full force and effect
furnish and supply

kind and character
known and described as
made and entered into
means and includes
null and of no effect
null and void
over and above
perform and discharge
relieve and discharge
remise, release, and forever quitclaim (except in states where statutorily required)
sole and exclusive
suffer or permit
then and in that event
true and correct
type and kind
understood and agreed

18.4 PRETENTIOUS AND VERBOSE EXPRESSIONS

Look closely at the lists that follow. The words in the *Don't Use* column are either pretentious or verbose. Replace them, as appropriate, with the words in the *Use* column.[11]

Don't Use	Use
above	[refer to the specific provision]
attains the age of	becomes. . .years old
at the time	when
below	[refer to the specific provision]
by means of	by
by reason of	by, because of
cease	stop
commence	begin
consequence	result
contiguous to	next to
dated as of even date hereof	dated the date of this Agreement
does not operate to	does not
during such time as	during
during the course of	during

continued on next page >

10. This list is from Reed Dickerson, *The Fundamentals of Legal Drafting* 208 (2d ed., Little, Brown & Co. 1986).

11. These lists are derived from lists in Reed Dickerson, *The Fundamentals of Legal Drafting* 209-213 (2d ed., Little, Brown & Co. 1986).

Don't Use	Use
effectuate	carry out
endeavor (verb)	try
enter into a contract with	contract with
for the duration of	during
for the purpose of holding	to hold
for the reason that	because
forthwith	immediately
in case	if
in cases in which	when, where (use "whenever" or "wherever" only when needed to emphasize the exhaustive or recurring applicability of the rule)
in lieu of	instead of, in place of
inquire	ask
institute	begin, start
in the event that	if
is able to	can
is authorized	may
is binding upon	binds
is unable to	cannot
loan (as a verb)	lend
mutually agree	agree
necessitate	require
notwithstanding anything to the contrary in this Agreement	despite any other provision in this Agreement
notwithstanding the foregoing	despite the previous [sentence]
party of the first part	[the party's name]
prior to	before
provision of law	law
purchase (as a verb)	buy
State of Kansas	Kansas
suffer (in the sense of *permit*)	permit
sufficient number of	enough
until such time as	until
utilize, employ (in the sense of "use")	use

CHAPTER EIGHTEEN

EXERCISES

In each of the following exercises, mark up the provision to eliminate the legalese. In addition, fix any other drafting errors.

Exercise 18-1

The following provision is from a shareholders' agreement:

> For purposes hereof, "Cause" with respect to the termination of any Shareholder's employment has the meaning set forth in said Shareholder's employment agreement with the Company.

Exercise 18-2

> The term of this Agreement commences as of the date set forth in Section 8.6 hereof.

Exercise 18-3

> No later than 90 days after the end of each fiscal year, the Borrower shall provide the Bank a copy of the Borrower's year-end financial statements. Such financial statements shall be certified by the Borrower's chief financial officer to fairly present the financial condition of the Borrower.

Exercise 18-4

> Except as herein to the contrary provided, each party releases, remises, and forever discharges the other from any and all actions, suits, debts, claims, and obligations whatsoever, both in law and equity, that either of them ever had, now has, or may hereafter have, against the other by reason of any matter, cause, or thing to the date of the execution of this Agreement.[12]

---

12. This provision is based on a general release in Gary N. Skoloff, Richard H. Singer, Jr., and Ronald L. Brown, *Drafting Prenuptial Agreements* VII-61 (Aspen 2003).

Exercise 18-5

In the event of the failure of the Borrower aforesaid to comply with the terms of the aforementioned Note, the undersigned Guarantor waives notice of acceptance of this Guaranty, diligence, presentment, notice of dishonor, demand for payment, any and all notices of whatever kind or nature, and the exhaustion of legal remedies available to the holder of said Note.

Exercise 18-6

The Lessor leases to the Lessee, and the Lessee leases from the Lessor, all the machinery, equipment, and other property described in

(a) the schedule executed by the parties concurrently herewith; and

(b) any schedule hereafter executed by the parties hereto.

All said machinery, equipment, and other property described in all said schedules are hereinafter collectively called the "equipment," and all said schedules are hereinafter collectively called the "schedules."

Exercise 18-7

The Merger's consummation does not violate the Communications Act or the rules and regulations promulgated thereunder.

Clarity Through Format

19.1 INTRODUCTION

Imagine if this book had no page numbers, no paragraphs separating ideas, and no chapters—instead, from start to finish, it was all one long, continuous, dense block of words. Daunting—a nightmare to read. But the publisher has spent considerable money and effort to enhance the book's clarity through format. Many lawyers, however, expend little effort enhancing their contracts' clarity through format.

In the remainder of this chapter, you will learn formatting techniques that will improve the clarity of the contracts you draft.

19.2 SECTIONS AND SUBSECTIONS

One of the easiest ways of formatting a contract is to use sections and subsections. By using more but shorter sections, a contract becomes easier to read.

Look at the following provision from a joint venture agreement. It sets forth the procedure for appointing officers and indemnifies the officers.

Wrong

> **9.3 Officers of the Joint Venture.** The Managing Venturer shall appoint the chief executive officer, chief financial officer, and other officers of the Joint Venture. The officers are to perform those duties and have those responsibilities that the Managing Venturer assigns to them. The Non-Managing Venturer must approve the appointment and replacement of the chief executive officer and shall not unreasonably withhold or delay its approval. The Managing Venturer may appoint one or more officers of either Venturer to be an officer of the Joint Venture, but only if that officer intends to devote substantially full time to the Joint Venture. If that officer fails to devote substantially full time to the Joint Venture, the Managing Venturer shall terminate that officer's employment. The Managing Venturer may determine, in its sole discretion, the benefits to be offered to any officer appointed

continued on next page >

in accordance with this subsection. The Joint Venture shall indemnify and defend each officer of the Joint Venture against all claims, losses, damages and liabilities, including reasonable attorneys' fees, relating to any act or failure to act by that officer, but only if the officer's act or failure to act was in good faith and, in both cases, in a manner that officer reasonably believed to be in, or not opposed to, the Joint Venture's best interests; or if the officer relied upon the opinion or advice of competent legal counsel. Any indemnity under this Section is to be paid from the Joint Venture's assets, and no Venturer has any individual liability on account of the indemnity under this Section.

No doubt, this provision gave you MEGO—*mine eyes glaze over.* Truth be told, did you even finish the provision? Provisions drafted like this make it difficult, if not impossible, to carefully analyze and comment on a contract. What follows is the same provision, but formatted. No other changes have been made. It is now much easier to read because it has been broken down into multiple sections, each section separated from the next by white space, and each with a heading to signal its substance. It is still long and not as interesting as a Tom Clancy novel, but it is better.

Correct

9.3 The Joint Venture's Officers.

9.3.1 Appointment of Officers. The Managing Venturer shall appoint the chief executive officer, chief financial officer, and other officers of the Joint Venture. The officers are to perform those duties and have those responsibilities that the Managing Venturer assigns to them.

9.3.2 Approval of Chief Executive Officer's Appointment. The Non-Managing Venturer must approve the appointment and replacement of the chief executive officer and shall not unreasonably withhold or delay its approval.

9.3.3 Appointment of a Venturer's Officer. The Managing Venturer may appoint one or more officers of either Venturer to be an officer of the Joint Venture, but only if that officer intends to devote substantially full time to the Joint Venture. If that officer fails to devote substantially full time to the Joint Venture, the Managing Venturer shall terminate that officer's employment. The Managing Venturer may determine, in its sole discretion, the benefits to be offered to any officer appointed in accordance with this subsection.

9.3.4 Indemnity of Officers.

9.3.4.1 The Indemnity. The Joint Venture shall indemnify and defend each officer of the Joint Venture against all claims, losses, damages and liabilities, including reasonable attorneys' fees, relating to any act or failure to act by that officer, but only if

9.3.4.1.1 the officer's act or failure to act was in good faith and, in both cases, in a manner that officer reasonably believed to be in, or not opposed to, the Joint Venture's best interests; or

> **9.3.4.1.2** the officer relied upon the opinion or advice of competent legal counsel.

9.3.5 **Source of Funds**. Any indemnity under this Section is to be paid from the Joint Venture's assets, and no Venturer has any individual liability on account of the indemnity under this Section.

19.3 TABULATION

19.3.1 EXPLANATION OF TABULATION AND WHEN TO USE IT

Look again at Section 9.3.4.1 in the provision in the previous section of this chapter. In that section, a long sentence is broken down into two subsections, each of which is grammatically independent of the other, although they are conceptually related—which is why they are subsections of the same section. Subsections can also be used to join two or more related sentences. This reduces the length of the contract and aids the reader by showing how the sentences are related. In both cases, each subsection is indented and separated from the other by white space. This formatting is known as **tabulation**. It takes its name from the use of the keyboard *Tab* key that is used to indent the tabulated material.

The following example shows how tabulation can be used to join two related sentences. The sentences are from a noncompetition agreement.

Version 1—Untabulated Sentences

Noncompetition. For a one-year period after the Term, the Executive shall not employ any person who was an employee during the Term. In addition, during that period, the Executive shall not interfere with the relationship between the Company and any of its employees.

Version 2—Tabulated Sentence

Noncompetition. For a one-year period after the Term, the Executive

(a) shall not employ any person who was an employee during the Term; and

(b) shall not interfere with the relationship between the Company and any of its employees.

Here is a long, untabulated sentence from a construction contract[1] and the same sentence, but tabulated.

---

1. This provision is based on a provision from Stanley P. Sklar & Gregory R. Andre, *Design and Construction Contracts*, in *Commercial Contracts: Strategies for Drafting and Negotiating*, vol. 2, ch. 29, 29-85 (Morton Moskin, ed., Aspen 2006).

Version 1—Untabulated Sentence

Contractor's Right to Terminate. The Contractor may terminate this Agreement for cause if work is stopped for 30 days or more through no fault of the Contractor or because of a court order, if the Architect unjustifiably refuses to approve a payment request, or if the Owner refuses to pay a payment request that the Architect approved.

Version 2—Tabulated Sentence

Contractor's Right to Terminate. The Contractor may terminate this Agreement for cause if

(a) work stops for 30 days or more through no fault of the Contractor or because of a court order;

(b) the Architect unjustifiably refuses to approve a payment request; or

(c) the Owner refuses to pay a payment request that the Architect approved.

Deciding when to use tabulation requires a judgment call. If you are deciding whether to join two or more sentences through tabulation, the subject matter of the sentences should be related. For example, if both sentences relate to the rights of a bank on its borrower's default, tabulation is probably appropriate. If the subject matter is not related, create separate sections and insert them in the appropriate place in the contract. If you are deciding whether to break down one sentence into a tabulated format, any sentence with a compound or a series is a candidate. For these purposes, a **compound** refers to two items in a sentence joined by *and* or *or.* A **series** refers to three or more items in a sentence joined by *and* or *or.*

The length and complexity of the sentence are also considerations. Any sentence that is already a candidate becomes a stronger candidate if it is three lines or longer—the so-called **three-line rule**. The ultimate deciding factor is whether tabulation makes it easier for a reader to assimilate the information.

Beware of tabulation overkill. Tabulating a sentence just because it has a compound or series is inappropriate. The following sentence should not have been tabulated; it is short and easy to understand in its untabulated state.

Version 1—Untabulated Sentence

Corporate Power and Authority. The Licensor has full corporate power and authority to execute, deliver, and perform this Agreement.

Version 2—Tabulated Sentence

Corporate Power and Authority The Licensor has full corporate power and authority to

(a) execute,

(b) deliver, and

(c) perform

this Agreement.

19.3.2 HOW TO TABULATE

The guidelines for tabulating are relatively simple.

General Tabulation Guideline 1

Use parallel drafting to construct the tabulated sentence.[2] To do this, draft the language that introduces the tabulated subsections and the language of each subsection so that the introductory language creates a coherent, grammatically correct sentence when joined with each subsection. In addition, if the sentence continues after the tabulated subsections, then that concluding language must also create coherent sentences when joined with the introductory language and each subsection.

Look at the tabulated sentence that follows. It uses parallel drafting. To test this, join together the introductory language with each of the subsections and create two separate sentences. Do not change any of the words. The sentence is from an agreement between a company and a software developer.[3]

Version 1—Tabulated Sentence

    Developer's Representations and Warranties. The Developer represents and warrants that the Software

      (a) is unique and original;

      (b) is clear of any claims or encumbrances; and

      (c) does not infringe upon the rights of any third parties.

Version 2—Untabulated Sentences

- The Developer represents and warrants that the Software is unique and original.
- The Developer represents and warrants that the Software is clear of any claims or encumbrances.
- The Developer represents and warrants that the Software does not infringe upon the rights of any third parties.

The following sentence also uses parallel drafting. Test it the same way. Remember: Join the introductory language, a subsection, and the concluding language.

Version 1—Tabulated Sentence

Employee Sanctions. Each time an Employee

      (a) is absent from work for an unexcused reason,

      (b) takes a coffee break longer than 15 minutes, or

---

2. *See* §23.11 for a discussion of parallel drafting as craftsmanship.

3. The provision is from Gregory J. Battersby & Charles W. Grimes, *License Agreements: Forms and Checklists* 3-10 (Aspen 2003).

(c) smokes a cigarette in a designated nonsmoking area,

that Employee loses one vacation day.

Version 2—Untabulated Sentences

■ Each time an Employee is absent from work for an unexcused reason, that Employee loses one vacation day.

■ Each time an Employee takes a coffee break longer than 15 minutes, that Employee loses one vacation day.

■ Each time an Employee smokes a cigarette in a designated nonsmoking area, that Employee loses one vacation day.

The following tabulated sentence does not use parallel drafting. Why?

Version 1—Wrong

Landlord's Rights upon Termination. If this Lease terminates because of a default by the Tenant, the Landlord may

(a) immediately enter the Premises by any legal proceeding; and

(b) has the right to evict any person on the Premises.

The problem is with subsection (b). When joined with the introductory language, it creates an incoherent sentence.

Version 1—Wrong

Landlord's Rights upon Termination. If this Lease terminates because of a default of the Tenant, the Landlord *may has the right to* evict any person on the Premises.

To fix the tabulated sentence so that it uses parallel drafting and makes sense, drop the words *has the right to* from subsection (b).

Version 2—Correct

Landlord's Rights upon Termination. If this Lease terminates because of a default of the Tenant, the Landlord may

(a) immediately enter the Premises by any legal proceeding; and

(b) evict any person on the Premises.

General Tabulation Guideline 2

The grammar of the sentence determines its punctuation. The application of this guideline breaks down tabulated sentences into two formats:

1. The **sentence format** in which each tabulated subsection creates a full sentence when joined with the introductory language.
2. The **list format** in which the introductory language is a complete sentence and each tabulated subsection is part of an enumerated list. A strong clue that a list format is appropriate is if the introductory language includes some form of the word *follow*.

Each tabulated sentence that was used as an example in the discussion of Guideline 1 used the sentence format. The following example of tabulation uses the list format.

> **Events of Default**. Each of the following events is an Event of Default:
>
> (a) The Borrower has failed to pay interest when due.
>
> (b) The Borrower has failed to pay principal when due.
>
> (c) Any representation or warranty of the Borrower set forth in Article 3 was false when made.
>
> (d) The Borrower has breached any covenant in Article 4.

Sometimes, with a little editing, a provision can be drafted using either the list format or the sentence format. Look at the following provision. It is drafted using the sentence format.

> **Version 1—Sentence Format**
>
> **Employee Sanctions.** Each time an Employee
>
> (a) is absent from work for an unexcused reason,
>
> (b) takes a coffee break longer than 15 minutes, or
>
> (c) smokes a cigarette in a designated non-smoking area,
>
> that Employee loses one vacation day.

This sentence can also be drafted using the list format.

> **Version 2—List Format**
>
> **Employee Sanctions.** An Employee loses one vacation day each time the Employee does any one of the following:
>
> (a) The Employee is absent from work for an unexcused reason.
>
> (b) The Employee takes a coffee break longer than 15 minutes.
>
> (c) The Employee smokes a cigarette in a designated non-smoking area.

In this instance, the list format is preferable because it is easier to read. The sentence format has introductory language, subsections, and concluding language—three separate components that must be joined before the reader can take in all the information. But the list format has only two components, the introductory language and the enumerated items in the subsections. The less work that a reader has to do, the easier it is for the reader to assimilate the information.

Now for the specific guidelines applicable for each of the formats. If a sentence is to be tabulated using the sentence format, the following guidelines apply. Examples follow the guidelines.

Guidelines for Sentence Format Tabulation

1. *Include in the introductory language all the words common to each tabulated subsection, with four exceptions.* First, do not separate an article (e.g., *the, a,* or *an*) from the noun it precedes. Doing so makes the reading of the tabulated subsections awkward. The second exception is stylistic and not followed by all drafters: If the tabulated subsections are a series of negative covenants introduced with *shall not,* put *shall not* with each subsection, rather than in the introductory language. This change acts as a reading aid, reminding the reader that the provision prohibits the acts in each of the subsections. The third exception is also stylistic, and its use depends upon the specific provision. Sometimes a provision is easier to read if the *to* of an infinitive is kept together with the present form of its verb (e.g., to see, to walk, to draft). But this is not always the case. The final exception requires a drafter to analyze how the tabulation affects a provision's substance: If putting all the common words in the introductory language affects a subsection's substantive meaning, then repeat the words in each subsection.

2. *Punctuate the introductory language as you would if the sentence were untabulated.* If you would not put punctuation after the last word in the introductory language if the sentence were untabulated, then do not use any punctuation when the sentence is tabulated. But if the introductory language would end with a comma if the sentence was untabulated, then that comma should remain when the sentence is tabulated.

3. *Begin each tabulated subsection with a lowercase letter.*

4. *If no concluding language is common to each subsection, do the following:*

    (a) *End each tabulated subsection (other than the last) with a semicolon.* This way, each tabulated subsection results in a complete sentence when combined with the introductory language. A semicolon signals the conclusion of each such sentence.

    (b) *Insert* and *or* or *as appropriate after the semicolon of the next to last subsection.*

    (c) *End the last tabulated subsection with a period.*

5. *If concluding language is common to each subsection, do the following:*

    (a) *End each tabulated subsection with whatever punctuation would be used (if any) if the sentence were untabulated.* To determine the punctuation, join the introductory language with each subsection to see if any punctuation is appropriate.

    (b) *Insert* and *or* or *as appropriate after the punctuation of the next to last subsection.*

    (c) *Begin the concluding language at the left margin so that it has the same margin as the introductory language.*

    (d) *End the concluding language with a period.*

As noted earlier, a tabulated sentence with both introductory and concluding language is more difficult for a reader to take in than a tabulated sentence that has only introductory material. If your initial draft includes concluding language, try to redraft the provision to eliminate it.

Example 1 is a classic example of a provision tabulated using the sentence format: All the common words are in the introductory language; that language does not conclude with any punctuation; and each subsection, other than the last, ends with a semicolon.

> **Example 1**
>
> **Architect's Obligations**. The Architect shall
>
> (a) consult with the Owner at least once a week; and
>
> (b) deliver to the Owner an accounting of expenses incurred each month in connection with the Project, no later than five business days after the end of each month.

Example 2 is a variation on Example 1. It differs in that the introductory language ends with a comma because that language is a prepositional phrase that would end with a comma if the sentence were untabulated. In addition, although *the* is common to both subsections, it is omitted from the introductory language as articles should be kept with their nouns.

> **Example 2**
>
> ***Force Majeure* Event**. If a *Force Majeure* Event occurs,
>
> (a) the Contractor shall advise the Owner of its existence as soon as possible after its occurrence; and
>
> (b) the Contractor's obligation to perform is suspended until the *Force Majeure* Event ends.

In Example 3, unlike Examples 1 and 2, the provision has both introductory and concluding language. Although no punctuation ends the first subsection (because there would be none if the sentence were untabulated), a comma ends the second subsection because the sentence would have a comma if it were untabulated.

> **Example 3[4]**
>
> **Type of Film**. The Photographer shall use
>
> (a) black and white film or
>
> (b) color film,
>
> as requested by the Client.

Example 4 revises Example 3 and demonstrates how a tabulated provision with concluding language can be drafted to eliminate that language.

---

4. This provision is sufficiently simple that it would not be tabulated in an agreement. It is used here to demonstrate how to tabulate this type of provision.

> **Example 4**
>
> **Type of Film**. The Photographer shall comply with the Client's request to use
>
> (a) black and white film or
>
> (b) color film.

If a sentence is to be tabulated using the list format, the following guidelines apply:

Guidelines for List Format Tabulation

1. *Draft the introductory language so that it includes the phrase* as follows *or* the following *or otherwise incorporates that concept and end it with a colon.*

2. *Draft the introductory language, if appropriate, so that it signals whether the items in each subsection are cumulative or alternative.*

3. *Begin each subsection with a capital letter and end it with a period.*

4. *Do not insert* and *or* or *after the next to last subsection.*

The following examples show how introductory language can signal whether the items in each subsection are cumulative or alternative.

> **Example 1**
>
> **Termination**. The Company may terminate the Executive for any one or more of the following reasons:
>
> **Example 2**
>
> **Notice**. When the Company sends a notice, it shall use one of the following methods, but it may choose which one:
>
> **Example 3**
>
> **Duties**. During the Term, the Executive shall perform all of the following duties:

19.3.3 MULTILEVEL TABULATION

Some sentences are sufficiently complex that they require more than one level of tabulation. If so, follow the numbering system for the sublevels as set out in Section 19.4. The following termination provision is in both untabulated and tabulated formats.[5] The tabulated version has two levels of subsections.

> **Version 1—Untabulated Sentence**
>
> **9.1 Termination**. Either party may terminate this if the other party breaches any covenant in this Agreement, but only if that breach remains

---

5. A real termination provision would include other termination events.

uncured for 30 days after written notice of it to the breaching party, and as a result of that breach, the nonbreaching party cannot substantially realize the benefits that it would have realized from this Agreement absent that breach, or if the other party files a petition for bankruptcy in any court pursuant to any statute of the United States or any state.

Version 2—Tabulated Sentence

9.1 Termination. Either party may terminate this Agreement if the other party

   (a) breaches any covenant in this Agreement, but only if

   (i) that breach remains uncured for 30 days after written notice of it to the breaching party and

   (ii) as a result of that breach, the nonbreaching party cannot substantially realize the benefits that it would have realized from this Agreement absent that breach;

or

   (b) files a petition for bankruptcy in any court pursuant to any statute of the United States or any state.

When drafting a multilevel tabulated sentence, indent each subordinate level five more spaces than the previous level so that the reader can see the subordinate relationship between one level and the next. In establishing the relative relationship between the levels, make each section or subsection parallel with its subordinate subsection to prevent a garbled or ambiguous provision. Finally, note the placement of the bolded *or*. Although some drafters would place this *or* after the semicolon in subsection (ii), others put it on its own line at the same indentation of the subsections that it joins. This placement is preferable because it provides another visual clue as to how the levels relate to each other. Of course, the *or* would not be bolded in an actual contract.

19.3.4 DOUBLE TABULATION

Double tabulation occurs in a sentence that has two or more independent sets of subsections at the same level. In the following representation and warranty from a loan agreement, the double tabulation occurs because subsections (i) and (ii) are not subsections of either subsection (a) or (b). Subsections (i) and (ii) are not labeled (c) and (d) because that would mislead the reader. It would suggest that the introductory language that applies to subsections (a) and (b) also applies to subsections (i) and (ii).

Leases. Schedule 3.11 lists each lease to which the Borrower is a party. With respect to each lease listed in **Schedule 3.11**,

   (a) no default has occurred and is continuing, and

   (b) no event has occurred and is continuing which, with notice or lapse of time or both, would constitute a default on the part of the Borrower,

except for those defaults and events of default, if any, that

> (i) are not material in character, amount, or extent; and
>
> (ii) do not, severally or in the aggregate, materially detract from the value of or materially interfere with the present use of the property subject to the lease.

Although you may use double tabulation if necessary, it is unwieldy. You can usually avoid it by breaking down the sentence into two or more sentences, as has been done in the following redraft.

> **Leases.**
>
> (a) **Borrower's Leases**. Schedule 3.11(A) lists each lease to which the Borrower is a party.
>
> (b) **Defaults**. Schedule 3.11(B) lists each lease to which the Borrower is a party and where either
>
> > (i) a default has occurred and is continuing; or
> >
> > (ii) an event has occurred and is continuing which, with notice or lapse of time or both, would constitute a default by the Borrower.
>
> (c) **Materiality of Defaults**. The defaults and events listed in Schedule 3.11(B)
>
> > (i) are not material in character, amount, or extent; and
> >
> > (ii) do not, severally or in the aggregate, materially detract from the value or materially interfere with the present use of the property subject to the lease.

19.4 NUMBERING SYSTEMS

In the same way that a brief or a memorandum can be organized into main ideas and subsidiary ideas, so too can a contract. To reflect the different organizational levels in a contract, use one of the common numbering systems. Most firms have templates for numbering systems, as do most word-processing applications. The key is to use an outline format, white space, and indentations to clarify the relative relationship between the provisions. Three common numbering systems follow:

Numbering System 1

Article 1 — How to Format a Contract

One of the most common numbering systems divides an agreement into articles, each article comprising a set of related provisions. The Asset Purchase Agreement in Appendix A uses this numbering system. So, for example, Article 3 sets forth the Seller's representations and warranties, and Article 4 sets forth the Buyer's representations and warranties.

Each article number and its title are bolded and centered. Although many drafters number the articles using roman numerals, Arabic numerals are easier for a reader.

1.1 Sections. Each article is broken down into sections and then subsections. Each section number has a heading, and both are in bold. A period follows the heading. The word *Section* should not precede a section's number, although many lawyers do include it. They feel that the slightly longer bolded heading helps the reader find a specific section. Drafters using a more contemporary style usually omit *Section.* The provision is in the regular font.

    (a) **Subsections.** The formatting of subsections resembles the formatting of sections. If a subsection includes one or more sentences, it should have its own heading as should every other subsection at that level. But if the subsections are part of a tabulation,

        (i) do not use a heading; and

        (ii) follow the punctuation guidelines for tabulation stated in §19.3.2.

    (b) **Indentation of Subsections.** All subsections at the same level should be indented relative to the indentation of the section or subsection that precedes it. This visually shows the reader the logical relationship between the contract's parts.

    (c) **More on Subsections.** In the same way an outline must have a subsection 2 if it has a subsection 1, a contract must have at least two subsections at each level.

1.2 More on Numbering System 1. If additional levels of subsections are required beyond the first level, those subsections should adhere to the following numbering system:

    (a)

        (i)

        (ii)

            (A)

            (B)

                (1)

                (2)

    (b)

Numbering System 2

1. How to Format a Contract. This level is the equivalent of an Article in Numbering System 1.

    1.1 Using Numbering System 2. The guidelines with respect to headings and fonts are the same for both formats. Only the numbering differs. It adheres to the following system:

    1.2

        1.2.1

        1.2.2

            1.2.2.1

            1.2.2.2

    1.3 Why Some Drafters Use this Numbering System. Some drafters prefer this numbering system because of its precision. Specifically, it helps a reader who flips through a contract looking for a particular provision. Rather than a page having merely a series of subsection referents (for example, (c) and (d)), each referent tells the reader a provision's location relative to the contract's other provisions.

    1.4 Variation. Some drafters modify this numbering system by using lettered and numbered subsections after the third level. After this level, the referents become long and harder to follow.

        1.4.1

            (a)

                (i)

Numbering System 3

1.   **Short Contracts.** Some contracts are relatively short and do not require articles. For these contracts, the provisions can be set up as a series of numbered sections, each section with a bolded heading. If subsections are required, they should adhere to the following numbering system:

    (a)   Some drafters refer to provisions using this numbering system as *paragraphs* and *subparagraphs,* perfectly acceptable alternative nomenclature.

        (i)

        (ii)

            (A)

            (B)

                (1)

                (2)

    (b)

2.   **Second Section.**

Contract provisions in this book use all three numbering systems.

19.5 HEADINGS

Integral to any numbering scheme are the headings that identify to the reader the substance of the provision. Readers often flip through contracts looking for a specific provision. Headings that accurately relate a provision's substance facilitate a reader's review.

When choosing a heading, take care that it accurately describes the provision's contents. Although many contracts include a general provision that states that headings do not affect the contract's construction or interpretation, relying on that provision results in sloppy drafting.

Headings are sometimes too short. Look at the following provision from an agreement between a publisher and a photographer.

> **Too Short**
>
> **Copies.** Upon publication of the Book, the Publisher shall provide the Photographer with five free copies of the Book.

Although the heading *Copies* is descriptive, it could be more so. By changing the name to *Free Copies,* just one more word, the heading becomes more informative.

> **Better**
>
> **Free Copies.** Upon publication of the Book, the Publisher shall provide the Artist with five free copies of the Book.

Headings, of course, can also be too long, trying to encapsulate too much of a provision. If to be accurate the heading must list more than two topics, divide the provision into two or more sections.

19.6 TABLE OF CONTENTS

A table of contents is particularly handy in long contracts. It permits a reader to find a specific provision quickly.

Most sophisticated word-processing applications can automatically create a table of contents if you use its numbering system.

CHAPTER NINETEEN

EXERCISES

All of the following Exercises are available on the *Drafting Contracts* Website.

Exercise 19-1

Mark up the following provision to indicate how you would tabulate it. Do not change anything else.

6.1 Audit by Licensor. With respect to each Royalty Period, the Licensor may cause an independent accounting firm to audit or review all the Licensee's books and records and to issue a report pertaining to the Royalties earned in that Royalty Period. The Licensor shall give the Licensee reasonable prior written notice of the audit or review. The Licensee shall make its books and records available to the Licensor during normal business hours. If the Licensor wants to object to the Licensee's determination of Royalties for a Royalty Period, it must deliver to the Licensee a statement describing its objections not later than 60 days after the Licensor receives the applicable report obtained. Each party shall use reasonable efforts to resolve the Licensor's objections. If the parties do not resolve all objections on or before the 30th day after the Licensee received the statement of the Licensor's objections, the parties shall promptly submit those objections for resolution to an independent accounting firm acceptable to both parties. If the parties cannot agree upon an independent accounting firm, the parties shall select a "big-four" accounting firm by lot. Each party may eliminate one firm by objecting to it in writing. The determination of the independent accounting firm selected in accordance with this provision is conclusive and binding upon the parties. The following provisions apply with respect to each audit or review pursuant to this Section 6.1: If an audit or review as finally determined pursuant to this Section 6.1 determines that the Licensee has underpaid Royalties for a Reporting Period, the Licensee shall promptly pay to the Licensor the amount equal to the Royalties owing *minus* the Royalties paid *plus* interest of 10 percent per year on that amount, accruing from and including the date on which that amount was due to, but excluding, the date on which that

amount is paid. If an audit or review as finally determined pursuant to this Section 6.1 determines

that the Licensee has overpaid Royalties for a Reporting Period, the Licensor shall promptly pay to

the Licensee the amount equal to the Royalties paid *minus* the Royalties owing. With respect to each

audit and review conducted in accordance with this Section 6.1, the Licensor shall pay the fees of the

independent accounting firm that conducted that audit or review and the fees of any other indepen-

dent accounting firm selected in accordance with this Section 6.1. Despite the immediately preceding

sentence, if the audit or review, as finally determined, determines that the Royalties for the applicable

Reporting Period are understated by 2 percent or more, then the Licensee shall pay the fees of the

independent accounting firm that audited or reviewed the Licensee's books and records and the fees

of any other independent accounting firm selected in accordance with this Section 6.1.

Exercise 19-2

Tabulate each of the following provisions, and correct any drafting errors.

Termination of Agreement. Upon the termination or expiration of this Franchise Agreement,

the Franchisee shall immediately cease to operate the Franchised Business. The Franchisee further

covenants that it will no longer represent to the public that it is a franchisee of the Franchisor.[6]

Limitations upon Dividends. etc. No dividend or other distribution or payment shall be

declared, paid, or made by the Seller in respect of shares of its capital stock. No purchase, redemp-

tion, or other acquisition shall be made, directly or indirectly, by the Seller of any outstanding shares

of its capital stock.

Use of Premises. The Tenant shall use and occupy the Premises for the purposes of a sand-

wich café, and the Tenant's use of the space will be for the sale of quality food for consumption on or

---

6. This provision is based on a provision from Andrew J. Sherman, *Franchise Agreements,* in *Commercial Contracts: Strategies for Drafting and Negotiating,* vol. 2, ch. 21, 21-58 (Morton Moskin ed., Aspen
2006).

off the Premises or for take-out or for delivery, for the operation of catering services and for the sale of

nonalcoholic beverages for consumption on or off the Premises or for take-out or delivery.

Exercise 19-3

Mark up the following provision to correct any drafting errors.

Covenants of the Borrower. From and after the Effective Date and through the end of the

Lending Term, the Borrower hereby agrees to

    (a)   provide the Lender with fiscal year-end financial statements no later than 60 days after the

          end of each fiscal year; and

    (b)   the insurance currently in place will continue throughout the term of the Agreement.

Exercise 19-4

Tabulate the following provision from a settlement agreement, and correct any drafting errors. In addition, determine what substantive changes you would recommend
to a client making these representations and warranties.[7]

Each of the Parties warrants and represents for itself that each has been represented by legal

counsel of their own choice in the negotiation and joint preparation of this Agreement, has received

advice from legal counsel in connection with this Agreement and is fully aware of this Agreement's

provisions and legal effect, that all agreements and understandings between the Parties are embod-

ied and expressed in this Agreement, and that each of the Parties enters into this Agreement freely,

without coercion, and based on each of the Parties' own judgment and not in reliance upon any

representations or promises made by any of the other Parties, apart from those expressly set forth in

this Agreement.

---

7. This provision is excerpted from CD Form 7, *Settlement Agreement with Detailed Provisions Deal-ing with Potential Claims-by-Non-Settling Entities,* in *Settlements Agreements in Commercial Dis-putes: Negotiating, Drafting & Enforcement,* vol. 1 (Richard A. Rosen, ed., Aspen 2003).

Clarity Through Sentence Structure

20.1 INTRODUCTION

Chapter 19 examined how an agreement's formatting can affect its clarity. In this chapter, we examine how an individual sentence's organization can affect its clarity.

20.2 SHORT SENTENCES

In Chapter 19, you learned one aspect of **the three-line rule**: Any sentence longer than three lines is a good candidate for tabulation if it includes a compound or a series. A variation on the three-line rule is that any sentence longer than three lines is also a candidate for being recast as two or more sentences. As with tabulation, the shorter sentences facilitate a reader's assimilation of a sentence's substance.

The following sentence comes from a lease. Compare it to the corrected version. Note how much easier the latter is to read.

Wrong

Termination upon Fire or Casualty. If a fire or other casualty destroys the Building, the Landlord may terminate the Lease by notifying the Tenant in writing, and then, all Base Rent and Additional Rent due under this Lease ceases as of the date of the casualty, and the Tenant shall remove its trade fixtures and personal property from the Premises no later than 35 calendar days after it receives the Landlord's termination notice, whereupon both parties are released from all further obligations under this Lease, except for any obligations previously incurred.

Correct

Termination upon Fire or Casualty. If a fire or other casualty destroys the Building, the Landlord may terminate the Lease by notifying the Tenant in writing. In that event, all Base Rent and Additional Rent due under this Lease ceases as of the date of the casualty. The Tenant shall remove its trade fixtures and personal property from the Premises no later than 35 calendar

---

> days after it receives the Landlord's termination notice. Upon completion of that removal, both parties are released from all further obligations under this Lease, except for any obligations previously incurred.

20.3 SENTENCE CORE

20.3.1 KEEP THE CORE TOGETHER

Every sentence has core words: the subject, verb, and object. These words convey a sentence's critical information. In the sentence, *Bob ate a sandwich, Bob* is the subject, *ate* is the verb, and *sandwich* is the object. A writer could expand the sentence by telling the reader the kind of sandwich and when Bob ate it, but the core words have conveyed the sentence's essence.

To facilitate a reader's understanding of a sentence, keep the core words next to each other. If they are separated, a reader must work harder to synthesize a sentence's information. This is especially so when the subject is separated from the verb. Instead of reading all the core information at once, a reader must put the core information on hold while wading through the noncore information. By the time the reader reaches the remainder of the core words, she may have lost the thread of the sentence.

In the provision that follows, underscore the core words of the sentence. Notice how the *if* clause inserted in the middle of the core words interrupts the sentence's flow.

Wrong

Revised Architectural Plans. The Architect shall, if the Owner agrees to pay the Architect's additional fee pursuant to Section 2.2, revise the Final Plans for the house.

This sentence can easily be revised either by beginning or ending the sentence with the *if* clause. Ending the sentence with the *if* clause is preferable because of its length.

Correct

Revised Architectural Plans. If the Owner agrees to pay the Architect's additional fee pursuant to Section 2.2, the Architect shall revise the Final Plans for the house.

Better

Revised Architectural Plans. The Architect shall revise the Final Plans for the house, if the Owner agrees to pay the Architect's additional fee pursuant to Section 2.2.

20.3.2 REDUCE THE NUMBER OF WORDS PRECEDING THE CORE WORDS

A sentence's core words should be as close to the beginning of a sentence as possible. If they are not, the reader becomes overburdened with the ancillary information that precedes them. By reducing the number of words preceding the core words, a reader can more readily absorb all the information in the sentence.

Drafters sometimes have problems adhering to this rule because they begin a sentence with a long introductory clause that precedes the sentence's core words. For example:

Wrong

Bankruptcy. If a party makes a general assignment of all or substantially all of its assets for the benefit of creditors, or applies for, consents to, or acquiesces in, the appointment of a receiver, trustee, custodian, or liquidator for its business or all or substantially all of its assets, the other party may immediately terminate this Agreement by sending written notice.

In the preceding provision, the sequence of clauses makes logical sense because it establishes an *if/then* relationship. If *x* condition exists, then *y* consequence follows. The sequence reflects the temporal order in which the events must occur. But because the core information comes so late in the sentence, a reader will have difficulty assimilating the sentence's information. The remedy is to flip the clauses' sequence.

Correct

Bankruptcy. A party may immediately terminate this Agreement upon written notice if the other party makes a general assignment of all or substantially all of its assets for the benefit of creditors, or applies for, consents to, or acquiesces in, the appointment of a receiver, trustee, custodian, or liquidator for its business or all or substantially all of its assets.

This provision becomes even clearer when the rearranged sentence structure is tabulated.

Better

Bankruptcy. A party may immediately terminate this Agreement upon written notice if the other party

(a) makes a general assignment of all or substantially all of its assets for the benefit of creditors; or

(b) applies for, consents to, or acquiesces in, the appointment of a receiver, trustee, custodian, or liquidator for its business or all or substantially all of its assets.

20.4 SHORT BEFORE LONG

20.4.1 PUT SHORT PHRASES BEFORE LONG PHRASES

Often a drafter may choose the order in which two or more phrases appear in a sentence. Generally, you should put the short phrase first. Again, this helps the reader assimilate information by reducing what must be remembered before the second phrase appears. Read the two versions of the following sentence and notice where the italicized language appears in each:

> **Version 1**
>
> **Maintenance of the Building**. The Landlord shall maintain the Building's Common Areas, including lobbies, stairs, elevators, corridors, and restrooms, the windows in the Building, the mechanical, plumbing, and electrical equipment serving the Building, and the structure of the Building *in reasonably good order and condition*.[1]
>
> **Version 2**
>
> **Maintenance of the Building**. The Landlord shall maintain *in reasonably good order and condition* the Building's Common Areas, including lobbies, stairs, elevators, corridors, and restrooms, the windows in the Building, the mechanical, plumbing, and electrical equipment serving the Building, and the structure of the Building.

While either version is grammatically correct, the latter version is preferable. In its new location in Version 2, the italicized language is easy to assimilate and does not impede the assimilation of the other information in the sentence.

The sentence can be further improved by tabulating it.

> **Version 3**
>
> **Maintenance of the Building**. The Landlord shall maintain *in reasonably good order and condition*
>
>   (a) the Building's Common Areas, including lobbies, stairs, elevators, corridors, and restrooms;
>
>   (b) the windows in the Building;
>
>   (c) the mechanical, plumbing, and electrical equipment serving the Building; and
>
>   (d) the structure of the Building.

20.4.2 PUT THE SHORT EQUIVALENT AS THE SUBJECT IN A DECLARATION

Some declarations are drafted as if the verb is a mathematical equal sign, making the language before and after it equivalents. Definitions are an example: "**Alphabet**" means the letters "a" through "z." Thus, *alphabet* equals *the letters "a" through "z."* If this type of sentence occurs outside of the definition section, putting the shorter equivalent before the verb generally facilitates a reader's comprehension.

---

1. This provision is based on a provision from Mark A. Senn, *Commercial Real Estate Leases: Preparation, Negotiation, and Forms* 17-4 (3d ed., Aspen 2004).

Version 1

    Exclusive Remedy. After the Closing, a party's sole remedy with respect to any claim relating to this Agreement and the Transaction Documents, including torts, is the indemnity pursuant to Article 10.

Version 2

    Exclusive Remedy. After the Closing, the indemnity pursuant to Article 10 is a party's sole remedy with respect to any claim relating to this Agreement and the Transaction Documents, including torts.

CHAPTER TWENTY

EXERCISES

Mark up the provision in each exercise to create clarity through sentence structure. If appropriate, make other drafting changes that improve the provision. All of the following exercises are available on the *Drafting Contracts* Website.

Exercise 20-1

"Agreement" means this Manufacturing Agreement, as it may from time to time be amended.

Exercise 20-2

Updating of Disclosure Schedules. The Seller shall, in the event of any omission or misstatement in the Disclosure Schedules, or any change in the underlying facts with respect to any matter disclosed in the Disclosure Schedules, amend and update the Disclosure Schedules so that they are at all times true and correct.

Exercise 20-3

Reproduction of Documents. This Agreement and all documents relating thereto, including, without limitation, (a) consents, waivers, and modifications that may hereafter be executed, (b) documents received by the Lender on the Closing Date (except the Notes themselves), and (c) financial statements, certificates, and other information previously or hereafter furnished to the Lender, may be reproduced by the Lender by any photographic, photostatic, microfilm or other process and the Lender may destroy any original document so reproduced.

Exercise 20-4

Share Ownership. Upon the transfer of the certificate or certificates evidencing the Shares owned by each Seller to the Buyer, each Seller will have transferred good and valid title to the Shares to the Buyer, free and clear of all Liens.

Exercise 20-5

Increase to Contract Price. If the Contractor is required to pay or bear the burden of any new federal, state, or local tax, or of any rate increase of an existing tax (except a tax on net profits) taking effect after May 30, 20XX, the Contract Price increases by the amount of the new tax or the increased tax resulting from the rate increase.[2]

Exercise 20-6

Set-off.[3] In addition to any rights and remedies of the Bank provided by law, the Bank shall have the right, without prior notice to the Company, any such notice being expressly waived by the Company to the extent permitted by applicable law, upon the filing of a petition under any of the provisions of the federal bankruptcy act or amendments thereto, by or against; the making of an assignment for the benefit of creditors by; the application for the appointment, or the appointment, of any receiver of, or of any of the property of; the issuance of any execution against any of the property of; the issuance of a subpoena or order, in supplementary proceedings, against or with respect to any of the property of or the issuance of a warrant of attachment against any of the property of; the Company, to set-off and apply against any indebtedness, whether matured or unmatured, of the Company to the Bank, any amount owing from the Bank to the Company, at or at any time after, the happening of any of the above-mentioned events, and the aforesaid right of set-off may be exercised by the Bank against the Company or against any trustee in bankruptcy, debtor in possession, assignee for the benefit of creditors, receiver or execution, judgment or attachment creditor of the Company, or

---

2. This provision is based on a provision in Glower W. Jones, *Alternative Clauses to Standard Construction Contracts* 455 (2d ed., Aspen 1998).

3. This provision is from a bank loan agreement. It describes when a bank has a **set-off right.** It provides that if a borrower owes money to the bank and has money on deposit with the bank, the bank may use the money on deposit to reduce the principal amount of the loan. For example, if a borrower owes a bank $10,000 and has $3,000 on deposit with the bank, the bank may *set off* the $3,000 against the $10,000 and reduce the borrower's outstanding principal to $7,000.

against anyone else claiming through or against the Company or such trustee in bankruptcy, debtor

in possession, assignee for the benefit of creditors, receiver, or execution, judgment or attachment

creditor, notwithstanding the fact that such right of set-off shall not have been exercised by the Bank

prior to the making, filing or issuance, or service upon the Bank of, or of notice of, any such petition;

assignment for the benefit of creditors; appointment or application for the appointment of a receiver;

or issuance or execution of a subpoena, order or warrant.

Ambiguity

21.1 INTRODUCTION

Ambiguity can be expensive. If parties dispute the meaning of a provision, they must either renegotiate it or litigate. In either event, clients pay attorneys' fees and bear the cost of time not spent on more productive matters. In this context, the old adage that an ounce of prevention is worth a pound of cure was never more true. You should derive little solace from canons of interpretation that may resolve an ambiguity. Those canons are most useful when parties are disputing a provision's meaning, but your job is to draft to preclude that dispute. In the remainder of this chapter, you will learn about common causes of ambiguity and how to prevent them.

21.2 AMBIGUITY AND VAGUENESS

21.2.1 DEFINITION OF AMBIGUITY

An ambiguity arises when a provision can be interpreted in two or more mutually exclusive ways. Imagine a contract between a Canadian manufacturer of ski equipment and a United States retailer that provides for payment of $10,000 upon the retailer's receipt of the merchandise. But what kind of dollars? United States or Canadian? This type of ambiguity, which arises because a word has multiple dictionary meanings, is known as **semantic** ambiguity.[1]

The two other types of ambiguity are **syntactic** and **contextual** ambiguity. Syntactic ambiguity occurs when it is unclear what a word or phrase refers to or modifies. In the following example, it is unclear whether each Seller is obligated to sell its Shares to the Buyer, or whether the Sellers are obligated to sell their jointly owned Shares to the Buyer.

> **Sale of Shares**. The Sellers shall sell their Shares to the Buyer.

---

1. Not all words that have multiple dictionary meanings create ambiguities. Some words necessarily reveal their meaning in context. "Examples of these multipurpose words abound: 'If the bear escapes, the owner shall bear the cost.'" Reed Dickerson, *Materials on Legal Drafting* 55 (West 1981). These words are known as *homonyms*.

Contextual ambiguity occurs when two provisions are inconsistent. The two provisions can be in the same or different agreements. The following example is more obvious than most ambiguities, but demonstrates the point:

> **Provision 1**
>
> **Tenant's Obligations.** The Tenant shall maintain the entire Building.
>
> **Provision 2**
>
> **Landlord's Obligations.** The Landlord shall maintain the lobby of the Building.

In the long run, it does not matter whether you can name the three types of ambiguity. What matters is developing a sensitivity to ambiguities, so that you do not draft them, and so that you can recognize them.

21.2.2   VAGUENESS DISTINGUISHED FROM AMBIGUITY

Vagueness is not the same as ambiguity. A word or a phrase is vague if its meaning varies depending upon the context or if its parameters are not plainly delineated. For example, *reasonable* is vague. What is reasonable in one context may be wholly unreasonable in another. *Blue* is also vague. It could be anything from a pale, robin's egg blue to midnight blue. One blue shades into the next.[2]

In his contract drafting treatise, Reed Dickerson distinguishes ambiguity from vagueness:

> Language can be ambiguous without being vague. If in a mortgage, for example, it is not clear whether the word "he" in a particular provision refers to the mortgagor or the mortgagee, the reference is ambiguous without being in the slightest degree vague or imprecise. Conversely, language can be vague without being ambiguous. An example is the written word "red."[3]

Vagueness is neither inherently good nor bad. It depends on what concept best expresses the parties' agreement and on what best protects your client or advances his interests. Assume that you represent a senior executive in the negotiation of his employment agreement with a large, privately held company. The company's first draft of the employment agreement states that it will lend the executive "$500,000 at 3.5 percent per year for the purchase of a house in Manhattan." *House* is problematic. It is too specific. Manhattan has very few houses. It has cooperatives, condominiums, townhouses, and lofts. While *house* might be perfectly appropriate in most parts of the country, in Manhattan, a more vague, more inclusive term such as *residence* or *home* is more appropriate.

21.3   AMBIGUITIES ARISING FROM SENTENCE STRUCTURE

21.3.1   MODIFIERS OF ITEMS IN A COMPOUND OR SERIES

Whenever a modifier precedes or follows a compound or a series, an ambiguity may be created. The issue is whether the qualifier modifies each item in the compound or series or only the closest item.

---

2. See Reed Dickerson, *The Fundamentals of Legal Drafting* 39 n. 3 (2d ed., Little, Brown & Co. 1986).

3. *Id.* at 40.

In the following representation and warranty, the qualifier, *to the knowledge of the Borrower,* follows *pending or threatened.*

> **Wrong**
>
> **Litigation**. No litigation against the Borrower is pending or threatened to the knowledge of the Borrower.

This provision's meaning differs significantly depending upon whether the knowledge qualifier modifies both *pending* and *threatened* or only *threatened.* Usually, a bank insists that a borrower give a flat representation and warranty with respect to pending litigation. It will argue that the borrower should know what litigation is pending and if it does not know, then it should perform the necessary due diligence so that it can give a flat representation and warranty. In contrast, a bank will usually accept a knowledge qualifier with respect to threatened litigation. It recognizes that a borrower might not know that a third party has been injured and is threatening to sue. To make the representation and warranty reflect the agreed-upon risk allocation, *to the knowledge of the Borrower* needs to be moved so that it follows the *or* and immediately precedes *threatened.*

> **Correct**
>
> **Litigation**. No litigation against the Borrower is pending or, to the knowledge of the Borrower, threatened.

21.3.2 THE MEANINGS OF *AND* AND *OR*

Grade school grammatical rules often state as axioms that *and* is **conjunctive** and inclusive, meaning that it joins two or more things, and that *or* is **disjunctive**, meaning that it establishes alternatives between two or more things. Look at the following two sentences:

> **Conjunctive *and***
>
> Fred likes cake *and* cookies.
>
> **Disjunctive *or***
>
> Samantha may have a dog *or* a cat as a pet.

The first sentence uses *and* in its traditional role, conjunctively, to signal that Fred likes both cake and cookies. The second sentence uses *or* in its traditional role, disjunctively, to signal that Samantha may have only one pet, either a dog or a cat. This is the exclusive use of *or.* But contract drafting is rarely so simple. Both *and* and *or* can be used in ways that your sixth-grade English teacher never mentioned.

In addition to being used disjunctively, *or* can signal that matters that seem to be exclusive alternatives may also exist concurrently, creating an additional alternative. Look at the following provision:

> **Wrong**
>
> **Default**. If the Landlord makes a misrepresentation or breaches a covenant, then the Tenant may pursue all remedies to which it is entitled under the law.

If *or* is only disjunctive, this provision permits the Tenant to sue for damages if the Landlord either makes a misrepresentation or breaches a covenant. But what happens if the Landlord does both? Has the Tenant lost all its remedies? That makes no business sense. Instead, the parties probably intended that if the Landlord both misrepresented and breached, the Tenant would have two causes of actions and that it could pursue all its remedies. This interpretation results in three alternatives, instead of two, that will give rise to remedies: a misrepresentation, a breach of covenant, and a misrepresentation and a breach of covenant. The following revised provisions reflect the parties' actual intent:

> **Correct—Version 1**
>
> **Default**. If the Landlord makes a misrepresentation, breaches a covenant, or makes a misrepresentation and breaches a covenant, then the Tenant may pursue all remedies to which it is entitled under the law.
>
> **Correct—Version 2**
>
> **Default**. The Tenant may pursue all remedies to which it is entitled under the law if the Landlord does one or both of the following:
>
> (a) Makes a misrepresentation.
>
> (b) Breaches a covenant.

Which of the "Correct" provisions do you prefer? Why?

This use of *or* is known as the **inclusive** use. Some contracts include an interpretive provision that any use of *or* is inclusive rather than exclusive. As contract provisions do use *or* in its exclusive sense, such an interpretive provision could wreak havoc within an agreement. Adding the phrase, *unless the context otherwise requires*, renders the interpretive provision a nullity. One side can always contend that the context otherwise requires. Instead, scrutinize each use of *or* and draft the provision so it says what you intend. One easy way to indicate the exclusive sense of *or* is to use *either* in conjunction with *or*.

> **Purchase Price Payment**. The Buyer shall pay the Seller *either* $8 million in immediately available funds on the Closing Date *or* $10 million in immediately available funds on the third anniversary of the Closing Date.

Although *and* is often used conjunctively, it can have the same connotation as the inclusive *or*. In the following example, both provisions permit the Contractor to use employees, subcontractors, or both employees and subcontractors to paint the house.

> **Version 1**
>
> **Painters**. The Contractor may use its employees or subcontractors to paint the House.
>
> **Version 2**
>
> **Painters**. The Contractor may use its employees and subcontractors to paint the House.

Because *and* and *or* have alternative meanings, look carefully at each use of these words to determine whether it creates an ambiguity.

21.3.3 MULTIPLE ADJECTIVES

An ambiguity can arise if two or more adjectives or adjectival phrases modify the same noun. For example, the phrase *charitable and educational institutions* is ambiguous.[4]

> **Original**
>
> **Identity of Donee**. The Trust may donate funds only to charitable and educational institutions.

The issue is how the two adjectives, *charitable* and *educational,* relate to each other and to the noun *institutions.* The phrase may contemplate institutions that are both charitable and educational. If so, then the adjectives are cumulative, the typical interpretation of a string of adjectives modifying a noun.

> **Revision 1**
>
> **Identity of Donee**. The Trust may donate funds only to an institution that is both charitable and educational.

Alternatively, however, the phrase could contemplate two types of institutions: charitable institutions and educational institutions.

> **Revision 2**
>
> **Identity of Donee**. The Trust may donate funds only to an institution that is either charitable or educational.

21.3.4 *AND* AND *OR* IN THE SAME SENTENCE

When *and* and *or* appear in the same sentence to join items in a series, their joint presence almost always creates an ambiguity. To demonstrate how the ambiguity arises, we will work with the following provision:

---

4. This example is from Reed Dickerson, *The Fundamentals of Legal Drafting* 110 (2d ed., Little, Brown & Co. 1986).

> **Wrong**
>
> **Registration for Litigation Clinic.** A student may register for the litigation clinic only if that student has taken evidence or advanced civil procedure and is a third-year student.

This sentence has three standards: the taking of evidence, the taking of advanced civil procedure, and being a third-year law student. The ambiguity stems from the different ways in which the standards can be combined. Looking at the alternatives as mathematical symbols can be helpful.

- A = the taking of evidence
- B = the taking of advanced civil procedure
- C = being a third-year student

Using the letter equivalents, the provision, as drafted, can be restated as follows:

- A or B and C

Now, using parentheses to establish the relationship between the letter equivalents, here are the two possibilities:

> **Version 1**
>
> (A or B) and C = the student must have taken either evidence or advanced civil procedure and, in addition, must be a third-year student
>
> **Version 2**
>
> A or (B and C) = the student must have taken evidence, or, as an alternative, must have taken advanced civil procedure and must be a third-year student

Tabulation easily cures an ambiguity arising from *and* and *or* appearing in the same sentence by showing the relative relationship between the sentence's parts.

> **Correct—Version 1**
>
> **Registration for Litigation Clinic.** A student may register for the litigation clinic only if that student
>
> (a) has taken either evidence or advanced civil procedure
>
> and
>
> (b) is a third-year student.[5]

---

5. An alternative redraft is the following:

Only third-year students who have taken either evidence or advanced civil procedure may register for the litigation clinic.

Some readers may find this version more difficult to understand because of the long *who* clause that separates *students* from *may*.

> **Correct—Version 2**
>
> **Registration for Litigation Clinic.** A student may register for the litigation clinic only if that student
>
> (a) has taken evidence
>
>   or
>
> (b) has taken advanced civil procedure and is a third-year student.

21.3.5 SENTENCE ENDING WITH A *BECAUSE* CLAUSE

Sentences that end with a *because* clause are often ambiguous. As explained by Reed Dickerson:

> A terminal "because" clause is often ambiguous in that it is not clear whether the clause applies to the entire statement or merely to the phrase immediately preceding. For example, in the sentence, "The union may not rescind the contract because of hardship," it may not be clear whether the draftsman intends to say, "The union may not rescind the contract, because to do so would cause hardship," or "The union may not rescind the contract, using hardship as the justification."[6]

When faced with such an ambiguity, redraft the sentence to clarify the intent.

21.3.6 SUCCESSIVE PREPOSITIONAL PHRASES

Ambiguity can occur when one prepositional phrase immediately succeeds another. In such a case, the provision generally does not indicate whether the second prepositional phrase modifies only the immediately preceding prepositional phrase or the preceding prepositional phrase and that which came before it. For example, the following sentence is ambiguous in the absence of any other context. Specifically, does the second prepositional phrase, *in New York,* modify *cooperative apartment* or *owner of a cooperative apartment?* Once you know the answer, you can easily rewrite the provision.

> **Wrong**
>
> **Entitlement to Tax Rebates.** Every owner of a cooperative apartment in New York is entitled to a tax rebate.
>
> **Correct—Version 1**
>
> **Entitlement to Tax Rebates.** Every owner of a cooperative apartment *that* is in New York is entitled to a tax rebate.
>
> **Correct—Version 2**
>
> **Entitlement to Tax Rebates.** Every owner of a cooperative apartment *who* is in New York is entitled to a tax rebate.

---

6. Reed Dickerson, *The Fundamentals of Legal Drafting* 103 (2d ed., Little, Brown & Co. 1986).

Although the redraft cured the ambiguity caused by the successive prepositional phrases, a second ambiguity remains: the use of *New York*. That could refer to New York State, New York City (which includes its five boroughs), or Manhattan (one of the five boroughs).

21.4   DATES, TIME, AND AGE

Drafters regularly cause ambiguities by the ways in which they express dates, age, and time. A modicum of care can banish these ambiguities from an agreement.

21.4.1   DATES

21.4.1.1   The Problems

Misuse of prepositions causes many of the ambiguities with respect to dates. Common problem prepositions are *by, within, between, from,* and *until.* Here are some examples. Section 21.4.1.2 sets out correct revisions of each of the following provisions.

> **Provision 1—by [a stated date]**
>
> **Samples**. The Manufacturer shall submit a sample *by* November 15, 20XX.

This use of *by* raises the issue of whether November 14 or November 15 is the last day on which the Manufacturer may submit the sample.

> **Provision 2—within [x days of]**
>
> **Notice to the EPA**. The Buyer shall notify the Environmental Protection Agency of the sale *within* 30 days of the Closing.

Here, it is unclear whether the 30 days precedes or follows the Closing, or both. In addition, it is unclear whether the 30 days includes the day of the Closing.

> **Provision 3—between [date 1] and [date 2]**
>
> **Tender of Bids**. A potential buyer may tender bids for the Target *between* November 1, 20XX and November 15, 20XX.

The ambiguity is whether the dates are bookends surrounding the dates on which a party may tender bids, or whether the dates are also dates on which a party may tender bids.

> **Provision 4—from [date 1] until [date 2]**
>
> **Tender of Bids**. A potential buyer may tender bids for the Target *from* November 1, 20XX *until* November 15, 20XX.

This provision creates the same ambiguity as does *between:* Are the stated dates also dates on which a party may tender bids, or are they bookends?

21.4.1.2 The Cures

To prevent ambiguities in provisions with dates, state the beginning and ending dates and, if appropriate, specify the time on each date. As an alternative, use one of the following:

- Before
- On or before
- After
- On or after
- No later than

> **Provision 1, Corrected—by [a stated date]**
>
> **Samples**. The Manufacturer shall submit a sample
>
> - *no later than* November 15, 20XX.
> - *on or before* November 15, 20XX.
> - *before* November 16, 20XX.

Although each of the three alternatives cures the ambiguity, clients often prefer the first and second alternatives as they state the last permissible date for submission, the date a client will circle in red on its calendar. The third alternative, however, requires a client to determine (albeit rather easily) the deadline.

> **Provision 2, Corrected—within [x days of]**
>
> **Notice to the EPA**. The Buyer shall notify the Environmental Protection Agency of the sale
>
> - *no later than* 30 days before the Closing.
> - *no later than* 30 days after the Closing.

Determining which alternative to include in the contract requires a review of the statute and knowing the business deal. In either alternative, the 30-day period excludes the day of the Closing.

> **Provision 3, Corrected—between [date 1] and [date 2]**
>
> **Tender of Bids**. A potential buyer may tender bids for the Target *beginning on* November 1, 20XX at 9:00 a.m. and *ending on* November 15, 20XX at 5:00 p.m.

The inclusion of the time on each of the two days avoids any issues as to how early or late in the day a potential buyer may tender a bid.

> **Provision 4, Corrected—from [date 1] until [date 2]**
>
> **Tender of Bids**. A potential buyer may tender bids for the Target *beginning on* November 1, 20XX at 9:00 a.m. and *ending on* November 15, 20XX at 5:00 p.m.

As *from/until* creates the same ambiguities as does *between,* the same cure works.

21.4.2 TIME

Time ambiguities fall into two broad categories: the measurement of a time period and the statement of the time of day.

21.4.2.1 Measurement of Time Periods

Parties often need to refer to time periods—for example, the length of a loan or the number of days' notice to be given. The best alternative is to use exact dates. But precedents sometimes try to limit the number of blanks to be filled in by expressing time periods in words. To avoid any ambiguity when doing so, follow these rules:

When measuring years:

- Use the concept of an anniversary date.
- Refer to calendar years only to refer to the period from and including January 1 through December 31 of the same year.
- Check the ramifications of leap years.
- Confirm that a future date is a Business Day by using a perpetual calendar or provide that the event must occur on the next Business Day.

For example:

> **Version 1**
>
> **Due Date**. The Note is due on May 6, 20XX.
>
> **Version 2**
>
> **Due Date**. The Note is due on the day immediately preceding the fifth anniversary of its issuance, except if that day is not a Business Day, then it is due on the next Business Day.

When measuring months, determine which of the following possibilities the parties intend and draft accordingly:

- Calendar months
- 30-day periods
- The period beginning on a specific date and ending on the day in the next month which is one day earlier than the day in the starting month (March 18, 20XX through April 17, 20XX)

Also consider whether changing the reference from a number of months to a number of days clarifies an ambiguity or makes the provision easier to draft. Here are some examples:

> **Version 1**
>
> **Term**. The term of this Lease is *six calendar months*. If the parties sign this Lease on the first day of a calendar month, then the term begins on that

date, and the month in which the Lease is signed is the first calendar month. If the parties do not sign this Lease on the first day of a calendar month, then the term begins on the first day of the next calendar month, which is then the first calendar month of the term. In either event, the term ends at 5:00 p.m. on the last day of the sixth calendar month of the term.

Version 2

Term. The term of this Lease is *six months*. The first day of the term is the date that the parties sign this Lease. If that date is

(a) the first day of a calendar month, the term ends at 5:00 p.m. on the last day of the sixth calendar month of the term; and

(b) not the first day of a calendar month, the term ends at 5:00 p.m. in the sixth month following the month in which the parties signed this Lease, on the day of the month that precedes the day of the month on which the term began.

Version 3

Term. The term of this Lease is 180 days, beginning on the date that the parties sign this Lease and ending at 5:00 p.m. on the 180th day.

Version 4

Term. The term of this Lease begins on March 14, 20XX and ends on September 13, 20XX.

When measuring weeks, determine which one of the following possibilities the parties intend:

- The seven-day period beginning on Sunday and ending on Saturday.
- The seven-day period beginning on a specific day and ending one day before the same day in the following week (Wednesday through Tuesday)
- The five-day period beginning on Monday and ending on Friday

Also, think through the effect of holidays, and consider whether changing the reference from a number of weeks to a number of days clarifies an ambiguity or makes the provision easier to draft. Compare the following provisions:

Version 1

Beginning of Production. The Manufacturer shall begin production of the Item no later than two weeks after the Retailer approves the Item. The two-week period begins on the day after the Manufacturer's receipt of the Retailer's approval and ends at 5:00 p.m. on the 14th day, including weekends and holidays.

Version 2

Beginning of Production. The Manufacturer shall begin production of the Item no later than 5:00 p.m. on the 14th day after the Manufacturer's receipt of the Retailer's approval. The 14-day period includes weekends and holidays.

When measuring days, determine the following:

- Which is the first day and which is the last
- Whether days should be limited to business days
- Whether a time of day should be specified

In making these determinations, parties often rely on interpretive provisions and definitions. For example, when a mathematical formula includes the number of days in a time period, an interpretive provision can prevent disputes by resolving what are the first and last days of the period. The following provision is from a credit agreement.

> **Number of Days in an Interest Period**. When calculating the amount of interest owed, the number of days as to which interest accrues includes the first day of a period but excludes the last day of that period.

Similarly, to avoid disputes as to whether weekends and holidays are part of a time period, parties often define *business day* to distinguish it from other days. These definitions usually use local bank holidays as their starting point because a bank holiday in Hawaii might not be a bank holiday in Nebraska.

> *Definition*
>
> **"Business Day"** means a day other than a Saturday, Sunday or other day on which commercial banks in [insert location] are authorized or required by law to close.
>
> *Provisions*
>
> **Version 1**
>
> **Response to Notice of Arbitration**. If a party gives the other party a Notice of Arbitration, the other party shall respond no later than *five days* after the date of its receipt of the Notice of Arbitration.
>
> **Version 2**
>
> **Response to Notice of Arbitration**. If a party gives the other party a Notice of Arbitration, the other party shall respond no later than *five Business Days* after the date of its receipt of the Notice of Arbitration.

If a time period keys off the date of a notice's receipt, many parties include the following two interpretive provisions in the notice section of the general provisions:

> **Date of Receipt**. If a party receives a notice on a day that is not a Business Day or after 5:00 p.m. on a Business Day, it is deemed received at 9:00 a.m. on the next Business Day.
>
> **Rejection or Nondelivery**. If a party rejects a notice, or the notice cannot otherwise be delivered in accordance with this Agreement, then the notice is deemed received upon its rejection or the inability to deliver it.

21.4.2.2 Time of Day

When stating the time of day as of when something should be determined, state whether it is a.m. or p.m. Do not use 12:00 a.m. or 12:00 p.m. as they can be ambiguous.[7] To deal with what day midnight belongs to, write either 11:59 p.m. or 12:01 a.m. If the two minute differential matters (which it generally does not), write 11:59:59 p.m. or 12:00:01 a.m.

21.4.3 AGE

When referring to a person's age,

- state the age as of which a right begins; or
- refer to the *celebration* of a particular birthday.

> **Authority of Officers.** Only a corporate officer who is 21 or older may bind a party.

21.5 USING *IF/THEN* FORMULATIONS TO DRAFT CONDITIONS

When drafting a condition using an *if/then* formulation, an ambiguity can be created if the *if* clause includes a time or date.

> **Wrong**
>
> **Additional Air-conditioning.** If the Landlord provides Additional Air-conditioning before 5:00 p.m. on any day, then the Tenant shall pay Additional Rent as computed in accordance with Exhibit C.

As *before 5:00 p.m. on any day* immediately precedes *then,* the Landlord could argue that the Tenant owes the Additional Rent on the day the Landlord provides the Additional Air-conditioning. The following redraft eliminates the ambiguity by deleting *then* and stating how to determine the time of payment, although only a general statement.

> **Correct**
>
> **Additional Air-conditioning.** If the Landlord provides Additional Air-conditioning on any day, the Tenant shall pay Additional Rent in accordance with the provisions of this Agreement, including Exhibit C.

21.6 PLURALS

Using the plural form of nouns invites ambiguity. Whenever possible, contracts should be drafted using singular nouns rather than plural nouns.

---

7. *See State v. Hart*, 530 A.2d 332, 333-334 (N.J. Super. App. Div. 1987) (noting the inconsistency of New Jersey opinions deciding the meaning of 12:00 p.m.). *See also Warshaw v. City of Atlanta*, 299 S.E.2d 552, 554 (Ga. 1983) (finding that zoning ordinance's use of "12:00 p.m." referred to midnight).

Look at the three circles below and notice how they intersect with each other. Imagine that Circle A represents the knowledge of Seller A, that Circle B represents the knowledge of Seller B, and that Circle C represents the knowledge of Seller C.

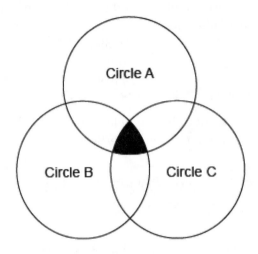

Now assume that the Buyer has drafted the following representation and warranty for the Sellers.

Wrong

Defaults. To the knowledge of the Sellers, the Target is not in material default under any contract.

To determine whether the representation and warranty is true, we would need to know what constitutes the knowledge of the Sellers. A reasonable argument could be made that the knowledge of the Sellers is not the aggregate knowledge of the Sellers, as represented by the aggregate area of the three circles, but instead is only the knowledge that all three Sellers share, as represented by the shaded area where the three circles intersect. To prevent this latter interpretation, the knowledge qualifier must be rewritten to clarify that the Buyer is asking about the knowledge of each Seller.

Correct

Defaults. To the knowledge of each Seller, the Target is not in material default under any contract.

Here is another example of ambiguity caused by plurals. In the original version, it is unclear whether each shareholder must exchange only that shareholder's shares or whether the shareholders must also exchange the shares they own jointly. The revised provision contemplates that some shares might be jointly owned but by fewer than all the shareholders.

> **Wrong**
>
> **Exchange of Shares**. On December 31, 20XX, the Shareholders shall exchange their preferred shares for common shares.
>
> **Correct**
>
> **Exchange of Shares**. On December 31, 20XX, each Shareholder shall exchange for common shares all of the preferred shares that Shareholder owns, whether individually or jointly with one or more other Shareholders.

In the next example, the ambiguity is whether the schedule must list agreements to which not all of the Sellers are a party. The revision refers to *each* agreement but could have referred to *all* agreements or *every* agreement without creating any ambiguity.

> **Wrong**
>
> **Agreements. Schedule 3.6** lists and describes all agreements to which the Sellers are a party.
>
> **Correct**
>
> **Agreements. Schedule 3.6** lists and describes, with respect to each Seller, each agreement to which that Seller is a party.

Ambiguity can also arise when parties are listed individually but joined by *and*. For example:

> **Wrong**
>
> **Notice of Borrowing Amount**. Borrower A and Borrower B shall notify the Bank of the Borrowing Amount at least three days before the Borrowing Date.

The ambiguity is whether each Borrower is obligated to notify the Bank or whether the Borrowers must act jointly.

> **Correct—Version 1**
>
> **Notice of Borrowing Amount**. Borrower A and Borrower B shall each notify the Bank of the Borrowing Amount at least three Business Days before the Borrowing Date.
>
> **Correct—Version 2**
>
> **Notice of Borrowing Amount**. Borrower A and Borrower B shall jointly notify the Bank of the Borrowing Amount at least three Business Days before the Borrowing Date.

21.7 PROVISOS

Drafters use provisos for three purposes:

- To state a condition
- To state an exception to a rule
- To add additional material

All these uses might suggest that provisos are an indispensable drafting tool. They are not. Instead, the multiplicity of purposes creates serious problems for a drafter because of their potential for ambiguity—as in the following provision:

> **Wrong**
>
> **Disclosure of Assets.** Mr. Nowicki shall disclose all of his assets to Mrs. Nowicki, *provided* that Mrs. Nowicki discloses all of her assets to Mr. Nowicki.

The proviso in this provision has two possible meanings: first, that as a condition to Mr. Nowicki's disclosures, Mrs. Nowicki must first disclose her assets. Alternatively, the proviso is merely a reciprocal covenant, requiring that Mrs. Nowicki must also disclose her assets.

A second problem with provisos is that they often travel in packs—like wolves. Where one resides, another lurks. This results from the usual back and forth of negotiation. First, the drafter crafts a provision, believing that it memorializes the parties' agreement. The other party readily agrees—with one proviso. The drafter then acknowledges that the proviso seems right, except for one issue that can be cured—with another proviso. And on it goes until the provision has three or even four provisos. The accumulation of provisos makes the provision difficult to understand: The reader gets lost trying to puzzle out what each proviso means (condition, exception, or additional material) and how each proviso relates to the others and to the main provision.

In contemporary commercial drafting, provisos should be expunged. They may have been a staple of commercial drafting for centuries, but they are a staple destined for the wastebasket.

When faced with a provision that typically might be handled with a proviso, first determine each proviso's purpose. Then, redraft each proviso, but use the alternative, appropriate language:

Rule 1

To state a condition, use *must, if,* or *it is a condition that.*

Rule 2

To state an exception to a rule, use *except that, but,* or *however.*

Rule 3

To add additional material, use a new sentence or subsection or a connective such as *furthermore* or *and.*

If a provision has more than one proviso, determine how each one relates to the other and to the main purpose of the provision. Then use formatting to establish how they relate to each other. Depending upon the provision, tabulation, multiple sentences, multiple sections, or multiple subsections may be appropriate.

The following are examples of improperly drafted provisos and appropriate redrafts.

Proviso as a Condition

Wrong

Change Order. The Owners may change the bathroom tile, *provided that* the new tile does not cost more than the original tile.

Correct

Change Order. The Owners may change the bathroom tile, if the new tile does not cost more than the original tile.

Provisos as an Exception to a Rule

Wrong

Consents. The Contractor shall obtain all Consents; *provided, however,* the Owners shall obtain the Community Board's Consent.

Correct

Consents. The Contractor shall obtain all **Consents**, *except* that the Owners shall obtain the Community Board's Consent.

Provisos as Additional Material

Wrong

Consents. The Contractor shall obtain the Consent of the Housing Department *provided, however,* it shall obtain also obtain the Community Board's Consent.

Correct

Consents. The Contractor shall obtain the Consent of both the Housing Department and the Community Board.

Drafters typically underscore *provided, provided that,* and *provided, however* as a way of making an exception prominent. Keeping with this practice, drafters may italicize *except*.

21.8 SAY THE SAME THING THE SAME WAY

21.8.1 ESTABLISHING STANDARDS AND CRAFTSMANSHIP

Practically every word or phrase in a contract establishes a standard, and by changing a few words, a drafter can change that standard. For example, when you learned about covenants, you learned different ways to express how hard a party must try to accomplish a goal. A party could be obligated to exert *best efforts* or *commercially reasonable efforts*. Each of these ways of stating the degree of obligation represents a different standard. So, by changing the adjective *best* to *commercially reasonable*, you change the standard and substantially reduce a party's degree of obligation.

Because a change of a word can change the meaning of a contract provision, a cardinal principle of good drafting is to **say the same thing the same way**. If you do not, a court may hold that the difference in wording is substantive, even if sloppy drafting caused it.

Here is a lawyer's nightmare:

You are drafting the purchase agreement in connection with your client's purchase of a chain of gyms. During a negotiation, you agreed to add a knowledge qualifier to four of the Seller's representations and warranties. When redrafting the contract, you use the phrase *to the knowledge of each of the Seller's officers* in the first three representations and warranties, but in the fourth you use *to the knowledge of each of the Seller's executive officers*. (The fourth is a more lenient standard from the Seller's perspective because the Seller is liable for the knowledge of a smaller group of people.) In the real world, this could occur inadvertently (but inexcusably) because you copied and pasted the fourth representation and warranty from another contract and failed to notice the different knowledge qualifier.

Now, the disaster. Post closing, your client discovers that the fourth representation and warranty is materially false, and that one of the Seller's officers knew it at the time of the contract's signing. Outraged, your client tells you to draft the complaint and to claim $100,000 in damages. You are now in a most unfortunate predicament. The fourth representation and warranty, as drafted, stated that none of the Seller's *executive* officers knew that the representation and warranty was false. That representation and warranty is, in fact, true. It was a lower-level officer who knew of the falsity. Therefore, your client has no cause of action against the Seller. If you had used the same qualifier in all four representations and warranties *(to the knowledge of each of the Seller's officers)*, the representation and warranty would have been false, and your client would have had a viable cause of action.

Although saying the same thing the same way is generally a matter of substance, it is not always. Sometimes, it is a matter of craftsmanship. For example, no substantive consequences will result if you use both the following phrases in a contract: *includes, without limitation* and *including, but not limited to*. However, by using only one of these phrases throughout a contract, you show the attention to detail that is the hallmark of a careful lawyer.

In the following sections, we will look at some of the more sophisticated ways that drafters use the say the same thing the same way principle.

21.8.2 ISSUES IN ACQUISITION AND CREDIT AGREEMENTS: REPRESENTATIONS AND WARRANTIES VS. COVENANTS

In acquisition agreements, representations and warranties, on the one hand, and covenants, on the other, often deal with the same subject matter. For example, in the representation and warranty on property, plant, and equipment, a seller states the current condition of those assets. Then, in the covenants, the seller promises how it will maintain those assets from signing to closing. If the standards in the representations and warranties and the covenants differ, a seller could be obligated to upgrade the condition of the assets. A parallel issue arises in a credit agreement in which a borrower often makes representations and warranties on a topic that is also a subject of a borrower covenant.

Look at the following provisions from the perspective of the seller and determine what modifications you would ask the buyer for and why.

> **From the representations and warranties**
>
> **4.12. Condition of Property**. Except as set forth in **Schedule 4.12**, the property, plant, and equipment of the Seller are in customary operating condition, subject only to ordinary wear and tear.
>
> **4.13. Insurance**. A list and brief description of all the Seller's insurance policies are set forth in **Schedule 4.13**. Except as set forth in **Schedule 4.13**, the Seller has insured all its properties
>
> (a) for its benefit;
>
> (b) in amounts the Seller's management deems adequate;
>
> (c) against all risks usually insured against by persons operating similar properties in the localities where the properties are located; and
>
> (d) under enforceable policies issued by insurers of recognized responsibility.
>
> **From the covenants**
>
> **5.10 Maintenance of Properties, etc**. The Seller shall maintain
>
> (a) all of its properties in good order, reasonable wear and tear excepted; and
>
> (b) insurance upon all of its properties in such amounts and of such kinds comparable to that in effect on the date of this Agreement.

21.8.3 SIMILAR PROVISIONS IN MORE THAN ONE AGREEMENT

In the same way that different standards in representations and warranties and covenants can create a problem, different standards in different agreements can create a problem. The classic scenario occurs when a buyer of a business borrows money to fund the acquisition. In the acquisition agreement, the seller makes representations and warranties to the buyer. In the financing agreement, the buyer turns into the borrower who makes representations and warranties to the lender. Although the representations and warranties in the two agreements will be similar, they will not be the same. For example, compare the following representations and warranties from an acquisition agreement and a financing agreement.

> **The Seller's Representation and Warranty to the Buyer:**
>
> **Condition of Property**. The Seller's equipment and machinery are in the condition that industry standards require.
>
> **The Borrower's Representation and Warranty to the Lender:**
>
> **Property, Plant, and Equipment**. All of the Borrower's properties are in good order, reasonable wear excepted.

If the buyer/borrower believes that the two standards materially differ and that the financing agreement standard is tougher, the buyer/borrower must decide whether it otherwise knows enough facts to make a truthful statement to the lender. If it does not, the buyer/borrower has four options. First, it can ask the seller to change its representation and warranty so that it mirrors the one that the buyer/borrower must give in the financing agreement. Second, it can ask the lender to change its representation and warranty so that it mirrors the one the buyer/borrower receives in the purchase agreement. Third, it can ask the lender for some other change in the representation and warranty, such as a qualification. Fourth, it can leave the representation and warranty unchanged, but only after performing additional due diligence so that it can truthfully make the representation and warranty.

The same issue can arise when memorializing a transaction requires multiple contracts. For example, imagine the repercussions if two agreements in an integrated transaction unintentionally had different governing law provisions. To prevent these mistakes, always take the time to conform all the general provisions in each of a transaction's agreements.

21.8.4   CONTRACT PROVISIONS AND DOCUMENTS BASED UPON STATUTORY PROVISIONS

Contract provisions and documents are sometimes based upon statutory provisions. For example, a certificate of incorporation reflects the requirements of the statute authorizing corporations. Although most drafters use a treatise form as the basis of a certificate of incorporation, that form, when it was first created, was based on the statute.

When creating a provision or a document based on a statute, parrot the words of the statute: say exactly what it says. Although a difference between the two may not cause a difference in substance, it could. And if it does, it may prevent your firm from opining that the document meets the statute's requirements.

The following example shows a provision from a certificate of incorporation based upon the statutory provision.

> **Delaware General Corporation Law §102 (a)(3)** *(contents of certificate of incorporation)*
>
> The certificate of incorporation shall set forth: . . . The nature of the business to be conducted or promoted. It shall be sufficient to state, either alone or with other businesses or purposes, that *the purpose of the corporation is to engage in any lawful act or activity for which corporations may be organized under the General Corporation Law of Delaware* . . . (emphasis added)
>
> **Statement of Purpose in Certificate of Incorporation**
>
> *The purpose of the Corporation is to engage in any lawful act or activity for which corporations may be organized under the General Corporation Law of Delaware* (emphasis added).

CHAPTER TWENTY-ONE

EXERCISES

Exercise 21-1

Read the following provision. Two words are vague, and one phrase is ambiguous. What are they? Markup the provision to clarify the ambiguity.

> **Assignment.** Neither party may assign any right under this Agreement to any Person without the prior written consent of the other party. Manufacturer consents, without any further consent being required, to the assignment by Purchaser to any affiliate of Purchaser that is as creditworthy as Purchaser.

Exercise 21-2

Mark up the following provisions to clarify the ambiguities and to correct any drafting errors.

> **Compliance with Applicable Law.** The Borrower has complied with all Laws and is currently in compliance with all Laws, except for any noncompliance which would not have a material adverse effect on the Borrower.

> **Conditions to Closing.** The Buyer's obligation to perform is subject to the fulfillment of each of the following conditions: The representations and warranties of the Seller must be true on and as of the Closing Date with the same force and effect as if made on the Closing Date. The Seller must have complied with the covenants to be complied with by the Closing Date. The Seller must have delivered to the Buyer a certificate to the foregoing effect.

> **Redemption of Shares.** The Seller shall not purchase, redeem, or otherwise acquire, directly or indirectly, any outstanding shares of its capital stock.

Exercise 21-3

The following provision comes from a website development agreement. Determine how *and* and *or* are used in it and whether their use creates any ambiguities. Mark up the provision to clarify any ambiguities.

Third-Party Content. The Developer shall use commercially reasonable efforts to secure for the Client the broadest possible rights to any third-party content that the Developer incorporates into the Website. The Developer may either purchase the third-party content or license it. Any use of third-party content is subject to the Client's final approval. The Client shall pay all costs or fees for third-party content, either by directly paying the third party or by reimbursing the Developer, after receiving appropriate documentation.

Exercise 21-4[8]

On December 15, 20XX, Bertha Ellsworth (Ellsworth) was admitted to the Home for the Aged (the Home) and signed an agreement setting forth the terms of her stay at the Home. The agreement provided that for the first two months of her stay she would be a probationary member and that afterwards she would become a life member. On the same day, Ellsworth paid $100,000 to the Home by a check which stated: "In Payment of Life Membership for Bertha Ellsworth in the Home, as specified in the Agreement dated December 15, 20XX."

Ellsworth died on December 29, 20XX, before her probationary period ended. The administrator of the estate wants to recover the $100,000 gift as Ellsworth never became a life member. The Home claims it is entitled to keep the money. The agreement is ambiguous. Assume that you represented Ellsworth when the contract was negotiated. How would you have drafted the following provisions to protect her?

The lines of the provisions are numbered to facilitate class discussion. The provisions are available on the *Drafting Contracts* Website.

```
1        1.1. Ellsworth having this day given the Home,
2    without reservation, the sum of $100,000 to be used and
3    disposed of in the furtherance of its benevolence and
4    charitable work as it may deem best, the Home admits
5    Ellsworth into the Home as a member thereof during the
6    period of her natural life.
7        1.5. It is clearly understood that Ellsworth has been
8    received in accordance with the new regulations on a
9    probation period of two months in which time she has the
10   opportunity of finding out whether she desires to remain in
11   the Home. If it should be found advisable to discontinue her
12   stay in the Home, then her gift, with the exception of $2,000
13   per month shall be refunded.
14       12.1. Probationary membership means a short trial
15   period while the member becomes adjusted to life at the
16   Home. The probationary membership shall not continue for
17   a longer period than two consecutive months. If for any
```

---

8. This exercise is based on *First Nat. Bank of Lawrence v. Methodist Home for the Aged*, 309 P.2d 389 (Kan. 1957).

18	reason the trial member does not desire to remain in the
19	Home, she shall have the privilege of leaving. Only
20	members who do not have the money to pay for their life
21	Membership shall be granted the privilege of paying by the
22	month.

Exercise 21-5[9]

Big Ten University (Big Ten) entered into a collective bargaining agreement with the Local Union (the Local Union) on January 1, 20XX.

1. As drafted, do the following provisions require Big Ten to contribute to the Welfare Fund and the Employees Pension Fund on behalf of each probationary employee? What do you think was the parties' intent?

2. Redraft the provisions to clarify that the agreement does not require a contribution with respect to any probationary employee.

The provisions are available on the *Drafting Contracts* Website.

2.2 New Employees. New employees may be disciplined or discharged with or without cause for a trial period of sixty days. New employees must become members of the Local Union by the sixty-first day of their employment, at which time they shall be deemed to be regular employees covered by this Agreement and entitled to all health and retirement benefits of this Agreement. Trial period employees will sometimes be referred to as probationary employees.

[Provisions Intentionally Omitted]

10.1 Contributions to Benefit Funds. Big Ten will contribute to the Employees Welfare Fund and the Employees Pension Fund on behalf of each employee.

Exercise 21-6

Mark up the following sentence from an employment agreement to correct the ambiguity and any other drafting errors. Assume that the Closing Date is not January 1, 20XX and that the parties intend a term based on the number of days in a calendar year.

Term. This Agreement and the employment hereunder shall commence upon the Closing Date

(as such term shall be defined in the Purchase Agreement) and shall continue in effect for a period of

five calendar years from such Closing Date.

---

9. This exercise is based on *Teamsters Indus. Employees Welfare Fund v. Rolls-Royce Motor Cars, Inc.*, 989 F.2d 132 (3d Cir. 1993).

Exercise 21-7

Mark up the following provisions to clarify the ambiguities and correct any other drafting errors.

Due Date. The Note is due one year from its date of issuance. Interest is to be computed on the basis of a 360-day year.

Interest Accrual. Interest accrues on the Note from the date of the Note's issuance until the Prepayment Date.

Acceptance of Bids. Seller shall accept all bids (for the purchase of Blackacre) delivered to its offices between April 3, 20XX, and April 16, 20XX.

Trust. Never trust anyone over 30.

Expiration of Option. This option expires at 12:00 midnight Tuesday, July 9, 20XX.

Exercise 21-8

Mark up the following provision to eliminate the provisos and to correct any other drafting errors.

Nonsolicitation. During the Noncompetition Period, Wagner shall not employ or seek to employ any employee of Sugarcane Corp.; provided, however, Wagner may employ or seek to employ Mark Bender, provided that Wagner first notifies Sugarcane Corp. in writing at least 10 days prior to contacting him with respect to any such employment; provided further, that this provision does not apply to the employment of any hourly employee.

Exercise 21-9

Mark up the following provisions to correct the drafting errors. The provisions create a substantive business issue. What is it?

Provision 1

Article 5   The Landlord's Covenants

Throughout the term of the Lease, the Landlord agrees as follows:

[Provisions Intentionally Omitted]

5.4 Alterations. The Landlord shall not unreasonably withhold permission from the Tenant in determining whether the Tenant may proceed with making alterations to the Premises.

Provision 2

Article 6   The Tenant's Covenants

Throughout the Lease Term, the Tenant agrees as follows:

[Provisions Intentionally Omitted]

6.6 Alterations. The Tenant shall not make any changes or alterations to the Premises without the Landlord's prior written consent.

Exercise 21-10

Memorandum

To: Andrew McKenzie

From: Sasha Petrov

Our client, Coffee & Cream Corp. (Coffee), owns a chain of high-end, company-operated retail stores that sell and serve coffee. They are merging with Tea for Two, Inc. (Tea), a similar chain of stores, but one that sells and serves tea. The parties signed the Merger Agreement on April 18, 20XX. Tea agreed to merge into Coffee, making Coffee the surviving corporation.

Both Tea and Coffee are Delaware corporations. Between now and the Closing, which will be on June 1, 20XX, each of the parties will submit the Merger Agreement to its stockholders in accordance with the requirements of Section 251 of the Delaware General Corporation Law. Instead of filing and recording the Merger Agreement as required by Section 251(c), Coffee has decided to file a certificate of merger as permitted by Section 251(c). Please draft the Certificate of Merger. Attached as Exhibit A are the relevant statutory provisions. In your draft you may assume that each of the constituent corporations will comply with all of the statutory provisions relating to mergers and that there will be no amendments or changes to the certificate of incorporation of HHI. HHI's principal place of business is located at 445 Tenth Avenue, New York, New York 10022.

The President of Coffee is Carla Cappuccino, and the President of Tea is Larry Lipton.

Exhibit A

Delaware General Corporation Law §251(c)

The agreement required by subsection (b) of this section shall be submitted to the stockholders of each constituent corporation at an annual or special meeting for the purpose of acting on the agreement. Due notice of the time, place, and purpose of the meeting shall be mailed to each holder of stock, whether voting or nonvoting, of the corporation at the stockholder's address as it appears on the records of the corporation, at least 20 days prior to the date of the meeting. The notice shall contain a copy of the agreement or a brief summary thereof, as the directors shall deem advisable. At the meeting, the agreement shall be considered and a vote taken for its adoption or rejection. If a majority of the outstanding stock of the corporation entitled to vote thereon shall be voted for the adoption of the agreement, that fact shall be certified on the agreement by the secretary or assistant secretary of the corporation. If the agreement shall be so adopted and certified by each constituent corporation, it shall then be filed and shall become effective, in accordance with §103 of this title. In lieu of filing the agreement of merger or consolidation required by this section, the surviving or resulting corporation may file a certificate of merger or consolidation, executed in accordance with §103 of this title, which states:

(1) The name and state of incorporation of each of the constituent corporations;

(2) That an agreement of merger or consolidation has been approved, adopted, certified, executed, and acknowledged by each of the constituent corporations in accordance with this section;

(3) The name of the surviving or resulting corporation;

(4) In the case of a merger, such amendments or changes in the certificate of incorporation of the surviving corporation as are desired to be effected by the merger, or, if no such amendments or changes are desired, a statement that the certificate of incorporation of the surviving corporation shall be its certificate of incorporation;

(5) In the case of a consolidation, that the certificate of incorporation of the resulting corporation shall be as set forth in an attachment to the certificate;

(6) That the executed agreement of consolidation or merger is on file at an office of the surviving corporation, stating the address thereof; and

(7) That a copy of the agreement of consolidation or merger will be furnished by the surviving corporation, on request and without cost, to any stockholder of any constituent corporation.

Delaware General Corporation Law §103

(a) Whenever any instrument is to be filed with the Secretary of State or in accordance with this section or chapter, such instrument shall be executed as follows:

(1) The certificate of incorporation, and any other instrument to be filed before the election of the initial board of directors if the initial directors were not named in the certificate of incorporation, shall be signed by the incorporator or incorporators (or, in the case of any such other instrument, such incorporator's or incorporators' successors and assigns). If any incorporator is not available by reason of death, incapacity, unknown address, or refusal or neglect to act, then any such other instrument may be signed, with the same effect as if such incorporator had signed it, by any person for whom or on whose behalf such incorporator, in executing the certificate of incorporation, was acting directly or indirectly as employee or agent, provided that such other instrument shall state that such incorporator is not available and the reason therefor, that such incorporator in executing the certificate of incorporation was acting directly or indirectly as employee or agent for or on behalf of such person, and that such person's signature on such instrument is otherwise authorized and not wrongful.

(2) All other instruments shall be signed:

   a. By any authorized officer of the corporation; or

   b. If it shall appear from the instrument that there are no such officers, then by a majority of the directors or by such directors as may be designated by the board; or

   c. If it shall appear from the instrument that there are no such officers or directors, then by the holders of record, or such of them as may be designated by the holders of record, of a majority of all outstanding shares of stock; or

   d. By the holders of record of all outstanding shares of stock.

Exercise 21-11

Mark up the following provision to clarify the ambiguity.

Allocation of Losses. Losses shall be borne by the General Partner and the Limited Partners in equal shares.

Numbers and Financial Provisions

22.1 INTRODUCTION

Clients may forgive many things, but getting the monetary provisions wrong is not one of them. To draft them properly often requires an understanding not only of the business deal, but also accounting and tax law. Therefore, drafting these provisions is generally a collaborative effort, involving the client's accountants and tax lawyers. You should bring these specialists into the process as early as possible, so that any business issues related to the monetary provisions can be resolved as early on as possible.

This chapter teaches you how to draft numbers and mathematical formulas. In addition, the final section discusses how to draft provisions involving financial statement concepts.

22.2 HOW TO DRAFT NUMBERS

Historically, drafters have written numbers both in words and Arabic numerals.

> **Wrong**
>
> **Samples**. The Licensee shall deliver to the Licensor a sample of any Product that it wants to manufacture at least thirty (30) days before manufacturing is to begin.

This unnecessary duplication makes a contract more difficult to read. *Write the numbers one through ten in words and the numbers higher than ten in Arabic numerals, unless the first word of a sentence begins with a number and other numbers are in the sentence. Then, write out all of the numbers in words.*

Although many drafters have stopped drafting numbers in both words and Arabic numerals, they continue to draft dollar amounts both ways. Instead, generally, only Arabic numerals should be used.

Wrong

> **Payment of Rent**. The Tenant shall pay the Landlord Ten Thousand Dollars ($10,000.00) for each calendar month of the Term, no later than the first Business Day of each calendar month of the Term.

Correct

> **Payment of Rent**. The Tenant shall pay the Landlord $10,000 for each calendar month of the Term, no later than the first Business Day of each calendar month of the Term.

The reiteration of dollar amounts is ingrained in our everyday habits. Think of the checks that you write. You write the amount both in numbers and in words.

The rationale for the duplication is that the words act as a safety net in case, inadvertently, an extra numeral is added, numerals are transposed, or some other error occurs. Indeed, a statutory canon of construction addresses this possibility and provides that the words are to be given effect if the words and the numbers differ.[1] But what happens if the number is correct and the words are wrong (60 v. six)? The better approach is to *draft dollar amounts using only numerals* and to proofread what you have written—carefully. Some drafters who generally follow this rule make an exception for promissory notes and mortgages and use both numerals and words for these documents.

You can reduce the likelihood of miswriting dollar amounts in two ways. First, omit the .00 of any dollar amount that has no cents. Write $345,286, rather than $345,286.00. Second, for dollar amounts greater than $1 million, express the millions or billions of dollars in words if the last three numbers of the dollar amount are all zeros. Write $103.25 million, rather than $103,250,000.

22.3 HOW TO DRAFT MATHEMATICAL FORMULAS

Mathematical calculations are commonplace in contracts. Parties must calculate royalties, cost-of-living adjustments, bonuses, purchase price adjustments, profit and loss allocations, earn-outs, mandatory prepayments, and financial covenants. Drafting these provisions requires an understanding of the business purpose of the formula as well as the ability to express mathematical concepts unambiguously.

22.3.1 BASIC MATHEMATICAL OPERATIONS

A formula begins with the four basic mathematical operations: addition, subtraction, multiplication, and division. Signal these operations by using mathematical terms to avoid any ambiguity that might arise from the use of colloquial expressions. For example, the mathematical operation of six over two can be interpreted two ways. If a court interprets it to signal subtraction, the result is four. But, six over two could also signal a

---

1. U.C.C. §3-114, U.L.A. §3-114 (2004) states: "If an instrument contains contradictory terms, typewritten terms prevail over printed terms, handwritten terms prevail over both, and words prevail over numbers." *See Yates v. Commercial Bank & Trust Co.*, 432 So. 2d 725, 726 (Fla. Dist. Ct. App. 3d Dist. 1983) ($10075.00 v. Ten hundred seventy-five dollars).

ratio, the numerator of which is six and the denominator of which is two. If that is how a court interprets the language, the result would be three, not four.

Addition

the *sum* of (a) _____ *plus* (b) _____

Subtraction

the *difference* of (a) _____ *minus* (b) _____

Multiplication

the *product* of (a) _____ *times* (b) _____

Division

the *quotient* of (a) _____ *divided* by (b) _____

In addition to the four basic mathematical operations, you may need to express a fraction or a percentage. For example, an executive fired without cause might be entitled to a percentage of her previously agreed-upon bonus. Although the contract could refer to a prorated percentage of the bonus, the following language is more precise, thereby reducing the likelihood of a dispute as to the calculation.

Version 1

Ratio: Expressed as a Fraction

the fraction, the numerator of which is _____ and the denominator of which is _____

Version 2

Ratio: Expressed as a Percentage

the fraction, expressed as a percentage, the numerator of which is ____ and the denominator of which is _____

When writing a formula, bold or italicize the mathematical terms. The emphasis makes it easier for a reader to follow the mathematical operations. Do not precede a mathematical term with a comma.

22.3.2 THE ORDER OF MATHEMATICAL OPERATIONS

If calculating a result requires more than one mathematical operation, indicate the order in which the operations are to occur. A change in the order might result in a change in the answer. For example:

Formula:	$6 + 3 \div 3$
Alternative 1	$(6 + 3) \div 3$
	$9 \div 3 = 3$
Alternative 2	$6 + (3 \div 3)$
	$6 + 1 = 7$

As discussed in the next section, tabulation is an excellent way to indicate the order in which mathematical operations are to be performed as it shows the relative relationship between the operations. Absent any directions in the contract as to the order of operations, perform them in the following order: multiplication, division, subtraction, and addition.

22.3.3 DRAFTING THE FORMULA

You can draft a formula three different ways:

- Using **an algebraic equation** in which each component of the formula is defined and mathematic notation is used to indicate the operations.
- Using **narration and tabulation** to indicate each component of the formula and the order of the operations.
- Using **a narrative cookbook approach** "to list in chronological order the steps leading to the intended result."[2]

To illustrate how these different approaches work, we will use a simple hypothetical based upon a provision for annual rent increases under a lease.[3] Many long-term leases include such provisions to protect landlords from cost-of-living increases resulting from inflation. As part of analyzing how to draft the formula that calculates the rent increase, we will look at some of the business considerations that might arise during the drafting process.

Before drafting any formula, understand how it works. To test your understanding, make up numbers and plug them into the tentative formula. Always test whether the result of the formula could be a negative number.

For example, assume that the base rent at the time a lease begins is $100 per month. In addition, the rent increases by the same percentage that the cost of living increases from the lease's commencement date. So, if as of the first anniversary of the lease's commencement date, the cost of living has increased by 5 percent, then the base rent increases by 5 percent, or $5 (.05 x 100), for a total of $105. Similarly, if as of the second anniversary of the lease's commencement date the cost of living has increased by 8 percent from the commencement date (not from the first anniversary of the commencement date), then the base rent of $100 increases by 8 percent, or $8, for a total of $108. Because these increases could be substantial over the course of a long-term lease, a tenant might want to negotiate a cap, that is, a limit by which the base rate could be increased.

But what happens if the cost of living decreases between the first and second anniversaries, so that the increase from the commencement date is 3 percent? The parties must decide between two possibilities. The rent could remain at $105 (no decreases allowed), or it could decrease to $103 to reflect the decreased cost of living. Let's assume that decreases are permitted. The parties must next address whether the rent could decrease below the base rent on the commencement date. Although a tenant would love that, a landlord might insist that the base rent established a floor below which the rent could not fall. If the tenant agrees to this, the rent to be paid beginning on the second anniversary of the commencement date could be less than $105 per month (the monthly rent paid between the first and second anniversaries), but not less than $100.

With that background, let us turn to the drafting of the provision. Based on the discussion in the previous paragraphs, you now know that the formula must

---

2. Reed Dickerson, *The Fundamentals of Legal Drafting* 202 (2d ed., Little, Brown & Co. 1986).

3. For a detailed discussion of cost-of-living adjustments in real estate leases, see Mark A. Senn, *Commercial Real Estate Leases: Preparation, Negotiation, and Forms* §6.04 (3d ed. Aspen 2004).

(a) calculate the percentage increase in the cost of living from the commencement date to a specific anniversary date; and

(b) use that percentage to calculate the increase in the base rent.

Here's a quickie math review: To determine a percentage change between two numbers, first determine the amount of the increase or decrease. Then, divide that amount by the original number. So, for example, if you have six oranges and buy two more for a total of eight, the percentage increase is calculated as follows: 8 *minus* 6, which is equal to 2; then 2 *divided by* 6, which is 1/3, which may also be stated as 33.33 percent or .333.)

To determine the cost-of-living increase, parties typically rely on the Consumer Price Index (CPI), an index that "represents changes in prices of all goods and services purchased for consumption by urban households."[4] That index provides data by geographic regions, permitting parties to choose the most applicable index. Each index establishes a base year with a value of 100. All increases in an index are keyed off the base year. Therefore, to determine a change in the CPI, you need calculate the difference in the value as of any two dates. So, if the CPI in 2006 is 140, the CPI has changed by 40 (140-100), resulting in a 40 percent increase (40/100) since the base year.

With this background, you can begin to draft.

To draft a formula, break down the financial business deal into its components, determine the mathematical operation for each component, and then state the formula using one of three methods: algebraic equation, narration and tabulation, and the cookbook approach. You will see how each of these methods works as you read through the following examples.

No matter which method you include in a contract, always draft the formula using an algebraic equation first. It will test your understanding of the formula. If you cannot draft it, you will probably also have a difficult time drafting both narrative methods, as each one expresses the equation in words.

The following provisions show how the rent increase formula can be drafted using each of the three methods:

Algebraic Equation

Rent.

(a) **Definitions.** For the purposes of this Section, each of the following terms has its assigned meaning:

   (i) **CPI 1** means the value of the Consumer Price Index on January 1, 2006.[5]

   (ii) **CPI 2** means the value of the Consumer Price Index on January 1 of the term year with respect to which the annual rent is being calculated.

(b) **Annual Rent.** The annual rent for the term year beginning on January 1, 2006, is $45,000. The annual rent for each subsequent term year is $45,000 *plus* the rent increase calculated by the formula set forth in subsection (c) (the "Rent Increase"). If the calculation of the Rent

continued on next page >

---

4. U.S. Dept. of Labor, *Bureau of Labor Statistics,* Consumer Price Indexes, http://www.bls.gov/cpi/cpiovrvw.htm#item1 (last modified date October 16, 2001).

5. An actual provision would specify the CPI to be used and detail what the parties should do if the government stopped publishing the chosen CPI.

Increase for any term year results in a negative number, the annual rent for that term year is $45,000.

(c) **Payment of Annual Rent.** Beginning on January 1, 2006, and through the end of the term, the Tenant shall pay the Landlord the annual rent in twelve approximately equal monthly installments, each installment being due no later than the first business day of each month.

(d) **Calculation of the Rent Increase.** The formula for calculating the Rent Increase is as follows:

$$\frac{CPI\,2 - CPI\,1}{CPI\,1} \times 45{,}000 = \text{Rent Increase}$$

By tinkering with this formula, you can calculate the new annual rent, rather than the amount of the increase. To do this, put the formula for the Rent Increase inside a set of parentheses (which means that the formula inside the parentheses is a separate calculation) and precede the parentheses with the following: *45,000 +*

Narration and Tabulation

Rent.

(a) **Annual Rent.** [The same as with the algebraic formula.]

(b) **Payment of Annual Rent.** [The same as with the algebraic formula.]

(c) **Calculation of the Rent Increase.** With respect to any term year, the amount of the Rent Increase is equal to *the product* of $45,000 *times* the amount equal to

(i) the value of the Consumer Price Index on January 1 of the term year with respect to which the annual rent is being calculated *minus* the value of the Consumer Price Index on January 1, 2006

divided by

(iii) the value of the Consumer Price Index on January 1, 2006.

The Cookbook Approach

Rent.

(a) **Annual Rent.** [The same as with the algebraic formula.]

(b) **Payment of Annual Rent.** [The same as with the algebraic formula.]

(c) **Calculation of the Rent Increase.** With respect to any term year, the amount of the Rent Increase is calculated as follows:

(i) *Subtract* the value of the Consumer Price Index on January 1, 2006 from the value of the Consumer Price Index on January 1 of the term year with respect to which the annual rent is being calculated (the difference, the "CPI Difference").[6]

---

6. Note that the defined terms in subsection (b) are used only once. Although, generally, you should not create a defined term unless you will use it more than once, here, the use of the defined terms clarifies the substance by making the calculations easier to understand.

(ii) *Divide* the CPI Difference by the value of the Consumer Price Index on January 1, 2006 (the quotient, the "Percentage Change").

(iii) *Multiply* the Percentage Change times $45,000.

You could also draft the cookbook approach provision by adding the definitions from the algebraic provision and using those defined terms.

Which provision did you find it the easiest to understand? Why?

After drafting the formula, review it with the client and get its approval. Because of the consequences of a mistake in a formula, you must be sure that the client understands and approves it. Do more than merely sending the contract provision. Also send multiple examples of how the formula works, including examples demonstrating what could happen in unusual circumstances (e.g., a decrease in the cost of living). Then, obtain the client's approval. If it arrives by e-mail, put a copy of it in the client file. If you speak with the client, write a memo to the file memorializing your discussion. These contemporaneous documents may help you if the client ever claims it did not approve the formula.

Once the client approves the formula, with its permission, send it and the examples of the formula's application to the other side. If they agree with what you have drafted and the examples, consider including those examples as an exhibit to the contract. If they are included, the parties and the court will be able to refer to those examples—as a type of legislative history—when later determining the parties' intent.

22.4 HOW TO DRAFT PROVISIONS INVOLVING FINANCIAL STATEMENT CONCEPTS

If you have not had an accounting course, you may have difficulty understanding some of the discussion in this section. But by reading it, you should come away with two points: You need to take an accounting course to be a business lawyer, and drafting provisions using financial statement concepts can be tricky.

Many contract provisions that require calculations use accounting concepts. For example, a publisher will pay an author based upon a book's **net sales**, an accounting concept; and a bank will have the right to declare a default if a company's **net worth** (another accounting concept) falls below an agreed-upon dollar amount. You cannot draft those provisions without understanding those concepts. However, a minicourse in financial statement concepts is beyond the scope of this book. Nonetheless, this section will address the role that **GAAP** plays in drafting provisions using financial concepts.

GAAP is the acronym for *generally accepted accounting principles.* These principles guide the preparation of financial statements. All public companies are required to report their results using GAAP, and many private companies do so, even though they are not required to. This agreed-upon set of principles benefits users of financial statements by making companies comparable.

GAAP does not establish just one set of principles to which all companies must adhere. GAAP is like a four-lane highway. Some GAAP principles are very conservative (the far right lane), while others are very aggressive (the far left lane). Companies may choose which lane to drive in. These choices determine a company's financial reporting personality—some are consistently aggressive; others, consistently conservative.[7]

Many unsophisticated drafters react with a knee-jerk response to drafting provisions involving accounting principles: They require all calculations to be made in accordance with GAAP. Unfortunately, that approach may deprive the drafter's client of a contractual advantage that a more thoughtful analysis could have created.

Among the points to be considered are the following:

■ GAAP is an evolving set of principles and practices.
■ GAAP allows different accounting treatments for the same event.
■ A non-GAAP principle may better protect your client.

22.4.1   GAAP AS AN EVOLVING STANDARD

GAAP is an evolving set of principles, one that tries to stay current in a changing commercial environment. Thus, new disclosures of financial information and new methods of accounting for transactions and events are constantly being mandated.[8] As many calculations required by an agreement are not made on the date of signing, contractual provisions dealing with GAAP-based calculations must contemplate the consequences of changes in GAAP. The types of provisions in which this issue arises include purchase price adjustments, contingent earn-outs, financial covenants in loan agreements, and buy-sell agreements in partnership and stockholder agreements.

Parties can address the fact that GAAP evolves over time in several ways. First, parties can ignore the changes. In this case, the parties would provide for *calculations to be made in accordance with GAAP as in effect as of the date of this Agreement.* Many parties, especially borrowers, prefer this formulation. It provides certainty. The borrower knows what GAAP is as of the contract date and that it can comply with the financial covenants. While this may provide the borrower with a business advantage, it does have a disadvantage: The borrower's record keeping becomes more onerous. Specifically, its records for reporting to the SEC and others must comply with whatever GAAP is in effect from time to time. In addition, it must also keep whatever records are necessary to compute the financial covenants in accordance with GAAP as it existed on the date the parties signed the contract.

As an alternative, the parties can provide that the calculations be made *in accordance with GAAP as in effect from time to time;* that is, whatever the evolving GAAP is on the calculation date. While this method avoids the record-keeping issue, it creates a different problem for borrowers: They must be able to comply with financial covenants based on a future GAAP that they neither know nor control.

Although these uncertainties may generate angst for borrowers, the borrower's "friendly" banker may not be similarly perturbed. While the lender cannot be certain how GAAP may change, the change in GAAP may require a more conservative presentation of the borrower's financial position—a result that appeals, of course, to a banker's conservative nature. This issue's resolution depends on many factors, but many borrowers accede to lenders' provisions because of their superior bargaining power.

---

7. Companies with conservative reporting practices tend to report lower rates of income than their more aggressive peers do, but are considered to have "high-quality" earnings.

8. For example: GAAP has evolved to recognize the **fair value** of intangible assets, such as intellectual property. Fair value is what an asset is worth in the marketplace. This recognition of fair value departs from GAAP's long-standing focus on **historical cost**—what a company paid for an asset.

Other alternatives for resolving the issue of which GAAP to use include the following:

- With respect to a proposed change in a generally accepted accounting principle, the parties may agree during their original negotiations how the change, once implemented, will affect the agreement's calculations.
- The parties may agree to negotiate in good faith the contractual consequences of any change in GAAP that materially affects any calculation in the agreement. Be careful with this provision. It is only an agreement to negotiate. The parties may not reach agreement. To deal with this possibility, some agreements provide that if the negotiations fail, the change in GAAP will not be automatically implemented.

22.4.2 GAAP'S AUTHORIZATION OF ALTERNATIVE PRINCIPLES

GAAP's flexibility in permitting users to choose among alternative acceptable principles can help or harm your client. Which it is generally depends upon whom you represent.

Imagine that a borrower's loan agreement requires it to earn a minimum level of net income, as determined in accordance with GAAP. Unfortunately, our hypothetical borrower has had a dismal year, and it seems likely that it will breach the minimum net income covenant.

The borrower's chief financial officer (CFO) has, however, carefully reviewed the loan agreement and has hit on an idea to boost the bottom line: By changing the principle it uses to account for sales, the borrower can recognize sufficient revenues[9] to meet the income test. Although the borrower's chief executive officer (CEO) professes concern that this principle differs from the one that the borrower is using, the CFO reassures the CEO that the change presents no problem. ("It's just a small 'lane change,'" he explains.) He reminds the CEO that GAAP does not mandate a particular way to recognize revenue, but instead permits users to choose among allowable alternatives. Moreover, the loan agreement gave the company this flexibility by failing to prohibit changes from one GAAP method to another.

Most lenders are, of course, sufficiently sophisticated to avoid this type of manipulation. Thus, their standard form agreements invariably require that the generally accepted accounting principles to be used are those that are consistent with past practice. Lenders do not always insist, however, that the requirement be applied to all principles in all instances. Sometimes, a lender will permit a borrower to deviate from past practice and use an alternative GAAP principle for a particular calculation.

For example, some companies value their inventory on a LIFO[10] basis. Assuming that inflation is causing the price of inventory to increase, LIFO reduces a company's net income and taxes by maximizing its reported cost of sales. It also simultaneously minimizes the reported value of the company's inventory.[11] This minimization is in many instances irrelevant. It can, however, be a distinct disadvantage. For example, a low reported value of inventory may limit the amount a company can borrow under

---

9. Accountants use the term **revenue recognition** to describe the rules for determining when (or if) a sale has taken place. If a company has not met the rules' requirements, it cannot include the additional income on its income statement.

10. **LIFO** is the acronym for *last in, first out*. It assumes that the most recent items that the company manufactured or bought for resale are the ones sold.

11. This may not be the case with respect to a product new to the market. In this case, rather than the cost of the product increasing over time to reflect inflation, the price may fall because of increased manufacturing efficiencies and the debugging of the product.

its loan agreement. In this situation, the borrower will probably want to report a higher inventory number to increase the amount it can borrow. A borrower can often achieve this goal by negotiating for the right to revalue its inventory using the FIFO method[12]—but only to calculate the amount it can borrow.

22.4.3 NON-GAAP ALTERNATIVES

In the same way that parties may need to replace one generally accepted accounting principle with another to reflect the true economic substance of a business deal, sometimes parties need to use a non-GAAP principle in valuing an asset or in making a calculation. Imagine that the buyer of a business has agreed to pay the seller the value of its assets, as stated on its balance sheet, plus $100,000. Included among these assets is a building that the seller has owned for 20 years. As GAAP requires buildings to be depreciated, the building's low book value may not reflect its real value. In this instance, the seller could reasonably insist that the building be valued at fair market value, even though that does not accord with GAAP.

22.4.4 AGREEMENTS USING BALANCE SHEET ACCOUNTS

Typical provisions that rely on calculations based on balance sheet accounts include the following:

- Purchase price adjustment provisions keyed into changes in **net worth**[13] or **working capital**[14]
- Financial covenants requiring borrowers to maintain minimum net worth, working capital, or current ratio
- Borrowing base formulas

When negotiating the accounting-related provisions in any of these contexts, the lawyer and her client must track through the balance sheet and think through on a line-item basis whether any one or more of the accounts requires special treatment. For example, the purchase price in some acquisition agreements is based on the seller's reported or book net worth, which in turn is based on the seller's total reported assets and its total reported liabilities. Thus, the value attributed to each asset and each liability directly impacts purchase price.

When you represent a seller in such a case, think through which assets on the balance sheet do not reflect that asset's true fair market value. Because GAAP is conservative, it tends towards understating assets. For that reason, parties may prefer to value assets using something other than GAAP. As noted before, buildings can be revalued to their fair market value.

While sellers want to maximize value, buyers fear being saddled with unforeseen liabilities. Therefore, they seek to ensure that the net worth calculation accurately reflects all the company's liabilities—not only those on the balance sheet, but also those that GAAP does not require a company to report. Significant areas of concern include the following:

---

12. **FIFO** is the acronym for *first in, first out.* It assumes that the first items that the company manufactured or bought for resale are the first ones sold.

13. **Net worth** is often used synonymously with equity in describing the value of the owners' interest in a business.

14. **Working capital** is shorthand for the result of the following calculation: the aggregate of a company's current assets (cash, accounts receivable, and inventory) *minus* the aggregate of its current liabilities (accounts payable, notes payable, and the current portion of long-term debt).

- Pending litigation
- Environmental cleanup liabilities
- Guaranties
- Purchase obligations

If you represent a buyer, consider dealing with these contingent liabilities by establishing a reserve, even though GAAP would not require one. Of course, the parties must work through the specifics of such an approach collaboratively with their lawyers and accountants.

22.4.5 AGREEMENTS USING REVENUE AND EARNINGS CONCEPTS

Revenues and earnings formulas appear in a wide variety of agreements, including:

- Purchase price provisions in acquisition agreements
- Compensation provisions in employment agreements
- Royalty provisions in license and franchise agreements
- Buy-out provisions in partnership and stockholder agreements
- Profit and loss sharing in joint ventures or partnerships

In these situations, the amount being paid or received can be significantly affected by the accounting choices made in the documents. To make certain that the documents reflect the deal, the formulas need to be carefully crafted.

A salient concern for parties is who controls the accounting. If your client controls it, then, generally, a bottom-line, profits-based formula is best; if it does not, the superior alternative is a top-line, revenues-based formula.

The theory behind this dichotomy is that the party lacking control risks the bottom line being artificially reduced—either by the inclusion of expenses that might be GAAP, but not reflective of the business deal, or by the acceleration of expenses. If the formula is tied to gross revenues, rather than profits, the party who controls the accounting is much less able to manipulate the payment due. Obviously, if you represent the party with control, the ability to "refine" the bottom line has a certain attraction.

If you represent the party without control and are unsuccessful in negotiating a revenue-based formula, all is not lost. Prophylactic countermeasures can be negotiated. Specifically, negotiate covenants limiting the types of expenses and the amount of each expense included in the net income computation. The goal is to reduce the other side's flexibility as much as possible, thereby putting your client in a position as close to a revenue-based formula as possible.

For example, a seller who is negotiating a contingent payout in connection with an acquisition might argue that the impairment of goodwill in connection with the acquisition should be an excluded expense. Analytically, this expense arises wholly because of the acquisition and, therefore, arguably, distorts the real earnings picture. From the seller's perspective, any other expenses new to the business (e.g., additional overhead) would also be fair game for excluding. Finally, consider including language that requires the accounting to be consistent with prior years, thus precluding artificial expense or revenue recognition in selected periods.

Obviously, if you represent the buyer, resist any attempt to shackle your client's flexibility. Your client now owns the business, and it should have the ability to run it, including the accounting.

CHAPTER TWENTY-TWO

EXERCISES

Exercise 22

Shareholders A, B, C, and D wish to enter into a shareholders' agreement, but they would like to see one provision before you draft the entire agreement. They want the agreement to provide that if any shareholder wants to sell shares to a third party, that shareholder must first offer the shares to the other shareholders. (This is known as a **right of first refusal**.) The shareholders were not terribly good at explaining how to determine the number of shares each nonselling shareholder could buy. Instead, they gave the following example. Assume that the corporation has 50 shares issued and outstanding, and that A wants to sell the 10 shares she owns. B, who owns 20 shares, could purchase 50% of those 10 shares because B owns 50 percent of the shares not being sold. Draft the formula for determining the number of shares that each nonselling shareholder may purchase. Use the method that you think will make it the easiest for the reader to understand the provision's purpose and how it functions.

A Potpourri of Other Drafting Considerations

23.1 GENDER-NEUTRAL DRAFTING

When drafting a contract that has parties who are individuals (rather than entities), make all pronouns referring to individuals gender specific. So, in an employment agreement between a corporation and its executive Sadie Kendler, make sure that *she* and *her* appear wherever appropriate, and not *he* or *him.* If you are working with a precedent on a computer, you can easily do this. Use your word processor's "Find and Replace" function to help you find all the instances that need to be changed. Alternatively, keep two versions of the precedent on your computer, one for men and the other for women.

The drafting becomes a little more complicated if both men and women are parties, or if men, women, and entities are parties. It is awkward to use *he, she,* and *it* and *him, her,* and *it.* Instead, replace the pronouns with the defined term used to refer to these parties.

> **Awkward**
>
> **Shareholder Eligibility.** To be eligible to vote for the members of the Board of Directors, a Shareholder shall submit *his, her, or its proxy* no later than 5:00 p.m., May 18, 20XX.
>
> **Better**
>
> **Shareholder Eligibility.** To be eligible to vote for the members of the Board of Directors, a Shareholder shall submit *that Shareholder's proxy* no later than 5:00 p.m., May 18, 20XX.

As an alternative, delete unnecessary pronouns.

> **Awkward**
>
> **Transfer of Shares.** A Shareholder proposing to transfer his, her, or its Shares . . .
>
> **Better**
>
> **Transfer of Shares.** A Shareholder proposing to transfer Shares . . .

Do not use a plural form of a defined term. While this works perfectly well in narrative writing, it can create ambiguity in a contract, as in the following provision:

> **Wrong**
>
> **Deadline.** The Students shall submit their exercises no later than 5:00 p.m., Friday, June 10, 20XX.

At least four interpretations of this provision are possible:

> **Correct—Version 1**
>
> **Deadline.** Each Student shall submit **that Student's *exercise*** no later than 5:00 p.m., Friday, June 10, 20XX.
>
> **Correct—Version 2**
>
> **Deadline.** Each Student shall submit **that Student's *exercises*** no later than 5:00 p.m., Friday, June 10, 20XX.
>
> **Correct—Version 3**
>
> **Deadline.** Each team of Students shall submit ***its exercise*** no later than 5:00 p.m., Friday, June 10, 20XX.
>
> **Correct—Version 4**
>
> **Deadline.** Each team of Students shall submit ***the Students' exercises*** no later than 5:00 p.m., Friday, June 10, 20XX.

If individuals are not parties to an agreement, gender-neutral drafting issues still arise if any of the contract's provisions refer to individuals. For example, references to *firemen, policemen,* and *workmen* are no longer appropriate. Contract provisions should use gender-neutral terms, such as *firefighters, police officers,* and *workers.*

23.2 THE CASCADE EFFECT

The **cascade effect** occurs when the drafting of a business term in one provision requires a change in, or the addition of, a second business term. A simple example: Assume that you are drafting an employment agreement that requires your client to pay its executive an annual salary of $100,000. The contract also includes an endgame provision that obligates the company to pay the executive his salary through his last day of employment upon his termination for cause. Now assume that after the first round of negotiations, the client agrees to pay the executive a $10,000 annual bonus. Here is where the cascade effect kicks in. You will need to make two changes. First, you will need to change the compensation provision in the action section to provide for the bonus. Second, you will need a new endgame provision that spells out how much of the bonus, if any, the client will pay if it fires the executive for cause. One change causes another.

23.3 EXCEPTIONS

When drafting or reviewing an agreement, a lawyer must carefully analyze each provision to determine whether it should apply in all circumstances. When it does not, and it often does not, the contract must provide for an exception.

23.3.1 HOW TO SIGNAL AN EXCEPTION

Exceptions are signaled in several ways: *except, except as otherwise provided, other than, unless, provided,* and *provided, however.* All of these signals, other than *provided* and *provided, however* are acceptable. These two terms have multiple meanings that create the possibility of ambiguity.[1]

23.3.2 PLACEMENT OF THE EXCEPTION

As a general rule, when drafting a provision that includes an exception, put the rule first, then the exception. If the order is reversed, the provision often becomes more difficult to understand because the reader does not have the context to understand the exception. In addition, with a long exception, the reader has too much information to remember before getting to the provision's main point.

Wrong

Enforceability. Except to the extent that enforcement is limited by

(a) applicable bankruptcy, insolvency, reorganization, moratorium, or other similar laws affecting creditors' rights generally, or

(b) general equitable principles, regardless of whether the issue of enforceability is considered in a proceeding in equity or at law,

this Agreement is the legal, valid, and binding obligation of the Publisher, enforceable against the Publisher in accordance with its terms.

Correct

Enforceability. This Agreement is the legal, valid, and binding obligation of the Publisher, enforceable against the Publisher in accordance with its terms, except to the extent that enforcement is limited by

---

1. See §21.7.

> (a) applicable bankruptcy, insolvency, reorganization, moratorium or other similar laws affecting creditors' rights generally; or
>
> (b) general equitable principles, regardless of whether the issue of enforceability is considered in a proceeding in equity or at law.

Although you should generally put the exception at the end of a provision, sometimes it may work at the beginning of a provision if

- it is short and quickly alerts the reader of the exception; or
- it provides helpful context.

In the following examples, the first version is acceptable, while the second is preferred.

Correct

> **Investments**. Except for a $400,000 investment in a subsidiary, the Borrower shall not make any investments.

Better

> **Investments** The Borrower shall not make any investments, except for a $400,000 investment in a subsidiary.

If a provision and its exception result in a long sentence, consider breaking it down into subsections. Put the general rule in the first subsection and the exception in the next. The captions for the subsections should signal their content: *General Rule* and *Exception*.

Correct

> **Duty of Nondisclosure.**[2]
>
> (a) **General Rule**. The Executive shall not disclose any item of Confidential Information in any form to any Person.
>
> (b) **Exception.** Despite subsection (a), the Executive may disclose Confidential Information to any one or more of the following Persons:
>
> (i) Any member, manager, or agent of the LLC.
>
> (ii) Any person to whom the LLC has authorized the Executive to make disclosure.

If a rule and its exception are in separate sentences or subsections, their relationship should be explicitly stated in one of the two sentences or subsections:

---

2. This provision is based upon a provision in John M. Cunningham, *Drafting Limited Liability Company Operating Agreements* Form 17, §7.1 (Wolters Kluwer 2006).

> Except as set forth in the next [sentence] [subsection], [state the general rule]
>
> *or*
>
> Despite the previous [sentence] [subsection], [state the exception]

Although you can generally draft the exception either way, use the second format if the contract states the general rule in a section or subsection captioned *General Rule*. *General rules* do not include exceptions. Of course, if the provision were rewritten without subsections and captions, the sentence with the general rule could contain the reference to the exception, as in the following provision.

> **Correct**
>
> **Duty of Nondisclosure.** The Executive shall not disclose any item of Confidential Information in any form to any Person, except in accordance with the following sentence. The Executive may disclose Confidential Information to any one or more of the following Persons:
>
> (a) A member, manager, or agent of the LLC.
>
> (b) A person to whom the LLC has authorized the Executive to make disclosure.

Putting an exception at the end of a provision or a sentence may create an ambiguity. If the exception follows a compound or a series, it may be unclear whether the exception modifies only the word or phrase immediately adjacent to it, or whether it modifies each of the items in the compound or the series.[3] To cure any potential ambiguity, tabulate the compound or the series and then, after the last item, put the exception on a new line at the margin. If the exception is short, then use it to begin the provision. In the provision that follows, the ambiguity is whether the exception, including its reasonableness requirement, applies only to subletting.

> **Wrong**
>
> **Assignments and Sublets.** The Tenant shall not assign its rights under this Lease or sublet the Apartment, except with the prior written consent of the Landlord, which consent the Landlord shall not unreasonably withhold.
>
> **Correct**
>
> **Assignments and Sublets.** The Tenant shall not
>
> (a) assign its rights under this Lease or
>
> (b) sublet the Apartment,
>
> except with the prior written consent of the Landlord, which consent the Landlord shall not unreasonably withhold.

---

3. See §21.3 for a discussion of how modifiers following a compound or series can create ambiguity.

Drafters sometimes put exceptions both at the beginning of a sentence and at the end. Instead, put all of the exceptions together at the end of the sentence and, if necessary to enhance clarity, tabulate them.

Wrong

Assignments and Sublets. Except as permitted by Section 4.7, the Tenant shall not assign its rights under this Lease or sublet the Apartment, except with the prior written consent of the Landlord, which consent the Landlord shall not unreasonably withhold.

Correct

Assignments and Sublets. The Tenant shall not assign its rights under this Lease or sublet the Apartment, except that it may assign its rights in each of the following circumstances:

(a) As permitted by Section 4.7.

(b) With the prior written consent of the Landlord, which consent the Landlord shall not unreasonably withhold.

23.3.3   EXCEPT AS OTHERWISE PROVIDED

The phrase *except as otherwise provided* signals an exception. The exception, however, appears not in the provision being read, but elsewhere in the contract. Some drafters specify where the other provision is, but others do not. Those who do not generally do not articulate a persuasive reason for not including a section reference. The proffered rationale often focuses on the danger of an incorrect cross-reference or on the flexibility to argue later that the contract includes more than one exception—even if the parties contemplated only one at the time of drafting. Include the cross-reference. To prevent an incorrect cross-reference, keep it in brackets or in a large, bold font until you finalize the agreement. Then, check the cross-reference, insert it, and delete any brackets or return it to its regular font, as the case may be.

23.4   NOTWITHSTANDING ANYTHING TO THE CONTRARY

The phrase *notwithstanding anything to the contrary in this Agreement* signals a reader that one provision trumps all of the others. No matter what those other provisions say, this provision supersedes them. This phrase may also be used in a more limited way: *notwithstanding anything to the contrary in Section X.*

Be careful when you use this phrase, especially if the contract uses it more than once. If the two instances contradict each other, an ambiguity will result.

A contemporary alternative to *notwithstanding anything to the contrary in this Agreement* is *despite any other provision of this Agreement.*

23.5   WITHOUT LIMITING THE GENERALITY OF THE PRECEDING

The phrase *without limiting the generality of the preceding [section, sentence]* signals the reader that the examples that follow are illustrative and not intended to restrict the breadth of the preceding statement of a general rule. For example:

> **Duties**. The Company shall employ the Performer as a broadcast anchor for sports programming on the Station. In this capacity, the Performer shall render those services that the Company requires, subject to its direction, control, rules, and regulations. *Without limiting the generality of the preceding sentence*, the Performer's services include
>
> (a) preparing for, rehearsing, delivering, and performing on the Station's programs, whether live or recorded;
>
> (b) operating all kinds of technical equipment; and
>
> (c) writing, producing, and directing programs and announcements on which the Performer is to appear.[4]

The phrase *without limiting the generality of the preceding [section, sentence]* is a contemporary alternative to *without limiting the generality of the foregoing*. Do not use the traditional formulation. In addition to being legalese, it can cause ambiguity because *foregoing* does not specify to what it refers; it could be one or more sentences or sections.

23.6 *EJUSDEM GENERIS*

Ejusdem generis, a Latin phrase, means *of the same kind or class*. Courts apply this canon of construction where a list of specific items concludes with general language intended to expand that list. In determining how that list should be expanded, courts limit the breadth of the general language by finding it embraces only other items of the same kind or class as those already listed. The preceding specific words limit the scope of the general language.

A classic application of *ejusdem generis* arises in the context of a *force majeure* definition. For example:

> **"*Force Majeure* Event"** means storm, flood, washout, tsunami, lightning, drought, earthquake, volcanic eruption, landslide, cyclone, typhoon, tornado, or any other event beyond a party's control.

Although the concluding language *any other event beyond a party's control* is broad, a court would look to the characteristics of the specific events preceding that language to determine what other events would be within its scope. As the listed events are all natural catastrophes, a court, relying on *ejusdem generis*, could reasonably find that a hurricane fits within the general language, but that a war does not. This may be exactly what the parties intended.

Parties can attempt to overcome the application of *ejusdem generis* by stating that it does not apply.

---

4. This provision is based on a provision in *Williams v. Nationwide Communications, Inc.*, 1988 WL 138919 *2 (Tenn. Ct. App. Dec. 30, 1988).

23.7 *EXPRESSIO UNIUS EST EXCLUSIO ALTERIUS*

Expressio unius est exclusio alterius, another Latin phrase, means *the expression of one thing excludes the other.* When used as a canon of construction, it limits a provision to what it states expressly.

Suppose, for example, that a contract obligates a breaching party to pay damages, including consequential damages. Would the breaching party also be obligated to pay punitive damages? Does the expression of consequential damages exclude punitive damages? The answer depends upon the meaning of *including.* Is it intended to introduce illustrative examples,[5] or is it restrictive language limiting the provision to the specifics that follow?[6] To avoid this problem, many drafters explicitly expand the meaning of *including* by using either of the following phrases: *including, without limitation* or *including, but not limited to.* Other drafters include an interpretive provision stating that *including* is deemed to be followed by *without limitation.*

23.8 DEEM

Use *deem* or *deemed* to turn something contrary to reality into a contractual reality. *Deem* creates the fiction that something is true, even though it is not.

> **Example 1**
>
> Wrong
>
>   **Notice.** A notice *is deemed effectively given* only if the notice is in writing and the intended recipient receives it.
>
> Correct
>
>   **Notice.** A party gives an effective notice only if the notice is in writing and the intended recipient receives it.
>
> **Example 2**
>
> Correct
>
>   **Notice.** Any notice or instruction received after 5:00 p.m. on a Business Day or on a day that is not a Business Day is deemed received at 9:00 a.m. on the next Business Day.

23.9 SCHEDULES AND EXHIBITS

23.9.1 INTRODUCTION

Schedules and exhibits are additional materials not within the body of a contract, but that are nonetheless part of it. Although some drafters use the terms interchangeably, they have different purposes.

---

5. *See St. Paul Mercury Ins. Co. v. Lexington Ins. Co.,* 78 F.3d 202, 206-207 (5th Cir. 1996).
6. *See P. Adams v. Dole,* 927 F.2d 771, 776-777 (4th Cir. 1991).

Schedules and exhibits generally gain their status by being referred to in the definition of *Agreement*. Some drafters, however, refer to them in an agreement without explicitly incorporating them. Drafters generally do not separately define these terms, although they often appear with their first letters capitalized.

> **"Agreement"** means this Power Purchase Agreement, as amended, and the Schedules and Exhibits to it.

This definition intentionally does not state that the schedules and exhibits are attached. Sometimes these documents are so large that attaching them becomes unwieldy. As drafted, this definition prevents any technical interpretive problems that might arise because the documents are not physically attached to the agreement.

23.9.2 SCHEDULES

Parties use **schedules** to disclose information that would otherwise be in representations and warranties. Sometimes the schedules contain additional information that supplements a party's representations and warranties; other times it lists exceptions.

> **Example 1**
>
> **Material Contracts. Schedule 3.10** lists all the material contracts to which the Borrower is a party.
>
> **Example 2**
>
> **Defaults**. The Borrower is not in default under any agreement, except as specified in **Schedule 3.18**.

Properly or improperly scheduling information directly affects liability under an agreement. If a borrower fails to schedule a material contract to which it is a party, it will have misrepresented the facts, subjecting it to liability. Therefore, you must meticulously prepare schedules and vet them with the client.

Parties put information into schedules for several reasons.

- First, it unclutters the agreement and makes it easier to read.
- Second, it simplifies the logistics of preparing the agreement. The lawyers responsible for drafting the schedules are not usually the lawyers drafting the agreement. For example, a bank's lawyers invariably draft the loan agreement, but the borrower and its counsel compile and draft the schedules used to expand or qualify the borrower's representations and warranties. Having the schedules in a separate word-processing document simplifies the drafting process.
- Third, sensitive information can be kept from prying eyes. Specifically, schedules are not generally filed with the Securities and Exchange Commission, even though the related agreement is filed and made public. This allows a party to protect its confidential information (such as a customer list) by putting it in a schedule.[7]

---

7. *See* Lou R. Kling and Eileen T. Nugent, *Negotiated Acquisitions of Companies, Subsidiaries and Divisions*, vol. 2, §10.02, n. 2. (Law Journal Press 2006).

When drafting an agreement, do not provide for a schedule if it will not list any information. Similarly, if only one or two short items are to be listed, include them in the representation and warranty. Readers quickly become frustrated if they turn to a schedule that provides little or no information.

Each schedule in a contract is identified by a number. The number is usually the same as the section number of the provision that requires the schedule. So, if Section 4.12 requires the seller to disclose all litigations, the list of litigations will appear in Schedule 4.12. Drafters often bold schedule references to visually alert the reader to a schedule: **Schedule 4.12**.

Drafters should be aware that putting together a disclosure schedule can be a sophisticated task. Before finalizing any schedules, make sure that you assess the business and legal issues and deal with them appropriately.[8]

23.9.3 EXHIBITS

Exhibits are agreements or other documents relating to the contract that the parties want incorporated into the contract. They may or may not have already been signed when the parties sign the contract. For example, when a loan agreement is signed, it will include as exhibits a form for each of the following: the promissory note, the security agreement, the pledge agreement, and the opinion that borrower's counsel must deliver. By "attaching" the forms as exhibits at the contract's signing, the parties establish an objective standard as to the agreements' and the documents' content.[9] With luck, these exhibits will preclude any dispute as to their substance when they are eventually signed at the closing.

Exhibits of unsigned documents and agreements are often first referenced in the definition article.

> **"Pledge Agreement"** means the Pledge Agreement by the Borrower in favor of the Bank, *substantially in the form of* **Exhibit F.**

Drafters include the italicized language to handle the possibility that the Pledge Agreement might differ slightly from the exhibit. This could occur either because the parties must complete blanks in the form, such as the date, or because the parties agree to a minor change.

As indicated, parties may also include as an exhibit an agreement that has been previously signed. Parties often do this if the agreement directly relates to the agreement's purpose. For example, the parties might attach to an assignment and assumption agreement a copy of the contract being assigned. Again, the rationale is to prevent a dispute, in this instance, as to which contract is being assigned. In the United States, parties would not generally attach as an exhibit a letter of intent or a confidentiality agreement signed before the signing of the main agreement. Outside the United States, customs differ, so be sensitive to local practice.

Occasionally, parties also use exhibits to display technical information or to demonstrate how a mathematical formula works.[10] The sample computations act as a form of legislative history that the parties or a court can use to resolve disputes.

---

8. *See generally id.* at Chap. 10.

9. Recall that Supersonic and Fly-by-Night agreed to sign an escrow agreement that included an exhibit (Exercise 6-3). That exhibit specified the form of notice that the parties would need to sign to cause the release of the escrow funds.

10. See Chapter 22.

Exhibits are generally given sequential numbers or letters based upon the order in which they appear in an agreement. Exhibit A, Exhibit B, and Exhibit C or Exhibit 1, Exhibit 2, and Exhibit 3. To facilitate keeping track of the exhibits, some drafters bold the references to them: **Exhibit A**.

23.10 NOMINALIZATION

Nominalizing a word converts it from a verb into a phrase that includes the noun form of the verb. For example, the previous sentence could be rewritten by converting *nominalize* into *nominalization* and *convert* into *conversion*.

> The *nominalization* of a word is the *conversion* of a verb into a phrase that includes the noun form of the verb.

When you have a choice between using a verb or a noun phrase, choose the verb. It makes the sentence shorter and punchier by making it more direct. Here are two other examples:

Example 1—Wrong

Upon the expiration of the term of this Agreement . . .

Example 1—Correct

When this Agreement expires . . .

Example 2—Wrong

A party shall give the other party a notification . . .

Example 2—Correct

A party shall notify the other party . . .

Common nominalizations and their verb forms include the following:

Noun	Verb
administration	administer
alteration	alter
application	apply
compensation	compensate
consideration	consider
contribution	contribute
notification	notify
payment	pay
submission	submit
violation	violate

23.11 PARALLEL DRAFTING

In Chapter 19, you learned about parallel drafting in connection with tabulating a single sentence. Parallel drafting also applies to multiple sentences dealing with similar subject matter. To be parallel, the grammatical structure of each of those sentences must be the same. Fixing parallel structure sometimes also requires that you redraft the provisions so that they say the same thing the same way. Generally, an absence of parallel drafting in this context does not affect substance. Instead, the issue is one of craftsmanship.

Here are two provisions from an employment agreement that are not parallel, as well as a revision that fixes the problem. The caption dealing with death in the corrected version has been revised so that the two captions parallel each other.

Wrong

Disability during Employment. The compensation payable to the Executive is reduced by 50 percent if the Executive cannot perform his services by reason of illness or incapacity for more than six months.

Death Benefits. If the Executive dies during the term of this Agreement, the Employer shall pay to the Executive's estate the salary through the date of his death.

Correct

Disability during Employment. If the Executive cannot perform his services by reason of illness or incapacity for more than six months during the term of this Agreement, the Company shall reduce the Executive's salary by 50 percent.

Death during Employment. If the Executive dies during the term of this Agreement, the Company shall pay to the Executive's estate the salary through the date of his death.

23.12 RESPECTIVELY

Use *respectively* to establish that two or more items create concurrent relationships when joined with two or more other items in the same sentence: If A, B, and C occur, then D, E, and F are true, respectively. A relates to D, B relates to E, and C relates to F, all at the same time.

Example 1

Maximum Borrowings. Subsidiary A, Subsidiary B, and Subsidiary C may borrow a maximum of $2 million, $4.5 million, and $8 million, respectively.

Example 2

Election of Directors. The Group A Shareholders and the Group B Shareholders shall cast their votes for Group A Directors and Group B Directors, respectively.

23.13   AS THE CASE MAY BE

Use *as the case may be* to establish that two or more items create alternative relationships when joined with two or more other items in the same sentence. If A occurs, then B occurs, *or* if C occurs then D occurs. The relationships are alternative, not concurrent.

> **Allocation of Income and Losses**. All net income or net loss allocated to a Partner in accordance with the terms of this Article 6 is to be credited or charged, as the case may be, to that Partner's capital account.

Some drafters use *as the case may be* to clarify that an *or* in a sentence is being used in its exclusive sense. That clarification may be unnecessary as in the immediately following provision.

> **Wrong**
>
> **Death and Retirement Benefits**. The Partnership shall pay the amount calculated in accordance with **Exhibit A** in 60 equal monthly installments, beginning on the first day of the month following the month in which the Partner died or retired, as the case may be.
>
> **Correct**
>
> **Death and Retirement Benefits**. The Partnership shall pay the amount calculated in accordance with **Exhibit A** in 60 equal monthly installments, beginning on the first day of the month following the month in which the Partner died or retired.

23.14   *THERE IS* AND *THERE ARE*

You can often eliminate *there is* and *there are* from a sentence, making it tighter. Look for the sentence's core meaning, and use those words to create a new subject and verb.

> **Wrong**
>
> **Litigation**. There is no litigation pending or threatened against the Licensor with respect to the Trademark.
>
> **Correct**
>
> **Litigation**. No litigation is pending or threatened against the Licensor with respect to the Trademark.

23.15   THE POSSESSIVE

Many lawyers shy away from using a noun's possessive form. But its use shortens a sentence, making it easier to read while doing no harm to its substance.

> **Wrong**
>
> **Confidentiality**. During the term *of this Agreement* and afterwards, each party shall protect the secrecy of the Confidential Information *of the other party*. All Confidential Information remains the exclusive property *of the disclosing party*. *(33 words)*

> **Correct**
>
> **Confidentiality**. During this *Agreement's* term and afterwards, each party shall protect *the other party's* Confidential Information. All Confidential Information remains *the disclosing party's* exclusive property. *(24 words)*

23.16 *ANY* AND *EACH*

Any and *each* are adjectives whose improper use can change the meaning of a contract provision. Applying the following guidelines will help prevent errors.

1. *To create an affirmative covenant, use* each.

> **Additional Capital Contributions**. *Each* Limited Partner shall contribute $1 million to the Partnership no later than 30 days after its receipt of a Call Notice.

2. *To create discretionary authority, use* any.

> **Assignment of Cash Distributions**. *Any* Limited Partner may assign its rights to Cash Distributions without the consent of the General Partner.

3. *To create a negative covenant that has a single person as the subject of the sentence, use a* negative subject *and* may.

> **Assignment of Partnership Interest**. *No Limited Partner may* assign its Partnership Interest without the prior written consent of the General Partner.

4. *To create a representation and warranty that is an affirmative statement of fact, use* each. *Use* each *also if the knowledge qualifies representation and warranty.*

> **Example 1**
>
> **Authority**. *Each Selling Shareholder* has all power and authority necessary to execute, deliver, and perform this Agreement.

> **Example 2**
>
> **Consents**. *To the knowledge of each Selling Shareholder,* the Target has obtained all consents required in connection with the transactions that this Agreement contemplates.

If *each* were changed to *any* in the immediately previous example, then the representation and warranty would be true even if two of the three Selling Shareholders did not know whether the Target had obtained all the required consents.

5. *To create a representation and warranty that is a negative statement of fact, use* any.

> **Correct**
>
> **Capitalization.** The Target has not issued or granted *to any Selling Shareholder* any outstanding right of subscription, warrant, call, option, or other agreement to purchase or otherwise acquire any securities of the Target.

If *any* were changed to *each* in the immediately preceding example, the representation and warranty would be true so long as the Target had not the issued or granted any right or security to all of the Selling Shareholders.

6. *To create a representation and warranty that is a negative statement of fact subject to a knowledge qualifier, use a* negative subject.

> **Correct**
>
> **Misstatements and Omissions.** *No Selling Shareholder knows* of any material misstatement or omission with respect to the transactions that this Agreement contemplates.

CHAPTER TWENTY-THREE

EXERCISES

Exercise 23-1

The following provision comes from an employment agreement between Vera Ward and Scuba Vacations, Inc. Mark it up so that it applies only to Ward. What changes would you make so that it could be used in any employment agreement? If you were Vera Ward, which version would you prefer, and why?

> The Company shall provide Ward with the Company's full range of health and insurance benefits and shall provide him with an office suite similar to the one he had at his previous employer.

Exercise 23-2

Mark up the following provisions to correct the drafting errors.

> **Assignments.** Except for delegations to affiliates, the Contractor shall not assign its performance under this Agreement to any Person, other than Hughes Contracting Corp.

> **Severability.** If any provision of this Agreement is deemed by the final decree of a court to be unenforceable, the enforceability of the remaining provisions is unimpaired.

> **Power and Authority.** The Licensees have all requisite corporate power and authority to own, operate, and lease their respective properties and to carry on their business as now being conducted.

> **Consents.** Other than the approval of the Seller's shareholders, the Seller is not required to obtain any consent or approval or give any notice in connection with the execution and delivery of this Agreement or the consummation of the transactions contemplated hereby, except for notification to and consents and approvals from the persons listed in **Exhibit D.**

> **Claims against the Target.** To the knowledge of the Sellers, no basis exists for the assertion of any claim against the Target.

Books and Records. The General Partner is responsible for the maintenance of the Partnership's books and records and shall give each Limited Partner notice of each claim made by each Limited Partner of any inaccuracy in those books and records.

Existing Agreements. A list and brief description of all agreements to which the Borrowers are a party are set forth on **Schedule 6.1.**

New Agreements. The Sellers shall not enter into any new agreements without the prior written consent of the Buyer.

Deconstructing Complex Provisions

24.1 THE SIX-STEP PROCESS

In the preceding chapters, you learned multiple skills that will help you write clear and unambiguous provisions. Although each can be used separately, you can also use them together to deconstruct long, difficult provisions in a precedent or draft from the other side. Many times these provisions are so dense that you cannot be sure of their substantive effect. To understand them, you need to take them apart, reorganize them, and clean up the language. Only then can you find the ambiguities and incorrect statements of the business deal.

Deconstructing these provisions can be intimidating. Often, so much seems wrong. But by deconstructing a provision in steps, the process becomes manageable. This chapter describes a six-step process for deconstructing—and reconstructing—complex provisions. You already know five of the six steps, so learning the process should be relatively easy. As the chapter explains each of the steps, it will deconstruct a provision so you can see the process being applied.

Here are the six steps:

1. Explicate.
2. Create clarity through format.
3. Create clarity through sentence structure.
4. Clarify ambiguities.
5. Root out legalese.
6. Check substance.

We will now look at each of them in turn.

24.1.1 EXPLICATE

Explicating a provision breaks it down into its component parts. It permits you to look at each sentence, clause, and modifier and see how each relates to the other.

Before explicating a provision, copy, paste, and save it into a new document. Then, using the Enter key, begin breaking the provision down by separating each sentence from the others. Number each of the sentences. To break down a sentence, tab any introductory prepositional clause so that it appears on its own line. Also find each compound and series and tab each item. As your skill in explicating improves, you may decide not to tabulate every item in a compound or series, but do it in the beginning. Show the relative relationship of the items in the compound or series to the preceding language by indenting each item, just as you would if you were formatting. If a word or phrase qualifies the compound or series, put it on a separate line. Finally, put each proviso and exception on a separate line.

Here is an unexplicated provision and what it looks like after explication.

Unexplicated Provision

    Maintenance and Location. The Lessee shall, at its own expense, maintain the Equipment in good operating condition and repair and protect the Equipment from deterioration other than normal wear and tear. The Lessee shall not make any modification, alteration, or addition to the Equipment without the prior written consent of the Lessor, which shall not be unreasonably withheld, provided that no consent is required for engineering changes recommended by and made by the manufacturer; and shall keep the Equipment at the location shown in the Schedule, and shall not remove the Equipment without the prior written consent of the Lessor. The Lessee shall during the term of this Lease, at its own cost, enter into and maintain in force a contract with the manufacturer or other acceptable maintenance company, covering the maintenance of the Equipment.

Explicated Provision

Maintenance and Location.

1. The Lessee shall, at its own expense,
        maintain the Equipment in
            good operating condition and
            repair and
       protect the Equipment from deterioration
   other than normal wear and tear.

2. The Lessee
      shall not make any
          modification,
          alteration, or
          addition
      to the Equipment without the prior written consent of the Lessor, which shall not be unreasonably withheld,
      provided that no consent is required for engineering changes recommended by and made by the manufacturer;
      shall keep the Equipment at the location shown in the Schedule, and
      shall not remove the Equipment
      without the prior written consent of the Lessor.

3. The Lessee shall during the term of this Lease, at its own cost,
      enter into and
      maintain in force

a contract with
>   the manufacturer or
>   other acceptable maintenance company,
covering the maintenance of the Equipment.

24.1.2 CREATE CLARITY THROUGH FORMAT

Once you explicate a provision, it becomes relatively easy to format. First, look at each sentence and decide whether the subject matter of another sentence is sufficiently related that the sentences should be combined to create a section or joined into one tabulated sentence. In addition, look at each sentence to decide whether it deals with only one subject. If it does not, then two sentences or sections may be appropriate. Then, look at each indented item from a compound or series and decide whether it should be a subsection or joined with the rest of the sentence. If any indented items are preceded or followed by a qualifier, keep the qualifier on a separate line. Later you will decide whether its placement creates an ambiguity. Write yourself a note, so that you remember to check this point later. (For now, we will strictly adhere to the order of the six-step process. But as you become more proficient, you may decide to perform multiple steps at one time.)

Applying this analysis to our example, we see that sentences one and three both deal with maintenance of the equipment. So, the redraft will put them together into one section. The second sentence, however, covers two unrelated topics: changes to the Equipment and location of the Equipment. Thus, two sections should be created from this sentence.

Now we will look at the indented items for each sentence and decide whether they should become subsections. The first sentence has two levels of indentation. *Good operating condition* and *repair* should be rejoined with the preceding language. They both qualify *Equipment* which precedes them in the sentence, and they are short with no potential for ambiguity. Deciding whether to keep the remaining tabbed items as subsections is more difficult. Because the qualifier *other than normal wear and tear* follows the tabbed items, it creates an ambiguity: Does the language qualify each of the tabbed items or only the second? This issue of ambiguity can also be postponed.

In the second sentence, *modification, alteration,* and *addition* need not be tabulated as they are short. As to the other two indented items, we earlier decided that they should be in their own section. They are, however, long enough that they should be tabulated in that new section. The last line, *without the prior written consent of the Lessor,* also creates an ambiguity as to what it modifies. Does it modify each of the tabbed items or only the last? For now, we can postpone that decision and leave it as a separate line.

In the third sentence, neither set of indented items needs to be drafted as subsections, although that may be revisited when the sentence is moved to become a part of the first section.

Here's the reformatted provision.

7.1 Maintenance. The Lessee shall, at its own expense,

(a)   maintain the Equipment in good operating condition and repair and

continued on next page >

(b)   protect the Equipment from deterioration,

other than normal wear and tear. The Lessee shall during the term of this Lease, at its own cost, enter into and maintain in force a contract with the manufacturer or other acceptable maintenance company, covering the maintenance of the Equipment.

7.2   Alterations and Additions. The Lessee shall not make any modification, alteration, or addition to the Equipment without the prior written consent of the Lessor, which shall not be unreasonably withheld, provided that no consent is required for engineering changes recommended by and made by the manufacturer.

7.3   Equipment's Location. The Lessee

(a)   shall keep the Equipment at the location shown in the Schedule and

(b)   shall not remove the Equipment without the prior

written consent of the Lessor.

24.1.3   CREATE CLARITY THROUGH SENTENCE STRUCTURE

To create clarity through sentence structure, apply the rules that you learned in Chapter 20 as well as other rules that you have learned that deal with sentence structure. For example, redraft nominalizations, place exceptions after the general rule, use the active voice, and use possessives.

Let's look at each of the sections of the example provision. In the first sentence of Section 7.1, *at its own expense* appears in the middle of the verb, violating the rule that a sentence's core words should be kept together. That can be corrected by moving it to the beginning of that sentence. The second sentence has the same issue. In addition, *during the term of this Lease,* is superfluous. That phrase can be deleted. The remainder of the sentence is wordy and should be made more concise. (See the redraft.)

Section 7.2 violates the three-line rule. This fix is easy. The "proviso" can be turned into its own sentence and rewritten to omit *provided.* In the new first sentence, three changes must be made. First, the nominalizations *modification, alteration,* and *addition* must be changed to their verb forms. Second, *without the prior written consent of the Lessor* must be redrafted so that it uses the possessive. Third, *which shall not be unreasonably withheld* must be changed from the passive to the active voice. In addition, *recommended by and made by the manufacturer* must also be changed from the passive to the active voice.

In Section 7.3, *without the prior written consent of the Lessor* must be changed so that it uses the possessive form of *Lessor.*

Here's the redraft.

7.1   Maintenance. At its own expense, the Lessee shall

(a)   maintain the Equipment in good operating condition and repair and

(b)   protect the Equipment from deterioration,

other than normal wear and tear. At its own cost, the Lessee shall enter into and maintain in force an equipment maintenance contract with the manufacturer or other acceptable maintenance company.

7.2   Alterations and Additions. The Lessee shall not modify, alter, or add to the Equipment without the Lessor's prior written consent, which it shall not unreasonably withhold. Despite the previous sentence, no consent is required for engineering changes that the manufacturer recommends and makes.

7.3   Equipment's Location. The Lessee

(a)   shall keep the Equipment at the location shown in the Schedule; and

(b)   shall not remove the Equipment

without the Lessor's prior written consent.

24.1.4   CLARIFY AMBIGUITIES

Section 7.1 presents three issues of ambiguity.

- First, should the phrase *other than normal wear and tear* qualify only subsection (b) or both subsections (a) and (b)? It probably qualifies both, although that would have been hard to tell from the original version of the provision. As a drafting matter, the phrase (really an exception) could be left where it is. The alternative would be to include it with each of the subsections.
- Second, the second sentence seems inconsistent with the first. The first sentence requires the Lessee to maintain the Equipment, while the second sentence requires the Lessee to enter into a maintenance agreement so that someone else can maintain the equipment. One way to reconcile the two would be to state that the second covenant is in furtherance of the first.
- Third, the two sentences do not say the same thing the same way. The first sentence uses the phrase *at its own expense,* while the second sentence uses the phrase *at its own cost.*

A second issue of not saying the same thing the same way arises when we compare Section 7.2 to Section 7.3. Section 7.2 provides that the Lessor *shall not unreasonably withhold its consent,* while Section 7.3 does not have that limitation on the Lessor's granting of its consent. Before deciding on this redraft, you would need to consult with your client to find out whether a difference was intended.

Finally, the last phrase of Section 7.3 is ambiguous. Again, to what does it apply: both tabbed items or only the last? You should confirm it with the client, but it probably applies to both.

Here's this redraft:

7.1   Maintenance. At its own expense, the Lessee shall

(a)   maintain the Equipment in good operating condition and repair and

(b)   protect the Equipment from deterioration,

except for normal wear and tear. At its own expense and in furtherance of its obligations in the preceding sentence, the Lessee shall enter into and maintain in force an equipment maintenance contract with the manufacturer or other acceptable maintenance company.

7.2   Alterations and Additions. The Lessee shall not modify, alter, or add to the Equipment without the Lessor's prior written consent, which it shall not unreasonably withhold. Despite the previous sentence, no consent is required for engineering changes that the manufacturer recommends and makes.

7.3   Equipment's Location. The Lessee

(a)   shall keep the Equipment at the location shown in the Schedule and

(b)   shall not remove the Equipment without the Lessor's prior written consent

[, which it shall not unreasonably withhold].

24.1.5   ROOT OUT LEGALESE

When performing this step, ruthlessly delete legalese. In addition, clean up any language problems that you have not already fixed.

This provision did not have much legalese. The only triplet in the provision is found in Section 7.2: *modify, alter, or add. Modify* and *alter* are synonyms, but arguably not *add.* If the original equipment is left unchanged, but a new piece of equipment is added to it, that addition, in this business, might not be an alteration.

The provision's defined terms, *Lessor* and *Lessee,* are problematic. As discussed in the chapter on definitions, many readers find it difficult to read contracts with defined terms ending in *or* and *ee.* Alternative defined terms might be *Owner* and *Renter.* If the owner regularly leases equipment, it might nonetheless prefer to retain the traditional defined terms. In either event, the article *the* does not always precede *Lessor* and *Lessee.* The rewrite must use—or not use—*the* consistently.

This rewrite is minimal:

7.1   Maintenance. At its own expense, the Renter shall

(a)   maintain the Equipment in good operating condition and repair and

(b)   protect the Equipment from deterioration,

except for normal wear and tear. At its own expense and in furtherance of its obligations in the preceding sentence, the Renter shall enter into and maintain in force an equipment maintenance contract with the manufacturer or other acceptable maintenance company.

7.2   Alterations and Additions. The Renter shall not alter or add to the Equipment without the Owner's prior written consent, which it shall not unreasonably withhold. Despite the previous sentence, no consent is required for engineering changes that the manufacturer recommends and makes.

7.3   Equipment's Location. The Renter

(a)   shall keep the Equipment at the location shown in the Schedule and

(b)   shall not remove the Equipment without the Owner's prior written consent

[, which it shall not unreasonably withhold].

24.1.6   CHECK SUBSTANCE

Checking substance is the final step of the six-step process. At this stage, you must step back and look at the redrafted provision and confirm that it accurately states the business deal. You may have discovered earlier in the process that the provision was incorrect. Correcting it then makes sense. That way, the other changes can work with the new substance. Also use this step as an opportunity to see if anything else in the provision must be changed. Some changes do not fall neatly into one of the steps, but they must still be made.

For our purposes, we will assume that the provision comports with the business deal. One point that might be raised with the client is a standards issue.[1] Section 7.1 ends with the statement that the maintenance company must be *acceptable.* Presumably, that means *acceptable to the Owner.* If representing the Renter, you might suggest changing that standard to *reasonably acceptable.*

---

1. See §25.5.

EXERCISES

Exercise 24-1

Apply the six-step process to the following provisions. Both are available on the *Drafting Contracts* Website.

Section 8.4. Assignment. No assignment or delegation of the rights, duties, or obligations of this Agreement shall be made by either party except as provided herein without the express written approval of a duly authorized representative of the other party; provided, however, that the Company may assign any or all of its rights and obligations hereunder to a wholly owned subsidiary of the Company; and provided further that the Company may delegate certain of its duties hereunder to ABC Healthcare Systems, Inc.

Section 7.3 Use of Mark on Invoices, etc. The use of the Mark by Licensee on invoices, order forms, stationery, and related material and in advertising in telephone or other directory listings is permitted only upon Licensor's prior written approval of the format in which the Mark is to be so used, the juxtaposition of the Mark with other words and phrases, and the content of the copy prior to the initial such use of the Mark and prior to any material change therein, which approval shall not be unreasonably withheld and shall be granted or denied within ten (10) business days of the submission of such format; provided, however, that such use of the Mark is only in conjunction with the sale of Licensed Items pursuant to this Agreement and further provided that should Licensor require a change in such format due to a revision, change, or modification by Licensor of the Mark, Licensor shall provide Licensee with reasonable notice of any such change or modification of the Mark in order to afford Licensee a reasonable period of time to revise and substitute invoices, order forms, stationery or other material reflecting the new Mark and shall permit Licensee to use, until the earlier of six months or depletion, such existing invoices, order forms, stationery, or other material without objection.

PART FOUR

Drafting from the Client's Perspective

Adding Value to the Deal

25.1 INTRODUCTION

Drafting contracts is more than translating the business deal into contract concepts and writing clear, unambiguous contract provisions. Sophisticated drafting requires a lawyer to understand the transaction from a client's business perspective and to add value to the deal. Looking at a contract from the client's perspective means understanding what the client wants to achieve and the risks it wants to avoid. Adding value to the deal is a euphemism for finding and resolving business issues. These skills are problem-solving skills and are an integral component of a deal lawyer's professional expertise. They require an understanding not only of contracts, but of business, the client's business, and the transaction at hand. At a law firm, having these skills is generally the province of the partners, and not necessarily all of them.

In a totally unscientific survey, partners were asked how they identified business issues. The following are some of the responses:

- "Identifying business issues requires a sixth sense."
- "A business issue is any issue you find that the client should resolve."
- "You know one when you see one."

The nub of these answers is that the partners learned by experience how to discern business issues.

Although you will find no substitute for experience, this chapter proposes a framework that will help you learn how more experienced practitioners think. The framework consists of five prongs, each of which is a business issue that appears in almost every transaction—albeit in different guises. The prongs of the framework are:

- Money
- Risk
- Control
- Standards
- Endgame

The subsequent sections of this chapter discuss these prongs and show how they manifest themselves in transactions. Afterwards, you will work through a series of exercises in which you will apply the framework to fact patterns.

25.2   MONEY

25.2.1   AMOUNT TO BE PAID OR RECEIVED

The first money issue to consider is always whether a client is entitled to receive more money or to pay less. Although clients generally negotiate and agree upon the consideration in a transaction, lawyers can often add value because of their deal-specific expertise. For example, perhaps your client, a major bank, wants to purchase a corporate jet. The client's expertise is finance, not the purchase and sale of airplanes, your specialty. If the client consults you before it negotiates the purchase price of the plane, you may be able to add value by explaining that the plane's proposed purchase price exceeds current market value because of the glut of planes on the market.

As part of this analysis, consider whether any of the consideration should be contingent. For example, buyers and sellers may value a seller's business differently. This is especially true for a new business. The seller is sure that it is the next Google, and the buyer certainly hopes so, but questions the seller's valuation because its business has no track record of profitability. To bridge the difference in valuation, a buyer can pay the seller a small amount at closing and additional consideration in the future. The parties will determine that amount based upon a formula tied into the business's performance after the acquisition. This arrangement is known as an **earn-out**.[1]

25.2.2   TIMING OF PAYMENTS

When analyzing a transaction, think through any issues with respect to the timing of monetary payments. These are known as **time value of money**[2] issues. It is almost always better for a client to pay later, but to receive money sooner. The longer a client has the money, the longer that money can be invested earning more money. Of course, tax considerations or other matters might require postponing the receipt of money.

If your client must pay the other party, ask whether it can spread out the payments over time, or alternatively whether the other party will give your client a discount for immediate payment. If the other side must pay your client, negotiate for receipt of the payment as soon as possible. If the other side objects, find out from your client whether it could benefit from an immediate, but smaller payment. For example, if the client receives the funds immediately, it may be able to invest in a new deal.

25.2.3   CREDIT RISK

Credit risk is always a business issue when the other party is obligated to pay your client in the future. Although the other party may be flush with cash when the parties make their deal, it may be less strong when payment is due. Therefore, whenever your client has agreed to receive a delayed payment, consider whether the risk of a payment default is significant. If it is, then negotiate a mechanism to secure the payment.[3]

---

1. For a more detailed discussion of earn-outs, see Lou R. Kling & Eileen Nugent, *Negotiated Acquisitions of Companies, Subsidiaries and Divisions* § 17.01 (Law Journal Press 1992).

2. For an excellent discussion of time value of money, see Terry Lloyd, *Present Value Concepts and Applications,* in *Accounting for Lawyers 1996: Using Financial Data in Legal Practice* 257 (PLI Corporate Law & Practice, Course Handbook Series No. B-965, 1996).

3. For a detailed discussion of ways to minimize credit risk, see the materials on risk in §25.3.3.

25.2.4 ISSUES RELATING TO PAYMENT FORMULAS

Parties often use a formula to determine a contract's consideration. For example, formulas are used to calculate the following:

- Purchase price adjustment provisions in acquisition agreements
- Compensation provisions in employment agreements
- Royalty provisions in license and franchise agreements
- Buy-out provisions in partnership and stockholder agreements

When reviewing a formula, begin by analyzing whether the theoretical basis for the payment amount is analytically correct. Stated differently, is the formula neutral, or does it favor your client or the other party?

Buchwald v. Paramount Pictures Corp. brought the problem of a flawed formula into sharp relief.[4] That case made "Hollywood accounting" infamous. The trouble began when Alain Bernheim, the producer of *Coming to America,*[5] agreed that Paramount would pay him a percentage of the movie's net profits, in addition to a modest upfront fee. Apparently, Bernheim expected the movie to be a success and anticipated that he could earn much more money by receiving a percentage of net profits rather than a one-time upfront fee.

The movie was a huge hit. Bernheim, no doubt, was elated. Unfortunately, that elation was short-lived: The studio reported that it lost money on the movie and that Bernheim was entitled to no additional money. The problem stemmed from the way the studio accounted for the movie's expenses. It included as expenses not only the direct expenses of the movie, but also some of the studio's overhead expenses. Thus, Bernheim would have been far better off receiving a percentage of the movie's gross revenues—before any expenses were deducted. Alternatively, Bernheim and the studio could have agreed upon which expenses were allocable to the movie.

Assuming that your client and the other party have agreed upon a formula for calculating the payment amount, confirm that the formula is properly stated. Is each variable unambiguous? Is the formula as a whole unambiguous?

Some of the most common drafting errors occur when crafting a formula.[6] To make certain that a formula works as intended, run multiple hypotheticals to see what answers are obtained when numbers are plugged into the formula. Be sure to include in the hypotheticals numbers far outside the range that the client expects. Calculations sometimes result in negative amounts, and the parties need to address what happens in this circumstance.

After running the numbers, send the hypotheticals to your client to make sure that he understands how the formula will work, both when the transaction succeeds and when it fails. (Clients do not like surprises.) Once your client approves the formula and the hypotheticals, send them to the other side for their review and approval. With luck, this process will root out any differences at a time when they can be resolved—without litigation. As the final step in this process, with the approval of all the principals, annex the hypotheticals as an exhibit to the contract. They will become a legislative history of sorts, setting forth the parties' understanding of the formula at the time of contracting.

---

4. *See Buchwald v. Paramount Pictures Corp.*, 1990 WL 357611 (Cal. Super. Jan. 8, 1990). See also, Pierce O'Donnell and Dennis McDougal, *Fatal Subtraction: The Inside Story of* Buchwald v. Paramount, Appendix B (Doubleday 1992).

5. Eddie Murphy starred.

6. See Chapter 22 for a fuller discussion of formulas.

25.2.5 TRANSACTION EXPENSES

Parties do not always address the allocation of transaction expenses—especially at the preliminary stages of negotiation. As they can run to a tidy sum, you and your client should think through whether each party should pay its own expenses or whether the expenses should be shifted from one party to the other. Also, consider whether the prevailing party in a litigation should be contractually entitled to recover its attorneys' fees and other litigation expenses.[7]

25.2.6 ACCOUNTING AND TAX ISSUES

The accounting and tax issues in a contract can be quite sophisticated. These issues may determine the structure of the transaction and sometimes even whether the transaction can be done. If you do not have the background to address these issues, you *must* obtain the assistance of a qualified practitioner.[8]

25.2.7 WHO, WHAT, WHEN, WHERE, WHY, HOW, AND HOW MUCH?

As you may recall from Chapter 8 on the action sections, whenever you draft a provision dealing with the payment of money, you should always answer the questions, *Who, what, when, where, why, how,* and *how much?*[9]

25.2.8 ENDGAME

Every contract ends—either happily or unhappily. A borrower can repay the loan or default; a joint venture can conclude successfully or fail; and an acquisition can close or fail to be consummated. No matter which way a contract ends, the parties will have issues to address. Often, they include money. Therefore, when drafting endgame provisions, think through what should be the monetary consequences of the contract's end. *Follow the cash.* For example, when a real estate lease term ends, consider what should happen with the tenant's deposit: The landlord should be required to return it, but should be able to offset against it any costs incurred because of the tenant damaging the apartment.[10]

25.3 RISK

25.3.1 TYPES OF RISK

As we have seen, representations and warranties, covenants, and conditions are all risk allocation mechanisms. In addition, risk can manifest itself in multiple other ways in a transaction. First, a contract can raise the specter of tort liability—fraudulent inducement, product liability, and tortious interference with contract. Second, the provisions can create contract law risk. For example, a noncompetition provision could be unenforceable. Third, a contract can create statutory liability, such as liability under the securities laws. Fourth, a risk, such as credit risk, can be inherent in the transaction.

---

7. Under the common law, each litigant is responsible for its own attorneys' fees. The parties can, however, agree that the losing party (whether plaintiff or defendant) must pay the prevailing party's attorneys' fees.

8. See Chapter 22 for a discussion of accounting-related drafting issues.

9. See §8.3.

10. For a detailed discussion of endgame issues, see Chapter 15.

25.3.2 EVALUATING THE RISK

Lawyers are terrific at ferreting out risks in a transaction. Law school primes them to issue spot. If that is all they do, however, they will quickly earn justifiable reputations as deal killers.

Determining the risks only begins a lawyer's risk analysis. Next, she must assess the probability that the risk will occur. In addition, she should try to quantify the risk and do a risk/reward analysis. With this information, the client can evaluate the risk more completely. It may decide, for example, not to elevate the matter to a business issue because it believes that the risk will probably not occur and that the financial consequences would be relatively small. Alternatively, the client could decide that the benefit does not justify the risk, even with a low probability of occurrence.

Whether a risk develops into a business issue often depends upon a client's risk aversion profile. How comfortable is the client with taking risk? Is the client an entrepreneur ready to roll the dice, or is it a local bank willing to assume only minimal risks?

25.3.3 METHODS TO MITIGATE RISK

A lawyer's reputation as a deal maker often depends upon the ability to resolve risk issues creatively. Although a transaction may require an innovative solution, you can often rely on the techniques discussed in this section.

If credit risk is the concern, one party can take a **security interest** in the other party's assets. If you use this technique, determine which assets are the most valuable and which will be the easiest to liquidate. Be sure that the security interest applies to these assets. As an alternative (or additional) technique for reducing credit risk, a third party's credit can be added to the credit of the party with the payment obligation. Typically, the third party will agree to serve either as a **co-obligor** or as a **guarantor**. Of course, this party must be creditworthy.

Escrows are another technique that parties use to lessen credit risk. To create an escrow, the parties deposit cash or other property with a neutral third party, who agrees to release it only in accordance with the terms of the escrow agreement. Appendix C discusses escrow agreements, including their use and some of the salient business issues.

Other methods of reducing risk include **indemnity agreements, letters of credit, insurance**, and **deal-specific methods**. In an indemnity agreement one party promises to pay the other party for its losses, even if the indemnified party did not cause the loss. For example, when a lateral partner joins a firm, the firm generally indemnifies the lateral partner against any existing malpractice claims.

In a letter of credit transaction, a bank substitutes its credit for that of a party. For example, imagine a manufacturer in Italy wants to sell goods to a small company in New York but will not do so unless it can be assured of payment. To provide this assurance, the buyer arranges for a letter of credit under which a bank will pay the manufacturer upon the fulfillment of certain conditions.

Typically, the conditions require that the manufacturer deliver documents to the bank indicating that the proper goods are being shipped. The bank does not, however, undertake to inspect the goods. It *only* examines documents.[11] If the buyer wants an inspection of the goods, the buyer must arrange for a third party to inspect the goods

---

11. Because a bank will only look at documents, a letter of credit is sometimes referred to as a **documentary letter of credit.**

and issue a certificate that the inspected goods were the proper items in the appropriate condition.

After all the parties have agreed to the conditions, the bank issues its letter of credit in favor of the manufacturer. The letter of credit is the bank's promise to pay the manufacturer upon its presentation to the bank of the appropriate documents. Thus, the bank substitutes its credit for the buyer's. The buyer reimburses the bank after it pays the manufacturer.

Parties also use insurance to reduce risk. Companies generally purchase multiple kinds of insurance:

■ General liability insurance
■ Directors' and officers' insurance
■ Health insurance
■ Environmental insurance
■ Business interruption insurance

Knowing that a party has insurance is insufficient. You must know, among other things, the deductible (the amount the insured must pay before the insurer is liable), the maximum the insurer is obligated to pay, how much of that amount has already been paid, and whether the insurer is creditworthy.

As noted, parties sometimes need to rely on deal-specific methods to reduce risk. For example, the parties could reduce a buyer's risk by changing a stock acquisition to an asset acquisition. The risk is reduced because of the different structure. In an asset acquisition, a buyer chooses which assets it will buy and chooses which liabilities it will assume. If the buyer does not specifically assume a liability, it remains with the seller. So, if the seller had significant litigation liabilities, the buyer could choose not to assume those liabilities. In contrast, in a stock acquisition, no assets are assigned or liabilities assumed. Instead, the shareholders of the target sell their shares to the buyer who becomes the new shareholder. Nothing happens to the business. Thus, any liability of the target continues to be its liability. Only its shareholders have changed.

25.4 CONTROL

In analyzing control as a business issue, the initial inquiry must be whether having control is good or bad from a client's perspective. For example, limited partners are entitled to limited liability because they exercise no control over the limited partnership. In this context, lack of control is good. However, limited partners do not generally want to abdicate to the general partner all control over their investment. They want the ability to protect their investment. Thus, the limited partners will seek as much control as the general partner will tolerate and as much control as the limited partners can accrete without becoming a general partner under the relevant state law. Thus, control is actually a two-edged sword for limited partners.

Control is always an issue when your client is subject to a risk. Indeed, whenever your client worries about risk, ask yourself how the agreement can diminish or control it.

Control and risk business issues often coexist when negotiating and drafting covenants. With respect to each promise, determine whether your client can control the outcome. If not, it is gambling when it agrees to the covenant because it could end up in breach through no fault of its own. To protect your client, negotiate a covenant that reduces the risk by changing the degree of obligation. For example, a party may not want to promise that it will obtain an environmental permit because it cannot control the agency's decision. That party may be willing, however, to promise that it will prepare and submit the necessary papers by a certain date and that it will enter into good faith negotiations with the agency.

When thinking about control issues, think through which party is in control, whether that is the correct party, or whether control should be shared, and if so, how. Imagine two companies have entered into a joint venture to build a skyscraper. Should one party decide (that is, control) who the subcontractors will be? If the decisions are to be joint, how will the parties break a deadlock?

Once controls are in place, they need not remain at the same level throughout a relationship. For example, after first making a loan, a bank may justifiably insist that the agreement prohibit the borrower from making any capital expenditures. However, the bank may be willing to moderate this restriction once the borrower has repaid an agreed-upon percentage of the principal.

Parties can also increase controls. Preferred shareholders often negotiate for this. Generally, they have no voting rights. But if the parties agree, they could earn the right to have one or more board members if the company fails to pay dividends for three consecutive quarters.

25.5 STANDARDS

Almost every word or phrase in a contract establishes a standard. For example, every representation and warranty establishes a standard of liability. If the standard is not met, the recipient of the representation and warranty may sue the maker. This is a macro standard. However, that macro standard can be changed at the micro level. By changing a word or a phrase in a representation, the standard changes. Are property, plant, and equipment in *good repair, customary repair,* or *in compliance with statutory standards?* Covenants and conditions are also standards, as is every adjective (*good* repair) and adverb (*promptly* deliver). Definitions are also standards (how a financial ratio is defined determines the standard to be incorporated into a loan covenant). Thus, each time a definition changes, so do a party's rights and duties.

Once you determine what the standards are, determine whether the standard favors your client, and if not, how it can be modified.

Some drafters insist that vague standards are inherently wrong.[12] That is wrong. While vagueness may invite a dispute over a standard, sometimes it is the only way to bridge disparate positions or to provide a party with flexibility. Vagueness is the drafter's equivalent of the reasonable person standard. Parties use it to establish a facts and circumstances test. For example, if a *force majeure* event occurs, how quickly must the nonperforming party tell the other party of the occurrence? Immediately? Within 24 hours? What if the nonperforming party is cut off from all communication because of the *force majeure* event? Under those circumstances, the 24-hour cutoff is unreasonable. More equitable would be *as soon as feasible.*

Although vague standards may sometimes further a transaction, they can also disadvantage a client. It depends on the business deal. As noted earlier, sometimes a seller of a business will agree to an earn-out. To memorialize this arrangement, the purchase agreement will state the formula for determining the income on which the earn-out is based. The value of the seller's earn-out could be destroyed, however, if

---

12. See Chapter 21 for a more detailed discussion of vagueness.

that formula merely states that *revenues minus expenses equals income.* In that case, the vagueness of the standard *expenses* would permit the buyer to decrease the income by deducting inappropriate expenses. Therefore, do not start drafting with a preconceived notion that vagueness is good or bad. Instead, each time a provision establishes a vague standard, analyze whether it helps your client or whether a more specific, concrete standard would improve the client's position.

When you contemplate negotiating a change in a standard, think through the business risk of asking for that change. If your client has limited negotiating leverage, a request for a change will focus the other party's attention on that standard and could result in an even more stringent standard.

You and your client must also consider who should decide whether a standard has been met. Sometimes, a party decides. For example, a landlord and tenant could agree that the tenant may assign the lease to a third party, *but only if the landlord grants consent in its sole and absolute discretion.*

If the parties disagree as to whether a standard has been met, they have several options. They can adjudicate the matter in court, or they can arbitrate or mediate their disagreement. Alternatively, they can appoint an individual with subject matter expertise to resolve any disputes outside a proceeding. In sophisticated construction agreements, owners and contractors sometimes appoint a third-party engineer to settle any differences in a timely manner—sometimes in just a few days.

Contracts sometimes, but not always, address the consequences of breaching a standard. Chapter 15 discusses this matter in depth.

25.6 ENDGAME

As noted earlier in this chapter and as discussed in Chapter 15, every contractual relationship terminates in either a friendly or an unfriendly manner. Either way, the parties must think through the consequences. These critical provisions deserve your studied attention.

Before turning to the exercises in this chapter, review Chapter 15 and its discussion of the business issues that endgame provisions raise.

CHAPTER TWENTY-FIVE

EXERCISES

Exercise 25-1

On the next page is a short letter agreement between a broker and an owner of an apartment. The agreement raises multiple business issues. In order to analyze what those issues are, you will use the chart on the following pages.

The chart is composed of an X axis and a Y axis. Along the X axis, each in a separate column, are the five prongs of the framework. Going down the Y axis, each sentence of the letter agreement is separately set forth. To complete the chart, determine with respect to each sentence which of the five business issues is present and indicate the issue in the appropriate box. Thus, with respect to the first sentence, first consider if it raises any money issues. If so, note them in the appropriate box. Then consider whether the sentence raises any risk issues, and if so, note them in the appropriate box. Follow the same procedure with respect to each of the other prongs and then with respect to each of the other sentences. Not every sentence involves all of the prongs. In addition, an issue may straddle two or more prongs. If this occurs, just indicate that in your notes.

Two additional exercises follow Exercise 25-1. Complete them the same way.

Mr. Robert Best
Best Brokerage, Inc.
200 Real Estate Way
Burgeoning City, Wyoming

Dear Mr. Best:

This letter sets forth the agreement between Best Brokerage, Inc. ("Best"), and the undersigned.

By signing this letter, I grant Best the exclusive right to act as broker for the sale of my apartment for a three-month period (the "Brokerage Period") beginning the day you countersign this letter agreement. I will pay Best a commission of 5 percent of the sales price of the apartment if during the Brokerage Period the apartment is sold to someone other than someone I have already identified as a prospective purchaser.

Upon the signing of this letter agreement, I will give you a set of keys to my apartment. You promise to give me sufficient notice before bringing any prospective purchaser to the apartment. If any prospective purchaser damages my apartment or its furnishings in any way, Best agrees to indemnify me in full for the cost of replacement or repair.

If this letter correctly sets forth our agreement, please countersign this letter.

Sincerely yours,

_____
Oren Oglethorpe, Owner

AGREED:
BEST BROKERAGE, INC.

By: _____
    Robert Best, President

Exercise 25-1 Chart

	Money	Risk	Control	Standards	Endgame
By signing this letter, I grant Best the exclusive right to act as broker for the sale of my apartment for a three-month period (the "Brokerage Period") beginning the day you countersign this letter agreement.					
I will pay Best a commission of 5 percent of the sales price of the apartment if during the Brokerage Period the apartment is sold to someone other than someone I have already identified as a prospective purchaser.					
Upon the signing of this letter agreement, I will give you a set of keys to my apartment.					
You promise to give me sufficient notice before bringing any prospective purchaser to the apartment.					
If any prospective purchaser damages my apartment or its furnishings in any way, Best agrees to indemnify me in full for the cost of replacement or repair.					

Exercise 25-2

To: Alice Associate

From: Peter Partner

    Our client is Ralph Products LP (Ralph LP). Ralph LP owns all rights in the cartoon character Ralph—a short, frumpy, bespectacled, eight-year-old for whom life never goes quite right. For reasons that no one can fathom, anything with a likeness of Ralph on it sells like hotcakes. Ralph LP has been making millions by licensing the character to different companies who manufacture and then market products bearing Ralph's likeness.

    Earlier today, Ralph Randolph, the president of Ralph LP, called to tell me that he and Merchandisers Extraordinaire, Inc. (Merchandisers), had agreed to the salient terms of a license agreement with respect to Ralph merchandise. Randolph asked me whether I could foresee any business or legal issues with respect to the manner in which the parties had structured the royalty payments. I understand that aspect of the deal as follows: With respect to each year of the contract term, Merchandisers must pay royalties equal to 15 percent of all gross sales under $7 million; 10 percent with respect to sales that equal or exceed $7 million; but in no event less than an aggregate of $600,000 per year. In addition, Ralph LP will have the right to terminate the contract if Merchandisers' net worth is less than $10 million as of the end of its fiscal year.

    As you know, I am on my way to Paris and do not have time to analyze this issue now. Please think it through and be prepared to explain any problems when I call you from the plane. I know that there are lots of other issues with respect to this license agreement, but right now just stick to the money, standards, and endgame issues.

Exercise 25-2 Chart

	Money	Risk	Control	Standards	Endgame
With respect to each year of the contract term, Merchandisers must pay royalties equal to 15 percent of all gross sales under $7 million; 10 percent with respect to sales that equal or exceed $7 million; but in no event less than an aggregate of $600,000 per year.					
In addition, Ralph LP will have the right to terminate the contract if Merchandisers' net worth is less than $10 million as of the end of its fiscal year.					

Exercise 25-3

To: Leo Pard

From: Ty Gere

Subject: Clark Partnership Agreement

Two siblings, Margo and Bob Clark, have asked us to consider their plan to form a general partnership for their new business: Diets-Are-Us. DAU intends to manufacture and market a line of freshly cooked high-end diet meals. They will sell the meals directly to specialty food stores. The Clarks are confident that the business will do well. Their secret ingredient is a genetically engineered food supplement that makes you feel full—even though the amount consumed is relatively small. The inventor of the ingredient is their cousin Roberta who has given them the go-ahead to use the ingredient in the business.

The Clarks intend to capitalize the business with $100,000. Margo will contribute $75,000, and Bob will contribute $25,000.

Bob has significant experience in the diet food industry, having just completed a three-year stint as executive vice president of the company that is the industry leader—albeit in frozen foods. Accordingly, the plan is that he will run the business on a day-to-day basis. Margo will be in charge of advertising and back-office operations. Bob hopes that the new business will keep Margo's mind off her recent illness. He confided that the long-term prognosis is not good.

The business deal with respect to profits is that the first $75,000 goes to Margo, while the next $25,000 in cash that is distributed is Bob's. Thereafter, the money is split 50-50.

Please provide me with a list of the business issues that I should raise with the Clarks at my meeting with them later today. It would be helpful if your list comported with the framework we recently discussed.

Exercise 25-3 Chart

	Money	Risk	Control	Standards	Endgame
Two siblings, Margo and Bob Clark, have asked us to consider their plan to form a general partnership for their new business: Diets-Are-Us. DAU intends to manufacture and market a line of freshly cooked high-end diet meals. They will sell the meals directly to specialty food stores. The Clarks are confident that the business will do well.					
Their secret ingredient is a genetically engineered food supplement that makes you feel full—even though the amount consumed is relatively small. The inventor of the ingredient is their cousin Roberta who has given them the go-ahead to use the ingredient in the business.					
The Clarks intend to capitalize the business with $100,000. Margo will contribute $75,000, and Bob will contribute $25,000.					

continued on next page >

	Money	Risk	Control	Standards	Endgame
	Bob has significant experience in the diet food industry, having just completed a three-year stint as executive vice president of the company that is the industry leader—albeit in frozen foods. Accordingly, the plan is that he will run the business on a day-to-day basis.				
	Margo will be in charge of advertising and back-office operations. Bob hopes that the new business will keep Margo's mind off her recent illness. He confided that the long-term prognosis is not good.				
	The business deal with respect to profits is that the first $75,000 goes to Margo, while the next $25,000 in cash that is distributed is Bob's. Thereafter, the money is split 50-50.				

PART FIVE

Putting a Contract Together

Organizing a Contract and Its Provisions

26.1 INTRODUCTION

A well-written contract has an organizational framework that makes it easy to read. It has **structural integrity**.[1] A reader knows where to look for a provision and understands how the contract's provisions relate to each other. By ordering them in a "meaningful sequence,"[2] a drafter reduces a reader's work.

There is no single way to organize a contract. Drafters can conceptualize the same contract differently. If an approach facilitates a contract's reading, then it is a legitimate alternative. Nonetheless, over time, through custom and practice, the organization of some types of contracts has become standardized. An acquisition agreement is a paradigmatic example. If you were to look at a dozen precedents from a dozen different firms, their organization would be almost exactly the same. In instances like this, hewing to the accepted organization facilitates the contract's reading. Changing it requires the reader to hunt for a provision that is not in its usual place, a frustrating and time-wasting exercise. In addition, the client may refuse to pay for the time spent reorganizing the contract.

In practice, you will draft very few contracts from scratch. Instead, you will use a precedent—either one from your firm or one that you find in a secondary resource. Someone else will have already spent the time imposing order and organizing the contract's provisions. You may want to fine-tune that organization, but most of your organizational responsibilities will be limited to inserting new provisions in the appropriate place and organizing individual provisions. These are not insignificant tasks, and a reader will appreciate your careful rendering of this work.

The remaining sections of this chapter discuss the typical organization of a contract, how to organize the business provisions of a contract, and how to organize individual provisions.

---

1. I first heard the phrase *structural integrity* from Ernest Rubenstein, then a partner at Paul, Weiss, Rifkin, Wharton & Garrison LLP.

2. Alan Siegel, *Language Follows Logic: Practical Lessons in Legal Drafting,* Remarks made at Conference of Experts in Clear Legal Drafting, National Center for Administrative Justice, Washington, D.C., June 2, 1978, in Reed Dickerson, *Materials on Legal Drafting* 150 (West 1981).

26.2 A CONTRACT'S ORGANIZATIONAL STRUCTURE

Contracts are organized at both a macro and a micro level. The macro level is the organization of the contract as a whole: What are the beginning, middle, and ending provisions? Micro-level organization refers to the organization of the individual provisions—no matter where in the contract they occur.

26.2.1 ORGANIZATION AT THE MACRO LEVEL

At the macro level, the organization of contracts rarely differs, except for the organization of business provisions. As you have seen, virtually all contracts begin with the introductory provisions: the preamble, recitals, and words of agreement—in that order. (Exceptions exist, of course. Drafters sometimes omit recitals because they are superfluous for the particular contract.) Although practice varies, most drafters follow the introductory provisions with the definitions.

The next provisions are almost always the action sections, and their order is, again, fairly standard: Typically, the subject matter performance provision appears first, followed by the provision setting forth the consideration, whether monetary or otherwise. Then come the provisions relating to the agreement's term, date, time, and place of closing, and the closing deliveries (in each instance, if appropriate for the transaction).

The remaining business provisions follow the action sections. These provisions set out the parties' representations and warranties, covenants, conditions, rights, discretionary authority, and declarations. You will need to focus most on them as their organization varies from contract to contract.

Generally, the last business provisions are the endgame provisions. These provisions usually adhere to a common organizational scheme: first the defaults, then the remedies, and finally the termination provisions. The default provisions precede the remedies provisions because, chronologically, in the business world, defaults precede remedies.

After the endgame provisions are the general provisions, the final provisions of a contract. Most drafters insert these provisions without giving any thought to the order in which they should appear (but, one hopes, with some thought as to their substance). Nonetheless, you can organize these provisions by grouping them by subject matter: communication provisions, provisions determining the elements of the contract, provisions relating to third parties, financial and risk allocation provisions, interpretive provisions, and dispute resolution provisions. (The outline at the end of this section details the specific provisions.) In some agreements, a general provision may be of particular importance; for example, the indemnity provision or the *force majeure* provision. In that case, break the provision out and give it its own article or section, as appropriate.

Case law suggests that a contract's last provision should be the waiver of a right to jury trial. Although courts will enforce a jury waiver, they do so reluctantly and insist that a waiver be knowing, voluntary, and intentional.[3] In deciding whether this standard has been met, courts look at whether the provision was conspicuous, thereby making it more likely that the waiving party read it. Putting the jury waiver provision last is one way of making it conspicuous.

Of course, the contract ends with the parties' signatures.

---

3. See §16.5 for a detailed discussion of the waiver of jury trial provision.

An outline of a contract conforming to the structure just laid out looks as follows:

> Preamble
> Recitals
> Words of Agreement
> Definitions
> Action Sections
>   (a)   Subject matter performance provision
>   (b)   Monetary provisions
>   (c)   Term (if applicable)
>   (d)   Closing details: when and where (if applicable)
>   (e)   Closing deliveries (if applicable)
> Other Business Provisions
> Endgame Provisions
>   (a)   Defaults
>   (b)   Remedies
>   (c)   Termination
> General Provisions
>   (a)   Communication (notices, publicity, and confidentiality)
>   (b)   Third parties (assignment, delegation, successors and assigns, and third-party beneficiaries)
>   (c)   Financial and risk allocation (indemnities and *force majeure*)
>   (d)   Determination of contract elements (amendment, waiver, merger, counterparts, and severability)
>   (e)   Interpretive provisions (number, gender, and captions)
>   (f)   Dispute resolution (arbitration, mediation, governing law, choice of forum, service of process, cumulative remedies, and waiver of jury trial)
> Signature Lines

26.3 ORGANIZATION OF THE BUSINESS PROVISIONS AND INDIVIDUAL PROVISIONS

The five primary organizing principles for arranging a contract's business provisions are the following:

- Subject matter
- Relative importance
- Contract concepts
- Chronology
- Party

Many contracts use more than one of these principles, with one acting as the primary organizing principle and the other (or others) as subsidiary principles.

26.3.1 SUBJECT MATTER AND RELATIVE IMPORTANCE

Organizing a contract's business provisions by subject matter is the most common way to put together a contract at the macro level. The process resembles the process used when organizing an outline for a brief or a memorandum. For those documents, a writer first determines the main points and the subsidiary points, and then orders them to create a cohesive and persuasive document. Before settling on the final organizational scheme, the writer may try several different ones.

The parallel process in contract drafting begins with a drafter grouping together business terms on the same or similar topics and creating subject matter groups. These groups become provisions that must be further organized, often with the more important provisions appearing earlier in the contract. As noticed earlier, the end-game provisions are generally placed, however, towards the end of the contract. This reflects the transaction's chronology, as well as a nod toward the parties' psychological reaction to endgame provisions: Bad news should be deferred.

In determining the relative importance of provisions, consider, among other things, whether the parties will refer to a provision frequently (more important) or infrequently (less important). In addition, generally, the statement of a rule should precede its exception[4] to facilitate understanding of the exception. Knowing what the rule is puts the exception in context.

As a test of whether an agreement's organization works, determine the number of cross-references used in the agreement. Sometimes a cross-reference cannot be avoided. Two provisions must be read in conjunction with each other; one may supersede the other in limited circumstances, or the second provision qualifies the first. But if multiple cross-references relate to the same topic, consider reorganizing the contract or a creating a new section to deal with that topic. Assembling the related provisions in one place may make it easier for the reader.

To make these organizing principles concrete, imagine that your client is a chain of big-box stores (think Target) that is contracting with a photo-finishing lab. Your client informs you that the parties have agreed to the following business terms—in no particular order:

1. The lab will develop and print the photographs that each store's customers have dropped off for developing.
2. For non-digital photographs, the lab must use developer manufactured by Chelsea Photo Chemicals, which is located in New York City.
3. The lab must pick up film from each store every day but after 5:00 p.m.
4. The lab must provide a first-quality product.
5. The lab must return the finished photographs no later than noon the day after it picks up the film.
6. For non-digital photographs, the lab must use fixer manufactured by Berkshire Photo Materials, which is located in Egremont, Massachusetts.
7. All photographs are to be printed on Kodak photographic paper with a matté finish, unless a customer specifies otherwise.
8. If a customer of a store drops off more than 10 rolls of film on any day, the lab may return the photographs developed from that film later than noon the day after it picks up the film, but no later than 5:00 p.m.

To organize these eight business points, first group together related matters: Four points relate to the quality of the product and the materials to be used (#2, #4, #6, and #7); three relate to pickups and deliveries (#3, #5, and #8), and one (#1) is part of the subject matter performance provision. Next, determine in which order these groups should appear. The first decision—and an easy one—is to put the subject matter performance provision in with the other action sections. After this, you must decide which of the remaining provisions should be first: the provisions dealing with pickups and deliveries or the ones dealing with the product's quality.

---

4. See §23.3 for a more detailed discussion of how to draft exceptions.

In the hypothetical described above, timing may be the more important business term because of its primacy in the store's marketing efforts. A drafter could decide, however, that quality is more important because without it, timing does not matter. Both analyses are reasonable, and either order would be acceptable based on the facts available.

After deciding the order of these two provisions, you must organize the individual provisions. This is organization at the micro level. With respect to the provisions on pickups and deliveries, how could you order them to help a reader understand them? Chronological order is an obvious possibility. In addition, the general rule as to the delivery of the photographs by noon should precede the exception that permits delivery after noon but no later than 5:00 p.m. of that same day. In the draft of this provision that follows, note how the formatting enhances its clarity.

"Delivery Day" means, with respect to each roll of film, the day after the day that the Lab picks up that roll of film from a Store.

Schedule of Pickups and Deliveries.

(a) **Pickups.** The Lab shall

  (i)   pick up from each Store every day all rolls of film that its customers have deposited with that Store; and

  (ii) make that pickup after 5:00 p.m.

(b) **Deliveries.**

  (i)   **General Rule.** With respect to each roll of film picked up from each Store, the Lab shall return to that Store the photographs developed from that roll no later than noon of that roll's Delivery Day.

  (ii) **Exception.** Despite subsection (i), if a customer of a Store deposits more than 10 rolls of film on any one day, the Lab

    (A) may return the photographs developed from those rolls to that store later than noon of their Delivery Day, but

    (B) shall return them no later than 5:00 p.m. of their Delivery Day.

Next you must analyze and organize the provisions dealing with the quality of the photographs and the purchase of the materials. You must first decide whether the lab's obligation to deliver first-quality photographs should be drafted as one section or two—one for the general obligation as to quality and the other as to the lab's obligation to use specific products. As the obligation to deliver a quality product is short, it can be combined easily with its related business points. Again, formatting is used to enhance the provision's clarity.

Quality of the Finished Photographs. The Lab shall print first-quality photographs. Without limiting the generality of the preceding sentence, the Lab shall

(a) use, for all non-digital photographs,

  (i)   developer manufactured by Chelsea Photo Chemicals, located in New York, New York; and

---

continued on next page >

> (ii)   fixer manufactured by Berkshire Photo Materials, located in Egremont, Massachusetts;
>
> and
>
> (b)   print all photographs on Kodak photographic paper with a matté finish, unless a customer specifies a different finish.

This provision has two levels of micro-organization, both of which rely on chronology. The substance of subsection (a) appears before subsection (b) as the lab must use the chemicals to develop the photographs before it prints them. Subsections (a)(i) and (ii) list the developer first and the fixer second as developer is the first chemical used in the developing process.

26.3.2   CONTRACT CONCEPTS

Contract concepts rarely provide the overarching organizational scheme of a contract's business provisions. Acquisition and financing agreements are the exceptions. Nonetheless, a drafter will sometimes use a contract concept to organize part of a contract that is otherwise organized by subject matter. For example, drafters often appropriately put all of a party's representations and warranties in one section, as was done in Section 11 of the Website Development Agreement in Appendix B.

26.3.3   CHRONOLOGY

Drafters can use chronology to organize provisions, especially in situations where one party's actions depend upon the occurrence—or nonoccurrence—of the other party's actions. For example, suppose that a licensor must approve a sample of a trademarked product before its licensee may manufacture it. A well-drafted provision will need to provide a timetable for the approval process: When must the licensee submit a sample of the product? How soon afterwards must the licensor respond, and by when does the licensee need to address the licensor's response? Putting these provisions in chronological order provides the reader with an easy roadmap to follow.

26.3.4   PARTY

Modern contracts are not usually organized so that all of the provisions relating to one party precede all of the provisions relating to the second party. Instead, organization by party is often a secondary level of organization. For example, in an indemnity agreement, each party usually indemnifies the other party against certain risks. Although a drafter could craft the indemnity so that each party indemnifies the other in one section, often the drafter creates separate sections for each party's indemnification obligation. Generally, the remaining provisions of an indemnity agreement are organized by subject matter.

CHAPTER TWENTY-SIX

EXERCISES

Exercise 26-1

Determine the organizational scheme of the Asset Purchase Agreement in
Appendix A.

Exercise 26-2

The provisions in the following list regularly appear in employment agreements.
They are not in the order in which they would appear in a contract. Reorder the list
so that the provisions are in an appropriate order.

1. No oral amendments. _____

2. Antiassignment provision. _____

3. Bonus. _____

4. Change of control of the Company (what happens to the Executive upon a change
   of control of the Company: forced retirement, bonus to keep on working, nothing?). _____

5. Death and disability (financial and contractual ramifications of death or disability). _____

6. Duties (a description of the Executive's responsibilities). _____

7. Effects of the termination of the Executive's employment. _____

8. The Executive represents that entering into this employment agreement will not
   violate any other agreement to which the Executive is a party. _____

9. The Company agrees to employ the Executive, and the Executive agrees to work for
   the Company. _____

10. Merger (all prior writings and negotiations are merged into this contract)
    (sometimes referred to as the *integration* provision). _____

11. Expense account. _____

12. Extent of service (e.g., full-time or part-time). _____

13. Governing law. _____

14. Waiver of jury trial. _____

15. Insurance and other employee benefits. _____

16. Notices. _____

17. Salary. _____

18. Severability. _____

19. Successors and assigns. _____

20. Term of contract: 3 years. _____

21. Termination for cause.   _____

22. Working facilities (windowed, corner office, or claustrophobic cubicle?).   _____

The Drafting Process

27.1 INTRODUCTION

Despite the sarcastic comments of some of your colleagues, drafting a contract requires much more than pulling out a dog-eared precedent and changing the names and the dates. The drafting process is sophisticated. It requires you to integrate your knowledge of business, the business deal, the client's business, the law, and your writing skills. This task is not easy, and it is time-consuming. But it is intellectually rewarding.

This chapter describes the ideal drafting process—what you would do with unlimited time and financial resources. You will rarely have the luxury of being able to follow the process step by step. Instead, you will take shortcuts and find your own way of doing things. But by understanding the full process, you can create a process that works for you and your client.

27.2 AGREEING TO THE BUSINESS TERMS

Most contracts enter the world in the same way. They begin with the parties agreeing to do a deal. It may be as prosaic as the purchase and sale of a house, or as exceptional as a multibillion-dollar joint venture. In a transaction, the parties generally negotiate the key business terms, including price.[1] Once they have done so, each party contacts its lawyers. One of the lawyers will probably draw up a list of the main business points for all parties to review, so that they can confirm the deal's basic terms.

At this juncture, the parties decide whether to enter into a **letter of intent**, also known as a **term sheet** or a **memorandum of understanding**. In it, the parties state the business terms to which they have agreed.

When properly used, letters of intent save the parties time and money. By forcing the parties to think about the transaction's details early on, with luck, the parties will discover any deal-breakers or other roadblocks to completing the transaction.

---

1. Other scenarios are, of course, possible. Sometimes an unsophisticated client will meet with a lawyer at a deal's inception. The lawyer will then help the client structure and negotiate the transaction's material terms.

The list of business terms in a letter of intent can be quite short or very detailed, covering almost everything that would appear in a signed agreement. Which approach is chosen depends on how the parties intend to use the document.

Some parties use the letter of intent as a mini-agreement, intending to be bound, but also intending to memorialize the deal in a traditional, full-fledged agreement. Other parties use a letter of intent as a nonbinding, general statement of interest in a transaction on the listed terms. In this context, the letter of intent is the basis of future negotiations, rather than the culminating expression of the negotiations. Nonetheless, the parties may choose to include binding terms with respect to confidentiality, payment of expenses, and the obligation to negotiate in good faith.

If the lawyers do not properly draft the letter of intent, it can become the source of litigation. One party will claim that it bound the parties to the transaction; the other will claim it was merely a preliminary statement of interest. To prevent this, the lawyers must clarify the letter of intent's purpose. If the parties intend it to be nonbinding, it should state clearly that the parties have significant, substantive business issues to negotiate and that the transaction is not binding until memorialized in a definitive, written agreement.

27.3   DETERMINING WHO DRAFTS THE CONTRACT

Before drafting begins, the parties and their lawyers must decide who will draft the contract. Often, however, no one discusses this. Instead, custom and negotiating leverage are determinant. For example, the lender's lawyers always draft the credit agreement and any ancillary agreements; the employer's lawyers always the draft the employment agreement; and the publisher's lawyers always draft the book contract. They are risking their money, so they set the ground rules—subject to the negotiation.

If custom does not dictate who drafts the contract, and if the other side gives you the opportunity to draft the contract, take it—not because the billings will be greater, but because your client will gain a strategic advantage if you control the drafting process. Specifically, as you begin to incorporate the agreed-upon business points into the contract, you will face a myriad of issues that the parties did not discuss. For example, should a representation and warranty be flat or qualified, and if qualified, how? Because you are drafting the contract, you and your client can decide each of these issues in a way that advantages your client, yet without violating any ethical proscriptions. You are not changing the deal. You are addressing matters not previously negotiated.

Depending upon her caliber, the lawyer on the other side may not question any of the provisions you craft, giving your client a win at no cost. If she does spot an issue, she must ask for a change and negotiate. Although any redraft may tilt the provision toward the other side, the ultimate provision may still be more favorable to your client than if the other side had produced the first draft.

Drafting the contract also means that you can control the deal's tempo. If your client is eager to close the transaction, you can turn around drafts quickly. But if it wants to slow the tempo, you can take your time in drafting and distributing the first draft or revisions.

27.4   LEARNING ABOUT A TRANSACTION

Generally, you will learn about a transaction when a client or supervising lawyer calls you or sends you an e-mail. Although your responsibilities are similar in each situation, they are not the same. This section will first discuss your responsibilities if you are dealing directly with the client and then if you are dealing with a supervising lawyer.

27.4.1 LEARNING ABOUT A TRANSACTION FROM A CLIENT

When a client calls and announces a new transaction, listen carefully to the details. He will probably start by giving you headlines:

> We are hiring a new Executive Vice President, Antoine Johnson. He will be starting June 15th, and we are going to pay him $150,000 per year.

Although these are certainly salient facts, they are not all the facts that you will need to write the contract. If you have been practicing for several years and you specialize in employment law, you may be able to rattle off 10 questions without any further research. But if that is not the case, ask the questions that you can think of and then suggest a meeting to discuss the transaction in more detail. Before ending the call, ask the client to bring to the meeting any relevant documents, including any deal memo, letter of intent, correspondence, previous contracts, and notes.

A follow-up meeting is generally better than a follow-up phone call. At a meeting, the conversations tend to be more wide-ranging, and you are more likely to gain a thorough understanding of the deal and the client's goals. The reality, however, is that parties conduct a great deal of business by phone and e-mail.

To prepare for the client meeting, create a checklist of the questions that you want to ask. The checklist should cover all the business terms to be incorporated into the agreement. If you are working at a firm, it may have a checklist for each type of transaction that it regularly handles. You can add to this checklist (or create your own) by reviewing agreements from prior transactions. If you are creating your own checklist, always look at more than one agreement, so that you review as wide a variety of provisions as possible. Also, look at forms in treatises, continuing legal education materials, and industry association materials. In addition, you can find agreements online, but take care that they come from reputable sources, so that you can have confidence in their quality.

As part of your preparation for the meeting, draw a diagram of the transaction. If you are drafting a simple lease, the diagram will probably not be of much help. But, with a more sophisticated transaction with multiple parties and mini-transactions, the visual may help you see how these minitransactions fit together. For example, imagine that your client, a bank, intends to lend $100 million to a corporation. Because the borrower has had some financial trouble in the past, it has agreed to grant a security interest in its assets to the bank. In addition, each of its two subsidiaries will guarantee the borrower's debt and back up its guaranty by granting a security interest in its assets. This may sound complex, but it is actually a relatively simple transaction. Take a look at the diagram on the following page.

At the client meeting, begin by getting an overview of the transaction and the client's attitude towards it. If the client is eager to discuss the details of the transaction, then postpone this preliminary discussion or integrate it into the discussion of deal points.

Assuming that you begin with a general discussion about the transaction, some of the questions that you might ask are the following:

- What is the impetus behind the transaction?
- What are the client's business goals and expectations?
- What would constitute a big win?
- What does the client want to avoid?

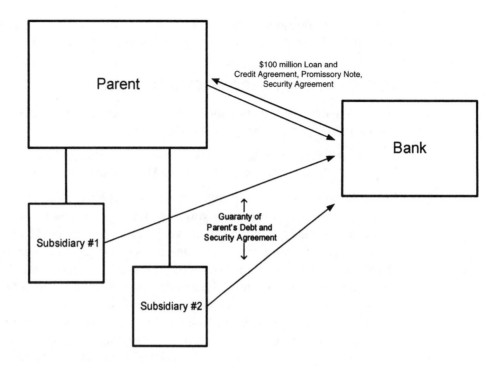

- What are the hot button issues and the deal breakers?
- Is the transaction necessary to the company's survival?
- Is timing a factor? Is time of the essence?
- Do the parties have a previous business relationship? Are they parties to any other agreements that will affect the new transaction?
- Is the price a bargain, or is it steep?
- Is it a good deal but one that the client will forego if the other side is unreasonable or intransigent?
- Which party has the negotiating leverage?
- How much risk will the client take?

Knowing the answers to these questions will help you to be more than a scrivener. Your advice will be more strategic, and you will be better able to craft a contract that serves the client's needs.

As part of this discussion, discuss negotiating strategy with the client. It may seem premature as you have not yet drafted the contract, but this is exactly the right time for the first of these discussions. A contract's first draft opens the bidding of the next round of the negotiations, so how you write its provisions affects how the other side responds. Does the client want to start out with extreme positions on the theory that you cannot get what you do not ask for? Or does the client want to start with more moderate positions to expedite final agreement? If the latter, the unstated message to the other side is that the moderate provisions are close to final, leaving little room for negotiation. In practice, the negotiation strategy will most likely differ depending upon the deal and the provision.

As part of the discussion of negotiating strategy, look at the contract from the other side's perspective. What does it need to make a deal? Much of this will already have been discovered in the earlier negotiations between the principals. But as you discuss the business issues with your client, discuss whether your client will be more likely to get what it needs if the contract's first draft reflects the other side's needs. At the same time, discuss how the other side may react to specific provisions. If you think that it will have a strong, negative reaction, it may be more strategic for the client to raise the issue directly with the other side's principal.

Next, ask the client how sophisticated the agreement should be. Should you "pull out all the stops" and address every business point that you can think of? If not, should you draft a "down and dirty" contract—that is, a contract that covers only the salient business points? If the latter, the answer may reflect concerns both as to timing and cost. If cost matters, discuss with your client the consequences of not dealing with certain issues. The associated risks may convince her that you should draft a more detailed contract. You could also decide that some points should be dealt with summarily and others, such as the endgame provisions, be drafted in detail. Of course, these decisions may change during the negotiation.

With these preliminary matters concluded, begin asking specific questions about the transaction. Be sure to keep accurate notes. You will discuss too many issues to rely on your memory.

Use your checklist as a guide for what needs to be discussed. Although the client will need to answer your specific questions, encourage expansive answers. The more you know, the better you can tailor the contract to the client's needs. If the client raises matters that are not on your list, explore them or add them to your list for follow-up. Also add to that list any questions that the client cannot answer.

As you go through the specific issues on your checklist, the client may instruct you not to address a specific business or legal matter. If so, explore the client's rationale. It may be a negotiating strategy. The client may lack negotiating leverage and fear that raising the issue means losing it. By omitting the issue from the contract, the client postpones the problem until a time when he may be in a stronger position.

The client may also see the risk as sufficiently remote or small that he does not want to spend time and money on it. If so, provide the client with the information needed to knowledgeably decide what to do, and then respect that business decision.

Alternatively, the client may tell you that he has established a terrific working relationship with the other side and can rely on their good faith to work out any issues. If so, gently remind the client that his contact person with the other side could change jobs, leaving him with just the contract and its provisions.

As you discuss this matter with the client, keep in mind that his focus on the relationship reflects a legitimate approach to negotiating and drafting contracts. Indeed, it prevails in Japan. Because the Japanese focus on the relationship, they usually put less emphasis on memorializing the deal and will agree to a much less detailed, shorter contract. Nonetheless, American contracts are negotiated in a different culture, where failing to address an issue can be dangerous. Ultimately, again, your client must decide.

Finally, a client may want to avoid contentious or unpleasant issues. This can be particularly true with endgame provisions. When putting together a deal, clients often want to focus on its success, not its potential failure. They will resist attempts to address the consequences of the deal foundering. Here, your objectivity can be quite valuable to a client. You can lay out the advantages and disadvantages of including the endgame provisions, as well as the relative merits of specific provisions. Again, the client must decide, but that decision will be a considered one if you do your job.

As part of this interview, you may also want to ask whether you or the client will take the laboring oar in the negotiations. Although lawyers often negotiate contracts, some business executives are excellent negotiators and want to take the lead on key business terms.

Before the meeting concludes, discuss timing. When does the client want to see a draft, and how quickly does he want to distribute it to the other side? In addition, review what you are to do and any matters on which the client should follow up.

The initial meeting will give you plenty of information with which to work. As you start using it and other information that you gather, you will think of more questions. This is as it should be.

27.4.2 LEARNING ABOUT A TRANSACTION FROM A SUPERVISING LAWYER

Learning about a new transaction from a supervising lawyer resembles, but is not the same as, learning about it from a client. As a junior lawyer, you should consider the more senior lawyers in the office your first clients. Therefore, your interactions with them will in many ways mirror the interaction that you will have with a client. But receiving an assignment is often a more passive interaction than meeting with a client. When you learn about a transaction from a supervising lawyer, she will probably have already discussed the transaction with the client. When you meet with her, your job is to ensure that she thoroughly and accurately transfers all that information to you.

Listen carefully to confirm that you understand the nature of the transaction. Are you to draft a sublease or a lease assignment? If you are to draft an employment agreement, should you also draft a noncompetition agreement? You should leave the meeting with all the information and documents that you would have had if you had been to a client meeting, including deal memos, letters of intent, correspondence, previous contracts, and notes. If you need other information, ask for it. Also ask questions if you do not understand something. Do not be embarrassed. As a junior lawyer, you can ask *almost* any question without others thinking it a dumb question. Senior lawyers expect you to ask questions at the initial meeting and to return later with more questions.

Before you leave, find out the deadline. The supervisor may give you any one or more of these three deadlines: the date by which you must submit your draft to the supervising lawyer, the date by which the supervising lawyer must submit a draft to the client, and the date by which your office must deliver the agreement to the other party.

27.5 PREPARING TO DRAFT A CONTRACT

27.5.1 RESEARCHING THE LAW AND OBTAINING THE ADVICE OF SPECIALISTS

Before beginning to draft, determine what legal issues the transaction raises. For example, will the endgame provisions include a liquidated damages provision? If so, you may need to research the law to help you and your client choose a dollar amount that adequately compensates the injured party, but does not convert the provision into an unenforceable penalty provision. Similarly, you must also consider whether any statutes affect the agreement. Must you deal with securities regulations, environmental laws, or U.C.C. provisions?

You cannot—and should not—research all of an agreement's legal issues before you begin drafting. First, you may not know about an issue until you are working on a specific provision. Second, the client may want to distribute a draft to the other side as quickly as possible. Third, others in your office may have subject matter expertise. Speaking with those lawyers will often save you time and the client money.

In any transaction, you *must* obtain the advice of an accountant or a tax lawyer, or both, unless you understand the subtleties of all the issues raised. Almost always, these issues require a specialist's expertise because of their implications. In more sophisticated transactions, these issues might require the transaction's structure to be changed or the deal abandoned. Because of these consequences, talk with the accountants and tax lawyers as early as possible in the transaction.

27.5.2 RESEARCHING THE PARTIES AND THE INDUSTRY

As this textbook repeatedly explains, before drafting a contract, you must fully understand the business deal. Often, to do this, you must research the client, the other side, and their industry. What you learn will enable you to add value to the deal because of your ability to find and resolve issues that you might otherwise have missed.

For example, assume that your client, a bank, has agreed to lend $5 million to a jewelry manufacturer. As part of the transaction, the borrower has agreed to grant the bank a security interest in its inventory. Taking the security interest may be more complicated than you would expect. In the jewelry industry, manufacturers often consign individual pieces of jewelry to their customers, retail stores. Sometimes, these consignments are properly documented with U.C.C. filings. Frequently, however, a manufacturer and its customer operate on a more informal basis. The manufacturer gives the retailer the jewelry "on memo," a short document that recites that the manufacturer has transferred the jewelry to the retailer. The parties file no U.C.C. forms. Without knowing how the borrower's industry functions, you could not draft the proper papers to document the bank's security interest.

With the advent of the Internet, researching a client, the other side, and the parties' industry has become much easier. By going online, you can find annual reports, recent articles, and research analysts' reports. As you sift through this information, try to determine the issues with which the industry—and the parties—are grappling. Then, assess the information and how you can use it to your client's advantage.

Also check the SEC's EDGAR database for agreements that the other side has entered into. If you find one for a transaction similar to the one you are working on, you may be able to use it against the other side during the negotiations. For example, if the other side insists on a materiality qualifier for a specific representation and warranty, but previously gave it flat, you can argue more forcefully that no qualifier is required.

27.6 DRAFTING WITH AND WITHOUT A PRECEDENT

27.6.1 CHOOSING A PRECEDENT

In a drafting context, **precedent** refers to a contract from an earlier transaction, but lawyers also use it to refer to forms. In both cases, lawyers use the precedent as the basis of a new agreement. Think of a precedent as a template that you tailor for each transaction.

Almost all drafting done today begins with a precedent for two reasons. First, it is efficient. Precedents save time and money. Rather than reinventing the wheel for each new deal, a lawyer gets a head start. Second, if the precedent is a good one, using it will reduce errors and improve a contract's quality.

Precedents abound. Generally, you will not have a problem finding them. The more difficult task will be choosing the right one. If you are working directly with a client, ask whether it has a preferred form that it would like you to use. Carefully review it, however, to confirm that it is appropriate for the new transaction. Clients generally are not lawyers and may not understand why a particular form is inappropriate.

If you are working for a supervising lawyer, ask that person to recommend a precedent. Lawyers tend to use the same precedent again and again because they are familiar with it and comfortable with its quality. If you use a different one, the supervising lawyer will compare your draft to her precedent, which may only result in your changing the draft so that it more closely resembles that precedent.

If no one gives you a precedent to use, you will need to look for one. If you work in a firm or a general counsel's office, ask your colleagues whether they have a contract from an earlier deal that would work for your transaction. In addition, find out whether your firm has a form bank. Many firms create forms for each type of transaction they handle. Some even annotate the form's provisions with explanations and instructions how to tailor them. These forms and contracts should be your first choice because of their quality. In addition, you may have ready access to the precedent's drafter who can explain the purpose behind provisions you do not understand.

If you do not obtain a precedent from someone in your office or the client, you can obtain forms from industry associations, treatises, continuing legal education materials, and online. Be wary of all these precedents. Quality varies.

In addition to finding forms online from various vendors, you can search the SEC's EDGAR database. It includes contracts that public companies have entered into and then filed to comply with their disclosure obligations.

When choosing between precedents, follow these guidelines:

GUIDELINES FOR CHOOSING PRECEDENTS

1. *Choose a precedent that is for the same type of transaction.* Do not choose a share purchase agreement if your transaction is a merger.

2. *Choose a precedent where the party in your client's position had the greater negotiating leverage.* For example, assume that you represent the landlord in the lease of a 35-story building at a time when demand for space is high and first-class space is generally unavailable. In this case, you would want to avoid leases that were negotiated when the real estate market was in the doldrums and tenants had the negotiating leverage. A more recent lease would probably include more landlord-friendly provisions.

3. *Do not use an executed agreement as a precedent.* It includes all the concessions that the party in your client's position made, so it is not a good place from which to start. Instead, look for a draft of the agreement, preferably one several iterations earlier than the executed agreement. If you can find it, the first draft sent to the other side makes a good precedent. It will include your colleagues' and the client's comments and will reflect your side's opening positions.

In addition to choosing a precedent to use as the base document for your draft, retain other good precedents. You can use them as additional resources as you draft. Analyzing multiple versions of the same provision will help you assess the precedent's provision and give you ideas on the different ways to draft its substance.

27.6.2 USING A PRECEDENT

A case precedent guides the court as it decides how to rule. But because a case is rarely on "all fours" with another, judges must find the similarities and the differences and tailor their opinions accordingly. You should approach a precedent's provisions the same way. They should *guide* you as you draft the agreement for your transaction. A precedent's words are not engraved in stone. If you are using a form, it represents what others have considered a good starting place. Those who created it intended drafters to modify it to memorialize each new transaction. Similarly, if you are using a contract from an earlier deal, the provisions are not specific to your deal, so you must change them.

Using a contract from an earlier deal can be a nightmare when you first begin working. At this stage in your career, you may have trouble discerning whether a provision is deal specific or simply something that you do not understand. You cannot punt and leave it in the contract, assuming that it must be correct. This would result in a "mindless mark-up." Neither can you just delete it, assuming that it is wrong or inapplicable. You must determine its purpose and then decide whether to keep it, modify it, or delete it. If you have access to several drafts of the agreement that you are using for a precedent, comparing them may help you determine a provision's role.

You will confront one other problem with precedents, many are poorly drafted from a stylistic perspective, even those whose substance is top-notch. In a perfect world, you would redraft each of these provisions, using what you have learned in your drafting course. Unfortunately, you generally will not have that option. Redrafting a provision is time-consuming, and you probably will not have that time in a fast-paced transaction. In addition, your firm will want to bill that time to the client, who may resist paying the firm for work it considered unnecessary.

When at a firm and confronted with a poorly drafted provision, determine whether the existing language creates an ambiguity. If it does, redraft it, but mention your change in the cover memo to the supervising lawyer.[2] Her perspective may differ from yours. If the provision is unambiguous, but otherwise poorly drafted, use the provision as is and then deal with its problems after the transaction finishes. Then, consult with the firm's "keeper of the forms," who will probably appreciate your input. Do not change the firm's master form without permission.

You may be able to change your approach to redrafting poorly drafted provisions as you become a more senior lawyer. As you gain the confidence of your supervising lawyers, they may give you greater latitude to rework a form's provisions.

If you have your own firm, even if you want to, you will probably be unable to clean up a precedent all at once because of the other demands on your time. Instead, redraft one or two provisions each time you use the precedent. By spreading out the work over time, you will be able to manage the task more easily.

27.6.3 DRAFTING WITHOUT A PRECEDENT

Occasionally, you may need to draft a contract for which you can find no precedent. If this occurs, take a step back and think about the substantive provisions that the contract will need. Do other contracts have similar provisions, even if they are not exactly on point? Can you draft the contract by patching together relevant provisions from different agreements?

For example, suppose a shareholder requests a new share certificate to replace the one that he has lost. Your client, the corporation that issued the share certificate, is willing to replace it, but does not want to be liable if someone subsequently presents the original. The corporation asks that you draft something to protect it. You agree to do so, but then cannot find a precedent.

Although you lack an exact precedent, you can borrow and modify the substantive provisions of other contracts. From a business perspective, your client has two goals. First, it wants the shareholder's assurance that he still owns the shares and that the reason the share certificate is "missing" is that he lost it, not because he transferred it to a third party. Second, your client wants to be able to sue the shareholder for damages if someone else presents the original certificate.

To accomplish these business goals, you can borrow substantive provisions from two agreements. To address your client's first concern, you could modify a representation and warranty on share ownership from a share purchase agreement.

---

2. See § 27.7.2.4.

> **Shareholder's Representations and Warranties**. The Shareholder represents and warrants to the Corporation that the Shareholder
>
> (a) owns the shares represented by Certificate No. 3345;
>
> (b) has not transferred to any third party the shares represented by Certificate No. 3345; and
>
> (c) has lost Certificate No. 3345.

To deal with your client's second concern, you could draft an indemnity provision, tailoring the subject matter performance provision of almost any indemnity agreement.

> **Indemnification**. The Shareholder shall indemnify and defend the Corporation against any liabilities and losses arising from the Shareholder's loss of Certificate No. 3345.

With these key business provisions in place, you can draft the remainder of the contract.

27.7 THE LOGISTICS OF DRAFTING A CONTRACT

If you are drafting a contract using a precedent, first copy the precedent and put the original aside. Always keep the precedent unchanged, so that it can be used again. Do this whether you are working with an electronic precedent or a hard copy.

If you are going to hand-mark changes to a hard copy of the precedent, photocopy the original onto 8½ by 14-inch paper and reduce the size of the print to 90 percent. This will give you more room for your mark-up and make it easier for you or your assistant to read the changes to be made.

Every draft of the contract that you distribute, whether internally where you work, to the client, or to third parties, should be numbered and dated, in the right or left header.

> **Draft #1**
> **June 13, 20XX**

This information not only distinguishes one draft from the next, but also may be some evidence that the draft was not intended as a final and binding agreement.[3]

Be sure to distinguish internal drafts from those sent to third parties. If you distribute two drafts at your firm before sending the agreement outside the firm, those distributions could be *Internal Draft #1* and *Internal Draft #2*. The first distribution outside the firm would be *Draft #1*.

Next, set up electronic and hard-copy file systems to keep track of the internal and external drafts. With respect to the electronic copies of the agreement, create a

---

3. *See In re Windsor Plumbing Supply Co., Inc.*, 170 B.R. 503, 522-523 (Bankr. E.D.N.Y. 1994); *Girardi v. Shaffer*, 2003 WL 23138445 at *7 (Bankr. E.D. Va. Jan. 17, 2003).

folder for each draft and keep in it the draft that was distributed and any electronic comments that you receive. By keeping a copy of each draft, you can always easily reinsert into Draft #4 the provision that you deleted from Internal Draft #2. In addition, you will have electronic precedents available for future transactions.

With respect to the hard-copy files, use one accordion-type expandable folder for each draft. In it, you would put a hard copy of the draft, along with all the comments that you received from your colleagues, whether electronically or on a hard copy of the agreement. In addition to keeping you organized, this system signals to your supervising lawyer that you are organized and in control of what you are doing. Partners and other supervising lawyers worry. They worry about every aspect of a transaction, including whether you know what you are doing. To the extent that you reduce their worry quotient, it will reduce the pressure on you.

27.8 DRAFTING THE CONTRACT

27.8.1 OTHER DRAFTERS

Although you may draft most of the contract, others in your office may be responsible for drafting portions of it. For example, when drafting a bank loan agreement, you might need inserts drafted by members of the environmental, labor, tax, and real estate departments. Those lawyers will appreciate your giving them as much lead time as possible.

27.8.2 TRANSLATING THE BUSINESS DEAL INTO CONTRACT CONCEPTS

Before beginning to draft, list all the provisions that you have to draft. Use the deal memo or letter of intent as a starting point. Then check your notes from discussions with the client or supervising lawyer, and go through the precedents and secondary materials. (You may have already done the latter if you created your own checklist or added to one that you obtained from your firm or elsewhere.) In addition, consider whether the cascade effect[4] will require you to draft any new provisions or change any existing provisions. Also, use the five-prong framework from Chapter 25 to analyze whether the contract must address any other deal-specific business issues. Finally, review the different ways that the parties' relationship could evolve, and confirm that you and the client have settled on a way to deal with each of them. All of this is time-consuming, but critical to the drafting process.

Once you have listed all the business terms, translate them into contract concepts. Then, reorganize the list so that the business terms appear in the order in which they will appear in the contract. Use your precedent and the principles that you learned in Chapter 26 to help you order the list. When you have finished all this, you are ready to draft. After you have practiced for awhile, you should be able to short-circuit this process. But, in the beginning, it will help you.

27.8.3 DRAFTING THE FIRST DRAFT

27.8.3.1 How to Begin

Where do you begin? How do you actually decide what to write? Drafters differ in their approach, and your approach may change depending upon the agreement. You may

---

4. See §23.2.

not want to start with the introductory provisions. You may have an idea for a tough provision and want to try drafting it right away. But absent a good reason to start somewhere else, start with the introductory provisions. Drafting these provisions first will establish the defined terms for the parties and will begin to put words on the page. Writer's block can be as much of a problem when writing contracts as when writing memos and briefs.

27.8.3.2 The Definitions

Although the definition article generally follows the words of agreement, drafting *all* the definitions is *not* the next thing to do. Many drafters prefer to skip the definition article entirely and deal with a definition only when they need the related defined term to draft a provision. This practice works well because it forces the drafter to see the definition in the context in which it will be used. It also works well for lawyers who place definitions in context.

Some drafters do draft some definitions before they turn to the contract's substantive provisions. Those who do generally work on definitions that they know they need to revise. These drafters then deal with the remaining definitions as needed.

Whether you skip the definitions or draft some early on, stay sensitive to the need to draft new ones. Draft them while you are working on the relevant provisions.

As you work with the definitions, remember that they are being incorporated into substantive contract provisions and that they will have substantive consequences. They are standards that, when changed, affect the business deal and the parties' rights and obligations. Accordingly, make sure that each definition works each time its defined term is used.

27.8.3.3 The Business Provisions

After the definitions, turn to your list of business points. If you have organized that list so that it coordinates with the sequence of the contract's provisions, you have a roadmap for working through the contract. But you will probably not stay on a straight path to the signature lines. Drafting is not linear.[5] Contracts evolve, and the process is often messy.

As you work through the contract, you will constantly refine your ideas and what you have drafted. You will see issues that were not apparent when you started drafting. You may decide on a new provision or do wholesale redrafts of provisions you thought you had finished. You may also decide not to revise all of the provisions your first time through the contract. You may prefer to make the easy changes in one round of revisions and then, in the next, return to the more sophisticated provisions. Or, you may draft all the points in the letter of intent in the first mark-up and turn to all the other provisions in the next. Most drafters go through three or four rounds of revisions before they have a first draft to distribute.

Some provision hopping should be part of your planned approach to drafting. Indeed, it is good practice to work on related provisions at the same time. For example, if you are drafting an acquisition agreement, you should draft the seller's representation and warranty about its equipment and the related covenant about maintaining that equipment at the same time. This will decrease the possibility that the provisions will have different standards and violate the *say the same thing the same way* rule.[6]

---

5. Scott J. Burnham, *Drafting and Analyzing Contracts* 318 (3d ed., LexisNexis 2003).
6. See § 21.8.

Similarly, provision hopping makes sense if you add a new provision that causes a cascade effect. If you choose not to draft related provisions at the same time, make a margin note in the precedent at the intended location of the second provision to remind you what you must do.

As you work through the contract, you will have questions. Do not stop drafting and wait to get an answer. Instead, do one or more of the following:

- Create a list of questions to ask your client or supervising lawyer. (Do not call every time you have a question.)
- Put the provision about which you have a question in brackets. (This option works well if you will not be able to ask a question before submitting your draft.)
- Craft two or more versions of the provision, putting each in brackets. (This shows the reader the options.)
- Describe the issue in the cover memo to your supervising lawyer or the client. (By explaining the issue, you may help the reader decide how to handle it.)

Also, set up a system to deal with cross-references. As you draft, you may find that one provision needs to refer to another. Because provisions will change their location as you work through the drafting process, you need to keep track of the cross-references so that you can update them properly when you finalize the contract. To deal with this, insert the correct cross-reference at the time of the initial drafting in a large bold font inside a set of brackets. Then, later, you can search for a bracket or the bold reference, and insert the correct provision.

Choosing the right words to express the deal is challenging—and fun. As you have seen throughout this book, the smallest change in a word or a phrase affects the parties' rights and obligations. Use your knowledge of the business and legal consequences of the contract concepts to guide you in tailoring the provisions. For example, draft a representation and warranty broadly and with no qualifiers if your client will receive the representations and warranties. The following list contains additional guidelines that you should take into account while drafting.

CONTRACT DRAFTING GUIDELINES

1. *Do not recut the deal.* Although you are more than a scrivener, you are not a principal. Do not draft a provision so that it favors your client more than the agreed-upon deal intended. Doing so could be an ethical violation.

2. *Determine whether one party will have more control.* If you represent the less powerful party, you may be able to protect it better with detailed provisions that spell out its rights.

3. *Determine whether vagueness or specificity will benefit your client.* The answer is usually provision specific.

4. *If the contract establishes a relationship that will exist for a term of years, build in flexibility so that each change in circumstances does not create a contractual crisis.*

5. *Use the canons of construction to give you insight into how a court might interpret a provision.* Then, rewrite the provision if the parties' intent differs.

6. *Do not rely on the canons of interpretation to put a gloss on what you are drafting.* Instead, clarify any unclear or ambiguous provisions. The canons of interpretation are a last resort—something to give you and your client comfort if a provision cannot be clarified because of the client's weak negotiating position. (Once you raise the problem with the provision, if the other party has superior negotiating leverage, they may try to strengthen the provision, so that it favors them even more.)

7. *Draft the contract to deal with all the possibilities of an* if/then *scenario.* As you have seen, covenants, discretionary authority, and declarations can be subject to conditions. When you draft a provision that sets out an *if/then* business term, think through what happens if the opposite fact pattern occurs. Does the contract already provide for this possibility? If not, discuss with your client how to handle this new situation. For example, the endgame provisions of most employment agreements deal with the possibility of a termination for cause.

> **Termination for Cause.** If the Company terminates the Executive for Cause, the Company shall pay the Executive . . .

This *if/then* scenario should make you think of another: termination without cause.

8. *Draft a real-world, pragmatic contract that reflects how the parties will interact.* Good writing alone does not make a good contract. If a contract's provisions are impractical and will not work on a day-to-day basis, redraft them.

As noted earlier, it may take three or four rounds of revisions to produce your "first draft." As you refine it to reflect the business deal as accurately as possible, also look at the contract from a good writing perspective and do the following:

- Create clarity through format.
- Create clarity through sentence structure.
- Eliminate legalese.
- Eliminate ambiguity.

27.8.3.4   Finalizing the Contract

To finalize the contract, run your word-processing application's spell-check. But beware: Spell-check does not pick up a misspelled word that creates another word (e.g., there v. their). Also, check that all cross-references are correct. Then, print out a hard copy and proofread it carefully. No matter how facile you are with a computer, you will find substantive errors and glitches when reviewing a hard copy that you will not find when looking at the contract on a computer screen. Read the contract slowly and look at what you wrote and see if it coincides with what you thought you wrote.

27.8.4   REDRAFTING THE CONTRACT

No contract is ever finished after the first draft. Most lawyers are inveterate revisers and cannot read a document without a pencil in hand to mark comments. Anyone who reads your draft, whether a supervising lawyer or a client, will have comments. Receiving comments does not mean that you did a poor job. It is part of the drafting process. Even senior lawyers will have other lawyers review their drafts. In a large firm, you may need to take comments from several lawyers—generally lawyers in other departments who did not give you their input as you were working on your first draft. By working through all these comments, the contract will improve, and you will learn a great deal about drafting.

Before taking comments from anyone, copy the draft onto 8½ by 14-inch paper and reduce the print to 90 percent. This creates room to annotate the provisions with comments. When you take comments, use a different color pen or pencil for each person.[7] By color-coding the comments, you will be able to report who made which comments. Your client or supervising lawyer may need this information to reconcile conflicting comments.

You will receive comments in several ways. Some readers mark their comments on their drafts and then give you the draft. Always follow up if you cannot decipher a notation. Others will use a word-processing application's comment function[8] or input changes on an electronic copy of the contract and give you a redlined version. (A redlined[9] document shows changes by underlining new language and striking through deleted language.) Other readers will talk through their comments with you. This can be helpful because it gives you an opportunity to ask questions.

As you receive or read through comments, think through whether they are correct. They may not be. You may have already dealt with a point elsewhere, or the comment may be inconsistent with your understanding of the business deal. If you disagree with a comment, discuss it with the person who made the comment.

Look carefully at each provision before you modify it. You may need to change additional language in that provision so that the requested change works properly. You may also need to change another provision or draft a new one because of the cascade effect. If you cut and paste in a new provision from another agreement, check that the relevant standards in the revised contract are consistent. Sometimes you will inadvertently introduce a new standard.

When you finish making the requested changes, read the entire contract. Inevitably, you will find glitches and substantive issues that you and others did not see. You may be the only one able to spot these problems because of your familiarity with the contract.

With that, you have completed your first draft for external distribution.

27.8.4.1 The Cover Memo

When you distribute the first draft of the contract (indeed any draft), send it with a cover memo that

- tells the reader where to find the provisions that deal with hot button issues;
- explains the risks and benefits of provisions not previously discussed; and
- describes open issues and proposes ways of resolving them.

If you take notes on these points as you draft, writing this memo will be much easier.

Spend time on the memo. Keeping the client (or supervising lawyer) informed is part of your job. Indeed, you have an ethical obligation to keep the client informed.[10] A short, well-written memo that highlights the salient issues will help you do that.

Choose the recipients of your memo carefully. If it contains privileged information, sending it to the wrong person could destroy the attorney/client privilege.

---

7. Professor Eric Goldman has a similar system that he uses when he negotiates a contract. He marks all of his comments and those of his colleagues with a red pen, and then uses a blue pen to mark the changes to which the other side agrees. *Contract Drafting: Course Materials* 44, Spring 2005, Marquette University Law School.

8. The comment function in Word permits a reader to insert a balloon in a document's margin and to write a comment in the balloon. Each balloon is connected to the relevant part of the document by a dotted line.

9. A synonym for *redlined* is *blacklined.*

10. Model R. Prof. Conduct 1.4(a)(3) (ABA 2006). See §30.3.

EXERCISES

Exercise 27-1

Your client has called and wants to come in for a meeting. She has decided to create a website for her business and must sign a contract with a marketing company. Create a checklist of questions to ask her. Use the Website Development Agreement in Appendix B as a starting place. In addition, find at least two other website development agreements and use their provisions to create additional checklist questions.

Exercise 27-2

Diagram the following transaction: A corporation (Parent) is the sole shareholder of Sub A and owns 51 percent of the outstanding shares of Sub B. The target (Target) is a wholly owned subsidiary of Target-Parent. Target is to merge into Sub A, with Sub A to be the surviving corporation. Sub A will pay Target-Parent with funds it borrows from Big Bank. Sub A has agreed to secure its debt by granting a security interest in all its assets to Big Bank. Parent will guarantee Sub A's debt and will back up the guaranty by pledging the shares it owns in Sub A and Sub B.

Exercise 27-3

Research letters of intent and then draft the language that you would use to clarify that a letter of intent did not bind the parties to consummate the transaction.

How to Review and Comment on a Contract

28.1 INTRODUCTION

Every contract has two drafters: the lawyer who writes the initial draft and the lawyer who reviews that draft. In some ways, reviewing a contract is more difficult than writing it. Not only must a reviewing lawyer prepare for that review in the same way a drafter prepares to draft, the reviewing lawyer must also try to determine what the drafter was thinking when the provision was written. A provision that seems reasonable on its face may be problematic. The drafting lawyer knows what was intended. The reviewing lawyer must divine that intent by reverse engineering. He must look at the finished product and figure out the thinking process that created it.

In this chapter, you will learn how to analyze a contract, identify key issues, and give comments. Just as drafting requires more than changing the names and dates in a precedent, analyzing a contract requires more than reading it. Here are the five steps:

1. Prepare.
2. Get your bearings.
3. Read and analyze the key business provisions.
4. Read and analyze the entire contract.
5. Mark up the contract and give comments.

28.2 PREPARE

Before you read the other side's draft, you must prepare in exactly the same way you would have if you had been the drafter. You must

- obtain all available information about the business deal;
- create a checklist of questions for the client;
- thoroughly interview the client;
- research the law, the other party, and the parties' industry;
- find appropriate precedents;
- create a list of business issues and deal terms (both those that the parties have agreed to and any new ones to be incorporated);

■ translate them into contract concepts; and

■ organize the business terms in the sequence in which you expect that they will appear in the contract.

Without this preparation, you cannot effectively review a contract. You will not have the knowledge of the business deal or the tools to determine whether the draft appropriately memorializes that deal.

28.3   GET YOUR BEARINGS

The first time you look at a contract, you should "eye-ball" it. "Eye-balling" a contract is less than skimming it. It means looking through the pages to obtain an overview. How is the contract organized? By subject matter? By contract concept? Is its organization similar to the precedents? How does it differ? Where are the action sections? Do the captions look familiar, or does the contract contain provisions that you had not expected?

With this information, you will gain a sense of the contract in the same way that you would gain the sense of a history textbook by looking at its table of contents and flipping through the pages. You will not have the details, but you will know where the details are and whether the contract at least appears to be within the expected norm.

28.4   READ THE KEY BUSINESS PROVISIONS

Once you have your bearings, review the key business provisions to see if the contract has correctly stated the most significant business terms. Clients frequently call shortly after you receive a contract—often before you could have reasonably been expected to have reviewed it fully. By looking at the key business provisions first, you will be able to address the client's immediate concerns. When reading, focus on the substance of the business deal, not on how you might change specific wording. You will deal with that when you do the mark-up.

Generally, you should read the consideration provisions in the action sections first. Clients often consider these to be a contract's most important provisions. Has the other side gotten the money right? If not, the contract has either been poorly drafted, or the parties have had a serious misunderstanding.

Next, look at the endgame provisions. Look at them from two perspectives: When does the other side have rights against your client, and when does your client have rights against the other side? Also, confirm that the contract ties up all the loose ends; for example, deposits returned and post-termination payments provided for. Finally, remember that endgame and money provisions often go hand in hand. Under what circumstances will your client lose the benefits of the contract, and how much will that cost?

Then, turn to the provisions dealing with the most significant other business terms. These may not be intuitively obvious. Sometimes, these points reflect concerns specific to your client. For example, assume that you represent an executive in connection with the negotiation and drafting of her employment agreement. The executive may have a special interest in a charity because of her family's circumstances (an illness, for example). As a partial inducement, the employer may have agreed to donate $50,000 a year to that charity. This issue probably does not appear on any treatise checklist or in any precedent, but it may matter greatly to your client.

28.5 READ THE ENTIRE CONTRACT

After reading the key business provisions, read the entire contract. Start from the beginning. Imagine that you are drafting the contract and marking up a precedent. As you look at each provision, think about what changes you would make. These provisions are not engraved in stone. Many are merely the other side's opening bid with respect to issues that the parties did not discuss. You cannot recut the business deal, but you can negotiate how it is memorialized.

If the contract includes a definitions article, you may take two different approaches to its review. If you have not previously drafted or reviewed this type of contract, consider initially skipping the article entirely, but then returning to it each time you confront a defined term. If you have previously drafted or reviewed this type of contract, look for key definitions and skim them to see if they seem relatively standard. If not, pay special attention to the provisions that include the related defined terms. The drafter may have made substantive changes to relatively standard provisions by changing the definitions. In either event, physically separate the definitions article from the rest of the contract. This will enable you to place it and the contract side by side, so that you can look at a definition and a provision at the same time.

As you continue through the contract, do not be tied in your review to the order of the contract provisions. Instead, mimic the drafting process. Provision hop as necessary so that you review related provisions at the same time. Once you deal with a point, go back to where you left off, so that you cover every provision. Some drafters check off each provision after they have read it.

As you go through the contract, you will analyze provisions as prosaic as the introductory provisions and as substantive as the action sections. To help you focus on the business issues, use the five-prong framework from Chapter 25 the same way you would have had you been the drafter. Review the contract slowly, or you will miss issues.

You may have stylistic comments: legalese, lack of formatting, etc. Generally, you should defer to the drafter on these matters. If she still drafts as if she were in eighteenth-century England, so be it. Do not spend negotiating capital on whether the contract should say *aforesaid* or *previously.* Although stylistic comments are generally inappropriate, some drafters appreciate them. It is bad form, however, to raise these points at a negotiating session, especially if clients are present. Instead, mark up the relevant provisions and give them to the drafter privately. You may appropriately note in these comments any misspellings, missing or incorrect words, or other "glitches."

Look not only at what is in the contract, but for what is missing. Reviewing lawyers tend to focus on the words on the page, not on what is absent. Use your checklist to determine whether all the business terms were included. Also, step back and think about your client's goals. Does the contract achieve those goals, or are other provisions needed?

As you go through the contract, make notes in the margin, circle problem language, or otherwise indicate any concern that you have with the language. Do not make the comments too cryptic, or you will have trouble recalling your point, especially if the contract is long. Also, do not do a detailed mark-up or draft inserts as you go through the contract this time. Subsequent provisions may affect your view of a provision. In addition, you will need the client's input.

That said, here are some questions that you should ask each time you review a contract.

1. Are the parties' names and other information in the preamble correct? Are the correct parties being bound? (See Chapter 6.)

2. Are the recitals accurate? What would be the effect on your client if they became stipulated facts in a lawsuit? Did the drafter put any substantive provisions in the recitals? (See Chapter 6.)

3. Does each definition work each time a provision uses its defined term?[1] Are any substantive provisions in the definitions? (See Chapter 7.)

4. Are the provisions in the action sections correct? (See Chapter 8.)

   (a) Carefully analyze the monetary provisions. Do they work? Does the contract appropriately restrict your client's obligation to pay? Should the other party be paying your client more? Is the other party creditworthy? Should the conditions to the other party's obligation to pay be more easily satisfied? In all instances, do the payment provisions answer the following questions: *who, what, when, where, why, how, and how much?* (See Chapter 8.)

   (b) Does the contract include an effective date? If it does, is the trigger for the effective date properly stated? (See Chapters 6 and 8.)

   (c) If the contract is for a stated term, what could prematurely terminate it?[2] Should the contract term automatically renew? (See Chapters 8 and 25.)

5. Are the representations and warranties that your client is being asked to make accurate? Do they allocate too much risk to your client? How can they be qualified to reduce the risk? Does the contract ask your client to make representations and warranties that are unrelated to the transaction? (See Chapters 3 and 9.)

6. Has the other side made representations and warranties? Are they too weak? If so, how can they be strengthened? What additional representations and warranties should they make? (See Chapters 3 and 9.)

7. Can your client perform its covenants? Are they too difficult? Does your client have control over the outcome of each of its covenants? What would decrease the degree of obligation? Should any of the covenants instead be conditions to the other party's obligation to perform? Do any of the covenants that your client is being asked to make need an exception? (See Chapters 3 and 10.)

8. Has the other side made the necessary covenants? If not, what additional or different covenants are needed? How should the degree of obligation be changed? Should any of the covenants include an exception? (See Chapters 3 and 10.)

9. Are any conditions to the other side's obligation to perform inappropriate? Should any condition to the other side's obligation to perform be recast as a covenant? (See Chapters 4 and 11.)

10. Should the conditions to the client's obligation to perform be more stringent? Should any of the client's covenants be recast as a condition? (See Chapters 4 and 11.)

---

1. To check, use your word processor's *Find* function.

2. Most contracts deal with this issue in the endgame provisions. Sometimes, however, drafters deal with it in the action sections.

11. Have you carefully examined the endgame provisions? Do they provide for early termination? What constitutes *default* or *cause?* What are the remedies? Does the contract provide for a friendly termination? Are all the loose ends tied up? Should one or more provisions survive the contract's termination? If an endgame provision involves money, does it answer the *who, what, when, where, why, how, and how much* questions? Should disputes be litigated, arbitrated, or mediated? (See Chapter 15.)

12. Does the contract include all the appropriate general provisions? If any are omitted, what are the consequences? Has each provision been tailored to reflect the parties' agreement? (See Chapter 16.)

13. Are the signature blocks properly set up? Are the names correct? Are they the same names as those in the preamble? If a party is an entity, does its signature line indicate the signatory's title? (See Chapter 17.)

14. Is there legalese that should be deleted? (See Chapter 18.)

15. Does the contract use formatting to enhance clarity? (See Chapter 19.)

16. Does each sentence's structure enhance its clarity? (See Chapter 20.)

17. Is any provision ambiguous? Are two or more provisions ambiguous when read together? (See Chapter 21.)

18. Do the contract provisions say the same thing the same way? If the standards differ, should they? (See Chapter 21.)

19. With respect to each mathematical formula, have you created hypotheticals to check whether the formula is properly stated? Have you received accounting and tax advice? (See Chapter 22.)

20. Have you used the five-prong framework to analyze the contract's provisions? (Chapter 25)

21. Does the contract's organization facilitate its reading? (See Chapter 26.)

22. Has each business point been incorporated? Does the contract deal with all the scenarios that you and the client discussed? If not, do you need to include any of the missing scenarios, or has the client reached a business judgment not to deal with them? Is your client adequately protected? (See Chapter 27.)

23. Do the contract's provisions reflect an understanding of the parties and their industry? (See Chapter 27.)

24. Does the contract raise any legal issues? Are all the provisions enforceable? Have the parties received all the required governmental approvals? (See Chapter 27.)

28.6 PREPARE COMMENTS

Once you have been through the contract and conferred with your client, you must prepare your comments for the other side. You have three choices, in declining order of preferability:

- A detailed mark-up of the contract, along with an accompanying memorandum. The mark-up will show the changes you want, while the memorandum will explain proposed changes and raise issues.
- A memorandum discussing the major points, plus a mark-up of small issues, glitches (typographical errors), and stylistic points (if appropriate).
- Oral comments, conveyed by telephone or at a meeting.

Before concluding which approach to take, talk with your client about these factors: time, cost, and the strategic benefits of one approach rather than another.

28.6.1 MARK-UPS

If you mark up the contract, you regain some of the leverage that you lost when the other side took on the role of drafter. Now, you and your client can shape the contract in ways both obvious and subtle. In addition, by making the comments in writing, you permit the drafter to concede the point without doing it in front of you, your client, and the drafter's client. It is easier on the ego, and the need to look tough in front of the client is not directly put into play. It also gives the other side time to think through your side's comments. A point that it might have rejected in person may be easier to win this way. You will not settle all the points with your mark-up. Key business issues will remain, but you may winnow down the issues, making it easier to complete the negotiations.

If your client is worried about the mark-up's cost, explain its strategic advantage. Point out the ability to shape the negotiation and the deal through drafting.

Mark-ups may be done by hand or by making changes using an electronic copy of the agreement. Ask the drafter which she prefers. Some drafters dislike electronic mark-ups because they lose control over the document. Others prefer it because it reduces the work of inputting agreed-upon changes.

Before marking up a contract electronically, check whether your firm permits you to do this. Some firms prohibit electronic mark-ups because their word-processing software allows the other side to track all the changes made, including any changes that were rejected before distribution. To prevent this from occurring, some firms use separate software applications that can input the changes without leaving a trail. Others turn the agreement into a PDF file.

The logistics of doing a hand mark-up are relatively easy. An example follows these instructions. To indicate that you wish to delete one or more words, put a straight line through those words. To indicate that you wish to insert words, put a **caret** where you want the words. (A caret is a proofreading mark that looks like an upside down "v.") Then, draw a line from the top of the caret into the margin. Write the words you want inserted, circle them to create a balloon, and connect the balloon to the line connected to the caret.

If an insert consists of more than a few words, type it on a separate page. Use a caret, a line, and a balloon to indicate where the insert goes. Rather than putting the proposed language in the balloon, put an **insert number**. An insert number consists of the page number on which the change is to be made and a capital letter to distinguish multiple inserts on the same page. Use the capital letters in alphabetical order. For example: *Insert 22A* and *Insert 22B*. Although each insert should appear on a separate page, you do need not to create a separate document for each insert. Instead, use a page break to move each insert onto its own page.

If you wish to move language to another page, circle it, draw a line from it to the margin, and attach it to a balloon. Inside the balloon, give the circled language an insert number, just as if you were adding language. Then, indicate the page to which the language should be moved: *Insert 22C to page 34.* On the page where the language is to be inserted, put a caret at the insertion point and attach it to a balloon in the margin. Inside the balloon, put language along the following lines: *Put Insert 22C here.*

When you add language or move it, the numbering of sections and subsections may change. Mark those changes too, or write a general comment.

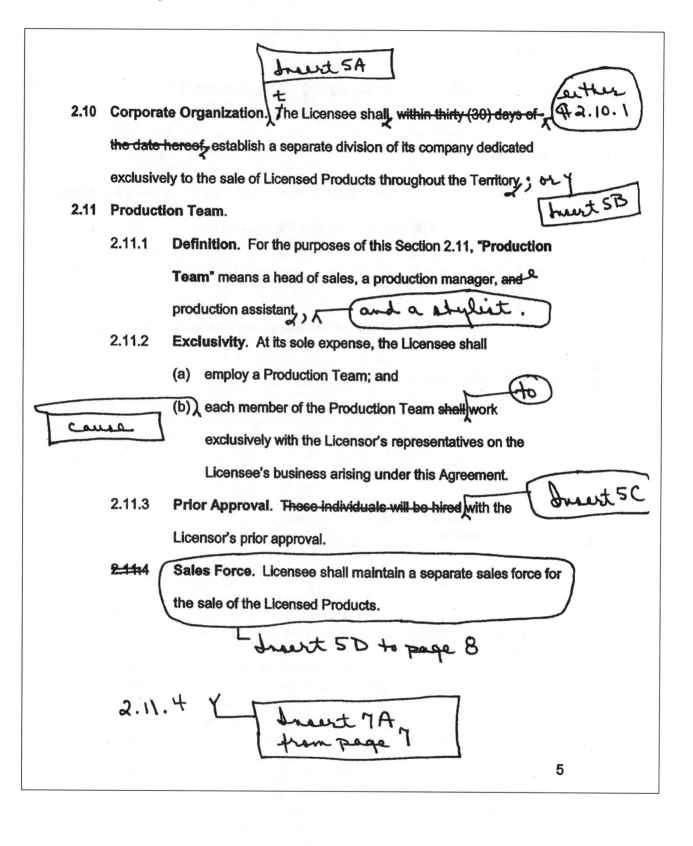

2.10 **Corporate Organization.** The Licensee shall ~~within thirty (30) days of~~
~~the date hereof,~~ establish a separate division of its company dedicated
exclusively to the sale of Licensed Products throughout the Territory ; or

[handwritten: Insert 5A]
[handwritten: t]
[handwritten: either ¶ 2.10.1]
[handwritten: Insert 5B]

2.11 **Production Team.**

    2.11.1 **Definition.** For the purposes of this Section 2.11, "Production
Team" means a head of sales, a production manager, ~~and~~ *[a]*
production assistant , *[handwritten: and a stylist .]*

    2.11.2 **Exclusivity.** At its sole expense, the Licensee shall

        (a) employ a Production Team; and

        (b) each member of the Production Team ~~shall~~ work *[to]*
exclusively with the Licensor's representatives on the
Licensee's business arising under this Agreement.

[handwritten: cause]

    2.11.3 **Prior Approval.** ~~These individuals will be hired~~ with the
Licensor's prior approval.

[handwritten: Insert 5C]

    ~~2.11.4~~ **Sales Force.** Licensee shall maintain a separate sales force for
the sale of the Licensed Products.

[handwritten: Insert 5D to page 8]

[handwritten: 2.11.4]
[handwritten: Insert 7A, from page 7]

Insert 5A

No later than 30 days after the signing of this Agreement,

Insert 5B

2.10.2   form a subsidiary company, but only if that company agrees in

writing to comply with this Agreement.

Insert 5C

The Licensee shall not employ a member of the Production Team, except

---

28.6.2   A MEMORANDUM

You can use a memorandum two ways: as a stand-alone document or as a supplement to a mark-up. If you use it as a stand-alone document, use it to explain the changes that you want and why. Put the most important ones first and then discuss the remainder in the order in which they appear in the contract. You can format the memorandum as follows:

1. **Section 7.2**—[Important change]
2. **Section 7.8**—[Important change]
3. **Section 2.4**—[Remaining changes; list in ascending section number order]

Use the memorandum as a negotiating tool, explaining the business and legal reasons for each change. Laying out the issues for the other side gives them the opportunity to think them through privately, without time pressure and without ceding the point in your presence or the clients'. A memorandum resembles a mark-up in this regard.

Tone is important, as in any negotiation. Diplomatic is generally best, but use a more aggressive tone if appropriate in the context of the transaction.

Although a memorandum allows you to argue your position, it does not, unfortunately, allow you to propose specific language changes. By not drafting the language, you cede a strategic advantage to the other side. But you may be able to regain some—subtly. As you draft the memorandum, phrase the discussion so it uses words or phrases that you think should be incorporated. The drafter might just use them as an easy way to make agreed-upon changes.

Some drafters accompany a stand-alone memorandum with a mark-up of glitches and minor points. This will advance the later negotiation by permitting the parties to focus on the primary business issues.

If you use the memorandum with a mark-up, do not elaborate on every change. Instead, use it as a negotiating tool, just as you would with a stand-alone memorandum.

28.6.3 ORAL COMMENTS

Oral comments are generally the least favorable option from a strategic point of view because you do not propose specific language. You can compensate—somewhat.

In preparing for the negotiation, draft inserts for key business provisions. This way, you know not only the substance of what you are asking for, but also the details. During the negotiation, make specific comments, using words and phrases from your inserts. As the other side takes notes, they may pick up your language and then, later, incorporate it into the contract. Having the draft inserts also enables you to offer them to the other side if they assent to a proposed change.

EXERCISES

Exercise 28-1

Before doing this exercise, read the material on termination provisions in Exhibit A to this chapter. Then, analyze the following contract using the steps described in this chapter.

Carrie Richards
210 East 21st Street
New York, New York

November 10, 20X5

Lydia Wright, Esq.
357 West 47th Street
New York, New York

Dear Lydia:

As I told you on the telephone, I landed the job with WXYZ, Channel 101, in New York. It's cable, but a coup. To get a broadcast job fresh out of college is beyond exciting. I met with two people: Rashad Hampton, Senior Vice President of USA Television Communications, Inc. (USA), and Alex Schroeder, Station Manager of WXYZ, USA's affiliate.

I'm going to be WXYZ's consumer affairs reporter. This is a great beat. There is never an emergency, which means that I will always get my weekends, and three-day holidays will really be holidays. I have committed to airing, on average, two segments a week. If I average three segments or more a week, they will pay me a $25,000 bonus. My salary is $100,000.

Here is a list of the other points that we negotiated:

1. I've agreed to a two-year term. They asked that I promise to negotiate with them exclusively for a 30-day period before the end of the term. I was leery about this, but I'm only promising to negotiate. It also seemed to be part of the price of admission, so I said, "yes."

2. They asked for a one-year noncompete after the term. That seems very long, but they said that it was standard industry practice. I temporized on that one. I said that I needed to talk to my lawyer.

3. They will give me a car and up to $600 a month to pay for insurance, parking, and repairs. I've promised to use the car principally for business. They will reimburse me for the expenses upon presentation to them of an itemized account of the expenses.

4. They will indemnify me if I get sued for anything in connection with the performance of my duties.

5. I told them that I planned to do about 30 hours a month volunteer work for the ASPCA.

They told me that was not a problem. Other broadcasters did similar volunteer work. They said we did not need to cover it in the contract; they never did for any of the other broadcasters.

6. Hampton said that the remainder of the contract would include their standard "boilerplate" clauses dealing with termination, confidentiality, adherence to company policy, etc.

7. They told me that they always investigate new employees, so I gave them my Social Security number, and I repeated what was on my resume: I graduated 10th in my class from Syracuse University in June 20X5 with a major in communications and that, while at Syracuse, I successfully completed the Renée Crown University Honors Program. I also told them that I was an unpaid intern at WTVH, Channel 5, the CBS affiliate in Syracuse, during the summers of 20X3 and 20X4.

I guess the contract must be fairly standard as I received a draft the day after I met with them. I would appreciate your giving me a call as soon as you have had a chance to look it over.

One last thing. Very strange. Hampton said that while it was usually not the practice for a commenting lawyer to give comments on style, their lawyer was new, so they would be delighted if we gave comments on style as well as substance.

Best,

Carrie

Employment Agreement

Employment Agreement, dated as of November 15, 20X5 between WXYZ, Channel 101, New York, New York (the "Station"), and Carrie Richards (the "Reporter").

The parties agree to the following terms of employment:

1. **Employment.** The Station shall employ the Reporter, and the Reporter shall work for the Station, under the terms of this Agreement.

2. **Salary.** The Station shall pay the Reporter at a rate of $100,000 per year in approximately equal weekly installments. If in any year the Reporter airs on average more than three segments per week, the Station shall pay the Reporter a bonus of $25,000 no later than March 31 of the following year.

3. **Term and Termination.**

   (a) **Term.** The term of the Reporter's employment under this Agreement is from January 1, 20X6 until 8:00 p.m. December 31, 20X7 (the "Term"), unless terminated earlier in accordance with the provisions of this Agreement.

   (b) **Extension of the Term.**

   (i) **Notice.** If the Station wants to extend the Reporter's employment beyond the end of the Term, then no later than 120 days before the end of the Term, the Station must notify the Reporter to that effect in writing.

   (ii) **Exclusive Negotiations.** If the Reporter receives the appropriate notice, then beginning 90 days before the end of the Term, the Reporter shall negotiate with the Station exclusively and in good faith for 30 days with respect to the contract terms for an

continued on next page >

extension of the Term. The Reporter shall not negotiate with any third party before this exclusive negotiating period.

(iii) **The Parties' Rights upon Failed Negotiations.** If the parties cannot reach an agreement during the exclusive negotiating period, the Reporter may negotiate with any third party during the remainder of the Term. If during the remainder of the Term a third party offers the Reporter a job that she wants to accept, she shall notify the Station in writing of the offer's terms no later than three days after she receives the offer. No later than three days after the Station receives the terms of the third-party offer, the Station shall notify the Reporter in writing whether it will match the offer. If it matches the offer, the Station and the Reporter shall enter into a new agreement pursuant to the terms of the offer. If the Station does not match the offer, the Reporter may accept it.

(c) **The Station's Right to Terminate.** The Station may terminate the Reporter's employment at any time for "cause." The following are illustrations of "cause," but the Station is not limited or bound by these illustrations:

(i) Misconduct.

(ii) Insubordination.

(iii) Failure to perform assigned work in a satisfactory manner.

(iv) Using, possessing, selling, or distributing intoxicants, illegal drugs, or controlled substances on the Station's property or any other violation of the Station's drug and alcohol abuse policy.

(v) Dishonesty or deceit.

(vi) On-air obscenity or impropriety, oral or visual.

(vii) Violation of any policy in the Station's Employee Handbook.

(viii) Conduct involving moral turpitude.

(ix) Conduct punishable as a felony under state or federal law;

(x) Any action involving a breach of the terms of this Agreement.

(xi) The Reporter's failure to conduct herself with due regard to social conventions, public morals, and decency.

(xii) Conduct that could jeopardize Station's license to operate.

(xiii) Violation of any Federal Communications Commission rule or regulation.

(xiv) Incompetence.

(xv) Violation of the Station's absenteeism policy.

The Station shall decide in its sole discretion whether particular conduct constitutes "cause," but it shall not exercise that discretion arbitrarily, capriciously, or in violation of law.

(d) **The Reporter's Right to Terminate.** The Employee may terminate this Agreement if the Station breaches this Agreement and has not cured the breach after notice and a 30-day opportunity to cure.

(e) **Death.** If the Reporter dies, her employment terminates, effective as of the date of her death, and the Station shall pay the Reporter's representatives her salary through that date.

4. **Duties.** The Reporter shall render personal services in the WXYZ designated market area as an on-the-air reporter. She shall diligently perform those duties that the Station reasonably assigns and that relate to on-the-air services, including planning, preparing, and broadcasting various news segments. The Employee shall air one to two segments per week on an average weekly basis. Nothing in this Agreement requires the Station to assign the Reporter any specific duties.

5. **Extent of Service.** The Reporter shall devote her entire professional time, attention, and energies to the performance of her duties for the Station.

6. **Insurance and Other Employee Benefits.** Employee is entitled to receive insurance, vacation, holidays, and other employee benefits as provided to other Station employees and as set out in the Station's Personnel Manual. The Station shall provide the Reporter with the use of a mid-size car of her choice for use during the Term.

7. **Working Facilities.** The Station shall give the Reporter an office suitable to her position and adequate for the performance of her duties.

8. **Scripts, Creative Material, Promotional Material.** The Reporter acknowledges that all scripts and creative material created by or performed by her are "work made for hire" as that term is used in the copyright laws of the United States, as set forth in 17 U.S.C. Section 101, et seq. In addition, all programs, program segments, titles and formats, scripts and outlines, and ideas and concepts, conceived and created for any program are the sole and exclusive property of the Station. The Reporter shall take all actions the Station requests to confirm ownership of the intellectual property in the Station. The Station may make or cause to be made likenesses, portraits, pictures, sketches, and caricatures of the Reporter and may use such likenesses, portraits, sketches, and caricatures of the Reporter as well as the Reporter's recorded voice and name in all forms of media for the purpose of publicizing, promoting, and advertising the Station and programs broadcast by the Station.

9. **Adherence to the Station's Policies.** The Reporter shall comply with the Station's Code of Business Conduct and any other policies, rules, or directives that the Station establishes.

10. **Confidentiality.** During the Term and thereafter, Employee shall keep secret and inviolate the terms of this Agreement, including without limitation the provisions of Paragraph 3 respecting compensation and all knowledge and information of a confidential nature that the Reporter knows now or subsequently comes to know as a result of her employment at the Station.

11. **Noncompetition.**

    (a) **Covenant Not to Compete.** The Reporter is familiar with

       (i)   the business of the Station;

       (ii) the commercial and competitive nature of the industry and its dependence upon public acceptability;

       (iii) the substantial commitment the Station makes in developing the Reporter as a personality with her extraordinary and unique services and abilities that enable him to seek and obtain similar employment outside the Station's market.

       The Reporter further recognizes that the value of the Station's business would be injured if the Reporter obtained comparable employment in the Station's market and that such injury could not be reasonably or adequately compensated by monetary compensation. For these reasons, upon the expiration or earlier termination of this Agreement, the Employee shall not, for a period of one year, perform services for, or otherwise be publicly identified with, any other television or cable television station, located in WXYZ's designated market area.

    (b) **Remedies.** The Reporter acknowledges that it is impossible to measure in monetary terms the damages that will accrue to the Station because of the Reporter's failure to perform the noncompetition covenant set forth in this Agreement. Accordingly, the Reporter acknowledges that if the Station institutes any litigation to enforce the noncompetition covenant, the Station is entitled to injunctive or other equitable relief to prevent the violation of the noncompetition covenant, in addition to damages, attorneys' fees, and costs.

12. **Content of Performance and Indemnification.** The Reporter shall not publicly disseminate or broadcast, or submit to others for that purpose, any material that a Station supervisor has not first approved. The Reporter shall not materially deviate from the script or other material furnished to her in connection with performance of her services. Except as provided below, the

continued on next page >

Station shall indemnify the Reporter from any and all claims, liabilities, and losses, including reasonable attorneys' fees, as a result of acts of the Reporter performed in the course and within the scope of the Reporter's employment. The Station's obligation under this paragraph shall not apply if the Reporter violates any of the Station's policies, if the Reporter has failed to promptly notify the Station of any claim made or litigation filed against him or the Reporter has settled or compromised the claim or litigation as to him without the Station's prior written consent.

13. **Representations and Warranties.** The Reporter represents and warrants as follows:

    (a) She graduated from Syracuse University in 20X5 with a major in communications and that while at Syracuse University, she successfully completed the course of study in the Renée Crown University Honors Program.

    (b) She was an employee at WTVH, Channel 5, the CBS affiliate in Syracuse, New York, during the summers of 20X3 and 20X4.

14. **General Provisions.**

    (a) **Assignment and Delegability.** The Station may assign its rights and delegate its performance under this Agreement. The Reporter shall not assign its rights or delegate its performance under this Agreement.

    (b) **Governing Law.** The laws of New York shall govern all matters arising under or relating to this Agreement.

    (c) **Severability.** If any provision of this Agreement is illegal or unenforceable, the other provisions of this provision remain in effect, if the essential provisions of this Agreement for each party remain valid, binding, and enforceable.

    (d) **Merger.** This Agreement contains the complete and final understanding of the parties and supersedes all other agreements, either oral or in writing, between the parties.

    (e) **Amendments.** This Agreement may be amended only by an agreement in writing signed by both parties.

To evidence the parties' agreement to this Agreement, they have executed and delivered it on the date set forth in the preamble.

WXYZ, Channel 101

_____

Alex Schroeder, Station Manager

_____

Carrie Richards

APPENDIX A

Termination Provisions in an Employment Agreement

Parties keenly negotiate the termination provisions of an employment agreement. These provisions are broken down into four main categories:

- Termination for *cause*
- Termination *without cause*
- Termination upon death
- Termination because of a disability

This appendix provides an overview of each of these categories.

Whether an employer terminates an employee with or without *cause* matters because it affects how much money the employer pays the employee upon termination. If an employee is terminated for *cause,* the employer generally pays the employee only her accrued salary and any expenses. If, however, the employee is terminated *without cause,* then, the employer generally must pay the employee her accrued salary, any expenses, bonus, and severance. In other words, the employer pays a good deal more money. With this in mind, the negotiation of what acts constitute *cause* has much more meaning.

Typically, employers want the definition of *cause* to include as many matters as possible and for each matter to be drafted as broadly as possible and with as few qualifications as possible. Employees, of course, want just the opposite. Common acts that constitute *cause* include misconduct, dishonesty, breach of contract, fraud, a conviction or pleading guilty to a felony, insubordination, and conduct involving moral turpitude. Employers will often try to include incompetence and failure to perform satisfactorily as *cause,* but sophisticated employee lawyers will resist those attempts and instead argue that those issues should constitute termination *without cause.* Contracts will also include as *cause* matters specific to an employer's business.

Two other common termination provisions are death and disability. Death is, of course, the ultimate termination provision. For junior level employees, their employer's obligations generally end upon the date of the employee's death. Companies are sometimes more gracious when dealing with the death of their senior executives. Then, the contract may provide that salary will continue to be paid through the last day of the month in which the executive dies, or some other period. The employment agreement typically provides that the employer will make its final salary payment according to its regular schedule. A senior executive might negotiate for the employer to pay his or her family a special death benefit payment. The parties will also need to negotiate whether the employer will pay a pro rata bonus, and when it should be paid.

Termination because of disability is more common than many people think. The issue of what constitutes disability is a difficult one. How many days absence: 30, 60, 90? Must they be consecutive? What if they occur within a five-month period? Any provision must be carefully drafted so that it complies with the Americans with Disabilities Act and the Family Medical Act. Once the definition of disability is negotiated, the payments (salary and pro rata bonus) must be determined, along with the timing of payments.

Amendments, Consents, and Waivers

29.1 INTRODUCTION

Business deals change: An existing provision no longer works, a new business issue arises, a party fails to perform, or a one-time event requires special handling. As the relationship between the parties evolves, so too must the agreement that memorializes their transaction. To deal with these changes, drafters rely on amendments, consents, and waivers.

29.2 AMENDMENTS

An amendment changes a contract. It can be on any topic covered—or not covered—by the contract. Under the common law, new consideration is necessary for an amendment to be enforceable. But the Uniform Commercial Code and other statutes in some jurisdictions include provisions that override the common law. They provide that an amendment is enforceable without consideration. But always check the law as these laws do not always apply or may not be enacted in the jurisdiction in which you practice.

As was discussed in Chapter 16, amendments can be either oral or written, and oral amendments are often enforceable—despite a no oral amendments provision. Because of this, in the appropriate situation, you should counsel your client to avoid any discussions or dealings that might be misconstrued as a contract amendment. In addition, if appropriate, consider sending a letter to the other side acknowledging negotiations with respect to an amendment but stating, for the record, that the parties reached no agreement.

An amendment may be drafted as an agreement or a letter. A letter is more informal and quicker, but it is just as binding. In both formats, the amending provisions are the same. They differ, however, with respect to the material that surrounds the amending provisions. Most letter agreements follow the format set out in Exhibit B to this chapter. They

- begin with the typical features of any letter, the addressee's name and address and a salutation;
- state that, when signed, the letter constitutes an amendment to the existing agreement;

- incorporate by reference the defined terms from the existing agreement;
- amend the existing agreement;
- request that the addressee indicate its agreement to the amendments by signing the letter and the enclosed duplicate original in the space provided at the end of the letter; and
- request that the addressee return one of the two originals to the sender.

The following sections detail how to draft an amendment in an agreement format. In this format, the amendments are the action sections, and the other contract parts play their usual, respective roles.

29.2.1 THE INTRODUCTORY PROVISIONS AND THE DEFINITIONS

When drafting the preamble of an amendment, name the agreement *Amendment* or *Amending Agreement*. If the parties have previously amended the existing agreement, the amendment's title should reflect the number of amendments: e.g., *Fourth Amendment*. The preamble should also state which agreement is being amended by including that agreement's name, its parties, and the original signing date or as of date. By properly titling the amendment and including the information about the existing contract, a drafter quickly conveys to the reader the contract's purpose. Some drafters exclude the information about the existing agreement from the preamble and put it in the recitals. But that style of preamble delays giving the reader critical information. The better style is to include all of the information on the existing agreement in the preamble. The following preamble is typical:

> **Second Amendment**, dated January 17, 2008, to the Employment Agreement, dated February 23, 2006, between Buckeye Pharmaceuticals Inc., an Ohio corporation (the "Company"), and Mohammed Ahmed, 322 Westland Road, Shaker Heights, Ohio 44120 (the "Executive").

Although recitals may be omitted from some agreements, they are often helpful in an amendment. Use them to explain why the parties are amending their agreement. This puts the amendment in context for the reader.

> **Background**
>
> 1. The Company has employed the Executive as Executive Vice President of Research for approximately two years and now desires to promote him to President.
> 2. The parties desire to amend the Employment Agreement, dated February 23, 2006, as amended (the "Existing Agreement"), to reflect the Executive's new duties, compensation, and other matters.

If the parties are not exchanging consideration for the amendment, do not state that they have. Keep the words of agreement simple:

Accordingly, the parties agree as follows:

When drafting the amendment, you may need to distinguish between the agreement as it exists before the amendment and the agreement that exists after it is amended. *Existing Agreement* is a good defined term to use for the agreement before the amendment. As suggested previously, *Amendment* or *Amending Agreement* works for the amendment, and *Resulting Agreement* can be used to refer to the Existing Agreement, as amended by the Amendment.

When drafting the definition of the Existing Agreement, be sure that it incorporates prior amendments. Do this whether you define the term in context, as in the recitals above, or in a separate definition.

> **"Existing Agreement"** means the Employment Agreement between the Company and the Executive, dated February 23, 2006, as amended to the date of this Amendment.

Other definitions may also be necessary. If so, the customary drafting guidelines apply. If the amendment uses terms defined in the existing agreement, do not redefine them. Instead, incorporate them into the amendment, using the following provision:

> **Definitions**. Capitalized terms used in this Amendment without definition have the meanings assigned to them in the Existing Agreement.

29.2.2 DECIDING WHAT TO AMEND

When discussing a proposed amendment with your client, focus the discussion on the business goal, rather than on specific provisions. Once you understand the goal, carefully review the *entire* contract for provisions that will need change. Often a change in one section leads to a change in another—the cascade effect.[1] You may need to change a cross-reference, rewrite a provision, or add another provision.

29.2.3 THE ACTION SECTIONS

The subject matter performance provision of an amending agreement comprises the amendments. To craft the amendments, drafters use two techniques: **inside-the-contract amendments** and **outside-the-contract amendments**.[2] With the former, a reader can theoretically cut and paste the changes into the existing agreement, resulting in an amended agreement that can be read from beginning to end. An outside-the-contract amendment does not amend specific words. Instead, it states the effect of the amendment, leaving the reader to figure out which words were actually changed. These amendments lack precision and invite litigation. You should avoid using them.

See Exhibit A to this chapter for an example of an amending agreement that uses inside-the-contract amendments and Exhibit B to this chapter for an example of a letter agreement that uses outside-the-contract amendments.

The remainder of this chapter discusses inside-the-contract amendments.

The following provisions are inside-the-contract amendments to an employment agreement. Although their form is correct, they include substantive drafting errors. You will analyze those errors as part of an exercise. For now, focus on the style of the amendments.

---

1. See §23.2.
2. My colleague Alan Shaw coined these phrases.

1. Section 2.2 (a) of the Existing Agreement is amended by deleting "Executive Vice President for Research" and inserting in its place "President."

2. Section 2.2 (b) of the Existing Agreement is amended by deleting the period at the end of the sentence and inserting in its place the following:

   > , except if the Company consents, and the Company shall not unreasonably withhold its consent.

3. Section 2.3 of the Existing Agreement is amended by deleting the period at the end of the sentence and inserting in its place the following:

   > , except that the Executive may perform volunteer work for the March of Dimes without violating this provision.

4. Section 2.4 of the Existing Agreement is amended by deleting that Section and inserting in its place the following:

   > **2.4 Term.** The term of employment under this Agreement is from March 1, 2006 through December 31, 2010 (the "Employment Term").

   (The employment term of the existing agreement was from March 1, 2006 through December 31, 2007.)

5. Section 2.5 is amended to read as follows:

   > **2.5 Salary.**
   >
   > (a) **March 1, 2006 through December 31, 2007.** The Company shall pay the Executive at a rate of $140,000 a year during the Employment Term. The annual salary is to be prorated for the period from March 1, 2006 through December 31, 2007. The Company shall pay the annual salary in approximately equal monthly payments on the last business day of each month. *(This is the original provision, now recast as a subsection with a caption.)*
   >
   > (b) **January 1, 2008 through December 31, 2010.** For the period beginning on January 1, 2008 through December 31, 2010, the Company shall pay the Executive an annual salary of $180,000. *(This is the new provision.)*

6. The Existing Agreement is amended by deleting Section 3 and inserting in its place "Section 3 has been intentionally omitted."

7. The Existing Agreement is amended by inserting the following provision as Section 6 after the end of the Existing Agreement's Section 5:

   > **6. The Company's Location.** The Company shall not locate its headquarters outside of the greater metropolitan Cleveland, Ohio, region without the Executive's consent, which consent the Executive shall not unreasonably withhold.

8. The Existing Agreement is amended to change the section numbers of Sections 6, 7, 8, 9, and 10 to Sections 7, 8, 9, 10, and 11, respectively.

Note the different ways in which an amendment can be effected. Paragraphs 1 and 2 are short. Neither includes the full amended provision, just the changes. This lack of context can obscure the amendment's effect, as in Paragraph 2.

Paragraphs 4 and 5 take a different approach. They include the entire provision, as amended. This method makes it easier for the reader but results in a longer amending agreement.

The amendment in Paragraph 6 deletes a section and inserts as a placeholder the statement that Section 3 was intentionally omitted. This language reduces a drafter's work by eliminating the need to renumber successive provisions and to revise cross-references that become incorrect because of the renumbering.

Paragraph 7 amends the existing agreement by adding a new section. It has the ancillary effect of throwing off the numbering of the subsequent sections. The amendment in paragraph 8 corrects that problem by renumbering the subsequent sections.

Some drafters put a new provision as the last provision of the existing agreement.[3] This keeps the numbering intact and avoids the need to change cross-references. Similarly, if a new subsection is added to a tabulated enumeration, drafters put it last. Then, the other changes to that provision will be limited to changes to the punctuation of the tabulated items. For example:

> Section 4 of the Existing Agreement is amended by
>
> (a) deleting "and" at the end of subsection (c);
>
> (b) deleting the period at the end of subsection (d) and inserting in its place "; and"; and
>
> (c) adding the following as a new subsection (e): "[insert new language]."

29.2.4 OTHER PROVISIONS

Amending agreements occasionally include representations and warranties. For example, each party might represent and warrant to the other that

- its board of directors has authorized the amendments;
- it has duly executed and delivered the amending agreement;
- the amending agreement is enforceable against it in accordance with its terms; and
- the representations and warranties made at the signing of the existing agreement are also true as of the signing of the amending agreement.

In addition to representations and warranties, amending agreements may also include conditions. These are usually directed towards postponing an amendment's effectiveness until the conditions have been satisfied. For example:

> **Amendments' Effectiveness**. The amendments in this Amendment are effective upon the satisfaction of the following condition: The Borrower's counsel must have delivered to the Bank an opinion that the Borrower's board of directors has duly authorized this Amendment and the amendments set forth in it. If this condition is not satisfied before June 1, 20XX, this Amendment terminates, and the Existing Agreement continues unchanged and in full force.

---

3. This should not be done, however, if you are restating the agreement or amending and restating it. See §29.3.

Drafters differ as to which of the general provisions should be included in an amending agreement. Some drafters incorporate all of them by reference; others restate the governing law provision, but no others.

One principled approach is to include only the following provisions: governing law, choice of forum, counterparts, severability, and merger. The governing law and choice of forum provisions are included to ensure that the amending agreement and the existing agreement are governed by the same law and can be adjudicated in the same court. The rationale for the last three provisions is that they deal directly with the amending agreement's creation. The language of all of these provisions should duplicate the language in the existing agreement. (Say the same thing the same way.)

If you follow this approach, the other general provisions do not need to be restated in the amending agreement. Once the parties execute and deliver the amending agreement, each of the general provisions applies to the resulting agreement—that is, the existing agreement after the amendments. But be careful. Make sure that the definition of *Agreement* in the existing agreement includes the phrase *as amended from time to time*. That way, each time the defined term *Agreement* is used in a general provision, or any other provision, it refers to the resulting agreement. If *Agreement* is not properly defined, add it to the list of needed amendments.

If you decide to incorporate by reference into the amending agreement all of the general provisions from the existing agreement, you may need to address a technical drafting issue. Specifically, when those provisions are incorporated, they will probably bring with them references to *this Agreement*. But those references will be wrong because they will be referring to the existing agreement. Instead, they should refer to the amending agreement as the general provisions are being incorporated so that they become part of the amending agreement. Therefore, to make the incorporation by reference work, add a sentence to the following effect in the provision that incorporates the general provisions from the existing agreement:

> Each reference to "this Agreement" in the provisions incorporated by reference from the Existing Agreement into this Amendment is deemed a reference to "this Amendment."

Amending agreements generally conclude with a provision along the following lines:

> **Continued Effectiveness of the Existing Agreement**. Except as amended by the amendments in this Amendment, the Existing Agreement continues unchanged and in full force.

This declaration precludes any inference that the amendments have caused a change to any provision in the existing agreement, other than those changed in the amending agreement.

29.3 RESTATED AGREEMENTS

Occasionally, parties enter into so many amendments that the then-existing agreement becomes difficult to read. Imagine trying to analyze a section of a contract whose subsections are in four different amending agreements! To deal with this event, parties can create a **restated** agreement or an **amended and restated** agreement.

To create a restated agreement, the drafter inserts all of the previous amendments into a master document, which then is the sole expression of the parties' agreement. An amended and restated agreement not only restates an agreement, but also amends one or more provisions at the same time.

When restating an agreement, move any provisions that were added to the end of the existing agreement—to keep numbering intact—to their appropriate place within the contract. Now that the agreement will exist on a stand-alone basis (without amendments), the contract's structural integrity should be restored. This will facilitate the reading and analysis of the contract because when a reader looks for a provision in its logical place, it will be there.

Before deciding to restate an agreement, consider whether the benefits of the restated agreement outweigh its disadvantages:

- The time and cost of preparing the restatement
- The possibility of introducing errors into the existing agreement
- The risk that the other side will see the restatement as an opportunity to renegotiate points that it conceded during the original negotiations

When drafting a restated or an amended and restated agreement, think through the effect of changing the date in the preamble from the date the parties signed the existing agreement to the date that the parties sign the restatement. One problem that this change causes relates to the representations and warranties. As you have learned, representations and warranties speak as of a moment in time, generally the date that the parties sign the contract.[4] When a restatement is signed, the date in the preamble is the date of that signing. But the existing agreement's representations and warranties should not speak as of the day of the restatement's signing. Instead, they should continue to speak as of the day of the existing agreement's signing. To preclude disputes on this matter, the introductory language to these representations and warranties should state explicitly that they continue to speak as of the original signing date.

> **Version 1**
>
> The Borrower represents and warrants to the Bank that the following statements were true as of [insert date of original signing of the contract]:

If the parties also want to add new representations and warranties or to have the existing representations and warranties also speak as of the date of the restatement's signing, additional language can be inserted.

> **Version 2**
>
> The Borrower represents and warrants to the Bank that the following statements were true as of the [insert date of original signing of the contract] and are true as of the date of this Restated Agreement:

---

4. See §3.2.1.

29.4 CONSENTS

29.4.1 DEFINITION

A **consent** permits something that the contract otherwise prohibits. For example, many contracts prohibit a party from delegating its performance under the contract without the other party's consent.

> **Delegation**. The Contractor shall not delegate any of the Work without the Owner's prior written consent.

If the Contractor wants to delegate the painting of the house without violating its covenant, the Contractor must obtain the Owner's consent.

29.4.2 DRAFTING THE REQUEST FOR CONSENT AND THE CONSENT

When drafting the request for a consent, keep the following guidelines in mind:

GUIDELINES FOR DRAFTING CONSENTS

1. *The first paragraph of the consent should refer to the agreement requiring the consent.*

> We refer to the Credit Agreement, dated November 12, 20X6, between Big Bank N.A. and Worldwide Shipping Inc.

2. *The second paragraph should state what your client wants and why.* Postponing these details to later in the letter will annoy the other side. Use the subsequent paragraphs to provide details.

3. *Draft the scope of the requested consent so that it meets your client's needs.* While your client might like the latitude of a broadly drafted consent, requesting that may not be the best strategy. If the other side perceives the consent as overreaching, it may reject the request.

4. *Make it as easy as possible for the other side to consent.*
   (a) Draft the consent and include it with the request.
   (b) Include a stamped, addressed return envelope or the appropriate materials for return by overnight courier.

5. *When drafting the consent, track the language*
   (a) in the agreement that prohibits the act for which your client is seeking consent; *and*
   (b) in the cover letter when explaining the scope of the consent.

29.5 WAIVERS

29.5.1 DEFINITION

From a practitioner's perspective, waivers typically arise in response to three events:

- The failure of a condition
- The occurrence of a misrepresentation, breach of warranty, or breach of covenant
- The likely breach of a covenant

If any of these offending events occurs, the party entitled to a remedy or walk-away right may choose to waive the event's occurrence. A **waiver** is a party's agreement that it will perform as if the event had not occurred and that it will not exercise its remedies or walk-away right. A waiver does not amend a contract. All of the agreement's provisions, including the problem provision, remain unchanged and enforceable. If the offending event occurs again, the party entitled to the remedy or walk-away right may once again choose whether to waive.

For example, imagine that a buyer of a house has bargained for the receipt of the house's architectural plans as a condition to closing. If the seller cannot deliver the plans, the buyer may decide not to close and to exercise his walk-away right, or he may waive the failure of the condition and purchase the house. If the seller also promised to deliver the plans, its nondelivery would be a breach of covenant. The buyer would then need to decide whether he also wanted to waive the breach and forego any remedies available to him.

As noted, a party may waive the application of a provision in anticipation of a breach. A bank might do this if its borrower announces that it will be unable to comply with one of its financial covenants. The pre-breach waiver would be advantageous to both parties. The bank would avoid having a borrower in default, and the borrower would avoid the ancillary consequences of a breach, such as a cross-default or disclosure obligations if it is a publicly held corporation.

Waivers can be drafted in the form of a letter or as a stand-alone agreement. In either case, the subject matter performance provision is the waiver. It is a self-executing provision,[5] effective upon the waiver's execution.

> **Waiver.** [By signing this Waiver] [By countersigning this letter], the Landlord waives the Tenant's failure to comply with Section 6.8 of the Lease.

To establish that the waiver is a one-time event, most waivers include language to the following effect:

> **Limited Waiver.** This Waiver is effective only on this occasion and only for the purpose given and is not to be construed as a waiver on any other occasion, for any other purpose, or against any other Person.

If the contract between the parties has a general provision dealing with waivers with language to this effect, parrot that language in the waiver. Remember: Say the same thing the same way.

29.6 CHOOSING BETWEEN A CONSENT AND A WAIVER

Consents and waivers are kissing cousins. Which is appropriate depends upon the contract's language. If a covenant absolutely prohibits something without exception, the piece of paper to be obtained is a waiver. It renders the prohibition unenforceable on this one occasion. If a covenant provides for an exception to the prohibition upon the other party's consent, then, in accordance with the contract, the piece of paper to be obtained is a consent.

---

5. See §8.2.

EXERCISES

Exercise 29-1

Review the inside-the-contract amendments in Section 29.2.3. What business and drafting issues do the amendments in paragraphs 4 and 5 raise? Read both provisions before trying to answer the question.

Exercise 29-2

Review Exhibit B to this Chapter. What business issues might there be because of the way the amendments are drafted? Use the information in Exhibit A to help you with your analysis.

Exercise 29-3

Using the information in the letter that follows, mark-up the Consent to Assignment that follows it. Alternatively, redraft the Consent using the Consent that is available on the *Drafting Contracts* Website.

January 26, 20X9

Mr. James Smith
425 West Haven Corp.
425 West Haven Avenue
El Paso, Texas 79905

Re: Request for Consent to Assignment and Release

Dear Mr. Smith:

We refer to the Lease (the "Lease"), dated July 1, 20X6, between 425 West Haven Corp. ("West Haven") and Maria's Muffins Inc. ("Muffins"). In accordance with Section 7.8 of the Lease, we request that West Haven consent to Muffins's assignment of its rights under the Lease to Sammy's Sweets Inc. ("Sweets").

Muffins is going out of business and desires to assign its rights under the Lease to Sweets. Sweets has agreed to assume all of Muffins's obligations under the Lease that arise and are due and payable on and after March 1, 20X9, the date that Muffins will assign its rights under the Lease to Sweets (the "Assignment Date").

Sweets manufactures and distributes chocolate truffles to candy stores in Texas. Enclosed for your information are (a) a description of Sweets's business and (b) Sweets's audited financial statements for the period ended December 31, 20X8.

Section 7.8 of the Lease prohibits the assignment of the Lease without West Haven's consent. Thus, in accordance with the Lease, Muffins requests that West Haven

(a)   consent to Muffin's assignment to Sweets, on March 1, 20X9, of all Muffins's rights under the Lease; and

(b)   release Muffins from all of its obligations under the Lease that arise and are due and payable on and after March 1, 20X9.

Muffins also requests that you acknowledge that no other consent or consideration is required for the assignment to be effective. Your consent and release will apply only to the transaction described in this letter and is subject to Sweets's assumption of all of Muffins's obligations under the Lease that arise and are due and payable on and after March 1, 20X9. We will mail you a copy of the assumption promptly after Sweets signs it.

To consent to the assignment and to grant the release, please

•   sign the two duplicate original consent forms accompanying this letter; and

•   return one of them in the enclosed, stamped and self-addressed envelope as soon as possible, but in no event later than February 20, 20X9.

If you desire any further information concerning the transaction, please do not hesitate to call me at (915) 555-5555. We appreciate your assistance in this matter.

Very truly yours,

Maria's Muffins Inc.

By: _____

Maria Rodriguez, President

Consent to Assignment

Subject to the proviso set forth in the last sentence hereof, West Haven Rental Corp. (the "Lessor") hereby consents to the assignment by Maria's Muffins Inc. ("Muffins") of all its right, title, and interest under the Lease, dated July 1, 20X6, (the "Lease") to Sammy's Sweets Inc. ("Assignee"), and Lessor hereby releases Muffins from all its obligations and liabilities under the Lease arising and due and payable on and after the date that Muffins assigns its rights under the Lease to the Assignee (the "Assignment Date"). Notwithstanding the foregoing, the consent and the release granted herein shall only be effective if, on the Assignment Date, Assignee shall have assumed all of Muffins's obligations

and liabilities under the Lease arising and due and payable on and after the Assignment Date.

425 West Haven Corp.

By: _____
James Smith, President

Dated: _____

EXHIBIT A TO CHAPTER 29

AN INSIDE-THE-CONTRACT AMENDMENT

Second Amendment[6]

Second Amendment, dated January 17, 2008, to the Employment Agreement, dated February 23, 2006, between Buckeye Pharmaceuticals Inc., an Ohio corporation (the "Company"), and Mohammed Ahmed, 322 Westland Road, Shaker Heights, Ohio 44120 (the "Executive").

Background

The Company has employed the Executive as Executive Vice President of Research for approximately two years and now desires to promote him to President. The parties desire to amend the Employment Agreement, dated February 23, 2006, as amended (the "Existing Agreement"), to reflect the Executive's new duties, compensation, and other matters.

Accordingly, the parties agree as follows:

1. **Definitions.**
   (a) Terms defined in the preamble and recitals have their assigned meanings, and capitalized terms used in this Amendment without definition have the meanings assigned to them in the Existing Agreement.
   (b) "Amendment" means this Second Amendment.

2. **Amendments.**
   (a) Section 2.2 (a) of the Existing Agreement is amended by deleting "Executive Vice President for Research" and inserting in its place "President."
   (b) Section 2.2 (b) of the Existing Agreement is amended by deleting the period at the end of the sentence and inserting in its place the following:
   , except if the Company consents, and the Company shall not unreasonably withhold its consent.
   (c) Section 2.3 of the Existing Agreement is amended by deleting the period at the end of the sentence and inserting in its place the following:

---

6. This fact pattern was inspired by one created by my colleague Alan Shaw.

, except that the Executive may perform volunteer work for the March of Dimes without violating this provision.

(d) Section 2.4 of the Existing Agreement is amended by deleting that section and inserting in its place the following:

Section 2.4 Term. The term of employment under this Agreement is from March 1, 2006 through December 31, 2010 (the "Employment Term").

(e) Section 2.5 is amended to read as follows:

Section 2.5 Salary.

(a) **March 1, 2006 through December 31, 2007.** The Company shall pay the Executive an annual salary of $140,000 during the Employment Term. The annual salary is to be prorated for the period from March 1, 2006 through December 31, 2007. The Company shall pay the annual salary in approximately equal monthly payments on the last business day of each month.

(b) **January 1, 2008 through December 31, 2010.** For the period beginning on January 1, 2008 through December 31, 2010, the Company shall pay the Executive an annual salary of $180,000.

(f) The Existing Agreement is amended by deleting Section 3 and inserting in its place "Section 3 has been intentionally omitted."

(g) The Existing Agreement is amended by inserting the following provision as Section 6 after the end of the Existing Agreement's Section 5:

Section 6. The Company's Location. The Company shall not locate its headquarters outside of the greater metropolitan Cleveland, Ohio region without the Executive's consent, which consent the Executive shall not unreasonably withhold.

(h) The Existing Agreement is amended to change the section numbers of Sections 6, 7, 8, 9, and 10 to Sections 7, 8, 9, 10, and 11, respectively.

3. Continuation of Existing Agreement. Except for the amendments made in this Amendment, the Existing Agreement remains unchanged and in full effect.

4. General Provisions.

(a) **Choice of Law.** [Intentionally omitted.]

(b) **Choice of Forum.** [Intentionally omitted.]

(c) **Counterparts.** [Intentionally omitted.]

(d) **Merger.** [Intentionally omitted.]

(e) **Severability.** [Intentionally omitted.]

To evidence their agreement to this Amendment's terms, the parties have executed and delivered this Amendment on the date set forth in the preamble.

Buckeye Pharmaceuticals Inc.

By: _____

Betsy Rice
Chief Executive Officer

_____

Mohammed Ahmed

EXHIBIT B TO CHAPTER 29

AN OUTSIDE-THE-CONTRACT AMENDMENT IN LETTER FORMAT

January 17, 2008

Mr. Mohammed Ahmed
322 Westland Road
Shaker Heights, Ohio 12345

Dear Mr. Ahmed:

Please refer to the agreement dated February 23, 2006 between Buckeye Pharmaceuticals Inc. (the "Company") and you relating to your employment by the Company (the "Existing Agreement"). When signed by you, this letter constitutes an amendment of the Existing Agreement.

Capitalized terms used in this letter without definition have the meanings assigned to them in the Existing Agreement.

1. You are promoted to President.
2. You may do volunteer work for the March of Dimes without breaching our agreement.
3. All references to December 31, 2007 are changed to December 31, 2010.
4. Your annual salary for the period January 1, 2008 through December 31, 2010 is $180,000.
5. As you will be President, you no longer have to report to the President.
6. The Company promises not to relocate its headquarters outside of Cleveland, Ohio without your consent. You have agreed not to withhold your consent unreasonably.
7. Except as set forth in this letter, the Existing Agreement remains unmodified and in full force.

To indicate your agreement to these amendments, please sign this letter and the enclosed duplicate original in the space provided at the end of the letter. In addition, please return one original to the Company in the enclosed, self-addressed envelope.

Very truly yours,

Buckeye Pharmaceuticals Inc.

By: _____
   Betsy Rice
   Chief Executive Officer

Agreed to on _____

_____
Mohammed Ahmed

PART SIX

Drafting Ethically

Ethical Issues in Drafting

30.1 INTRODUCTION

The ABA Model Rules of Professional Conduct (the Model Rules)[1] primarily address ethical issues that arise in litigation. This focus creates problems for deal lawyers who turn to them when faced with ethical dilemmas. They find, with limited exceptions,[2] no rule on point or one that applies only tangentially or by analogy.

The litigation bias of the Model Rules has its roots in the failures of its predecessors, the Model Code of Professional Responsibility[3] and the 1908 Canons of Ethics:[4]

> The [Model] Code's failure to state standards and objectives for the advisor is probably due to many factors. Perhaps the most easily understandable is historical. Traditionally the lawyer's function was almost solely that of a courtroom advocate, and as a result, the original Canons of Professional Responsibility [1908] dealt almost exclusively with the dilemmas of that role. . . .
>
> There are perhaps several reasons why this historical bias was not remedied. Whereas the result of the advocate's effort is often of extreme public import, and occasionally political in nature, the advisor's effort is generally private and seemingly important only to the immediate parties. Frequently the advisor's most important decisions are designed to remain confidential. Because the Code of Professional Responsibility serves partly as a public relations device, it is only natural that the Code should focus on the more public, and more publicized, role of an attorney.
>
> Another reason for the limited viewpoint . . . is that the advocate's role has been better defined by a well-delineated legal process. In contrast, the advisor performs many diverse functions for the client and generally is unconstrained by formal proce-

---

1. All citations to the Model Rules are to the 2006 American Bar Association Model Rules of Professional Conduct. Although most states have adopted the Model Rules, New York is a hold-out, having adopted the Code of Professional Responsibility. As so many sophisticated transactions occur in New York, this chapter also cites the relevant provisions in the New York Code of Professional Responsibility.

The full commentary to each Model Rule cited is at the end of this chapter in Exhibit A.

2. *See e.g.* Model R. Prof. Conduct 2.1 entitled "Advisor." "In representing a client, a lawyer shall exercise independent professional judgment and render candid advice. In rendering advice, a lawyer may refer not only to law but to other considerations such as moral, economic, social and political factors, that may be relevant to the client's situation."

3. Model Code of Prof. Responsibility (ABA 1981, as amended).

4. Canons of Prof. Ethics (ABA 1908, as amended).

dures. As a result, it is more difficult to state comprehensively the ethical considerations for an advisor.[5]

Exacerbating this paucity of rules is a paucity of case law and ethical opinions. This scarcity undoubtedly reflects the private nature of transactional work. Litigation is audible, visible, and takes place in a public forum where the proceedings are recorded. Transactions are generally negotiated in the privacy of a conference room, and contracts drafted in the privacy of an office. Because no record is made, disciplining a lawyer becomes much more difficult.

The remainder of this chapter highlights key ethical issues that contract drafters face. The exercises that follow take you past the generalities to specific, real-world applications of the ethics rules.

30.2 THE DRAFTER'S ROLE

Model Rule 1.2(a) allocates the responsibilities and authority of lawyers and their clients. It states:

> [A] lawyer shall abide by a client's decisions concerning the objectives of representation and, as required by Rule 1.4 shall consult with the client as to the means by which they are to be pursued. A lawyer may take such action on behalf of the client as is impliedly authorized to carry out the representation.[6]

Stated more colloquially, the client's role is to establish the representation's objective, while the lawyer's role is to determine the means to accomplish the objective and to take the actions necessary to accomplish it.

Comment 2 to Model Rule 1.2 adds a gloss on the objective/means dichotomy in the context of a lawyer and client disagreeing about the means the lawyer should use. Although the Comment does not state how lawyers and clients should resolve their disagreements, it notes the following:

> Clients normally defer to the special knowledge and skill of their lawyer with respect to the means to be used to accomplish their objectives, particularly with respect to technical, legal and tactical matters. Conversely, lawyers usually defer to the client regarding such questions as the expense to be incurred and concern for third persons who might be adversely affected.[7]

This gloss carefully hedges its assertion by including the adverbs *normally* and *usually.* In the transactional context, the gloss's applicability depends to some degree on the client's sophistication. The more sophisticated the client is, the more likely that the client will want to participate in technical, legal, and tactical matters. Sophisticated clients often have as much experience as their lawyers in negotiations and will have specific ideas on what to broach, how, and when. In addition, as more lawyers have moved out of the legal profession into business positions, more clients have legal expertise. In these situations, deferring to the client as to the means is appropriate. If you vehemently disagree with their decisions, consider resigning.[8]

---

5. Louis M. Brown & Harold A. Brown, *What Counsels the Counselor? The Code of Professional Responsibility's Ethical Considerations—A Preventive Law Analysis,* 10 Val. U. L. Rev. 453, 454-456 (1975-1976) (footnotes omitted).

6. Model R. Prof. Conduct 1.2(a). See N.Y. Code Prof. Resp. EC 7-7, 7-8.

7. Model R. Prof. Conduct 1.2 cmt. 2.

8. "If [efforts to reach agreement] are unavailing and the lawyer has a fundamental disagreement with the client, the lawyer may withdraw from the representation." *Id.*

Although no Model Rule deals directly with contract drafting, the objective/means dichotomy does provide some guidance as to the drafter's role. That role is to facilitate, through drafting (the means), an agreement between the parties (the client's objective). This role does not render the drafter a mere scrivener. By working with a client to flesh out the business deal, a drafter adds value to the deal and advances the client's objective. A drafter may not, however, recut the parties' business deal by adding or changing provisions to which the parties have agreed. Doing so steps over the line.

30.3 THE DRAFTER'S RESPONSIBILITIES

Model Rule 1.1 states that "[a] lawyer shall provide competent representation to a client."[9] This rule raises at least two issues for drafters. First, what body of knowledge must a drafter have to be competent, and second, may a lawyer draft a contract if the lawyer has no prior experience with that type of contract? Comment 2 to Model Rule 1.1 should give you *some* comfort as you begin your career:

> A lawyer need not necessarily have special training or prior experience to handle legal problems of a type with which the lawyer is unfamiliar. A newly admitted lawyer can be as competent as a practitioner with long experience. . . . A lawyer can provide adequate representation in a wholly novel field *through necessary study.*[10]

The italicized words are the key. You may represent a client despite little practical experience, but only if you gain the requisite knowledge through study. For a contract drafter, requisite knowledge means, at a bare minimum, a thorough grounding in contract law. (E.g., You should know the consequences of drafting a covenant rather than a condition.) In addition, according to some commentators, it includes an understanding of arbitration's role in dispute resolution.[11] It also entails subject matter expertise—either in a field of law or an industry. Finally, you must understand business, including financial statement concepts.[12] You cannot draft an agreement reflecting a business agreement if you do not understand business and the client's business. Remember: A failure to have (or gain) the requisite expertise could subject you not only to disciplinary action, but also to malpractice liability.

A drafter's responsibilities also include regularly informing the client about the status of the agreement and the transaction—how business and legal issues have been resolved and which issues remain open.[13] What this entails varies, depending upon what Comment 5 to Model Rule 1.4 calls the **guiding principle**: The degree of communication depends upon the client's expectations.[14] Some clients are hands-on and

---

9. Model R. Prof. Conduct 1.1. See N.Y. Code Prof. Resp. DR 6-101.

10. Model R. Prof. Conduct 1.1 cmt. 2 (emphasis added). See N.Y. Code Prof. Resp. EC 6-3, 6-4.

11. Donald Lee Rome, *It's a New Day for ADR: From Boilerplate to Professional Responsibility,* 8 Bus. L. Today 11, 12, 15 (Jan./Feb. 1999). David Hricik, *Infinite Combinations: Whether the Duty of Competency Requires Lawyers to Include Choice of Law Clauses in Contracts They Draft for Their Clients,* 12 Williamette J. Intl. L. & Disp. Res. 241, 258 (2004) (suggesting that in some circumstances, the duty of competency requires the inclusion of a choice of law provision).

12. Lawrence A. Cunningham, *Sharing Accounting's Burden: Business Lawyers in Enron's Dark Shadows,* 57 Bus. Law. 1421, 1449-1459 (2002).

13. "A lawyer shall . . . keep the client reasonably informed about the status of the matter." Model R. Prof. Conduct 1.4(a)(3). "A lawyer shall explain a matter to the extent reasonably necessary to permit the client to make informed decisions regarding the representation." Model R. Prof. Conduct 1.4(b). See N.Y. Code Prof. Resp. EC 7-8.

14. "The guiding principle is that the lawyer should fulfill reasonable client expectations for information consistent with the duty to act in the client's best interests, and the client's overall requirements as to the character of representation." Model R. Prof. Conduct 1.4 cmt. 5.

want to know everything about everything. Other clients are concerned only with the big picture. They want information on deal points, but not on other, subsidiary business issues. What and how much you communicate is client specific.

30.4   INTERACTIONS WITH THIRD PARTIES

Transactional lawyers deal with third parties on a regular basis, particularly in negotiations. These dealings are often strewn with ethical landmines through which you must navigate carefully, and they do not disappear because you are negotiating on paper through dueling drafts and mark-ups.

The key ethical proscriptions in connection with contract drafting are the following Model Rules:

- Model Rule 1.2(d)—A lawyer shall not counsel a client to engage, or assist a client, in conduct that the lawyer knows is criminal or fraudulent. . . .[15]
- Model Rule 4.1(b)—In the course of representing a client a lawyer shall not knowingly . . . fail to disclose a material fact to a third person when disclosure is necessary to avoid assisting a criminal or fraudulent act by a client, unless disclosure is prohibited by Rule 1.6.[16]
- Model Rule 8.4(c)—It is professional misconduct for a lawyer to . . . engage in conduct involving dishonesty, fraud, deceit or misrepresentation. . . .[17]

Model Rules 1.2(d) and 4.1(b) require an understanding of **intersectionality**.[18] Intersectionality determines whether a lawyer's actions are ethical by looking at where in the spectrum of behavior the client's actions fall. Imagine that the following diagonal represents the range of a client's actions, moving from legal and not fraudulent at Point A to criminal and fraudulent at Point D.

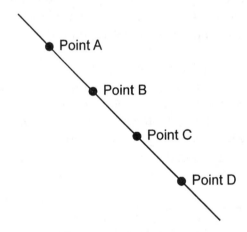

As the client's activities move down the diagonal, the lawyer's actions move in tandem from ethical to unethical. So, at Point A, when the client's actions are legal, his lawyer's actions are ethical. But at Point D, when the client's actions are criminal or fraudulent, the lawyer violates the ethical duty not to assist a client in criminal or fraudulent activities.

---

15. Model R. Prof. Conduct 1.2(d). See N.Y. Code Prof. Resp. DR 7-102(A)(7).
16. Model R. Prof. Conduct 4.1(b). See N.Y. Code Prof. Resp. DR 7-102(A)(3), DR 7-102(B).
17. Model R. Prof. Conduct 8.4(c). See N.Y. Code Prof. Resp. DR 1-102(A)(4).
18. Dean Mary C. Daly of St. John's University School of Law introduced me to the concept of *intersectionality*.

To apply the concept of intersectionality to drafting, imagine that the diagonal represents varying degrees of truthfulness in the client's representations and warranties. If the representations and warranties are true, then the lawyer's drafting of the contract does not violate any ethical proscriptions. But, if they are intentionally false, they constitute fraudulent misrepresentations, and drafting the contract assists the client in perpetrating a fraud.

Violation of Model Rule 8.4(c) does not require as a prerequisite that the client commit a crime or fraud. Instead, the focus is on the lawyer's actions. Has the lawyer done something, independently of the client's actions, that involves dishonesty, fraud, deceit, or misrepresentation? For example, one ABA Opinion concludes that a lawyer's failure to alert the drafter of a scrivener's error that the latter made would constitute fraud by the lawyer.[19] Although the opinion also adverts to Model Rules 1.2(d) and 4.1(b), the violation of Model Rule 8.4(c) is included as a separate violation.

30.5 REPRESENTATION OF MULTIPLE CLIENTS CONCURRENTLY

Although it is per se unethical to represent both parties in a litigation,[20] that is not the case with respect to transactions. In transactions, even if "there is a significant risk that the representation of one or more clients will be materially limited by the lawyer's responsibilities to another client,"[21] the clients may give their informed consent to the concurrent representation.[22]

The issue of joint representation commonly occurs in connection with the formation of a corporation and the drafting of a shareholders' agreement. Here, the interests of the clients are generally aligned, although their interests will differ in some matters. The lawyer works to resolve the clients' differences by focusing on their mutual interests.[23] This is sometimes known as being **the lawyer for the situation**.

30.6 MULTI-JURISDICTIONAL PRACTICE

Lawyers who draft contracts often travel outside their home states in connection with the transactions on which they are working. Previously when they did this, they were arguably engaged in the unauthorized practice of law as they were providing legal services in a state other than the one in which they were admitted.[24] In recognition of this recurring feature of contemporary practice, the ABA adopted Model Rule 5.5(c)(4). It provides, in pertinent part:

> A lawyer admitted in another United States jurisdiction, and not disbarred or suspended from practice in any jurisdiction, may provide legal services on a temporary basis in this jurisdiction . . . [if those services] arise out of or are reasonably related to the lawyer's practice in a jurisdiction in which the lawyer is admitted to practice.[25]

---

19. ABA Informal Op. 86-1518.

20. See Model R. Prof. Conduct 1.7(a) and 1.7(b)(3); N.Y. Code Prof. Resp. EC 5-15, DR 5-101(A).

21. Model R. Prof. Conduct 1.7(b).

22. See Model R. Prof. Conduct 1.7(b)(4); N.Y. Code Prof. Resp. DR 5-105(C).

23. See Model R. Prof. Conduct 1.7(d) cmt. 28 N.Y.C. Assn. B. Comm. Prof. Jud. Eth. Formal Op. 2001-2.

24. *See Birbrower, Montalbano, Condon & Frank, P.C. v. Super. Ct. of Santa Clara Co.*, 949 P.2d 1 (Cal. 1998).

25. Model R. Prof. Conduct 5.5(c)(4).

The tough issue, of course, is to determine the meaning of *arise out of or reasonably related to the lawyer's practice* in her home jurisdiction. Comment 14 to Model Rule 5.5 provides useful guidance. It states that the connection can be found in a variety of factors, including a prior representation of the client, the client's substantial contacts to the home jurisdiction, and legal issues relating to the law of the home jurisdiction.[26]

---

26. Model R. Prof. Conduct 5.5(c)(4) cmt. 14.

EXERCISES

Exercise 30-1

Skating on Thin Ice

Part A

Assume that you are Sandy Plage, an up-and-coming corporate partner at Good Ethics & Law. Over the years, you have developed an excellent business relationship with Bob Hansell. Bob has sent you substantial business over the years from whatever company was his then-current employer.[27] Currently, he is General Counsel (United States) at Speedskates, Inc. (Speedskates). Speedskates is the U.S. operating subsidiary of Speedskates International, Inc. (International), a privately held multinational corporation with its headquarters in Singapore.

The sole shareholders of International are two siblings (Robert and Sara Marlat), who are also the directors and officers of Speedskates. Although your law firm is not primary counsel to either International or Speedskates, you do have regular contact with the siblings on multiple issues—both with respect to International and Speedskates. Recently, you and your tax partner have been reviewing tax and corporate issues relating to International's operations both in the United States and worldwide.

Bob just called sounding somewhat distressed. He related the following:

1. Speedskates is in the midst of negotiating for a $50 million line of credit from Big Bank NA (Big Bank). International will guarantee the debt. (Speedskates already has $200 million in long-term debt from a multibank group.) The new line would provide Speedskates with some badly needed additional working capital. (See the diagram that follows this exercise.)

2. Speedskates is being represented in this transaction by Other Firm LLP (Other Firm). Liza Richardson, the former general counsel (United States) of Speedskates, is the deal partner at Other Firm.[28]

3. As a condition to the consummation of the Credit Agreement, Other Firm must deliver an opinion to Big Bank regarding certain matters. Other Firm has requested Bob as in-house counsel to deliver a back-up opinion on which Other Firm can rely. (This is common practice. The theory is that in-house counsel can deliver these opinions more cheaply because they have superior knowledge.) Bob wants you to review the Credit Agreement and his opinion to advise him whether the opinions he is being asked to give are appropriate. His initial inclination is that he should be able to give the opinions as they are all true. Those opinions are as follows:

---

27. Translation: Bob is important to you. You are paid not only for your brains but because you bring in business. Bob = business.

28. Translation: The relationship is professional and superficially cordial, but fraught with tension. Bob feels that Liza is always looking over his shoulder and reporting to his superiors. You, of course, are in competition with Other Firm for business and would like nothing better than to become regular outside counsel.

(a) Speedskates is duly incorporated and in good standing; the Credit Agreement is duly authorized, executed, and delivered.

(b) The consummation of this transaction does not violate any existing agreements to which Speedskates is a party.

Issue

Is it appropriate for you to take on this matter?

Part B

In your preliminary review of the Credit Agreement, you discover two representations warranties that raise concern:

- The draft of the Credit Agreement states that Speedskates has complied with all the covenants in the other loan agreement. That agreement requires Speedskates and its affiliates to meet certain net worth tests. Because of operating losses incurred during the past two years, Speedskates has failed to meet the net worth tests and has breached the loan agreement. Therefore, leaving the representation and warranty as is in the Credit Agreement would result in an untrue statement.

- In Section 5.7 of the Credit Agreement, Speedskates represents that International and each of its subsidiaries (including Speedskates) has filed the tax returns required to be filed and has paid all required taxes, other than those that could not have a material adverse effect.

  (i) Based upon the work that your firm has done, you know that Speedskates France, one of International's subsidiaries, may owe some taxes to the United States. No one yet knows whether the amount at stake is material as the detailed review and analysis that would be required to make such an assessment has not been done. An assessment of materiality would need to contemplate not only the effect of any payment on International's net worth but also on its liquidity. Neither the firm nor Speedstakes' auditors has the time to finish the assessment before the loan closes.

  (ii) Bob Hansell knows all about the tax issues as he has been acting as International's point person. Liza Richardson also knows as Bob has briefed her at International's request.

After reviewing these representations and warranties with several of your colleagues, you call Bob back.

Issues

1. What do you advise Bob about the legal consequences of Speedskates making the representation and warranty with respect to the no violation of other agreements? Why does this matter? If Speedskates makes the representation and warranty and you continue with your representation, will you violate your ethical duties?

2. What do you advise Bob about the legal consequences of Speedskates making the representation and warranty with respect to the tax payments and the financial statements? Why does this matter? If Speedskates makes the representation and warranty and you continue with your representation, will you violate your ethical duties?

3. May Bob deliver his opinion without violating any ethical rules?

4. Assume that

   (a) you and Bob have raised grave concerns about the tax returns with the President of International;

   (b) International's President tells Bob that the amount at stake with regard to the tax returns is not material, and that the materiality exception in the representation and warranty permits Speedskates to make the representation and warranty without further disclosure; and

   (c) Liza has concurred with the President's analysis.

Can you and Bob rely on what the President and Liza have said?

5. Assume that

   (a) Bob tells International's President that he will not deliver his opinion without changes to the representations and warranties; and

   (b) the President responds by telling Bob that if he fails to deliver the opinion, he will be in breach to International.

Bob then calls you and asks what his rights are if he quits, or in the alternative, if International fires him. You respond. . .

6. Bob goes home to mull over his options. The next morning he calls to report that the deal is closing and that Liza is delivering her opinion without any backup. May you tell the bank? What are your ethical obligations in terms of reporting this matter to the local disciplinary authority?

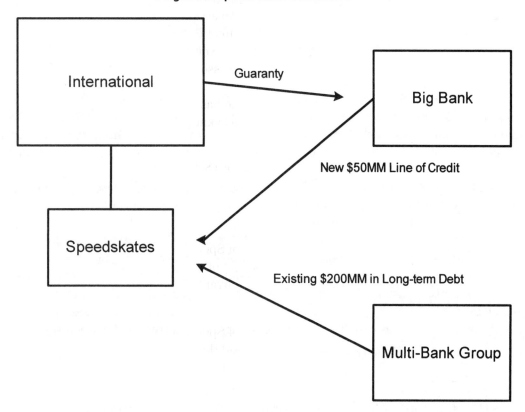

Diagram of Speedskates Transaction

Exercise 30-2

You're Too Kind

To: Exhausted, But Still Going, Associate

From: Compassionate, but Demanding, Corporate Partner

As you know, I am representing HiTech Inc. in the sale of substantially all of its assets. Unfortunately, in connection with that deal, I now have an ethical dilemma: Buyer's lawyers have crafted a provision that is too generous to our client. Specifically, they have drafted the representation and warranty with respect to defaults under existing contracts as follows:

"No material defaults exist under any material agreements."

According to my recollection of the negotiation (and also the recollection of our client), the representation and warranty was supposed to provide that no defaults exist under any material agreement. (No double dip on materiality.)

Our client insists that we say nothing. I am thinking that maybe we should say something. What are our ethical obligations? Do you have any suggestions as to how we should deal with our client on this matter?

I have no idea whether it will be helpful to you, but attached is ABA Informal Op. 86-1518. Do not do any other research on this matter; our client does not want to pay.

ABA Informal Opinion 86-1518
Notice to Opposing Counsel of Inadvertent Omission of Contract Provision
February 9, 1986

Where the lawyer for [A] has received for signature from the lawyer for [B] the final transcription of a contract from which an important provision previously agreed upon has been inadvertently omitted by the lawyer for [B], the lawyer for [A], unintentionally advantaged, should contact the lawyer for [B] to correct the error and need not consult [A] about the error.

A and B, with the assistance of their lawyers, have negotiated a commercial contract. After deliberation with counsel, A ultimately acquiesced in the final provision insisted upon by B, previously in dispute between the parties and without which B would have refused to come to overall agreement. However, A's lawyer discovered that the final draft of the contract typed in the office of B's lawyer did not contain the provision which had been in dispute. The Committee has been asked to give its opinion as to the ethical duty of A's lawyer in that circumstance.

The Committee considers this situation to involve merely a scrivener's error, not an intentional change in position by the other party. A meeting of the minds has already occurred. The Committee concludes that the error is appropriate for correction between the lawyers without client consultation.[1]

---

1. Assuming for purposes of discussion that the error is "information relating to [the] representation," under Rule 1.6 disclosure would be "impliedly authorized in order to carry out the representation." The Comment to Rule 1.6 points out that a lawyer has implied authority to make "a disclosure that facilitates a

A's lawyer does not have a duty to advise A of the error pursuant to any obligation of communication under Rule 1.4 of the ABA Model Rules of Professional Conduct (1983). "The guiding principle is that the lawyer should fulfill reasonable client expectations for information consistent with the duty to act in the client's best interests and the client's overall requirements as to the character of representation." Comment to Rule 1.4. In this circumstance there is no "informed decision," in the language of Rule 1.4 that A needs to make; the decision on the contract has already been made by the client. Furthermore, the Comment to Rule 1.2 points out that the lawyer may decide the "technical" means to be employed to carry out the objective of the representation, without consultation with the client.

The client does not have a right to take unfair advantage of the error. The client's right pursuant to Rule 1.2 to expect committed and dedicated representation is not unlimited. Indeed, for A's lawyer to suggest that A has an opportunity to capitalize on the clerical error, unrecognized by B and B's lawyer, might raise a serious question of the violation of the duty of A's lawyer under Rule 1.2(d) not to counsel the client to engage in, or assist the client in, conduct the lawyer knows is fraudulent. In addition, Rule 4.1(b) admonishes the lawyer not knowingly to fail to disclose a material fact to a third person when disclosure is necessary to avoid assisting a fraudulent act by a client, and Rule 8.4(c) prohibits the lawyer from engaging in conduct involving dishonesty, fraud, deceit, or misrepresentation.

The result would be the same under the predecessor ABA Model Code of Professional Responsibility (1969, revised 1980). While EC 7-8 teaches that a lawyer should use best efforts to ensure that the client's decisions are made after the client has been informed of relevant considerations, and EC 9-2 charges the lawyer with fully and promptly informing the client of material developments, the scrivener's error is neither a relevant consideration nor a material development and therefore does not establish an opportunity for a client's decision.[2] The duty of zealous representation in DR 7-101 is limited to lawful objectives. See DR 7-102. Rule 1.2 evolved from DR 7-102(A)(7), which prohibits a lawyer from counseling or assisting the client in conduct known to be fraudulent. See also DR 1-102(A)(4), the precursor of Rule 8.4(c), prohibiting the lawyer from engaging in conduct involving dishonesty, fraud, deceit, or misrepresentation.

Exercise 30-3

Lower than Loew

You are Lydia Grant, a senior associate at Good Ethics & Law LLP. Your client is Acquisitions Inc., a privately held investment firm. One of Acquisitions's subsidiaries, Newco, is purchasing substantially all of the assets of a candy manufacturer. To finance the purchase, Newco is borrowing the necessary funds from Megabank USA. You have been representing the subsidiary in connection with the loan negotiations. You've been working with Henry Loew, Vice President of Acquisitions.

---

satisfactory conclusion"—in this case completing the commercial contract already agreed upon and left to the lawyers to memorialize. We do not here reach the issue of the lawyer's duty if the client wishes to exploit the error.

2. The delivery of the erroneous document is not a "material development" of which the client should be informed under EC 9-2 of the Model Code of Professional Responsibility, but the omission of the provision from the document is a "material fact" which under Rule 4.1(b) of the Model Rules of Professional Conduct must be disclosed to B's lawyer.

The terms of the borrowing are fairly standard and include mandatory prepayments as determined by a formula.[29] Unfortunately, the formula does not work properly—based upon your understanding of the provision from earlier discussions with the bankers and their lawyers. It seems as if the formula's results significantly understate the amount Newco must prepay. As the parties did not draft a term sheet, you have no statement of terms with which to compare the provision. Moreover, as Acquisitions and Megabank have not done a deal before, you can't even look at an earlier deal for guidance.

Loew is adamant that you say nothing. To obtain an additional perspective, you speak with the Ralph Adams, the firm's partner responsible for legal ethics. He gives you the attached case, thinking that it might provide you with some much needed guidance.

Issues

1. Must you disclose the problem with the prepayment provision?

2. Assume that you conclude that you must disclose the problem with the prepayment provision. Upon hearing your conclusion, Loew marches into Ralph Adams's office and declares you to be "a lily-livered coward." Ralph is less abusive, but not much. He tells you and Loew that although it is a close question, he thinks the deal can go forward without disclosing the problem with the prepayment formula. What are your ethical obligations? May you follow your superior's instructions without violating your ethical obligations?

Stare v. Tate
98 Cal. Rptr. 264 (Cal. App. 2d Dist.1971)

KAUS, Presiding Justice.

Plaintiff appeals from an adverse judgment in an action to reform a property settlement agreement with her former husband, the defendant, and to enforce the agreement as reformed. . . .

The agreement in question was signed by both parties [who were divorcing] on February 21, 1968. It was the culmination of protracted negotiations which had been going on for several years. Both sides were represented by counsel at all times.[1]

. . . To sum up: if Joan was correct with respect to the value of the Holt property, her community property interest in it was about $25,000 higher than Tim conceded; if she were to succeed on her contentions with respect to the stock, Tim would have had to pay her roughly $40,000 more than he was willing.

In January, 1968, Joan's attorney prepared a document entitled "SECOND PROPOSAL FOR A BASIS OF SETTLEMENT—TATE v. TATE" which, among other things, arrived at a

---

29. Mandatory prepayment provisions generally provide that a borrower must repay the bank a percentage of any cash that it receives from an additional bank borrowing, the issuance of equity or debt securities, or the sale of substantially all of its assets.

---

1. The attorneys who represent the husband on this appeal did not act for him in the negotiations.

In the negotiations both sides apparently agreed that the community property was to be evenly divided. They did not agree, however, on the value of certain items and on the community property status of certain stocks which stood in the husband's name alone.

These disagreements centered principally on items which, it was understood, were to be retained by the husband.

suggested figure of $70,081.85 for the value of Joan's share in the Holt property. This value was arrived at by a computation set forth in the proposal. It is copied in the footnote.[4]

It is obvious that Joan's attorney arrived at the figure of $70,081.85 for the community equity in the property only by making two substantial errors. First, the net value after deducting the encumbrances from the asserted gross value of $550,000 is $241,637.01, not $141,637.01; second, one-half of $141,637.01 is substantially more than $70,081.85. The correct figure for the equity should have been $120,818.50 or, roughly $50,000 more.

The mistake did not escape Tim's accountant [who] discovered it while helping Tim's attorney in preparing a counteroffer. He brought it to the attention of the attorney who, in his own words, reacted as follows:

> I told him that I had been arguing with (the wife's attorney) to use the value that was on the— on the real property tax statement, but I knew that that was low and (he) would never go for it, that the appraisal had been $425,000.00 when the building had been purchased by said owners, and I thought that until we got it, that we would use something like a $450,000.00 value, and he said, "Fine." It is my recollection that I said to him, "You know, you might as well use the figure that Walker [the wife's attorney] has there because his mistake is a hundred thousand dollars and we value it at a hundred thousand dollars less, so it is basically the same thing, so give it a $70,000.00 equity," and that is what he did and that is how it came about.

A counteroffer was then submitted to Joan and her lawyer. It lists all of the community assets, with the property in question being valued at $70,082.00, rounding up the erroneous figure in Joan's offer to the nearest dollar. There can be no reasonable doubt that the counteroffer was prepared in a way designed to minimize the danger that Joan or her attorney would discover the mistake. While all other encumbered properties are listed at an agreed gross value, with encumbrances shown as a deduction therefrom, the only figure that appears next to the Holt property is the equity!

. . . The rule that the party who misleads another is estopped from claiming that the contract is anything but what the other is led to believe, appears to be quite generally accepted. Citing many cases from other jurisdictions and noting no contrary authority Corbin says: "Reformation may be a proper remedy even though the mistake is not mutual. If one of the parties mistakenly believes that the writing is a correct integration of that to which he had expressed his assent and the other party knows that it is not, reformation may be decreed. The conduct of the other party in permitting the first to execute the erroneous writing and later attempting to enforce it may be regarded as fraudulent; but it is enough to justify reformation that he knows the terms proposed by the first party and the meaning thereof and leads that party reasonably to believe that he too assents to those terms. This makes a contract; and the writing may be reformed to accord with it. The fact that the first party was negligent in failing to observe that the writing does not express what he has assented to does not deprive him of this remedy. The ground for estoppel is against the other and non-mistaken party, not against the mistaken party even though he is negligent." (3 Corbin on Contracts, s 614, pp. 730-732.) The rule is also in accord with the Restatement of Contracts. . . .

STEPHENS, and AISO, JJ., concur.

---

4. "888 East Holt Avenue, Pomona
(Note: value as per previous offer)
Total value $550,000.00
Less encumbrance - 308,362.99
Net value $141,637.01
One-half community $70,081.85"

Exercise 30-4

WCBA's Technical Problems

You are Pat E. Kake, a partner at Good Ethics & Law, a New York City law firm with 450 lawyers in the United States and abroad. You have a broad-ranging corporate practice, having successfully resisted several attempts by the firm to pigeon-hole you into a niche practice.

Part A

One of your clients is WCBA, one of New York City's premiere television stations. Your contact at WCBA is Lila Bartley, Senior Vice President and General Counsel.

Lila just called and related the following: WCBA's longtime sportscaster, Ray Statler, passed away recently. His death has created a significant business problem for WCBA as its ratings for the evening broadcasts have fallen precipitously since he died. Lila tells you that all is not lost, however. WCBA has learned through the grapevine that Bob Jacobs, WXYZ's longtime sportscaster, is disaffected with his present employer and wants to jump ship as soon as possible. As a result of the intervention of an intermediary, Bob gave his employment agreement to another employee of WCBA, and that agreement has been passed on to Lila.

Lila tells you that she has reviewed the contract and that one provision gives her pause. It states the following:

> **Noncompete**. During the Term and for a period of 90 days afterwards, Employee shall not
>
> (a)   accept employment from,
> (b)   negotiate for employment with, or
> (c)   solicit any proposal from,
>
> any Person in connection with a position as a radio or television sportscaster.[30]

She then states the obvious: If Bob were to sign a contract with WCBA, he will have violated his contract with WXYZ, and WCBA may be subject to a suit for tortious interference with contract. Lila then continues that WCBA is willing to accept the business risk of the lawsuit. Lila is worried, however, about the risk to her. Is she somehow acting unethically by participating in the negotiation and drafting of Bob's employment contract with WCBA?

Issues

1. What do you advise Lila? Should she alert Bob to the issue?

2. How (if at all) does this differ from aiding a client who intends to violate a law?

Part B

Lila calls you and informs you that WCBA has made the business decision to employ Bob. She asks that you negotiate the contract. You are, of course, delighted to do so (your hours this month have been a little low). Lila tells you that Dave Winslow will be negotiating on behalf of Bob.

---

30. For the purposes of this exercise, assume that this contract provision is enforceable.

After marking up an employment agreement from the firm's precedents files, you send a copy to Lila who blesses it. You then messenger over a copy of the agreement to each of Bob Jacobs and Dave Winslow.

About three days later, Dave calls to give you comments on the draft. Most of his comments are reasonable; others give you pause.

Issues

1. Dave asks for a bonus if ratings improve 5 percent or more within the first 30 days of the employment term. Lila approves the bonus. When you go to draft the bonus provision, you note that the parties did not address whether a pro rata bonus should be payable upon death or disability. Are you ethically obligated to provide for the pro rata bonus in the revised contract? What non-ethical reason could you give to Lila for raising the issue with Dave?

2. Dave states that the proposed noncompete provision is probably unenforceable both in time and geographic scope. You agree to a reasonable, smaller time period, but insist on a larger geographic scope arguing that it is the industry standard. It is, but it is also highly unlikely that a court would enforce it.

   (a) Will you be violating your ethical duties if the contract includes an unenforceable geographic scope provision?

   (b) Would your answer change if you were drafting a standard form contract that all of WCBA's employees would sign and you knew that the courts had held the provision unenforceable?

Exercise 30-5

Pine Greene

In addition to WCBA, one of your long-time clients is By'em Inc. (By'em). By'em buys undervalued companies and sells off the subsidiaries and divisions at prices that are, in the aggregate, greater than the value of the company as a whole. You have strong relationships with both the in-house counsel, Stanley Leech, and the Executive Vice President, Reena Pixley.

Reena called about two weeks ago to tell you about a new deal. By'em plans to purchase Conglomerate Inc. (Conglomerate). She asked that you mark up and distribute By'em's standard form purchase agreement. The deal is on a fast track. Negotiations and due diligence proceed apace and the closing is scheduled for the end of the month. The transaction is basically friendly; you even established a good working relationship with Roger Pine, President of Conglomerate.

As part of the negotiations, By'em and Conglomerate agree to a term. When drafting the insert, you craft the insert in such a way that Conglomerate arguably takes on more of the risk than had been agreed to. You blackline the entire provision so that Conglomerate's counsel will know that it has been changed. In your cover letter, as has been your practice, you point out the significant changes in the revised draft—other than this one provision.

Issue:

1. Did you violate your ethical duties by drafting the provision the way you did, or by failing to note the change in your cover letter?

2. Does your answer change if the client instructs you to make the change? Consider *In re Rothwell*, 296 S.E.2d 870 (S.C. 1982).

In re ROTHWELL

296 S.E.2d 870 (S.C. 1982)

PER CURIAM:

The Hearing Panel and the Board of Commissioners on Grievances and Discipline recommend respondent Donald Erwin Rothwell be publicly reprimanded for professional misconduct. We agree.

Respondent was retained by Richard Mowery to represent him in negotiations with Mowery's former employer, W.W. Williams Company, who had transferred Mowery from Columbus, Ohio to Columbia. To facilitate the transfer, Williams Company loaned Mowery $47,000 to purchase a house in Columbia.

Mowery was discharged from Williams Company after he moved to Columbia, but before he had repaid the $47,000. Williams Company offered to buy Mowery's Ohio house and apply the equity to the debt, leaving a deficiency of $7,201.04.

Williams Company prepared and mailed to respondent a deed along with a letter requesting that respondent have his client, Mowery, execute and return the deed to Williams Company for filing. The letter also stated, "[w]e will expect your call if there are any questions."

Respondent surreptitiously altered the deed by inserting a paragraph satisfying the entire debt from Mowery to Williams Company, and mailed the deed to Williams Company with a letter which stated only:

> We are returning herewith your package to you duly executed. Once you have filed the deed of record, please forward on a clocked copy of same for our files. Thank you.
> No notice was given Williams Company that the deed had been altered.

Williams Company filed the deed and sued Mowery for the deficiency. Respondent raised the altered deed as a defense.

Respondent contends the deed prepared by Williams Company was merely an offer, and his alteration of the deed constituted a counteroffer. Clearly, Williams Company expected respondent to either (1) have his client execute the deed or (2) telephone Williams Company. Respondent's letter to Williams Company gave no notice of the alteration, but rather, led Williams Company to believe he had complied with their request.

We agree with the Panel that respondent engaged in conduct involving dishonesty, fraud, deceit, and misrepresentation which is prejudicial to the administration of justice and adversely reflects on his fitness to practice law, all in violation of DR1-102(A)(1), (4), (5) and (6); DR7-102(A)(3); and sections 5(b) and (d) of the Rule on Disciplinary Procedure of the Supreme Court of the State of South Carolina. Accordingly, respondent Donald Erwin Rothwell stands publicly reprimanded for his acts of professional misconduct.

EXHIBIT A TO CHAPTER 30

Comments to the Model Rules of Professional Conduct (2006)

Rule 1.1 Competence—Comment

Legal Knowledge and Skill

[1] In determining whether a lawyer employs the requisite knowledge and skill in a particular matter, relevant factors include the relative complexity and specialized nature of the matter, the lawyer's general experience, the lawyer's training and experience in the field in question, the preparation and study the lawyer is able to give the matter and whether it is feasible to refer the matter to, or associate or consult with, a lawyer of established competence in the field in question. In many instances, the required proficiency is that of a general practitioner. Expertise in a particular field of law may be required in some circumstances.

[2] A lawyer need not necessarily have special training or prior experience to handle legal problems of a type with which the lawyer is unfamiliar. A newly admitted lawyer can be as competent as a practitioner with long experience. Some important legal skills, such as the analysis of precedent, the evaluation of evidence and legal drafting, are required in all legal problems. Perhaps the most fundamental legal skill consists of determining what kind of legal problems a situation may involve, a skill that necessarily transcends any particular specialized knowledge. A lawyer can provide adequate representation in a wholly novel field through necessary study. Competent representation can also be provided through the association of a lawyer of established competence in the field in question.

[3] In an emergency a lawyer may give advice or assistance in a matter in which the lawyer does not have the skill ordinarily required where referral to or consultation or association with another lawyer would be impractical. Even in an emergency, however, assistance should be limited to that reasonably necessary in the circumstances, for ill-considered action under emergency conditions can jeopardize the client's interest.

[4] A lawyer may accept representation where the requisite level of competence can be achieved by reasonable preparation. This applies as well to a lawyer who is appointed as counsel for an unrepresented person. See also Rule 6.2.

Thoroughness and Preparation

[5] Competent handling of a particular matter includes inquiry into and analysis of the factual and legal elements of the problem, and use of methods and procedures meeting the standards of competent practitioners. It also includes adequate preparation. The required attention and preparation are determined in part by what is at stake; major litigation and complex transactions ordinarily require more extensive treatment than matters of lesser complexity and consequence. An agreement between the lawyer and the client regarding the scope of the representation may limit the matters for which the lawyer is responsible. See Rule 1.2(c).

Maintaining Competence

[6] To maintain the requisite knowledge and skill, a lawyer should keep abreast of changes in the law and its practice, engage in continuing study and education and comply with all continuing legal education requirements to which the lawyer is subject.

Rule 1.2 Scope Of Representation And Allocation Of Authority Between Client And Lawyer—Comment

Allocation of Authority between Client and Lawyer

[1] Paragraph (a) confers upon the client the ultimate authority to determine the purposes to be served by legal representation, within the limits imposed by law and the lawyer's professional obligations. The decisions specified in paragraph (a), such as whether to settle a civil matter, must also be made by the client. See Rule 1.4(a)(1) for the lawyer's duty to communicate with the client about such decisions. With respect to the means by which the client's objectives are to be pursued, the lawyer shall consult with the client as required by Rule 1.4(a)(2) and may take such action as is impliedly authorized to carry out the representation.

[2] On occasion, however, a lawyer and a client may disagree about the means to be used to accomplish the client's objectives. Clients normally defer to the special knowledge and skill of their lawyer with respect to the means to be used to accomplish their objectives, particularly with respect to technical, legal and tactical matters. Conversely, lawyers usually defer to the client regarding such questions as the expense to be incurred and concern for third persons who might be adversely affected. Because of the varied nature of the matters about which a lawyer and client might disagree and because the actions in question may implicate the interests of a tribunal or other persons, this Rule does not prescribe how such disagreements are to be resolved. Other law, however, may be applicable and should be consulted by the lawyer. The lawyer should

also consult with the client and seek a mutually acceptable resolution of the disagreement. If such efforts are unavailing and the lawyer has a fundamental disagreement with the client, the lawyer may withdraw from the representation. See Rule 1.16(b)(4). Conversely, the client may resolve the disagreement by discharging the lawyer. See Rule 1.16(a)(3).

[3] At the outset of a representation, the client may authorize the lawyer to take specific action on the client's behalf without further consultation. Absent a material change in circumstances and subject to Rule 1.4, a lawyer may rely on such an advance authorization. The client may, however, revoke such authority at any time.

[4] In a case in which the client appears to be suffering diminished capacity, the lawyer's duty to abide by the client's decisions is to be guided by reference to Rule 1.14.

Independence from Client's Views or Activities

[5] Legal representation should not be denied to people who are unable to afford legal services, or whose cause is controversial or the subject of popular disapproval. By the same token, representing a client does not constitute approval of the client's views or activities.

Agreements Limiting Scope of Representation

[6] The scope of services to be provided by a lawyer may be limited by agreement with the client or by the terms under which the lawyer's services are made available to the client. When a lawyer has been retained by an insurer to represent an insured, for example, the representation may be limited to matters related to the insurance coverage. A limited representation may be appropriate because the client has limited objectives for the representation. In addition, the terms upon which representation is undertaken may exclude specific means that might otherwise be used to accomplish the client's objectives. Such limitations may exclude actions that the client thinks are too costly or that the lawyer regards as repugnant or imprudent.

[7] Although this Rule affords the lawyer and client substantial latitude to limit the representation, the limitation must be reasonable under the circumstances. If, for example, a client's objective is limited to securing general information about the law the client needs in order to handle a common and typically uncomplicated legal problem, the lawyer and client may agree that the lawyer's services will be limited to a brief telephone consultation. Such a limitation, however, would not be reasonable if the time allotted was not sufficient to yield advice upon which the client could rely. Although an agreement for a limited representation does not exempt a lawyer from the duty to provide competent representation, the limitation is a factor to be considered when determining the legal knowledge, skill, thoroughness and preparation reasonably necessary for the representation. See Rule 1.1.

[8] All agreements concerning a lawyer's representation of a client must accord with the Rules of Professional Conduct and other law. See, e.g., Rules 1.1, 1.8 and 5.6.

Criminal, Fraudulent and Prohibited Transactions

[9] Paragraph (d) prohibits a lawyer from knowingly counseling or assisting a client to commit a crime or fraud. This prohibition, however, does not preclude the lawyer from giving an honest opinion about the actual consequences that appear likely to result from a client's conduct. Nor does the fact that a client uses advice in a course of action that is criminal or fraudulent of itself make a lawyer a party to the course of action. There is a critical distinction between presenting an analysis of legal aspects of questionable conduct and recommending the means by which a crime or fraud might be committed with impunity.

[10] When the client's course of action has already begun and is continuing, the lawyer's responsibility is especially delicate. The lawyer is required to avoid assisting the client, for example, by drafting or delivering documents that the lawyer knows are fraudulent or by suggesting how the wrongdoing might be concealed. A lawyer may not continue assisting a client in conduct that the lawyer originally supposed was legally proper

but then discovers is criminal or fraudulent. The lawyer must, therefore, withdraw from the representation of the client in the matter. See Rule 1.16(a). In some cases, withdrawal alone might be insufficient. It may be necessary for the lawyer to give notice of the fact of withdrawal and to disaffirm any opinion, document, affirmation or the like. See Rule 4.1.

[11] Where the client is a fiduciary, the lawyer may be charged with special obligations in dealings with a beneficiary.

[12] Paragraph (d) applies whether or not the defrauded party is a party to the transaction. Hence, a lawyer must not participate in a transaction to effectuate criminal or fraudulent avoidance of tax liability. Paragraph (d) does not preclude undertaking a criminal defense incident to a general retainer for legal services to a lawful enterprise. The last clause of paragraph (d) recognizes that determining the validity or interpretation of a statute or regulation may require a course of action involving disobedience of the statute or regulation or of the interpretation placed upon it by governmental authorities.

[13] If a lawyer comes to know or reasonably should know that a client expects assistance not permitted by the Rules of Professional Conduct or other law or if the lawyer intends to act contrary to the client's instructions, the lawyer must consult with the client regarding the limitations on the lawyer's conduct. See Rule 1.4(a)(5).

Rule 1.4 Communication—Comment

[1] Reasonable communication between the lawyer and the client is necessary for the client effectively to participate in the representation.

Communicating with Client

[2] If these Rules require that a particular decision about the representation be made by the client, paragraph (a)(1) requires that the lawyer promptly consult with and secure the client's consent prior to taking action unless prior discussions with the client have resolved what action the client wants the lawyer to take. For example, a lawyer who receives from opposing counsel an offer of settlement in a civil controversy or a proffered plea bargain in a criminal case must promptly inform the client of its substance unless the client has previously indicated that the proposal will be acceptable or unacceptable or has authorized the lawyer to accept or to reject the offer. See Rule 1.2(a).

[3] Paragraph (a)(2) requires the lawyer to reasonably consult with the client about the means to be used to accomplish the client's objectives. In some situations—depending on both the importance of the action under consideration and the feasibility of consulting with the client—this duty will require consultation prior to taking action. In other circumstances, such as during a trial when an immediate decision must be made, the exigency of the situation may require the lawyer to act without prior consultation. In such cases the lawyer must nonetheless act reasonably to inform the client of actions the lawyer has taken on the client's behalf. Additionally, paragraph (a)(3) requires that the lawyer keep the client reasonably informed about the status of the matter, such as significant developments affecting the timing or the substance of the representation.

[4] A lawyer's regular communication with clients will minimize the occasions on which a client will need to request information concerning the representation. When a client makes a reasonable request for information, however, paragraph (a)(4) requires prompt compliance with the request, or if a prompt response is not feasible, that the lawyer, or a member of the lawyer's staff, acknowledge receipt of the request and advise the client when a response may be expected. Client telephone calls should be promptly returned or acknowledged.

Explaining Matters

[5] The client should have sufficient information to participate intelligently in decisions concerning the objectives of the representation and the means by which they are to be pursued, to the extent the client is will-

ing and able to do so. Adequacy of communication depends in part on the kind of advice or assistance that is involved. For example, when there is time to explain a proposal made in a negotiation, the lawyer should review all important provisions with the client before proceeding to an agreement. In litigation a lawyer should explain the general strategy and prospects of success and ordinarily should consult the client on tactics that are likely to result in significant expense or to injure or coerce others. On the other hand, a lawyer ordinarily will not be expected to describe trial or negotiation strategy in detail. The guiding principle is that the lawyer should fulfill reasonable client expectations for information consistent with the duty to act in the client's best interests, and the client's overall requirements as to the character of representation. In certain circumstances, such as when a lawyer asks a client to consent to a representation affected by a conflict of interest, the client must give informed consent, as defined in Rule 1.0(e).

[6] Ordinarily, the information to be provided is that appropriate for a client who is a comprehending and responsible adult. However, fully informing the client according to this standard may be impracticable, for example, where the client is a child or suffers from diminished capacity. See Rule 1.14. When the client is an organization or group, it is often impossible or inappropriate to inform every one of its members about its legal affairs; ordinarily, the lawyer should address communications to the appropriate officials of the organization. See Rule 1.13. Where many routine matters are involved, a system of limited or occasional reporting may be arranged with the client.

Withholding Information

[7] In some circumstances, a lawyer may be justified in delaying transmission of information when the client would be likely to react imprudently to an immediate communication. Thus, a lawyer might withhold a psychiatric diagnosis of a client when the examining psychiatrist indicates that disclosure would harm the client. A lawyer may not withhold information to serve the lawyer's own interest or convenience or the interests or convenience of another person. Rules or court orders governing litigation may provide that information supplied to a lawyer may not be disclosed to the client. Rule 3.4(c) directs compliance with such rules or orders.

Rule 1.7 Conflict Of Interest: Current Clients—Comment

General Principles

[1] Loyalty and independent judgment are essential elements in the lawyer's relationship to a client. Concurrent conflicts of interest can arise from the lawyer's responsibilities to another client, a former client or a third person or from the lawyer's own interests. For specific Rules regarding certain concurrent conflicts of interest, see Rule 1.8. For former client conflicts of interest, see Rule 1.9. For conflicts of interest involving prospective clients, see Rule 1.18. For definitions of "informed consent" and "confirmed in writing," see Rule 1.0(e) and (b).

[2] Resolution of a conflict of interest problem under this Rule requires the lawyer to: 1) clearly identify the client or clients; 2) determine whether a conflict of interest exists; 3) decide whether the representation may be undertaken despite the existence of a conflict, i.e., whether the conflict is consentable; and 4) if so, consult with the clients affected under paragraph (a) and obtain their informed consent, confirmed in writing. The clients affected under paragraph (a) include both of the clients referred to in paragraph (a)(1) and the one or more clients whose representation might be materially limited under paragraph (a)(2).

[3] A conflict of interest may exist before representation is undertaken, in which event the representation must be declined, unless the lawyer obtains the informed consent of each client under the conditions of paragraph (b). To determine whether a conflict of interest exists, a lawyer should adopt reasonable procedures, appropriate for the size and type of firm and practice, to determine in both litigation and non-litigation matters the persons and issues involved. See also Comment to Rule 5.1. Ignorance caused by a failure to institute such

procedures will not excuse a lawyer's violation of this Rule. As to whether a client-lawyer relationship exists or, having once been established, is continuing, see Comment to Rule 1.3 and Scope.

[4] If a conflict arises after representation has been undertaken, the lawyer ordinarily must withdraw from the representation, unless the lawyer has obtained the informed consent of the client under the conditions of paragraph (b). See Rule 1.16. Where more than one client is involved, whether the lawyer may continue to represent any of the clients is determined both by the lawyer's ability to comply with duties owed to the former client and by the lawyer's ability to represent adequately the remaining client or clients, given the lawyer's duties to the former client. See Rule 1.9. See also Comments [5] and [29].

[5] Unforeseeable developments, such as changes in corporate and other organizational affiliations or the addition or realignment of parties in litigation, might create conflicts in the midst of a representation, as when a company sued by the lawyer on behalf of one client is bought by another client represented by the lawyer in an unrelated matter. Depending on the circumstances, the lawyer may have the option to withdraw from one of the representations in order to avoid the conflict. The lawyer must seek court approval where necessary and take steps to minimize harm to the clients. See Rule 1.16. The lawyer must continue to protect the confidences of the client from whose representation the lawyer has withdrawn. See Rule 1.9(c).

Identifying Conflicts of Interest: Directly Adverse

[6] Loyalty to a current client prohibits undertaking representation directly adverse to that client without that client's informed consent. Thus, absent consent, a lawyer may not act as an advocate in one matter against a person the lawyer represents in some other matter, even when the matters are wholly unrelated. The client as to whom the representation is directly adverse is likely to feel betrayed, and the resulting damage to the client-lawyer relationship is likely to impair the lawyer's ability to represent the client effectively. In addition, the client on whose behalf the adverse representation is undertaken reasonably may fear that the lawyer will pursue that client's case less effectively out of deference to the other client, i.e., that the representation may be materially limited by the lawyer's interest in retaining the current client. Similarly, a directly adverse conflict may arise when a lawyer is required to cross-examine a client who appears as a witness in a lawsuit involving another client, as when the testimony will be damaging to the client who is represented in the lawsuit. On the other hand, simultaneous representation in unrelated matters of clients whose interests are only economically adverse, such as representation of competing economic enterprises in unrelated litigation, does not ordinarily constitute a conflict of interest and thus may not require consent of the respective clients.

[7] Directly adverse conflicts can also arise in transactional matters. For example, if a lawyer is asked to represent the seller of a business in negotiations with a buyer represented by the lawyer, not in the same transaction but in another, unrelated matter, the lawyer could not undertake the representation without the informed consent of each client.

Identifying Conflicts of Interest: Material Limitation

[8] Even where there is no direct adverseness, a conflict of interest exists if there is a significant risk that a lawyer's ability to consider, recommend or carry out an appropriate course of action for the client will be materially limited as a result of the lawyer's other responsibilities or interests. For example, a lawyer asked to represent several individuals seeking to form a joint venture is likely to be materially limited in the lawyer's ability to recommend or advocate all possible positions that each might take because of the lawyer's duty of loyalty to the others. The conflict in effect forecloses alternatives that would otherwise be available to the client. The mere possibility of subsequent harm does not itself require disclosure and consent. The critical questions are the likelihood that a difference in interests will eventuate and, if it does, whether it will materially interfere with the lawyer's independent professional judgment in considering alternatives or foreclose courses of action that reasonably should be pursued on behalf of the client.

Lawyer's Responsibilities to Former Clients and Other Third Persons

[9] In addition to conflicts with other current clients, a lawyer's duties of loyalty and independence may be materially limited by responsibilities to former clients under Rule 1.9 or by the lawyer's responsibilities to other persons, such as fiduciary duties arising from a lawyer's service as a trustee, executor or corporate director.

Personal Interest Conflicts

[10] The lawyer's own interests should not be permitted to have an adverse effect on representation of a client. For example, if the probity of a lawyer's own conduct in a transaction is in serious question, it may be difficult or impossible for the lawyer to give a client detached advice. Similarly, when a lawyer has discussions concerning possible employment with an opponent of the lawyer's client, or with a law firm representing the opponent, such discussions could materially limit the lawyer's representation of the client. In addition, a lawyer may not allow related business interests to affect representation, for example, by referring clients to an enterprise in which the lawyer has an undisclosed financial interest. See Rule 1.8 for specific Rules pertaining to a number of personal interest conflicts, including business transactions with clients. See also Rule 1.10 (personal interest conflicts under Rule 1.7 ordinarily are not imputed to other lawyers in a law firm).

[11] When lawyers representing different clients in the same matter or in substantially related matters are closely related by blood or marriage, there may be a significant risk that client confidences will be revealed and that the lawyer's family relationship will interfere with both loyalty and independent professional judgment. As a result, each client is entitled to know of the existence and implications of the relationship between the lawyers before the lawyer agrees to undertake the representation. Thus, a lawyer related to another lawyer, e.g., as parent, child, sibling or spouse, ordinarily may not represent a client in a matter where that lawyer is representing another party, unless each client gives informed consent. The disqualification arising from a close family relationship is personal and ordinarily is not imputed to members of firms with whom the lawyers are associated. See Rule 1.10.

[12] A lawyer is prohibited from engaging in sexual relationships with a client unless the sexual relationship predates the formation of the client-lawyer relationship. See Rule 1.8(j).

Interest of Person Paying for a Lawyer's Service

[13] A lawyer may be paid from a source other than the client, including a co-client, if the client is informed of that fact and consents and the arrangement does not compromise the lawyer's duty of loyalty or independent judgment to the client. See Rule 1.8(f). If acceptance of the payment from any other source presents a significant risk that the lawyer's representation of the client will be materially limited by the lawyer's own interest in accommodating the person paying the lawyer's fee or by the lawyer's responsibilities to a payer who is also a co-client, then the lawyer must comply with the requirements of paragraph (b) before accepting the representation, including determining whether the conflict is consentable and, if so, that the client has adequate information about the material risks of the representation.

Prohibited Representations

[14] Ordinarily, clients may consent to representation notwithstanding a conflict. However, as indicated in paragraph (b), some conflicts are nonconsentable, meaning that the lawyer involved cannot properly ask for such agreement or provide representation on the basis of the client's consent. When the lawyer is representing more than one client, the question of consentability must be resolved as to each client.

[15] Consentability is typically determined by considering whether the interests of the clients will be adequately protected if the clients are permitted to give their informed consent to representation burdened by

a conflict of interest. Thus, under paragraph (b)(1), representation is prohibited if in the circumstances the lawyer cannot reasonably conclude that the lawyer will be able to provide competent and diligent representation. See Rule 1.1 (competence) and Rule 1.3 (diligence).

[16] Paragraph (b)(2) describes conflicts that are nonconsentable because the representation is prohibited by applicable law. For example, in some states substantive law provides that the same lawyer may not represent more than one defendant in a capital case, even with the consent of the clients, and under federal criminal statutes certain representations by a former government lawyer are prohibited, despite the informed consent of the former client. In addition, decisional law in some states limits the ability of a governmental client, such as a municipality, to consent to a conflict of interest.

[17] Paragraph (b)(3) describes conflicts that are nonconsentable because of the institutional interest in vigorous development of each client's position when the clients are aligned directly against each other in the same litigation or other proceeding before a tribunal. Whether clients are aligned directly against each other within the meaning of this paragraph requires examination of the context of the proceeding. Although this paragraph does not preclude a lawyer's multiple representation of adverse parties to a mediation (because mediation is not a proceeding before a "tribunal" under Rule 1.0(m)), such representation may be precluded by paragraph (b)(1).

Informed Consent

[18] Informed consent requires that each affected client be aware of the relevant circumstances and of the material and reasonably foreseeable ways that the conflict could have adverse effects on the interests of that client. See Rule 1.0(e) (informed consent). The information required depends on the nature of the conflict and the nature of the risks involved. When representation of multiple clients in a single matter is undertaken, the information must include the implications of the common representation, including possible effects on loyalty, confidentiality and the attorney-client privilege and the advantages and risks involved. See Comments [30] and [31] (effect of common representation on confidentiality).

[19] Under some circumstances it may be impossible to make the disclosure necessary to obtain consent. For example, when the lawyer represents different clients in related matters and one of the clients refuses to consent to the disclosure necessary to permit the other client to make an informed decision, the lawyer cannot properly ask the latter to consent. In some cases the alternative to common representation can be that each party may have to obtain separate representation with the possibility of incurring additional costs. These costs, along with the benefits of securing separate representation, are factors that may be considered by the affected client in determining whether common representation is in the client's interests.

Consent Confirmed in Writing

[20] Paragraph (b) requires the lawyer to obtain the informed consent of the client, confirmed in writing. Such a writing may consist of a document executed by the client or one that the lawyer promptly records and transmits to the client following an oral consent. See Rule 1.0(b). See also Rule 1.0(n) (writing includes electronic transmission). If it is not feasible to obtain or transmit the writing at the time the client gives informed consent, then the lawyer must obtain or transmit it within a reasonable time thereafter. See Rule 1.0(b). The requirement of a writing does not supplant the need in most cases for the lawyer to talk with the client, to explain the risks and advantages, if any, of representation burdened with a conflict of interest, as well as reasonably available alternatives, and to afford the client a reasonable opportunity to consider the risks and alternatives and to raise questions and concerns. Rather, the writing is required in order to impress upon clients the seriousness of the decision the client is being asked to make and to avoid disputes or ambiguities that might later occur in the absence of a writing.

Revoking Consent

[21] A client who has given consent to a conflict may revoke the consent and, like any other client, may terminate the lawyer's representation at any time. Whether revoking consent to the client's own representation precludes the lawyer from continuing to represent other clients depends on the circumstances, including the nature of the conflict, whether the client revoked consent because of a material change in circumstances, the reasonable expectations of the other client and whether material detriment to the other clients or the lawyer would result.

Consent to Future Conflict

[22] Whether a lawyer may properly request a client to waive conflicts that might arise in the future is subject to the test of paragraph (b). The effectiveness of such waivers is generally determined by the extent to which the client reasonably understands the material risks that the waiver entails. The more comprehensive the explanation of the types of future representations that might arise and the actual and reasonably foreseeable adverse consequences of those representations, the greater the likelihood that the client will have the requisite understanding. Thus, if the client agrees to consent to a particular type of conflict with which the client is already familiar, then the consent ordinarily will be effective with regard to that type of conflict. If the consent is general and open-ended, then the consent ordinarily will be ineffective, because it is not reasonably likely that the client will have understood the material risks involved. On the other hand, if the client is an experienced user of the legal services involved and is reasonably informed regarding the risk that a conflict may arise, such consent is more likely to be effective, particularly if, e.g., the client is independently represented by other counsel in giving consent and the consent is limited to future conflicts unrelated to the subject of the representation. In any case, advance consent cannot be effective if the circumstances that materialize in the future are such as would make the conflict nonconsentable under paragraph (b).

Conflicts in Litigation

[23] Paragraph (b)(3) prohibits representation of opposing parties in the same litigation, regardless of the clients' consent. On the other hand, simultaneous representation of parties whose interests in litigation may conflict, such as coplaintiffs or codefendants, is governed by paragraph (a)(2). A conflict may exist by reason of substantial discrepancy in the parties' testimony, incompatibility in positions in relation to an opposing party or the fact that there are substantially different possibilities of settlement of the claims or liabilities in question. Such conflicts can arise in criminal cases as well as civil. The potential for conflict of interest in representing multiple defendants in a criminal case is so grave that ordinarily a lawyer should decline to represent more than one codefendant. On the other hand, common representation of persons having similar interests in civil litigation is proper if the requirements of paragraph (b) are met.

[24] Ordinarily a lawyer may take inconsistent legal positions in different tribunals at different times on behalf of different clients. The mere fact that advocating a legal position on behalf of one client might create precedent adverse to the interests of a client represented by the lawyer in an unrelated matter does not create a conflict of interest. A conflict of interest exists, however, if there is a significant risk that a lawyer's action on behalf of one client will materially limit the lawyer's effectiveness in representing another client in a different case; for example, when a decision favoring one client will create a precedent likely to seriously weaken the position taken on behalf of the other client. Factors relevant in determining whether the clients need to be advised of the risk include: where the cases are pending, whether the issue is substantive or procedural, the temporal relationship between the matters, the significance of the issue to the immediate and long-term interests of the clients involved and the clients' reasonable expectations in retaining the lawyer. If there is significant risk of material limitation, then absent informed consent of the affected clients, the lawyer must refuse one of the representations or withdraw from one or both matters.

[25] When a lawyer represents or seeks to represent a class of plaintiffs or defendants in a class-action lawsuit, unnamed members of the class are ordinarily not considered to be clients of the lawyer for purposes of apply-

ing paragraph (a)(1) of this Rule. Thus, the lawyer does not typically need to get the consent of such a person before representing a client suing the person in an unrelated matter. Similarly, a lawyer seeking to represent an opponent in a class action does not typically need the consent of an unnamed member of the class whom the lawyer represents in an unrelated matter.

Nonlitigation Conflicts

[26] Conflicts of interest under paragraphs (a)(1) and (a)(2) arise in contexts other than litigation. For a discussion of directly adverse conflicts in transactional matters, see Comment [7]. Relevant factors in determining whether there is significant potential for material limitation include the duration and intimacy of the lawyer's relationship with the client or clients involved, the functions being performed by the lawyer, the likelihood that disagreements will arise and the likely prejudice to the client from the conflict. The question is often one of proximity and degree. See Comment [8].

[27] For example, conflict questions may arise in estate planning and estate administration. A lawyer may be called upon to prepare wills for several family members, such as husband and wife, and, depending upon the circumstances, a conflict of interest may be present. In estate administration the identity of the client may be unclear under the law of a particular jurisdiction. Under one view, the client is the fiduciary; under another view the client is the estate or trust, including its beneficiaries. In order to comply with conflict of interest rules, the lawyer should make clear the lawyer's relationship to the parties involved.

[28] Whether a conflict is consentable depends on the circumstances. For example, a lawyer may not represent multiple parties to a negotiation whose interests are fundamentally antagonistic to each other, but common representation is permissible where the clients are generally aligned in interest even though there is some difference in interest among them. Thus, a lawyer may seek to establish or adjust a relationship between clients on an amicable and mutually advantageous basis; for example, in helping to organize a business in which two or more clients are entrepreneurs, working out the financial reorganization of an enterprise in which two or more clients have an interest or arranging a property distribution in settlement of an estate. The lawyer seeks to resolve potentially adverse interests by developing the parties' mutual interests. Otherwise, each party might have to obtain separate representation, with the possibility of incurring additional cost, complication or even litigation. Given these and other relevant factors, the clients may prefer that the lawyer act for all of them.

Special Considerations in Common Representation

[29] In considering whether to represent multiple clients in the same matter, a lawyer should be mindful that if the common representation fails because the potentially adverse interests cannot be reconciled, the result can be additional cost, embarrassment and recrimination. Ordinarily, the lawyer will be forced to withdraw from representing all of the clients if the common representation fails. In some situations, the risk of failure is so great that multiple representation is plainly impossible. For example, a lawyer cannot undertake common representation of clients where contentious litigation or negotiations between them are imminent or contemplated. Moreover, because the lawyer is required to be impartial between commonly represented clients, representation of multiple clients is improper when it is unlikely that impartiality can be maintained. Generally, if the relationship between the parties has already assumed antagonism, the possibility that the clients' interests can be adequately served by common representation is not very good. Other relevant factors are whether the lawyer subsequently will represent both parties on a continuing basis and whether the situation involves creating or terminating a relationship between the parties.

[30] A particularly important factor in determining the appropriateness of common representation is the effect on client-lawyer confidentiality and the attorney-client privilege. With regard to the attorney-client privilege, the prevailing rule is that, as between commonly represented clients, the privilege does not attach. Hence, it must be assumed that if litigation eventuates between the clients, the privilege will not protect any such communications, and the clients should be so advised.

[31] As to the duty of confidentiality, continued common representation will almost certainly be inadequate if one client asks the lawyer not to disclose to the other client information relevant to the common representation. This is so because the lawyer has an equal duty of loyalty to each client, and each client has the right to be informed of anything bearing on the representation that might affect that client's interests and the right to expect that the lawyer will use that information to that client's benefit. See Rule 1.4. The lawyer should, at the outset of the common representation and as part of the process of obtaining each client's informed consent, advise each client that information will be shared and that the lawyer will have to withdraw if one client decides that some matter material to the representation should be kept from the other. In limited circumstances, it may be appropriate for the lawyer to proceed with the representation when the clients have agreed, after being properly informed, that the lawyer will keep certain information confidential. For example, the lawyer may reasonably conclude that failure to disclose one client's trade secrets to another client will not adversely affect representation involving a joint venture between the clients and agree to keep that information confidential with the informed consent of both clients.

[32] When seeking to establish or adjust a relationship between clients, the lawyer should make clear that the lawyer's role is not that of partisanship normally expected in other circumstances and, thus, that the clients may be required to assume greater responsibility for decisions than when each client is separately represented. Any limitations on the scope of the representation made necessary as a result of the common representation should be fully explained to the clients at the outset of the representation. See Rule 1.2(c).

[33] Subject to the above limitations, each client in the common representation has the right to loyal and diligent representation and the protection of Rule 1.9 concerning the obligations to a former client. The client also has the right to discharge the lawyer as stated in Rule 1.16.

Organizational Clients

[34] A lawyer who represents a corporation or other organization does not, by virtue of that representation, necessarily represent any constituent or affiliated organization, such as a parent or subsidiary. See Rule 1.13(a). Thus, the lawyer for an organization is not barred from accepting representation adverse to an affiliate in an unrelated matter, unless the circumstances are such that the affiliate should also be considered a client of the lawyer, there is an understanding between the lawyer and the organizational client that the lawyer will avoid representation adverse to the client's affiliates, or the lawyer's obligations to either the organizational client or the new client are likely to limit materially the lawyer's representation of the other client.

[35] A lawyer for a corporation or other organization who is also a member of its board of directors should determine whether the responsibilities of the two roles may conflict. The lawyer may be called on to advise the corporation in matters involving actions of the directors. Consideration should be given to the frequency with which such situations may arise, the potential intensity of the conflict, the effect of the lawyer's resignation from the board and the possibility of the corporation's obtaining legal advice from another lawyer in such situations. If there is material risk that the dual role will compromise the lawyer's independence of professional judgment, the lawyer should not serve as a director or should cease to act as the corporation's lawyer when conflicts of interest arise. The lawyer should advise the other members of the board that in some circumstances matters discussed at board meetings while the lawyer is present in the capacity of director might not be protected by the attorney-client privilege and that conflict of interest considerations might require the lawyer's recusal as a director or might require the lawyer and the lawyer's firm to decline representation of the corporation in a matter.

Rule 2.1 Advisor—Comment

Scope of Advice

[1] A client is entitled to straightforward advice expressing the lawyer's honest assessment. Legal advice often involves unpleasant facts and alternatives that a client may be disinclined to confront. In presenting advice, a

lawyer endeavors to sustain the client's morale and may put advice in as acceptable a form as honesty permits. However, a lawyer should not be deterred from giving candid advice by the prospect that the advice will be unpalatable to the client.

[2] Advice couched in narrow legal terms may be of little value to a client, especially where practical considerations, such as cost or effects on other people, are predominant. Purely technical legal advice, therefore, can sometimes be inadequate. It is proper for a lawyer to refer to relevant moral and ethical considerations in giving advice. Although a lawyer is not a moral advisor as such, moral and ethical considerations impinge upon most legal questions and may decisively influence how the law will be applied.

[3] A client may expressly or impliedly ask the lawyer for purely technical advice. When such a request is made by a client experienced in legal matters, the lawyer may accept it at face value. When such a request is made by a client inexperienced in legal matters, however, the lawyer's responsibility as advisor may include indicating that more may be involved than strictly legal considerations.

[4] Matters that go beyond strictly legal questions may also be in the domain of another profession. Family matters can involve problems within the professional competence of psychiatry, clinical psychology or social work; business matters can involve problems within the competence of the accounting profession or of financial specialists. Where consultation with a professional in another field is itself something a competent lawyer would recommend, the lawyer should make such a recommendation. At the same time, a lawyer's advice at its best often consists of recommending a course of action in the face of conflicting recommendations of experts.

Offering Advice

[5] In general, a lawyer is not expected to give advice until asked by the client. However, when a lawyer knows that a client proposes a course of action that is likely to result in substantial adverse legal consequences to the client, the lawyer's duty to the client under Rule 1.4 may require that the lawyer offer advice if the client's course of action is related to the representation. Similarly, when a matter is likely to involve litigation, it may be necessary under Rule 1.4 to inform the client of forms of dispute resolution that might constitute reasonable alternatives to litigation. A lawyer ordinarily has no duty to initiate investigation of a client's affairs or to give advice that the client has indicated is unwanted, but a lawyer may initiate advice to a client when doing so appears to be in the client's interest.

Rule 4.1 Truthfulness In Statements To Others—Comment

Misrepresentation

[1] A lawyer is required to be truthful when dealing with others on a client's behalf, but generally has no affirmative duty to inform an opposing party of relevant facts. A misrepresentation can occur if the lawyer incorporates or affirms a statement of another person that the lawyer knows is false. Misrepresentations can also occur by partially true but misleading statements or omissions that are the equivalent of affirmative false statements. For dishonest conduct that does not amount to a false statement or for misrepresentations by a lawyer other than in the course of representing a client, see Rule 8.4.

Statements of Fact

[2] This Rule refers to statements of fact. Whether a particular statement should be regarded as one of fact can depend on the circumstances. Under generally accepted conventions in negotiation, certain types of statements ordinarily are not taken as statements of material fact. Estimates of price or value placed on the subject of a transaction and a party's intentions as to an acceptable settlement of a claim are ordinarily in this category, and so is the existence of an undisclosed principal except where nondisclosure of the principal

would constitute fraud. Lawyers should be mindful of their obligations under applicable law to avoid criminal and tortious misrepresentation.

Crime or Fraud by Client

[3] Under Rule 1.2(d), a lawyer is prohibited from counseling or assisting a client in conduct that the lawyer knows is criminal or fraudulent. Paragraph (b) states a specific application of the principle set forth in Rule 1.2(d) and addresses the situation where a client's crime or fraud takes the form of a lie or misrepresentation. Ordinarily, a lawyer can avoid assisting a client's crime or fraud by withdrawing from the representation. Sometimes it may be necessary for the lawyer to give notice of the fact of withdrawal and to disaffirm an opinion, document, affirmation or the like. In extreme cases, substantive law may require a lawyer to disclose information relating to the representation to avoid being deemed to have assisted the client's crime or fraud. If the lawyer can avoid assisting a client's crime or fraud only by disclosing this information, then under paragraph (b) the lawyer is required to do so, unless the disclosure is prohibited by Rule 1.6.

Rule 5.5 Unauthorized Practice Of Law; Multijurisdictional Practice Of Law—Comment

[1] A lawyer may practice law only in a jurisdiction in which the lawyer is authorized to practice. A lawyer may be admitted to practice law in a jurisdiction on a regular basis or may be authorized by court rule or order or by law to practice for a limited purpose or on a restricted basis. Paragraph (a) applies to unauthorized practice of law by a lawyer, whether through the lawyer's direct action or by the lawyer assisting another person.

[2] The definition of the practice of law is established by law and varies from one jurisdiction to another. Whatever the definition, limiting the practice of law to members of the bar protects the public against rendition of legal services by unqualified persons. This Rule does not prohibit a lawyer from employing the services of paraprofessionals and delegating functions to them, so long as the lawyer supervises the delegated work and retains responsibility for their work. See Rule 5.3.

[3] A lawyer may provide professional advice and instruction to nonlawyers whose employment requires knowledge of the law; for example, claims adjusters, employees of financial or commercial institutions, social workers, accountants and persons employed in government agencies. Lawyers also may assist independent nonlawyers, such as paraprofessionals, who are authorized by the law of a jurisdiction to provide particular law-related services. In addition, a lawyer may counsel nonlawyers who wish to proceed pro se.

[4] Other than as authorized by law or this Rule, a lawyer who is not admitted to practice generally in this jurisdiction violates paragraph (b) if the lawyer establishes an office or other systematic and continuous presence in this jurisdiction for the practice of law. Presence may be systematic and continuous even if the lawyer is not physically present here. Such a lawyer must not hold out to the public or otherwise represent that the lawyer is admitted to practice law in this jurisdiction. See also Rules 7.1(a) and 7.5(b).

[5] There are occasions in which a lawyer admitted to practice in another United States jurisdiction, and not disbarred or suspended from practice in any jurisdiction, may provide legal services on a temporary basis in this jurisdiction under circumstances that do not create an unreasonable risk to the interests of their clients, the public or the courts. Paragraph (c) identifies four such circumstances. The fact that conduct is not so identified does not imply that the conduct is or is not authorized. With the exception of paragraphs (d)(1) and (d)(2), this Rule does not authorize a lawyer to establish an office or other systematic and continuous presence in this jurisdiction without being admitted to practice generally here.

[6] There is no single test to determine whether a lawyer's services are provided on a "temporary basis" in this jurisdiction, and may therefore be permissible under paragraph (c). Services may be "temporary" even though the lawyer provides services in this jurisdiction on a recurring basis, or for an extended period of time, as when the lawyer is representing a client in a single lengthy negotiation or litigation.

[7] Paragraphs (c) and (d) apply to lawyers who are admitted to practice law in any United States jurisdiction, which includes the District of Columbia and any state, territory or commonwealth of the United States. The word "admitted" in paragraph (c) contemplates that the lawyer is authorized to practice in the jurisdiction in which the lawyer is admitted and excludes a lawyer who while technically admitted is not authorized to practice, because, for example, the lawyer is on inactive status.

[8] Paragraph (c)(1) recognizes that the interests of clients and the public are protected if a lawyer admitted only in another jurisdiction associates with a lawyer licensed to practice in this jurisdiction. For this paragraph to apply, however, the lawyer admitted to practice in this jurisdiction must actively participate in and share responsibility for the representation of the client.

[9] Lawyers not admitted to practice generally in a jurisdiction may be authorized by law or order of a tribunal or an administrative agency to appear before the tribunal or agency. This authority may be granted pursuant to formal rules governing admission pro hac vice or pursuant to informal practice of the tribunal or agency. Under paragraph (c)(2), a lawyer does not violate this Rule when the lawyer appears before a tribunal or agency pursuant to such authority. To the extent that a court rule or other law of this jurisdiction requires a lawyer who is not admitted to practice in this jurisdiction to obtain admission pro hac vice before appearing before a tribunal or administrative agency, this Rule requires the lawyer to obtain that authority.

[10] Paragraph (c)(2) also provides that a lawyer rendering services in this jurisdiction on a temporary basis does not violate this Rule when the lawyer engages in conduct in anticipation of a proceeding or hearing in a jurisdiction in which the lawyer is authorized to practice law or in which the lawyer reasonably expects to be admitted pro hac vice. Examples of such conduct include meetings with the client, interviews of potential witnesses, and the review of documents. Similarly, a lawyer admitted only in another jurisdiction may engage in conduct temporarily in this jurisdiction in connection with pending litigation in another jurisdiction in which the lawyer is or reasonably expects to be authorized to appear, including taking depositions in this jurisdiction.

[11] When a lawyer has been or reasonably expects to be admitted to appear before a court or administrative agency, paragraph (c)(2) also permits conduct by lawyers who are associated with that lawyer in the matter, but who do not expect to appear before the court or administrative agency. For example, subordinate lawyers may conduct research, review documents, and attend meetings with witnesses in support of the lawyer responsible for the litigation.

[12] Paragraph (c)(3) permits a lawyer admitted to practice law in another jurisdiction to perform services on a temporary basis in this jurisdiction if those services are in or reasonably related to a pending or potential arbitration, mediation, or other alternative dispute resolution proceeding in this or another jurisdiction, if the services arise out of or are reasonably related to the lawyer's practice in a jurisdiction in which the lawyer is admitted to practice. The lawyer, however, must obtain admission pro hac vice in the case of a court-annexed arbitration or mediation or otherwise if court rules or law so require.

[13] Paragraph (c)(4) permits a lawyer admitted in another jurisdiction to provide certain legal services on a temporary basis in this jurisdiction that arise out of or are reasonably related to the lawyer's practice in a jurisdiction in which the lawyer is admitted but are not within paragraphs (c)(2) or (c)(3). These services include both legal services and services that nonlawyers may perform but that are considered the practice of law when performed by lawyers.

[14] Paragraphs (c)(3) and (c)(4) require that the services arise out of or be reasonably related to the lawyer's practice in a jurisdiction in which the lawyer is admitted. A variety of factors evidence such a relationship. The lawyer's client may have been previously represented by the lawyer, or may be resident in or have substantial contacts with the jurisdiction in which the lawyer is admitted. The matter, although involving other jurisdictions, may have a significant connection with that jurisdiction. In other cases, significant aspects of the lawyer's work might be conducted in that jurisdiction or a significant aspect of the matter may involve the law of that jurisdiction. The necessary relationship might arise when the client's activities or the legal issues involve

multiple jurisdictions, such as when the officers of a multinational corporation survey potential business sites and seek the services of their lawyer in assessing the relative merits of each. In addition, the services may draw on the lawyer's recognized expertise developed through the regular practice of law on behalf of clients in matters involving a particular body of federal, nationally uniform, foreign, or international law.

[15] Paragraph (d) identifies two circumstances in which a lawyer who is admitted to practice in another United States jurisdiction, and is not disbarred or suspended from practice in any jurisdiction, may establish an office or other systematic and continuous presence in this jurisdiction for the practice of law as well as provide legal services on a temporary basis. Except as provided in paragraphs (d)(1) and (d)(2), a lawyer who is admitted to practice law in another jurisdiction and who establishes an office or other systematic or continuous presence in this jurisdiction must become admitted to practice law generally in this jurisdiction.

[16] Paragraph (d)(1) applies to a lawyer who is employed by a client to provide legal services to the client or its organizational affiliates, i.e., entities that control, are controlled by, or are under common control with the employer. This paragraph does not authorize the provision of personal legal services to the employer's officers or employees. The paragraph applies to in-house corporate lawyers, government lawyers and others who are employed to render legal services to the employer. The lawyer's ability to represent the employer outside the jurisdiction in which the lawyer is licensed generally serves the interests of the employer and does not create an unreasonable risk to the client and others because the employer is well situated to assess the lawyer's qualifications and the quality of the lawyer's work.

[17] If an employed lawyer establishes an office or other systematic presence in this jurisdiction for the purpose of rendering legal services to the employer, the lawyer may be subject to registration or other requirements, including assessments for client protection funds and mandatory continuing legal education.

[18] Paragraph (d)(2) recognizes that a lawyer may provide legal services in a jurisdiction in which the lawyer is not licensed when authorized to do so by federal or other law, which includes statute, court rule, executive regulation or judicial precedent.

[19] A lawyer who practices law in this jurisdiction pursuant to paragraphs (c) or (d) or otherwise is subject to the disciplinary authority of this jurisdiction. See Rule 8.5(a).

[20] In some circumstances, a lawyer who practices law in this jurisdiction pursuant to paragraphs (c) or (d) may have to inform the client that the lawyer is not licensed to practice law in this jurisdiction. For example, that may be required when the representation occurs primarily in this jurisdiction and requires knowledge of the law of this jurisdiction. See Rule 1.4(b).

[21] Paragraphs (c) and (d) do not authorize communications advertising legal services to prospective clients in this jurisdiction by lawyers who are admitted to practice in other jurisdictions. Whether and how lawyers may communicate the availability of their services to prospective clients in this jurisdiction is governed by Rules 7.1 to 7.5.

Rule 8.4 Misconduct—Comment

[1] Lawyers are subject to discipline when they violate or attempt to violate the Rules of Professional Conduct, knowingly assist or induce another to do so or do so through the acts of another, as when they request or instruct an agent to do so on the lawyer's behalf. Paragraph (a), however, does not prohibit a lawyer from advising a client concerning action the client is legally entitled to take.

[2] Many kinds of illegal conduct reflect adversely on fitness to practice law, such as offenses involving fraud and the offense of willful failure to file an income tax return. However, some kinds of offenses carry no such implication. Traditionally, the distinction was drawn in terms of offenses involving "moral turpitude." That concept can be construed to include offenses concerning some matters of personal morality, such as adultery and comparable offenses, that have no specific connection to fitness for the practice of law. Although a lawyer is personally answerable to the entire criminal law, a lawyer should be professionally answerable only

for offenses that indicate lack of those characteristics relevant to law practice. Offenses involving violence, dishonesty, breach of trust, or serious interference with the administration of justice are in that category. A pattern of repeated offenses, even ones of minor significance when considered separately, can indicate indifference to legal obligation.

[3] A lawyer who, in the course of representing a client, knowingly manifests by words or conduct, bias or prejudice based upon race, sex, religion, national origin, disability, age, sexual orientation or socioeconomic status, violates paragraph (d) when such actions are prejudicial to the administration of justice. Legitimate advocacy respecting the foregoing factors does not violate paragraph (d). A trial judge's finding that peremptory challenges were exercised on a discriminatory basis does not alone establish a violation of this rule.

[4] A lawyer may refuse to comply with an obligation imposed by law upon a good faith belief that no valid obligation exists. The provisions of Rule 1.2(d) concerning a good faith challenge to the validity, scope, meaning or application of the law apply to challenges of legal regulation of the practice of law.

[5] Lawyers holding public office assume legal responsibilities going beyond those of other citizens. A lawyer's abuse of public office can suggest an inability to fulfill the professional role of lawyers. The same is true of abuse of positions of private trust such as trustee, executor, administrator, guardian, agent and officer, director or manager of a corporation or other organization.

Additional Exercises

Exercise 31-1[1]

Revised Car Purchase Agreement

Please redraft your draft of the Car Purchase Agreement (Exercise 5-1) based on the material that you have covered so far this semester. In addition, include appropriate provisions to reflect the following changes to the transaction's terms:

1. The Buyer has decided that it is appropriate to do a bit of due diligence and not to rely solely on the Seller's representations and warranties. The Seller has agreed that the Buyer has the right not to close if a mechanic of the Buyer's choice determines that the car is not in the condition represented. (Think through the real-world steps that will be necessary for the Buyer to accomplish the inspection. Remember that during the gap period between signing and closing the Seller has control of the car.) The Buyer has agreed to pay for the inspection.

2. The Seller is insisting on a downpayment of 10 percent, plus an additional 10 percent after completion of the mechanic's inspection.

3. The car's Vehicle Identification Number is 23456.

4. The Buyer has been looking for a job as an associate at a law firm and has received an offer from Hie Power & Stress LLP. He wants to be able to call off the closing if he does not receive the promised $5,000 sign-on bonus. In order to induce the Seller to accept this proposal, the Buyer agreed that if the Buyer did not close because he did not receive his sign-on bonus, the Seller could keep the downpayment. The Seller would also like some assurance in the contract that the Buyer has received an offer from Hie Power.

5. The Seller has agreed to deliver the car, the keys, and any manuals to the Buyer's home no later than the Closing Date.

6. The Seller has told the Buyer that the car is still under the manufacturer's warranty and that she has its documentation. The Buyer was delighted to learn this but wants to know what the warranty provides. If it is not reasonably acceptable, he does not want to purchase the car. Without stating the details of the warranty, provide the Buyer with the comfort he has asked for.

---

1. This Exercise is based on an exercise that Alan Shaw created.

7. Make sure to follow the cash and provide for all appropriate contingencies as to its payment—both if the transaction closes and if it does not close. If you believe the agreement is unclear who is entitled to the money under a particular circumstance, choose one of the possibilities and draft a cover memo explaining your choice.

For the purposes of this exercise, assume that the contract has not yet been executed. Stated otherwise, each of these provisions is part of the original contract and are not amendments to an agreement that is already in effect.

Exercise 31-2

Aircraft Purchase Agreement

Memorandum

To: A. Barrister

From: H. Flighty

Date: October 10, 20XX

Re: Purchase of the G550

As you know, I have not finalized my deal with Rob Robertson. I think that deal will fall through. If it does, I suspect my entire net worth will be at risk as I have yet to find financing to consummate the G550 purchase from Samson's company.

Last evening, Sam called and asked why my lawyers hadn't sent out a draft agreement. I told him that I would see what was holding you up. Obviously, what was holding you up was that I hadn't asked you to draft the rest of the agreement. Now, however, we must go forward.

Please do not reinvent the wheel on this transaction. I have attached to this memo as **Exhibit A** a document that combines

(a) the draft I gave you that had the preamble, recitals, words of agreement, and definitions (the First Draft); and

(b) representations and warranties, covenants, and conditions from an Asset Purchase Agreement that a friend of mine used in another transaction.

I have also attached a photo of the G550 and its specifications. I thought you might be interested to see what I'm buying.

To complete the draft for my review, please do the following:

(i)   Redraft **Exhibit A** to take into account our prior discussion of the First Draft. If we didn't discuss something, but it needs revision, do it.

(ii) Insert the action sections that you previously worked on, making any necessary revisions.

(iii) Redraft the remaining provisions of **Exhibit A** to reflect our deal. They will probably need a fair amount of revision. Do not use any supplementary sources, other than those distributed to you in that drafting course you took at law school.

In order to save money, do not draft provisions other than the ones I've specifically asked for, or which are required because of the cascade effect.

In your redraft, please take into account the following:

1. Please carefully review the litigation representation and warranty. The first sentence seems overbroad to me. The issue is not that no one in the world is a party to litigation. Instead, we care if Wings is a party to a litigation or if a litigation involves the Aircraft. Please redraft this representation and warranty accordingly.

2. In our discussions, Sam advised me that Wings is not in default under the Pilot Agreement, but that it is in default under the Maintenance Agreement. The default has given rise to a $250,000 lien against the G550 in favor of Greasemonkeys, Inc. I told Sam that I considered this lien material. Sam specifically stated that no other liens had been filed against the Aircraft—material or otherwise. He then promised me that between now and the Closing the Greasemonkeys lien would be removed. Obviously, this point needs to be covered wherever appropriate in the Aircraft Purchase Agreement. If that lien is not removed by Closing, I would like the right not to close as well as the right to sue for damages.

3. Delete in whole or in part any representation and warranty, covenant, or condition that is inapposite, or change it to fit the facts as I have described them to you. One thing I am certain of is that I cannot represent and warrant that I have financing now. I doubt that Sam will go for it, but try drafting a financing out.

    As I'm sure you know, a financing out provides a buyer with a walk-away right if it is unable to obtain financing. Sellers generally dislike financing outs, fearing that they transform an obligation to purchase into an option to purchase. Specifically, they worry that a buyer may decide it dislikes a deal and then try to get out of it by claiming it could not obtain any financing or could not obtain financing on commercially reasonable terms. If that happens, a seller could end up losing other sale opportunities, while tied up for months in a contract with the buyer. If you can think of something that might make the financing out tolerable to Sam (but one that I could live with), please add it to the draft.

4. As far as I know, Wings's only tangible asset is the G550. Please make sure that the contract reflects this. I want it explicitly covered because if Wings does own any spare parts or anything else related to the Aircraft, I want them to be part of this deal. I'm certainly paying enough.

5. My recollection is that I inappropriately included at least one substantive provision in the definition article of the Aircraft Purchase Agreement. Please move it to the appropriate section in the body of the agreement. Also include whatever representations and warranties, covenants, and conditions that the Purchase Offer requires. If it is unclear whether a term is a covenant or a condition, I'd like to be able to sue as well as to get out of this deal.

6. Samson told me that the G550's maximum range with eight passengers and four crew members is 6000 nautical miles. That's a fabulous distance. Please make sure that the contract includes this information.

7. Sam has agreed to have the Aircraft's tail painted by the Closing with Fly-by-Night's logo. But, the paint shop may have trouble fitting in the G550 in between now and Closing. If the Aircraft is not painted on time, we've agreed that I don't have to close.

8. The draft attached as **Exhibit A** is rife with drafting errors. There's legalese; provisions are way too long; and there's a total lack of craftsmanship. Please clean it up.

9. Please spell out how the escrowed amount is to be distributed if we don't close. Figure out all the reasons we might not close and make sure that the escrow is distributed appropriately. Remember. *Follow the cash.* Also, my recollection is that the Purchase Offer requires me to pay $3 million if the deal doesn't close because of something I did wrong. Please figure out how this interacts with the financing out.

continued on next page >

10. It is very important that Wings maintain its status quo during the period between the signing of the contract and Closing. Except for ordinary course transactions, please be sure that they have to come to me if they even want to sneeze. It seems as if the types of transactions about which I'm worried are those listed in Section 5.5 of **Exhibit A.**

11. I always worry about government regulation. Is there any notice that has to be given to any governmental agency because Wings is selling the G550? If so, who has to give the notice and by when? Please draft the appropriate provisions.

12. I've also been worrying about the Engines. My mechanic didn't think that they were properly maintained. I don't think that the seller can say more than that they are in adequate condition. The rest of the Aircraft, however, was in good condition, except for ordinary wear and tear. Please provide that between now and the closing the Aircraft will be maintained and repaired in accordance with its FAA Approved Maintenance and Inspection Program. That should bring the Engines to an appropriate maintenance level before closing. Also, please make sure that the seller is obligated to keep the Aircraft's logbook and other flight maintenance records accurate, complete, and current.

13. Please make clear that this agreement supersedes the Purchase Offer. Do not draft any other "boilerplate" provisions. Sam and I have agreed to deal with those issues in a later draft.

14. Include the appropriate signature lines.

When you send me the finished agreement, please include a cover memo, highlighting any outstanding issues. In addition, use the cover memo to explain how you addressed any provision that you thought was ambiguous or any request that I made that was unclear to you.

Finally, please draft a fair agreement, one that you think the other side could accept. But, remember, you are my lawyer.

H.F.

Attachments
Exhibit A

Note to students: The following draft of the Aircraft Purchase Agreement is on the *Drafting Contracts* Website.

PERFORMANCE

*Maximum Range at Mach 0.80	6,750 nm	/	12,501 km
*Maximum Range at Mach 0.85	6,000 nm	/	11,112 km
*Maximum Range at Mach 0.87	5,000 nm	/	9,260 km

(8 passengers, 4 crew and NBAA IFR reserves)

Mmo (Maximum Operating Mach Number)			Mach 0.885
Takeoff Distance (SL, ISA, MTOW)	5,910 ft	/	1,801 m
Landing Distance (SL, ISA, MLW)	2,770 ft	/	844 m
Initial Cruise Altitude	41,000 ft	/	12,497 m
Maximum Cruise Altitude	51,000 ft	/	15,545 m

WEIGHTS

Maximum Takeoff Weight	91,000 lb	/	41,277 kg
Maximum Landing Weight	75,300 lb	/	34,156 kg
Maximum Zero Fuel Weight	54,500 lb	/	24,721 kg
**Basic Operating Weight (including 4 crew)	48,300 lb	/	21,909 kg
**Maximum Payload	6,200 lb	/	2,812 kg
**Payload with Maximum Fuel	1,800 lb	/	816 kg
Maximum Fuel Weight	41,300 lb	/	18,733 kg

DESIGN STANDARDS

Engines (2)			Rolls-Royce BR710 C4-11
Rated Takeoff Thrust (each)	15,385 lb	/	68.4 kN
Passengers: Maximum			19
Typical Outfitting			14 - 18

INTERIOR

Cabin Length	50 ft 1 in	/	15.27 m
Cabin Height	6 ft 2 in	/	1.88 m
Cabin Width	7 ft 4 in	/	2.24 m
Cabin Volume	1,669 cu ft	/	47.3 cu m
Baggage Compartment Volume	226 cu ft	/	6.4 cu m

EXTERIOR

Length	96 ft 5 in	/	29.39 m
Height	25 ft 10 in	/	7.87 m
Wingspan	93 ft 6 in	/	28.50 m

* NBAA IFR theoretical range. Actual range will be affected by ATC routing, operating speed, weather, outfitting options and other factors.

** Stated weights are based on theoretical standard outfitting configurations. Actual weights will be affected by outfitting options and other factors.

Gulfstream®
A GENERAL DYNAMICS COMPANY

10.5.5M

AIRCRAFT SALES AGREEMENT

AGREEMENT, dated October 30, 20XX, by and among Supersonic Wings Corp., a Delaware corporation, (the "Seller") and Fly-by-Night Aviation, Inc., a New York corporation having its principal place of business at 987 East 48th Street, New York, New York 12345 ("Buyer").

WHEREAS, the Seller desires to sell to Buyer, and Buyer desires to purchase from the Seller, the Aircraft; and

WHEREAS, the Buyer hereby agrees to pay the Seller $23,000,000 in immediately available funds.

NOW, THEREFORE, in consideration of the mutual promises herein set forth and subject to the terms and conditions hereof, the parties agree as follows:

Article 1. Definitions

1.1 Defined Terms. As used in this Agreement, terms defined in the preamble and recitals of this Agreement have the meanings set forth therein, and the following terms have the meanings set forth below:

"Agreement" means this Agreement of Sale and all Schedules and Exhibits hereto, as the same may be amended from time to time.

"Aircraft" means the Airframe, equipped with two Rolls-Royce Tay engines model number MK611-8 bearing Serial Numbers 72725 and 72726, together with all appliances, avionics, furnishings, and other components, equipment, and property incorporated in, attached to, or otherwise related to, the Airframe and engines.

"Airframe" means the Gulfstream Aerospace Corporation G550 aircraft, bearing United States Registration No. N765BW and Manufacturer's Serial No. 8181.

"Assigned Contracts" means the Maintenance Agreement (as hereafter defined) and the Pilot Agreement (as hereafter defined).

"Assumed Liabilities" means all liabilities and obligations that (i) arise under the Maintenance Agreement on or after the date hereof and (ii) arise under the Pilot Agreement on or after the date of the Closing.

"Aviation Fuel" means any gas or liquid that is used to create power to propel an aircraft. At the time of the Seller's delivery of the Aircraft to Buyer, the fuel gauge of the Aircraft shall register as full.

"Closing" means the closing of the sale of the Aircraft contemplated by this Agreement in New York, New York, on the Closing Date.

"Closing Date" has the meaning specified in Section 2.04(a).

"Consent" shall mean any consent, approval, authorization of, notice to, or designation, registration, declaration or filing with, any Person.

"Contract" shall mean any contract, lease, agreement, license, instrument, arrangement, commitment, or understanding to which the Buyer or any Seller is a party or by which it or any of its properties or assets may be bound or affected.

"Engines" means the two Rolls-Royce Tay engines model number MK611-8 bearing Serial Numbers 72725 and 72726.

"Laws" means all Federal, state, local or foreign laws, rules, and regulations.

"Lien" means any lien, charge, encumbrance, security interest, mortgage, or pledge.

"Maintenance Agreement" means that certain Maintenance Agreement, dated as of April 3, 2004, between Greasemonkeys, Inc., and Seller, as the same may be amended from time to time.

"Note" means the Buyer's 9 percent promissory note, payable to the order of the Seller, in the principal amount of $5,000,000, due on December 31, 2010, substantially in the form of **Exhibit A** to this Agreement.

"Order": any judgment, award, order, writ, injunction or decree issued by any Federal, state, local or foreign authority, court, tribunal, agency, or other governmental authority, or by any arbitrator, to which any Seller or its assets are subject, or to which the Buyer or its assets are subject, as the case may be.

"Person" shall mean any individual, a partnership, joint venture, corporation, trust, unincorporated organization, government (and any department or agency thereof) or other entity.

"Pilot Agreement" means that certain Pilot Agreement between Seller and Ace Pilots, Inc., dated as of May 12, 2005, as the same may be amended from time to time.

Article 2. Purchase and Sale

[To be inserted.]

Article 3. Representations and Warranties of the Seller

The Seller represents and warrants to the Buyer as follows:

3.1 Organization, Good Standing. The Seller is a corporation duly organized, validly existing and in good standing under the laws of the state of its incorporation as set forth in Schedule 2, with all requisite corporate power and authority to own, operate and lease its properties, and to carry on its business as now being conducted. The Seller is duly qualified to do business and is in good standing in each jurisdiction where the conduct of its business or the ownership of its property requires such qualification. The jurisdictions in which the Seller is qualified to do business are set forth in Schedule 2 hereto.

3.2 Authority. The Seller has full corporate power, authority and legal right to execute and deliver, and to perform its obligations under this Agreement and to consummate the transactions contemplated hereunder, and has taken all necessary action to authorize the purchase hereunder on the terms and conditions of this Agreement and to authorize the execution, delivery and performance of this Agreement. This Agreement has been duly executed by the Seller and constitutes a legal, valid, and binding obligation of the Seller enforceable against Seller in accordance with its terms, except as such enforceability may be limited by applicable bankruptcy, insolvency, or other similar laws from time to time in effect, which affect the enforcement of creditors' rights in general and by general principles of equity regardless of whether such enforceability is considered in a proceeding in equity or at law.

3.3 Absence of Undisclosed Liabilities. To the knowledge of the Seller, based upon facts known to it as of the date hereof, no basis exists for assertions against the Seller of any material claim or liability of any nature, other than any claim or liability disclosed to the Buyer herein.

3.4 Noncontravention; Adverse Agreements. Neither the execution and the delivery of this Agreement by Seller nor the consummation of the transactions contemplated hereby will (i) conflict with or result in any violation of the certificate of incorporation or the by-laws of the Seller, (ii) result in the violation of any Law or Order applicable to the Seller or any of its assets, or (iii) will conflict with, result in the breach of (with or without notice or lapse of time or both), or constitute a default under (with or without notice or lapse of time or both), any Contract to which the Seller is a party or to which the Seller or its assets is subject. The Seller is not a party to or subject to any Contract or any Law or Order that materially and adversely affects the business, operations, prospects, properties, assets or condition, financial or otherwise, of the Seller.

3.5 Governmental and other Consents, etc. No consent, approval or authorization of or designation, declaration or filing with any governmental authority or other persons or entities on the part of the Seller is required in connection with the execution or delivery of this Agreement or the consummation of the transactions contemplated hereby, except for notification to and consents from the persons specified in **Schedule 3.6.**

3.6 Title to Assets. A description of all real property owned by the Seller is set forth in Schedule 5. Except as set forth in said Schedule 5 or in any title insurance policy obtained by the Buyer prior to the execution of this Agreement by the Buyer, the Seller has good title to all its properties and assets, real, personal and intangible, subject to no mortgage, pledge, lien, security interest, lease, charge, encumbrance or conditional sale or other title retention agreement, except for such imperfections of title, liens, easements or encumbrances, if any, as are not material.

3.7 Agreements. A list and brief description of all agreements to which the Seller is a party is set forth in Schedule 6. All such agreements are valid and effective in accordance with their respective terms. Except as set forth in Schedule 6, there are no existing defaults or events which with notice or lapse of time or both would constitute defaults thereunder, the consequences of which in the aggregate would have a material adverse effect on the business and operations of the Seller.

3.8 Condition of Property. Except as set forth in Schedule 7, the plants, structures, and equipment of the Seller are in good operating condition and repair, subject only to ordinary wear and tear.

3.9 Litigation and Law Compliance. There is no suit, action or litigation pending or, to the best of Seller's knowledge, threatened. The Seller has complied with and is not in default under any Laws the violation of which could have a material adverse effect on the business, properties, assets, or operations, or on the condition, financial or otherwise, of the Seller. Seller agrees to comply in all material respects with any Law the violation of which could have a material adverse effect on the Seller.

Article 4. Representations and Warranties of the Buyer

The Buyer represents and warrants to the Seller as follows:

4.1 The Buyer is a corporation duly incorporated, validly existing and in good standing under the laws of its jurisdiction of incorporation and has all requisite corporate power and authority and legal right to own, operate and lease its properties and assets and to carry on its business as now being conducted.

4.2 Authority. The Buyer has full corporate power, authority and legal right to execute and deliver, and to perform its obligations under this Agreement and to consummate the transactions contemplated hereunder, and has taken all necessary action to authorize the purchase hereunder on the terms and conditions of this Agreement and to authorize the execution, delivery and performance of this Agreement. This Agreement has been duly executed by the Buyer, and constitutes a legal, valid and binding obligation of the Buyer enforceable against Buyer in accordance with its terms except as such enforceability may be limited by applicable bankruptcy, insolvency, or other similar laws from time to time in effect, which affect the enforcement of creditors' rights in general and by general principles of equity regardless of whether such enforceability is considered in a proceeding in equity or at law.

4.3 Compliance with Instruments, Consents, Adverse Agreements. Neither the execution and the delivery of this Agreement by Buyer nor the consummation of the transactions contemplated hereby will conflict with or result in any violation of or constitute a default under any term of the certificate of incorporation or the bylaws of the Buyer, or conflict with or result in any violation of or constitute a default under any Law or Contract by which the Buyer is, or its properties or assets are, bound. The Buyer is not a party to or subject to any Contract, or subject to any charter or other corporate restriction or any Law which materially and adversely affects the business, operations, prospects, properties, assets or condition, financial or otherwise, of the Buyer.

4.4 Financing. Buyer has all monies or appropriate binding commitments from responsible financial institutions to provide Buyer with funds sufficient to satisfy the obligations of Buyer to Seller under this Agreement.

Article 5. Covenants of the Seller

The Seller agrees that prior to the Closing:

5.1 Cooperation. To use its best efforts to cause the sale contemplated by this Agreement to be consummated, and, without limiting the generality of the foregoing, to obtain the Consents, permits and licenses that may be necessary or reasonably required in order for the Seller to effect the transactions contemplated hereby.

5.2 Transactions Out of Ordinary Course of Business. Except with the prior written consent of the Buyer, the Seller shall not enter into any transaction out of the ordinary course of business.

5.3 Maintenance of Properties, etc. To maintain all of its properties in customary repair, order and condition (taking into consideration the age and condition thereof), reasonable wear and tear excepted.

5.4 Access to Properties, etc. The Seller shall give to the Buyer and to its counsel, accountants, and other representatives access during normal business hours (upon reasonable prior notice) to copies of all of its Contracts and Permits, books and records, and shall furnish to the Buyer all such documents and information with respect to the affairs of the Seller as the Buyer may from time to time reasonably request.

5.5 Ordinary Course. The Seller shall not (i) enter into any contract to merge or consolidate with any other corporation, (ii) change the character of its business, or sell, transfer or otherwise dispose of any material assets other than in the ordinary course of business or (iii) declare or pay any dividend or other distribution in respect of shares of capital stock. In addition, the Seller agrees not to make any purchase, redemption or other acquisition, directly or indirectly, of any outstanding shares of its capital stock or purchase any assets or securities of any Person, except with the prior written consent of the Buyer.

Article 6. Covenants of the Buyer

The Buyer agrees that prior to the Closing:

6.1 Cooperation. The Buyer shall use its best efforts to cause the sale contemplated by this Agreement to be consummated, and, without limiting the generality of the foregoing, to obtain the Consents and Permits which may be necessary or reasonably required in order for the Buyer to effect the transactions contemplated hereby.

Article 7. Conditions to the Seller's Obligations

All obligations of the Seller under this Agreement are subject to the fulfillment, at the option of the Seller, at or prior to the Closing Date, of each of the following conditions:

7.1 Buyer's Representations and Warranties. The representations and warranties of the Buyer set forth herein shall be true in all material respects on and as of the Closing Date, except as affected by transactions contemplated or permitted by this Agreement.

7.2 Buyer's Covenants. The Buyer shall have performed all its obligations and agreements and complied with all its covenants contained in this Agreement to be performed and complied with by the Buyer prior to the Closing Date.

7.3 No Litigation. No action, suit or proceeding before any court or any governmental or regulatory authority shall have been commenced and still be pending, no investigation by any governmental or regulatory authority shall have been commenced and still be pending, and no action, suit or proceeding by any governmental or regulatory authority shall have been threatened against the Seller or the Buyer (i) seeking to restrain, prevent or change the transactions contemplated hereby or questioning the validity or legality of any of such transactions, or (ii) which if resolved adversely to such party would materially and adversely affect the financial condition, business, property, assets or prospects of any such Person.

7.4 Documentation. All matters and proceedings taken in connection with the Acquisition as herein contemplated, including forms of instruments and matters of title, shall be reasonably satisfactory to the Seller and to its counsel.

Article 8. Conditions to the Buyer's Obligations

All obligations of the Buyer under this Agreement are subject to the fulfillment, at the option of the Buyer, at or prior to the Closing Date, of each of the following conditions:

8.1 Seller's Representations and Warranties. The representations and warranties of the Seller contained herein shall be true and correct in all material respects on and as of the Closing Date, except as affected by transactions contemplated or permitted by this Agreement.

8.2 Seller's Covenants. The Seller shall have performed all of its obligations and agreements and complied with all of its covenants contained in this Agreement to be performed and complied with by it prior to the Closing Date.

8.3 No Litigation. No action, suit or proceeding before any court or any governmental or regulatory authority shall have been commenced and still be pending, no investigation by any governmental or regulatory authority shall have been commenced and still be pending, and no action, suit or proceeding by any governmental or regulatory authority shall have been threatened against the Seller or the Buyer (i) seeking to restrain, prevent or change the transactions contemplated hereby or questioning the validity or legality of any of such transactions or (ii) which if resolved adversely to such party, would materially and adversely affect the financial condition, business, Property, assets or prospects of any such Person.

8.4 Documentation. All matters and proceedings taken in connection with the Acquisition as herein contemplated, including forms of instruments and matters of title, shall be reasonably satisfactory to the Buyer and to its counsel.

Asset Purchase Agreement

Asset Purchase Agreement[1]

Asset Purchase Agreement dated as of December 2, 2002 by and among Ladder Maker, Inc., a New York corporation (the "Seller"), and Ladco LP, a limited partnership organized under the laws of the State of New Jersey (the "Buyer").

WHEREAS, the Seller desires to sell substantially all of its properties and assets to the Buyer and the Buyer desires to purchase substantially all of the properties and assets of the Seller;

NOW, THEREFORE, in consideration of the mutual promises herein set forth and subject to the terms and conditions hereof, the parties agree as follows:

Article 1. Definitions

1.1 **Definitions.** As used in this Agreement, the following terms shall have the meanings set forth below:

(a) **"Agreement"** shall mean this Asset Purchase Agreement and all Schedule and Exhibits hereto, as the same may from time to time be amended.

(b) **"Assumed Liabilities"** means all Liabilities of the Seller that

(i) are reserved for or disclosed in the Financial Statements or this Agreement to the extent so reserved for or disclosed (other than Retained Liabilities); or

(ii) arise after the date of the Financial Statements in the ordinary course of business and that are either disclosed, or not required to be disclosed, in this Agreement (other than Retained Liabilities); or

(iii) arise under Contracts of the Sellers (other than Retained Liabilities) which are (A) either disclosed, or not required to be disclosed, in this Agreement or (B) voluntarily assumed in writing by the Buyer; or

---

1. **WARNING:** This agreement is intended only as a teaching tool. The agreement is replete with substantive and drafting errors and has omitted important provisions.

(iv) are incurred to attorneys, accountants or others for services rendered in connection with the transactions contemplated by this Agreement; or

(v) are incurred for transfer taxes on the sale of the Purchased Assets (other than any such taxes which are Retained Liabilities);

(c) **"Cash Consideration"** has the meaning assigned in Section 2.2.

(d) **"Closing"** shall mean the closing of the transactions contemplated by this Agreement in New York, New York on the Closing Date.

(e) **"Closing Date"** shall mean December 30, 2002, or such other date, not later than December 31, 2002, as the Seller and the Buyer may agree to.

(f) **"Contract"** means any contract, lease, agreement, license, arrangement, commitment or understanding, oral or written, to which the Seller is a party or by which it or any of its properties or assets may be bound or affected.

(g) **"Excluded Assets"** shall mean the following assets and properties:

(i) The consideration delivered to the Seller pursuant to this Agreement for the Purchased Assets sold, transferred, assigned, conveyed, and delivered pursuant to this Agreement.

(ii) The Seller's right to enforce the Buyer's representations, warranties and agreements hereunder and the obligations of the Buyer to pay, perform or discharge the Liabilities of the Seller assumed by the Buyer pursuant to this Agreement and all other rights, including rights of indemnification, of the Seller under this Agreement or any instrument executed pursuant hereto.

(iii) The Seller's certificate of incorporation, corporate seal, minute books, stock books, and other corporate records having exclusively to do with the corporate organization and capitalization of the Seller.

(iv) The Seller's books of account, but the Seller agrees that the Buyer shall from time to time have the right to inspect said books and make copies thereof.

(v) Shares of the capital stock of the Seller, including shares held by the Seller as treasury shares.

(vi) The Properties or the proceeds received by the Seller from the sale of the Properties.

(vii) The properties, assets, and rights of the Seller set forth in **Schedule 1.1(g)** hereto.

(h) **"Financial Statements"** means the consolidated balance sheet of the Ladder Corporations as of December 31, 2001, and the related consolidated statements of earnings, changes in shareholders' equity and changes in financial position for the fiscal year then ended.

(i) **"Ladder Corporation"** shall be an individual reference to the Seller, New Jersey Ladder Makers, Inc., a New Jersey corporation and subsidiary of the Seller ("NJ Ladder Maker"), Stepladders, Inc., a New York corporation and a subsidiary of the Seller ("Stepladders"), and Construction Ladders, Inc., a former New York corporation and subsidiary of the Seller ("Construction").

(j) **"Ladder Corporations"** shall be a collective reference to the Seller, NJ Ladder Maker, Stepladders, and Construction.

(k) **"Liabilities"** shall mean all debts, liabilities, Contracts, commitments, taxes and other obligations of every kind and character of the Seller as each may exist at the Closing (whether accrued, absolute, contingent or otherwise and whether due or to become due) or which may arise in the future based upon events or a state of facts existing at the Closing.

(l) **"New Jersey Property"** shall mean the real estate and buildings owned by the Seller in Baltimore, Maryland, as described in **Schedule 1.1(l)** hereto.

(m) **"Purchased Assets"** shall mean all of the properties and assets (real and personal, tangible and intangible) of the Seller of every kind and wherever situated which are owned by the Seller or in which it has any right or interest (including, without limiting the generality of the foregoing and to the extent owned, its business as a going concern, its goodwill, franchises and all right, title and interest in and to the use of its corporate name and any derivatives or combinations thereof; its trademarks, trademark registrations and trademark applications, trade names, copyrights, copyright applications and copyright registrations, letters patent, patent applications, franchises, permits, licenses, processes, formulae, trade secrets, inventions and royalties (including all rights to sue for past infringement); its lands, leaseholds and other interests in land; its inventory, equipment and supplies; its cash, money on deposit with banks and others, certificates of deposit, commercial paper, stocks, bonds and other investments (other than the shares of capital stock of the Seller); its accounts receivable; its insurance policies; its causes of action, judgments, claims and demands of whatever nature; its tangible and intangible personal property of all kinds; its deferred charges, advance payments, prepaid items, claims for refunds, rights of offset and credits of all kinds; all credit balances of or inuring to the Seller under any state unemployment compensation plan or fund; its employment contracts, restrictive covenants and obligations of present and former officers and employees and of individuals and corporations; its contracts, rights under joint venture agreements or arrangements; and its files, papers and records relating to the aforesaid business, properties and assets), other than the Excluded Assets, and the Purchased Assets shall include without limitation all assets of the Seller reflected on the consolidated balance sheet of the Ladder Corporations as of December 31, 2001, examined by Ernst & Young, independent accountants, and all assets acquired since that date, except for the Excluded Assets and those assets which have been transferred or disposed of after December 31, 2001.

(n) **"Properties"** shall mean the New Jersey Property and the Virginia Property.

(o) **"Retained Liabilities"** means the following Liabilities:

(i) The Liabilities of the Seller described in Section 10.2(a) of this Agreement.

(ii)   Federal, state and local taxes on the gain on the sales of the Properties.

(iii) Liabilities that are secured by any lien upon the Properties, including transfer taxes, recording fees, title insurance premiums, attorneys fees and appraisal fees, expenses of sale of the Properties and amounts to be used by the Seller to discharge liens and encumbrances on the Properties.

(iv)   Liabilities or obligations of the Seller in connection with stock options or stock option plans.

(v)   Liabilities to the extent that they may be satisfied or paid by an insurer or insurers under an insurance policy issued to the Buyer or to the Seller.

(p) **"Virginia Property"** shall mean the real estate and buildings owned by the Seller in Richmond, Virginia, as described in **Schedule 1.1(p)** hereto.

Article 2. Purchase and Sale

2.1   Sale of Properties and Assets. At the Closing, the Seller shall sell, transfer, assign, convey and deliver to the Buyer, and the Buyer shall purchase, accept and acquire from the Seller, all of the Purchased Assets.

2.2   Purchase Price. The purchase price is $26,429,380 (the "Cash Consideration")[2] *plus* an assumption by the Buyer of the Assumed Liabilities of the Seller.

2.3   The Closing. The Closing will take place on the Closing Date at the offices of Workhard & Playlittle, counsel to the Buyer, 1180 Avenue of the Americas, New York, New York, beginning at 9:00 a.m. local time.

2.4   Instruments of Transfer; Payment of Purchase Price and Assumption of Liabilities; Further Assurances.

(a) **Seller's Deliveries.** At the Closing the Seller shall deliver to the Buyer:

(i)   A bill of sale, in a form satisfactory to the Buyer;

(ii)   An assignment of each lease under which the Seller is lessee, in a form satisfactory to the Buyer;

(iii) Assignments for all funds of the Seller on deposit with banks or other persons (other than Excluded Assets), in a form satisfactory to the Buyer; and

(iv)   Such other instrument or instruments of transfer as shall be necessary or appropriate to vest in the Buyer good and marketable title to the Purchased Assets of the Seller.

---

2. Cash Consideration is defined here to distinguish it from the second part of the purchase price, which is the Buyer's assumption of liabilities.

(b) **Buyer's Deliveries.** At the Closing, the Buyer shall deliver to the Seller the following:

(i) The Cash Consideration in immediately available funds;

(ii) An instrument, in a form satisfactory to the Seller, whereby the Buyer agrees to assume the Assumed Liabilities of the Seller;

(iii) Such further instruments as any creditor or other person to whom the Seller is obligated on any lease, agreement or instrument may timely and reasonably request as a condition to the release of the Seller from its obligation being assumed by the Buyer at the Closing, provided the Buyer shall not be required to deliver any such instrument

(A) if, in the reasonable opinion of the Buyer or the Buyer's counsel, the effect of the delivery of such instrument might be to modify, increase or otherwise adversely affect the Buyer's liability or obligation to such creditor or other person (expected to be incurred under this Agreement) or

(B) if delivery of such instrument would disclose any information which the Buyer reasonably desires not to disclose to such creditor or other person.

(c) **Further Assurances.** Following the Closing,

(i) at the request of the Buyer, the Seller shall deliver any further instruments of transfer and take all reasonable action as may be necessary or appropriate

(A) to vest in the Buyer good and marketable title to the Purchased Assets; and

(B) to transfer to the Buyer all licenses and permits necessary for the operation of the Purchased Assets;

and

(ii) at the request of the Seller, the Buyer shall deliver such further instruments as any creditor or other person to whom the Seller is obligated on any lease, agreement or instrument may timely and reasonably request as a condition to the release of the Seller from its obligation being assumed by the Buyer at the Closing, provided the Buyer shall not be required to deliver any such instrument

(A) if, in the reasonable opinion of the Buyer or the Buyer's counsel, the effect of the delivery of such instrument might be to modify, increase or otherwise adversely affect the Buyer's liability or obligation to such creditor or other person (expected to be incurred under this Agreement); or

(B) if delivery of such instrument would disclose any information which the Buyer reasonably desires not to disclose to such creditor or other person.

Article 3. Representations and Warranties of the Seller

The Seller represents and warrants to the Buyer as follows:

3.1 Organization; Good Standing. The Seller is a corporation duly organized, validly existing and in good standing under the laws of the state of its incorporation as set forth in **Schedule 3.1,** with all requisite corporate power and authority to own, operate and lease its properties, to carry on its business as now being conducted. The Seller is duly qualified to do business and is in good standing in each jurisdiction where the conduct of its business or the ownership of its property requires such qualification. The jurisdictions in which the Seller is qualified to do business are set forth in **Schedule 3.1** hereto. No person has any agreement, right, or option to acquire any share of stock of the Seller, other than as set forth in **Schedule 3.1.**

3.2 Subsidiaries. NJ Ladder Maker and Stepladders are the only subsidiaries of the Seller and neither NJ Ladder Maker nor Stepladders has any subsidiary corporations. The Seller owns all of the outstanding shares of NJ Ladder Maker and Stepladders free and clear of all liens, security interests, charges, and encumbrances. Neither NJ Ladder Maker nor Stepladder has any assets (other than the right to its corporate name) or any liabilities. The Seller had one subsidiary (Construction Ladders) which was liquidated after December 31, 2001 and before the date of this Agreement, and that subsidiary is not existing on the date of this Agreement.

3.3 Authority. The Seller has full corporate power and authority to execute and deliver this Agreement and to perform its obligations hereunder. The execution, delivery and performance of this Agreement have been duly authorized, or will have been duly authorized, by all necessary corporate action on the part of the Seller, and this Agreement has been duly executed and delivered by the Seller.

3.4 Enforceability. This Agreement is the legal, valid and binding obligation of the Seller, enforceable against the Seller in accordance with its terms, except to the extent that enforcement is limited by

(a) applicable bankruptcy, insolvency, reorganization, moratorium or other similar laws affecting creditors' rights generally; or

(b) general equitable principles, regardless of whether the issue of enforceability is considered in a proceeding in equity or at law.

3.5 Schedules, Exhibits and Other Information. All of the Schedules and Exhibits or other written material required under this Agreement do not and will not contain any statement which is false or misleading with respect to any material fact, and do not and will not omit to state a material fact necessary in order to make the statements therein not false or misleading.

3.6 Financial Statements. The consolidated balance sheets of the Ladder Corporations as of December 31, 2001, December 31, 2000, and December 31, 1999 and the related consolidated statements of earnings, changes in shareholders' equity and changes in financial position for each of the fiscal years then ended, including the related notes thereto, certified by Ernst & Young, independent accountants, have been prepared in accordance with generally accepted accounting principles applied on a basis consistent with that of the preceding years or periods and fairly present the financial position of the Ladder Corporations as of said date and the results of their operations for the period indicated. The Ladder Corporations' unaudited financial statements as of September 30, 2002 have been prepared in accordance with generally accepted accounting principles applied on a basis consistent with that of the preceding year or period and fairly present the financial position of the Ladder Corporations as of that date and the results of their operations for the period indicated.

3.7   Absence of Undisclosed Liabilities. Except to the extent reflected or reserved against in the financial statements dated December 31, 2001 referred to in Section 3.6, including the notes thereto, or as set forth in **Schedule 3.8** hereto, the Seller does not have any material liabilities or obligations of any nature, whether accrued, absolute, unliquidated, contingent or otherwise, and whether due or to become due, other than those incurred in the ordinary course of business.

3.8   No Material Adverse Change. Except as set forth in **Schedule 3.8,** since December 31, 2001, there has not been any one or more of the following:

(a)   Any material adverse change in the financial condition or in the operations, business, prospects, properties or assets of the Seller, from that shown on the Ladder Corporations' financial statements as of December 31, 2001.

(b)   Any material damage, destruction or loss to any of the properties or assets of the Seller, whether or not covered by insurance, which has materially and adversely affected or impaired or which does or may materially and adversely affect or impair the ability of the Seller to conduct its businesses.

(c)   Any labor trouble (including, without intending any limitation, any negotiation, or request for negotiation, for any representation or any labor contract) or any event or condition of any character which has materially and adversely affected or which does or may materially and adversely affect or impair the business of the Seller.

(d)   Any declaration, setting aside or payment of any dividend, or any distribution, in respect of the Seller's capital stock.

(e)   Any redemption, purchase or other acquisition by the Seller of any of the capital stock of the Seller or any other Ladder Corporation.

3.9   Tax Returns and Payments. Each Ladder Corporation has duly filed all federal, state and local tax returns and reports required to be filed and each has duly paid or established adequate reserves for the proper payment of all taxes and other governmental charges upon it or its properties, assets, income, franchises, licenses or sales. The charges, accruals and reserves shown in the financial statements referred to in Section 3.6 in respect of taxes for all fiscal periods to date are adequate, and the Seller does not know of any material unpaid assessment or proposal by any taxing authority for additional taxes for which it does not have adequate reserves for any such fiscal year. All monies required to be withheld by each Ladder Corporation from employees for income taxes, Social Security and unemployment insurance taxes have been collected or withheld, and either paid to the respective governmental agencies or set aside in accounts for such purpose, or accrued, reserved against, and entered upon the books of such Ladder Corporation. Neither the Seller nor its shareholders has adopted or taken any action in contemplation of any plan of liquidation or dissolution.

3.10   Title to Property and Assets. A description of all real property owned by the Seller is set forth in **Schedule 3.10.** Except as set forth in **Schedule 3.10** or in any title insurance policy obtained by the Buyer prior to the execution of this Agreement by the Buyer, the Seller has good title to all its properties and assets, real, personal and intangible, including all property and assets reflected in the financial statements referred to in Section 3.6 except as disposed of after December 31, 2001, subject to no mortgage, pledge, lien, security interest, lease, charge, encumbrance or conditional sale or other title retention agreement, except for such imperfections of title, liens, easements or encumbrances, if any, as are not material in character, amount or extent and do not, severally or in the aggregate, materially detract from the value or interfere with the present use of the property subject thereto or affected thereby or otherwise materially impair the business and operations of the Seller. The Seller has not disposed of any of its assets after December 31, 2001 (except for dispositions in the ordinary course of business which in the aggregate did not have a material adverse effect on the Seller).

3.11   Leases and Licensing Agreements. A list and brief description of all leases of real property, licensing agreements and leases of any substantial amounts of personal property, to which the Seller is a party, either as lessor or lessee, are set forth in **Schedule 3.11.** All such leases and licensing agreements are valid and effective in accordance with their respective terms. Except as set forth in **Schedule 3.11,** there are no existing defaults or events of default or events which with notice or lapse of time or both would constitute defaults thereunder, the consequences of which in the aggregate would have a material adverse effect on the business and operations of the Seller. Except as set forth in **Schedule 3.19,** the Seller has not received written notice and is not otherwise aware of any claimed default with respect to any lease or licensing agreement.

3.12   Condition of Property. Except as set forth in **Schedule 3.12,** the plants, structures, and equipment of the Seller are in good operating condition and repair, subject only to ordinary wear and tear.

3.13   Insurance. A list and brief description of all insurance policies of the Seller are set forth in **Schedule 3.13.** Except as set forth in **Schedule 3.13,** all properties of the Seller are insured for the benefit of the Seller, in amounts deemed adequate by the Seller's management, against all risks usually insured against by persons operating similar properties in the localities where such properties are located, under valid and enforceable policies issued by insurers of recognized responsibility.

3.14   Patents, Trademarks, Licenses, etc. Except as set forth in **Schedule 3.14,** the Seller owns or possesses the right to use all the material trademarks, service marks, trade names, brands, copyrights, letters patent, patent applications and licenses, and rights with respect to the foregoing, necessary for the continued conduct of its business as now conducted, without any known material conflict with the rights of others, and the Seller has received no written notice and is not otherwise aware of any claimed conflict with respect to any of the foregoing. The Seller has all material licenses, franchises, permits, and other authorizations necessary for the continued conduct of its business presently conducted.

3.15   Litigation, etc. Except to the extent set forth in **Schedule 3.15,** there is no suit, action or litigation, administrative, arbitration or other proceeding or governmental investigation or inquiry or any change in the environment, zoning or building laws, regulations or ordinances affecting the real property, leasehold property or business operations of the Seller, pending or, to the knowledge of the officers of the Seller, threatened which might, severally or in the aggregate, materially and adversely affect the financial condition, business, property, assets or prospects of the Seller. The Seller has materially complied with and is not in default in any material respect under any laws, ordinances, requirements, regulations or orders applicable to its business and properties, and the Seller has not received written notice and the Seller is not otherwise aware of any claimed default with respect to any of the foregoing.

3.16   Compliance with other Instruments, etc. Subject to obtaining the consents listed in **Schedule 3.16,** neither the execution nor the delivery of this Agreement nor the consummation of the transactions contemplated hereby will conflict with or result in any violation of or constitute a default under any term of the Certificate of Incorporation or By-laws of the Seller or any material agreement, mortgage, indenture, franchise, license, permit, authorization, lease or other instrument, judgment, decree, order, law or regulation by which the Seller is bound.

3.17 Governmental and other Consents, etc. Other than the approval of the Seller's shareholders, no consent, approval or authorization of or designation, declaration or filing with any governmental authority or other persons or entities on the part of the Seller is required in connection with the execution or delivery of this Agreement or the consummation of the transactions contemplated hereby except for notification to and consents from the persons specified in **Schedule 3.16.**

3.18 Adverse Agreements. The Seller is not a party to any agreement or instrument or subject to any charter or other corporate restriction or any judgment, order, writ, injunction, decree, rule or regulation which materially and adversely affects or, so far as the Seller can now foresee, may in the future materially and adversely affect the business operations, prospects, properties, assets or condition, financial or otherwise, of the Seller.

3.19 Agreements, etc. Set forth in **Schedule 3.19** are complete and accurate lists of the following: (a) all agreements, contracts, arrangements, commitments, understandings or obligations, oral or written, of the Seller except for (i) purchase and sale orders that may be canceled by the Seller within one year and involve expenditures of less than $100,000 on the part of the Seller and (ii) agreements that involve expenditures of less than $100,000 on the part of the Seller and are not material to the Seller or its business or financial condition; (b) all bonus, incentive, compensation, profit-sharing, retirement, pension, group insurance, death benefit or other fringe benefit plans, deferred compensation and post-termination obligations, trust agreements of each Ladder Corporation in effect or which were in effect prior to such Ladder Corporation's liquidation, or under which any material amounts remain unpaid on the date hereof or are to become effective after the date hereof; (c) all collective bargaining agreements of the Seller with any labor union or other representative of employees, including local, amendments, supplements, letters and memoranda of understanding of all kinds and all employment and consulting contracts not terminable at will without penalty to which is a party; (d) each instrument defining the terms on which debts (for borrowed money) of, or guarantees by the Seller aggregating more than $75,000 have been or may be issued; (e) all letters patent, patent applications, trademarks, service marks, trade names, brands, copyrights and licenses both domestic and foreign, and rights with respect to the foregoing, now owned or used by the Seller; (vi) any agreement limiting the Seller's freedom to compete in any line of business or with any person; (f) all other agreements, contracts, arrangements, commitments, understandings, or obligations, oral or written, relating to the Seller, its business, operations, prospects, properties, assets or condition (financial or otherwise) in which any officer or director of the Seller has any interest, direct or indirect, including a description of any transactions between the Seller with any of such officers and directors or with any entities in which such officers and directors have any interest; and (g) any agreements, contracts, arrangements, commitments, understandings, or obligations, oral or written, which are otherwise material to the Seller or its business or financial condition. Except as set forth in **Schedule 3.16,** all instruments set forth in **Schedule 3.19** are fully assignable without the consent of any third party. Except as set forth in **Schedule 3.19,** the Seller has no knowledge of any material default or claimed or purported or alleged material default or state of facts which with notice or lapse of time or both would constitute a material default on the part of any party in the performance of any obligation to be performed or paid by any party under any agreements, contracts, arrangements, commitments, understandings, or obligations, oral or written, plans or other instruments referred to in or submitted as a part of **Schedule 3.11** or **Schedule 3.19,** and the Seller has not received or given notice, and the Seller is not otherwise aware of any default or claimed or purported or alleged default or state of facts which with notice or lapse of time or both would constitute a default on the part of any party in the performance or payment of any obligation to be performed or paid by any party under any agreements, contracts, arrangements, commitments, understandings, or obligations, oral or written, plans or other instruments or arrangements referred to in or submitted as a part of **Schedule 3.11** or **Schedule 3.19.**

3.20   ERISA. Except as set forth in **Schedule 3.20,** the Seller is in compliance in all material respects with all applicable provisions of ERISA and other federal and state statutes and regulations relating to employee benefit plans.

3.21   Brokers. All negotiations relative to this Agreement and the transactions contemplated hereby have been carried on without the intervention of any other person in such manner as to give rise to any valid claim against the Seller for a finder's fee, brokerage commission or other like payment.

Article 4. Representations and Warranties of the Buyer

The Buyer represents and warrants to the Seller as follows:

4.1   Organization; Good Standing. The Buyer is a validly existing limited partnership organized under the laws of the State of New Jersey composed of two partners, NewLadder, Inc., a Delaware corporation ("NewLadder"), and Limited Partner Corp., a Delaware corporation ("LPC"). The Buyer has all requisite power and authority to own, operate, and lease its properties and assets and to enter into this Agreement and perform its obligations hereunder. At the Closing Date, the Buyer will have duly filed all instruments required as a limited partnership to do business in each of the foreign jurisdictions listed in **Schedule 4.1** and will have all requisite power and authority to own or lease the Purchased Assets and to carry on its intended business. Since its formation, the Buyer has not engaged, and it will not at any time prior to the Closing Date engage, in any business activities except in furtherance of and as contemplated by this Agreement. A copy of the Buyer's partnership agreement and all amendments thereto, which has heretofore been delivered to the Seller, is complete and correct. NewLadder is duly organized, validly existing and in good standing under the laws of its jurisdiction of incorporation with all requisite corporate power and authority to own, operate and lease its properties and assets and to enter into this Agreement and perform its obligations hereunder.

4.2   Litigation. Except as set forth in **Schedule 4.2,** there is no suit, action or litigation, administrative, arbitration or other proceeding or governmental investigation pending or, to the knowledge of the officers of the Buyer, threatened which might, severally or in the aggregate materially and adversely affect the financial condition or prospects of the Buyer.

4.3   Authority. The Buyer has taken, or will have taken prior to the Closing, all necessary action to approve this Agreement and the performance of its obligations hereunder.

4.4   Compliance with Instruments, Consents, Adverse Agreements. Neither the execution nor the delivery of this Agreement nor the consummation of the transactions contemplated hereby will conflict with or result in any violation of or constitute a default under any term of the partnership agreement of the Buyer or any material agreement, mortgage, indenture, license, permit, lease or other instrument, judgment, decree, order, law or regulation by which the Buyer is bound. No consent, approval or authorization of or designation, declaration of filing with any governmental authority or other persons or entities on the part of the Buyer is required in connection with the execution or delivery of this Agreement or the consummation of the transactions contemplated hereby. The Buyer is not a party to or subject to any agreement or instrument, or subject to any judgment, order, writ, injunction, decree, rule or regulation which materially and adversely affects or, so far as the Buyer can now foresee, may in the future materially and adversely affect, the business operations, prospects, properties, assets or condition, financial or otherwise, of the Buyer.

4.5   Brokers. All negotiations relative to this Agreement and the transactions contemplated hereby have been carried on without the intervention of any other person in such manner as to give rise to any valid claim against the Buyer for a finder's fee, brokerage commission or other like payment.

Article 5. Covenants of the Seller

The Seller agrees that prior to the Closing:

5.1   Cooperation. The Seller shall use its best efforts to cause the sale contemplated by this Agreement to be consummated, and, without limiting the generality of the foregoing, to obtain all consents and authorizations of third parties and to make all filings with and give all notices to third parties which may be necessary or reasonably required in order to effect the transactions contemplated hereby. The Seller shall use its best efforts to preserve its business organization intact and to keep available the services of its employees and representatives and to preserve the good will of its respective employees, customers, suppliers and others having business relations with it.

5.2   Transactions Out of Ordinary Course of Business. Except with the prior written consent of the Buyer, the Seller will conduct its businesses only in the ordinary course.

5.3   Maintenance of Properties, etc. The Seller will maintain all of its properties in customary repair, order and condition, reasonable wear excepted, and will maintain insurance upon all of its properties and, with respect to the conduct of its business, in such amounts and of such kinds comparable to that in effect on the date of this Agreement.

5.4   Maintenance of Books, etc. The Seller will maintain its books, accounts, and records in the usual manner on a basis consistent with prior years. The Seller will duly comply in all material respects with all material laws and decrees applicable to it and to the conduct of its businesses.

5.5   Access to Properties, etc. The Seller will give or cause to be given to the Buyer and to the Buyer's counsel, accountants, investment advisors and other representatives full access during normal business hours to all of the properties, books, tax returns, contracts, commitments and records of any Ladder Corporation and will furnish to the Buyer copies of all such documents, certified if requested, and all such information as the Buyer may from time to time reasonably request with respect to the affairs of the Ladder Corporations.

5.6   Limitation on Debt. Except with the prior written consent of the Buyer, the Seller shall not issue or contract to issue debt or guarantees of debt, except for trade debt incurred in the ordinary course of business and borrowings in the ordinary course of business under the Seller's existing bank line not to exceed $12,250,000 at any one time.

5.7   Dispositions or Encumbrances on Assets. The Seller shall not, directly or indirectly, dispose of or encumber any of its assets except in the ordinary course of business or as otherwise provided in this Agreement.

5.8   Limitations upon Dividends, etc. No dividend or other distribution or payment will be declared, paid or made by the Seller in respect of shares of its capital stock. No purchase, redemption, or other acquisition will be made, directly or indirectly, by the Seller of any outstanding shares of its capital stock.

5.9   Amending Schedules and Exhibits. From time to time prior to the Closing Date, the Seller shall promptly supplement or amend the Schedules and Exhibits with respect to any matter hereafter arising which, if existing or occurring at the date of this Agreement, would have been required to be set forth or described in the Schedules and Exhibits. No such supplement or amendment shall have the effect of curing any misrepresentations or breach of warranty for the transactions contemplated by this Agreement.

Article 6. Covenants of the Buyer

The Buyer agrees that prior to the Closing, it shall use its best efforts to cause the sale contemplated by this Agreement to be consummated, and, without limiting the generality of the foregoing, to obtain all consents and authorizations of third parties and to make all filings with and give all notices to third parties which may be necessary or reasonably required in order to effect the transactions contemplated hereby. The Buyer will not, prior to the Closing, engage in any business activities except such as are related to this Agreement.

Article 7. Conditions to the Seller's Obligations

All of the Seller's obligations under this Agreement are subject to the fulfillment, on or before the Closing Date, of each of the following conditions. The Seller may waive any failure to satisfy any one or more of the conditions.

7.1   Buyer's Representations and Warranties. The representations and warranties of the Buyer herein contained shall be true on and as of the Closing Date with the same force and effect as though made on and as of said date, except as affected by transactions contemplated hereby.

7.2   Buyer's Covenants. The Buyer shall have performed all its obligations and agreements and complied with all its covenants contained in this Agreement to be performed and complied with by the Buyer prior to the Closing Date.

7.3   Buyer's Closing Certificate. The Seller shall have received a certificate of the Buyer, executed on behalf of the Buyer by a general partner of the Buyer, dated the Closing Date, in form and substance satisfactory to counsel for the Seller, certifying as to the fulfillment of the matters mentioned in Section 7.1 and 7.2.

7.4   Buyer's Counsel's Opinion. Workhard & Playlittle, counsel to the Buyer, shall have delivered to the Seller an opinion, dated the Closing Date, substantially in the form of **Exhibit 7.4** hereto. In giving such opinion such counsel may rely, as to matters of fact, upon certificates of the Buyer and, as to matters governed by the laws of any jurisdiction, upon the opinions of local counsel satisfactory to the Seller, provided that such counsel shall state that they believe that they are justified in relying upon such certificates and opinions of local counsel and deliver copies thereof to the Seller.

7.5   Shareholder Approval. The transactions contemplated by this Agreement shall have been authorized and approved by the shareholders of the Seller. The Seller's shareholders shall have approved the transactions contemplated by this Agreement by the affirmative vote of the holders of two-thirds of the outstanding shares of the Seller as well as the affirmative vote of the holders of at least a majority of the shares present in person or by proxy and voting at the meeting other than the shares owned on the record date by officers and directors of the Seller, members of their immediate families, certain family trusts and shares in the Seller's Senior Executive Employee Deferred Stock Incentive Plan.

7.6   No Litigation. Except as set forth in **Schedule 3.15** of the Agreement, no action, suit or proceeding before any court or any governmental or regulatory authority shall have been commenced, no investigation by any governmental or regulatory authority shall have been commenced and no action, suit or proceeding by any governmental or regulatory authority shall have been threatened against the Seller, the Buyer, NewLadder or LPC (i) seeking to restrain, prevent or change the transactions contemplated hereby or questioning the validity or legality of any of such transactions, or (ii) if resolved adversely to the Seller would materially and adversely affect the financial condition, business, property, assets or prospects of the Seller.

7.7   Sale of Properties. The Properties shall have been sold by the Seller or the Seller shall have executed a contract for the sale of the Properties in a form satisfactory to the Seller.

7.8   Seller's Counsel. All matters and proceedings taken in connection with the sale of the Purchased Assets by the Seller to the Buyer and the assumption of the Liabilities by the Buyer as herein contemplated shall be satisfactory in form and substance to the Seller and to its counsel.

Article 8. Conditions to the Buyer's Obligations

All of the Buyer's obligations under this Agreement are subject to the fulfillment, on or before the Closing Date, of each of the following conditions. The Buyer may waive any failure to satisfy any one or more of the conditions.

8.1   Seller's Representations and Warranties. The representations and warranties of the Seller herein contained shall be true on and as of the Closing Date with the same force and effect as though made on and as of said date, except as affected by transactions contemplated hereby.

8.2   Seller's Covenants. The Seller shall have performed all of its obligations and agreements and complied with all of its covenants contained in this Agreement to be performed and complied with by it prior to the Closing Date.

8.3   Seller's Closing Certificate. The Buyer shall have received a certificate of the Seller, executed on behalf of the Seller by the President or any Vice President of the Seller, dated the Closing Date, in form and substance satisfactory to Buyer's counsel, certifying as to the fulfillment of the matters mentioned in Section 8.1 and 8.2.

8.4   Consents. The Buyer shall have received evidence, satisfactory to the Buyer and counsel for the Buyer, that all of the consents disclosed in **Schedule 3.16** have been duly obtained, and that all material permits, licenses, franchises and other authorizations necessary to the operation of the businesses of the Seller have been transferred to or issued to the Buyer.

8.5   Seller's Counsel's Opinion. Counsel for the Seller shall have delivered to the Buyer an opinion, dated the Closing Date, substantially in the form of **Exhibit 8.5** hereto. In giving such opinion such counsel may rely, as to matters of fact, upon certificates of officers of the Seller and, as to matters governed by the laws of any jurisdiction, upon the opinion of local counsel satisfactory to the Buyer, provided that such counsel shall state that they believe that they are justified in relying upon such certificates and opinions of local counsel and deliver copies thereof to the Buyer.

8.6   Seller's Trademark and Patent Counsel's Opinion. Seller's trademark and patent counsel shall have delivered to the Buyer an opinion, dated the Closing Date, in form and substance reasonably satisfactory to Buyer's counsel.

8.7   Comfort Letter. There shall have been delivered to the Buyer a letter from Ernst & Young, dated not earlier than three business days immediately preceding the date of the Closing and addressed to the Buyer, in form and substance satisfactory to the Buyer and to counsel for the Buyer.

8.8   Buyer's Financing. The Buyer shall have obtained the financing necessary to consummate the transactions contemplated hereby; and all matters and proceedings, including form of instruments and matters of title, shall be satisfactory to Buyer's lenders and their counsel. The Buyer shall have received such certificates from the Seller relating to the transactions contemplated by this Agreement or to the businesses of the Seller as shall be necessary to consummate the Buyer's financing or as shall otherwise be reasonably requested by the Buyer.

8.9   No Litigation. Except as set forth in **Schedule 3.15** no action, suit or proceeding before any court or any governmental or regulatory authority shall have been commenced, no investigation by any governmental or regulatory authority shall have been commenced and no action, suit or proceeding by any governmental or regulatory authority shall have been threatened against the Seller, the Buyer, NewLadder or LPC (i) seeking to restrain, prevent or change the transactions contemplated hereby or questioning the validity or legality of any of such transactions, or (ii) if resolved adversely to the Seller severally or in the aggregate, would materially and adversely affect the financial condition, business, property, assets or prospects of the Seller.

8.10   Employment and Management Agreements. On the Closing Date, the Buyer will enter into a Management Agreement with Michael M. Ladder and Employment Agreements with Michael M. Ladder, Nicholas Martin and William Smith, each in form satisfactory to Buyer.

8.11   Sale of Properties. The Properties shall have been sold by the Seller or the Seller shall have executed a contract for the sale of the Properties in form satisfactory to the Buyer. The Properties shall have been leased to the Buyer on terms satisfactory to the Buyer.

8.12   Shareholder Approval. The transactions contemplated by this Agreement shall have been authorized and approved by the shareholders of the Seller. The Seller's shareholders shall have approved the transactions contemplated by this Agreement by the affirmative vote of the holders of two-thirds of the outstanding shares of the Seller as well as the affirmative vote of the holders of at least a majority of the shares present in person or by proxy and voting at the meeting other than the shares owned on the record date by officers and directors of the Seller, members of their immediate families, certain family trusts and shares in the Seller's Senior Executive Employee Deferred Stock Incentive Plan.

8.13   Buyer's Counsel. All matters and proceedings taken in connection with the sale of the Purchased Assets by the Seller to the Buyer and the assumption of the Liabilities by the Buyer as herein contemplated shall be satisfactory in form and substance to Buyer and to its counsel.

Article 9. Termination

Either party may terminate this Agreement by written notice if the Closing has not occurred on or before December 31, 2002.

Article 10. Indemnities and Survival of Representations and Warranties

10.1   Survival of Representations and Warranties. All representations and warranties made in this Agreement by the Seller

(a)   survive the execution and delivery of this Agreement and the consummation of the transactions contemplated by this Agreement; and

(b)   may be relied on by the Buyer notwithstanding

(i)   any right of the Buyer to investigate fully the affairs of the Seller; and

(ii)   any knowledge of any facts determined or determinable by the Buyer's investigation or right to investigate.

10.2   Indemnity.

(a)   **The Seller's Indemnity Obligation.** The Seller shall indemnify and hold harmless the Buyer from and against any loss, liability, obligation, damage, cost or expense (including without limitation, attorney's fees and expenses) resulting from or relating to any

(i)   misrepresentation,

(ii)   breach of warranty, or

(iii)   failure to perform any covenant in this Agreement to be performed by the Seller.

(b)   **The Buyer's Indemnity Obligation.** The Buyer shall indemnify and hold harmless the Seller from and against any loss, liability, obligation, damage, cost or expense (including without limitation, attorney's fees and expenses) resulting from or relating to any

(i)   misrepresentation,

(ii)   breach of warranty, or

(iii)   failure to perform any covenant in this Agreement to be performed by the Buyer.

Article 11. Change of Corporate Names; Noncompetition

11.1   Names. Promptly after the Closing, the Seller shall change its corporate name to that set forth in **Exhibit 11.1** hereto. From and after the Closing the Seller consents to the use by the Buyer or Buyer's designees of the names "Ladder," "Maker," and "Construction" or any of the corporate names or names of the Seller or any subsidiaries or divisions of the Seller, or any variation thereof.

11.2   Noncompete. At no time during the five-year period subsequent to the Closing will the Seller engage in any business within the United States which is directly competitive with that sold to the Buyer hereunder.

Article 12. Miscellaneous

12.1   Confidentiality. The Seller and the Buyer shall, and shall cause their respective officers, subsidiaries and authorized representatives to hold in strict confidence, and not disclose to any other party without the prior written consent of the Buyer or the Seller, as the case may be, all information acquired from the Buyer or the Seller in connection with the transactions contemplated hereby, except as may be required by applicable law or as otherwise contemplated herein.

12.2   Brokerage. The Seller agrees to indemnify the Buyer and hold it harmless from and against any and all claims for any broker's or finder's fee or commission arising out of or based on any act of any Ladder Corporation. The Buyer agrees to indemnify the Seller and hold it harmless from and against any and all claims for any broker's or finder's fee or commission arising out of or based on any act of the Buyer.

12.3 Waivers. The Buyer may, by written notice to the Seller, and the Seller may, by written notice to the Buyer, at any time prior to consummation of the sale of the Purchased Assets to Buyer pursuant hereto, whether before or after authorization thereof by the shareholders of the Seller: (a) extend the time for the performance of any of the obligations of the other party under this Agreement; (b) waive any inaccuracies in the representations or warranties of the other party contained in this Agreement; (c) waive compliance with any of the covenants of the other party contained in this Agreement; (d) waive or modify performance of any of the obligations of the other party under this Agreement; or (e) waive satisfaction of any of the conditions specified herein to the performance of such party's obligations under this Agreement. The waiver by either of the parties of a breach of any provision of this Agreement shall not operate or be construed as a waiver of a breach of any other provision of this Agreement.

12.4 Amendments, Supplements, etc. This Agreement may be amended, modified and supplemented, whether before or after the vote of the shareholders of the Seller, by written agreement of the Buyer and the Seller at any time prior to the Closing Date with respect to any of the terms contained herein; provided, however, that after the approval of this Agreement by the shareholders of the Seller, no such amendment, modification or supplement shall reduce the amount or change the form of the consideration to be delivered to the Seller pursuant to Section 2.2 hereof, or otherwise change Section 2.2 hereof in any manner adverse to the Seller.

12.5 Antiassignment. Neither party may assign this Agreement or any obligations under this Agreement. Any purported assignment is null and void.

12.6 Notices. All notices, consents, demands, requests, approvals and other communications which are required or may be given hereunder shall be in writing and shall be deemed to have been duly given if delivered or mailed certified first-class mail, postage prepaid:

(a)   If to the Seller:

Ladder Maker, Inc.

94 Madison Avenue

New York, New York 10016

(b)   If to the Buyer:

Ladco

c/o NewLadder, Inc.

285 Entrepreneur Avenue

Hopenaprayer, New Jersey 00000

or to such other person or persons at such address or addresses as may be designated by written notice to the other parties hereunder.

12.7 Merger. This Agreement embodies the entire agreement and understanding of the parties hereto and supersedes any prior agreement and understanding between the parties.

12.8 Choice of Law. This Agreement shall be governed by the laws of the State of New York.

12.9 Binding Effect. This Agreement is binding upon and inures to the benefit of the parties hereto and their respective successors and assigns.

12.10 Severability. Any provision of this Agreement which is prohibited or unenforceable in any jurisdiction shall, as to such jurisdiction, be ineffective to the extent of such prohibition or unenforceability without invalidating the remaining provisions hereof, and any such prohibition or unenforceability in any jurisdiction shall not invalidate or render unenforceable such provision in any other jurisdiction.

IN WITNESS WHEREOF, the parties have executed this Agreement as of the date first written above.

LADDER MAKER, INC.

By: _____

　　Title: Executive Vice President

LADCO LP, a limited partnership

By: NEWLADDER, INC., General Partner

By: _____

　　Title: President

Website Development Agreement

This **Website Development Agreement** is dated January 8, 20XX and is between Go-Karts Corp., a California corporation (the "Client"), and Website Designs, Inc., a Michigan corporation (the "Consultant").

This Agreement provides for the Consultant's development of a website for the Client.

The parties agree as follows:

1. **Definitions.** Terms defined in the preamble have their assigned meanings and each of the following terms has the meaning assigned to it.

    1.1. **"Agreement"** means this Website Development Agreement, as amended from time to time.

    1.2. **"Business Day"** means any day other than a day that a bank in San Jose, California is required or permitted to be closed.

    1.3. **"Change Order"** means an agreement that changes or supplements the Services.

    1.4. **"Content"** means all text, images, sound, graphics, and other materials describing the Client's business and industry.

    1.5. **"Developer Programming"** has the meaning assigned to it in Section 9.1.

    1.6. **"Down Payment"** has the meaning assigned to it in Section 4.2.

    1.7. **"Effective Date"** means the date that is the second to occur of the following dates:

        1.7.1. The date the Developer receives the Down Payment.

        1.7.2. The date the first party to sign this Agreement receives the fully signed Agreement from the other party.

    1.8. **"Services"** means the services listed in Scope of Services section in **Exhibit A,** as changed from time to time.

1.9. **"Team"** means the employees the Developer assigns to perform the Services.

1.10. **"Works"** means the Website and all other deliverables, including without limitation, all derivative deliverables, resulting from the performance of the Services.

1.11. **"Website"** means a collection of interconnected web pages on the Internet, pertaining to the Client.

2. **Hiring of the Developer.** By signing this Agreement, the Client hires the Developer to design and develop a Website for the Client.

3. **Design and Development of the Website.** Subject to the provisions of this Agreement, the Developer shall design and develop the Website by performing the Services.

4. **Fees.**

4.1. **Estimate and Cap.** The Developer estimates that its fee for performing the Services will be between $12,000 and $15,000. Despite the preceding sentence, the maximum that the Client is obligated to pay the Developer for the Services, as described in Exhibit A on the Effective Date, is $17,000. If the parties agree to a Change Order, the new cap is the amount the parties agree to at that time. If the parties do not agree to a new cap, then it is the higher number of any estimate plus 10 percent of that number.

4.2. **Down Payment.**

4.2.1. **Amount of the Down Payment.** The down payment is $6,000 (the **"Down Payment"**).

4.2.2. **The Developer's Bank Account.** Immediately after the Developer signs and delivers this Agreement, it shall notify the Client of the bank account into which the Client is to wire the Down Payment.

4.2.3. **Obligation to Pay the Down Payment.** The Client shall pay the Down Payment to the Developer by wire transfer of funds immediately available in San Jose, California, no later than one Business Day after the second to occur of the following dates:

(a) The date the Client receives notice of the bank account into which it is to wire transfer Down Payment.

(b) The date the first party to sign this Agreement receives the fully signed Agreement from the other party.

4.3. **Additional Payments.**

4.3.1. **Billing Rates.** The billing rates for Team members range from $75 to $225 an hour. The Developer may increase these rates only after having given the Client at least 30 days prior notice.

4.3.2. **Amount to be Paid.** The Client shall pay the Developer for each quarter hour that a Team member works, except if the cap has been reached. In that event, the Client's obligation to pay any amount in excess of the cap is discharged. In determining the amount that the Client is obligated to pay, the Developer shall give the Client a credit equal to the amount of the Down Payment.

4.3.3. **Form of Invoice.** With respect to each month that the Developer provides Services, the Developer shall send an invoice to the Client indicating

(a)   the number of hours each Team member worked;

(b)   the billing rate for each Team member;

(c)   the aggregate invoiced fee for each Team member;

(d)   the aggregate invoiced fee for the Team; and

(e)   the amount by which the invoice has been reduced to reflect any outstanding credit arising from the Down Payment.

If the cap has been reached, the Developer shall continue to send invoices to the Client, but it shall indicate on the invoice that the Client is not obligated to pay the invoiced amount.

4.3.4. **Form and Timing of Payment.** The Client shall pay each month's invoice by company check or by wire transfer, in either case, payment to be received no later than 10 Business Days after the Client's receipt of that month's invoice.

5.   **Effective Date.** This Agreement is effective on the Effective Date.

6.   **Provision of Services.**

6.1.   **Quality of Services.** The Developer shall perform the Services using sound professional practices and in a competent and professional manner by knowledgeable and qualified employees.

6.2.   **Content.** The Client shall not deliver any Content to the Developer that

6.2.1.   it does not own or have a right to use; or

6.2.2.   is defamatory, libelous, or otherwise actionable.

6.3.   **The Developer's Employees.** No later than the Effective Date, the Developer shall assign the following employees to be the Team members providing the Services to the Client: Omar Adams, Kyla Rubin, and Marla Wojinsky. The Developer may replace one or more of these employees with other employees, but only after it receives the Client's prior consent. The Client shall not unreasonably withhold its consent.

6.4.   **Schedule.** The Developer shall use commercially reasonable efforts to provide the Services as efficiently as possible with the goal of completing the Services no later than April 30, 20XX.

6.5.   **Liens.** The Developer shall perform the Services so that each Work is free of any liens or other encumbrances at the time that it is delivered.

6.6.   **Change Orders.** If from time to time the Client wants to change or supplement any Service, the parties must sign a Change Order. A Change Order is effective when the first party to sign the Change Order receives the fully signed Change Order from the other party. If the provisions of a Change Order and this Agreement conflict, the provisions of this Agreement govern.

6.7.   **Compliance with Laws.** In performing the Services, the Developer shall comply with all federal, state, local, or foreign laws, rules, and regulations, as each is in effect from time to time.

7.   **Client Representative.** No later than the Effective Date, the Client shall assign a representative to work with the Team and notify the Developer who that representative is. The Client shall give the representative the authority to sign Change Orders and to make all other decisions concerning the Website and the Services. At any time, the Client may remove the then current representative and assign another representative to work with the Team.

8.   **Content.**

8.1.   **Initial Content.** No later than 10 Business Days after the Effective Date, the Client shall deliver to the Developer the following:

8.1.1.   The Website's URL.

8.1.2.   The Content that it wants incorporated into the Website.

8.2.   **Additional Content.** If the Client wants to change the Content after the Developer has incorporated it into the Website, the Developer is entitled to an additional fee, all of which must be documented by a Change Order that both parties sign.

9.   **Ownership.**

9.1.   **Definition. "Developer Programming"** means any programming or software that the Developer creates, or has created, outside of this Agreement but uses in the Works.

9.2.   **Work for Hire.**

9.2.1.   **Rights to the Works.** The Works are works made for hire and all rights to them vest in the Client. The Developer has no right to them or any interest in them and shall not use them to benefit anyone other than the Client.

9.2.2.   **Assignment of Rights in the Works.** By signing this Agreement, the Developer assigns to the Client

(a)   all rights in each Work that do not vest in the Client by operation of law; and

(b)   all copyright interests in each Work for the entire period of that Work's copyright protection.

9.3.   **Developer Programs.** The Developer retains all rights to all Developer Programming, but grants to the Client a perpetual, nonexclusive license to use all Developer Programming in connection with the Works.

10.   Warranties. The Developer warrants that the Works will

10.1.   be useable by the Client for the purposes for which they were intended;

10.2.   operate in conformity with the specifications listed in Exhibit A; and

10.3.   be free of viruses, Trojan horses, and other software that could damage the Website or the computer of any user of the Website.

11.   Representations and Warranties.

11.1.   **Developer.** The Developer represents and warrants to the Client as follows:

11.1.1.   **Organization.** The Developer is a corporation duly organized, validly existing, and in good standing under the laws of its jurisdiction of incorporation.

11.1.2.   **Corporate Power and Authority.** The Developer has all requisite corporate power and authority

(a)   to own, operate, and lease its properties, and to carry on its business as now being conducted; and

(b)   to sign, deliver, and perform this Agreement.

11.1.3.   **Authorization.** The Developer has taken all necessary corporate action to authorize the signing, delivery, and performance of this Agreement.

11.1.4.   **Enforceability.** This Agreement has been duly signed by the Developer and constitutes its legal, valid, and binding obligation. It is enforceable against the Developer in accordance with its terms, except to the extent that enforcement is limited by either one or both of the following:

(a)   Applicable bankruptcy, insolvency, reorganization, moratorium or other similar laws affecting creditors' rights generally.

(b)   General equitable principles, regardless of whether the issue of enforceability is considered in a proceeding in equity or at law.

11.1.5.   **Team Members.** The Team members listed in Section 6.3 are knowledgeable and qualified to perform the Services.

11.2.   **Client.** The Client represents and warrants to the Developer as follows:

11.2.1.   **Organization.** The Client is a corporation duly organized, validly existing, and in good standing under the laws of its jurisdiction of incorporation.

11.2.2.   **Corporate Power and Authority.** The Client has all requisite corporate power and authority

(a)   to own, operate, and lease its properties, and to carry on its business as now being conducted; and

(b)   to sign, deliver, and perform this Agreement.

11.2.3. **Authorization.** The Client has taken all necessary corporate action to authorize the signing, delivery, and performance of this Agreement.

11.2.4. **Enforceability.** This Agreement has been duly signed by the Client and constitutes its legal, valid, and binding obligation. It is enforceable against the Client, except to the extent that enforcement is limited by either one or both of the following:

(a)   Applicable bankruptcy, insolvency, reorganization, moratorium or other similar laws affecting creditors' rights generally.

(b)   General equitable principles, regardless of whether the issue of enforceability is considered in a proceeding in equity or at law.

12. **Development Credit.** The Client shall acknowledge the Developer as the Website developer on the Website page entitled "About the Site." The Client may remove the acknowledgment if it materially changes the Website after this Agreement terminates.

13. **Termination.**

13.1. **Termination.** This Agreement terminates when the Developer has completely performed the Services and the Client has paid all fees in accordance with Section 4.

13.2. **Termination for Cause.** Despite the provisions of Section 13.1, a party may earlier terminate this Agreement by giving 10 Business Days notice to the other party, if that latter party materially misrepresented a fact or materially breached a warranty or covenant. In that event, the terminating party has all rights and remedies that law and equity provide.

14. **General Provisions.**

14.1. **Governing Law.** The laws of California govern all matters relating to this Agreement, including torts.

14.2. **Assignment and Delegation.** The Developer shall not assign its rights or delegate its performance under this Agreement without the Client's prior consent. The Client may assign its rights and delegate its performance. For the purposes of this Section, an assignment includes a change of control.

14.3. **Successors and Assigns.** This Agreement binds and benefits the parties and their respective permitted successors and assigns.

14.4. **Notices.** The parties must send all notices in writing and give all consents in writing. A notice or consent occurs is effective when the intended recipient receives it.

14.5. **Merger.** This Agreement is the final, complete, and exclusive statement of the parties' agreement on the matters contained in this Agreement. It supersedes all previous negotiations and agreements.

14.6. **Amendments.** The parties shall not amend this Agreement, except by an agreement in writing signed by both parties.

To evidence the parties' agreement to this Agreement, they have signed and delivered it on the date set forth in the preamble.

WEBSITE DESIGNS, INC.

By: _____
    Walter Kelley, President

GO-KARTS CORP.
By: _____
    Esther Grant, President

Scope of Services

- Creative consulting
- Creation of site map
- Three mock-ups of home page
- Two revisions of chosen home page
- Three mock-ups of secondary page
- Two revisions of chosen secondary page
- Programming for 30 static pages
- Launch and testing of Website

Specifications

- Website to work with multiple browsers, including Internet Explorer, Mozilla Firefox, and Opera
- Website to work with multiple operating systems, including Windows and Mac
- Client to be able to make changes to the Website using Dreamweaver

Escrow Agreements

Parties use escrow agreements to safeguard property. They deposit the property with a neutral third party, the escrow agent, to ensure that neither party has access to the property, except under agreed upon circumstances. The escrow agent holds the escrowed property until it distributes it in compliance with the escrow agreement's terms. Escrowed property may be cash, securities, or other property.

The reasons for using an escrow are transaction specific. In connection with the purchase of a house, the buyer usually places his deposit in escrow with an escrow agent. Typically, the escrow agent will release the deposit to the seller if the transaction closes or to the buyer if it does not. In a business acquisition, the parties may deposit a portion of the purchase price in escrow to secure the seller's post-closing indemnification obligations.

The parties to an escrow agreement are the escrow agent and the parties to the primary transaction. The escrow agreement does not set out the terms of the primary transaction (e.g., the purchase and sale of the house), although its recitals will describe the transaction. The escrow agreement does do the following:

- It details the circumstances under which the escrow agent will take the property and how it will invest it.
- It establishes the terms in accordance with which the escrow agent will distribute the escrowed property.
- It requires the parties to the primary transaction to pay the escrow agent's fees and to indemnify it for any losses arising out of its service as escrow agent.

The key provisions in the escrow agreement set out the circumstances under which the escrow agent will distribute the escrowed property. Typically, escrow agents require either joint written instructions if the parties agree as to the property's disposition, or, if they do not, a court order that cannot be appealed. Some escrow agents insist on being able to resign if the parties cannot resolve a dispute. In addition, they may require the right to begin a lawsuit seeking a declaratory judgment as to which party is entitled to the escrowed property. If they require such a provision, the escrow agreement usually also provides that the escrow agent may deposit the escrowed property with the court and resign without further liability.

Drafters get into trouble with escrow agreements two ways. First, they fail to think through all of the scenarios under which the property might need to be distributed. Second, they do not sufficiently explain to the client the circumstances under which the escrowed property will remain undistributed.

Exercise 6-3 includes a Purchase Offer for the sale of an aircraft and an Escrow Agreement pursuant to which the escrow agent will hold the buyer's $300,000 deposit. Section 2 of the Escrow Agreement provides for the escrow agent's distribution of the deposit. Note the use of the Exhibit as a means of establishing the content of the notice that the parties must deliver. How does this protect the escrow agent?

Index

A CONTRACT'S BUILDING BLOCKS

	DEFINITION	BUSINESS PURPOSE	REMEDY
Representation	Statement of fact as of a moment of time intended to induce reliance.	To induce reliance; to establish standards of liability; to allocate risk.	For a material, innocent or negligent misrepresentation, avoidance and restitutionary recovery. For a fraudulent misrepresentation, either • avoidance and restitutionary recovery or • damages (either out-of-pocket or benefit of the bargain) and possibly punitive damages.
Warranty	A promise that a statement is true.	To provide an indemnity if a statement is not true; to allocate risk.	Damages.
Covenant	A promise to do or not to do something. A covenant establishes a duty, also called an obligation to perform.	To require or prohibit action; to establish standards of liability; to allocate risk.	Damages and, if appropriate, specific performance. If the breach is so material that it is a breach of the whole contract that cannot be cured, then a party may have a right to cancel as well as other remedies.
Right	A party's entitlement to the other party's performance of a covenant. A right is the flip side of a covenant.	To require or prohibit action; to establish standards of liability; to allocate risk.	The same as for a covenant.
Condition to an Obligation	A state of facts that must exist before a party is obligated to perform. The occurrence of the condition must be uncertain.	To establish when a party is obligated to perform a covenant; to allocate risk.	A condition to an obligation cannot be breached. Its failure to occur means that the obligation to perform is not triggered. If the failed condition does not affect the parties' ongoing relationship, the condition is an ongoing condition. If the failed condition permits one party to choose whether to perform, the condition is a walk-away condition that creates a walk-away right.
Discretionary Authority	The right to choose what action to take; permission to act.	To provide choice or permission; to allocate risk.	Not applicable.

	DEFINITION	BUSINESS PURPOSE	REMEDY
Condition to Discretionary Authority	A state of facts that must exist before a party may exercise discretionary authority.	To establish when discretionary authority may be exercised; to allocate risk.	Not applicable.
Declaration	Statement of fact as to which the parties agree.	To create definitions and establish policies.	Not applicable.
Condition to a Declaration	A state of facts that must exist before a policy has substantive consequences.	To establish when a policy is applicable.	Not applicable.